AF473856

WHY ME? FIRST, ACCOUNT FOR ME

For my friends pictured within,
especially Eva Menuhin who rescued my text
and Lucy Duckworth who tolerated my indecision.

WHY ME? FIRST, ACCOUNT FOR ME

Adventures in the Music and Film Trade

"These days, newspapers and television pour out opinions with a frenzy that marked the production of spitfires during the last war. Phone-ins proliferate, choked with calls from the semi-literate, the bigoted and the barmy. And opinion polls, the entrails of democracy, are now picked over for prophetic insight. We have become a nation of babbling, back-seat cab-drivers".

John Osborne

"I don't want to be working in ballet or opera or things where it's like, 'Hey, keep this thing alive even though ... no one cares about this anymore.'"

Timothée Chalamet

TONY PALMER

Published in 2026 by Unicorn
an imprint of Unicorn Publishing Group
Charleston Studio
Meadow Business Centre
Lewes BN8 5RW
www.unicornpublishing.org

ISBN: 978-1-917458-94-8

Insides typeset by Mach 3 Solutions
Printed by Bell and Bain, Scotland

Contents

Prologue

When I read this book, the biography famous,
And is this then (said I) what the author calls a man's life?
And so will some one when I am dead and gone write my life?
(As if any man really knew aught of my life,
When even I myself I often think know little or nothing of my real life,
Only a few hints, a few diffused faint clews and indirections
I seek for my own use to trace out here).

WALT WHITMAN, ***Leaves of Grass***

Courage. It's not a quality you can easily define, nor even a quality you would recognise in someone beforehand. It is certainly not a quality which can be predicted or predicated or even prejudged. Is it, therefore, a quality latent in every man or woman? And if not, why not? Does it define the person, in that he or she is aware of it at the time? Probably not. Does it inspire the person? Unlikely. Does it make the person more noble, more worthwhile? Very doubtful. But it is the one characteristic that all the people about whom I have made films exhibited, and sometimes in bucket loads.

What, then, is this quality called courage? Galileo certainly had it when he confronted the Catholic Church and its mistaken belief in the sun going round the earth. Beethoven, also, as he battled against his increasing deafness. Columbus, when he set off in a flimsy vessel across an unknown sea in search of he knew not what, had courage - even if inspired by greed; courage nonetheless. Likewise, Thor Heyerdahl. Likewise, Roald Amundsen, the greatest of all polar explorers. And Martin Luther King Jr, in his civil rights struggles on behalf of a third of the entire American population, definitely, in my view, had what has become loosely known as 'courage'.

Margot Fonteyn had courage. She explained to me the hazards of touring with a ballet company. 'You come to a theatre you do not know. Maybe the wooden stage has not been cleaned properly. Maybe there is a nail sticking up somewhere. Maybe the rake on the stage is greater than you are used to. But, come your cue and your music, you must make your grand entrance, literally a leap into the unknown. Your foot lands on that nail. You break your ankle. Your career is finished in an instant. So it does take a little courage to make that first entrance knowing what might be against you.'

Or Orson Welles; he had the courage to keep going even though no-one wanted to employ him as a director. Or Maria Callas. The greater her fame, the greater the expectations and demands being made upon her. Graziella Sciutti, the distinguished Italian soprano, told me that she was shocked when working with Maria to find that, before her first entrance, she was literally shaking with terror.

Benjamin Britten, one of the greatest pianists of his generation, besides being one of the greatest composers, was so overcome with terror before giving a recital, even with his long-time lover and inspiration Peter Pears, that he needed a tumbler full of brandy to calm his nerves before making his entrance upon the stage. I remember filming him once, and, looking through the lens of the camera at a close-up of his hands, being shocked that they were trembling. Janet Baker, the great mezzo-soprano, told me of her own early experience of Britten's nerves. 'When Ben came up onto the platform from the pit to take his bow, we held hands, as one does, and both bowed to the audience,' she told me. 'He was shaking like a leaf. I was shaking like a leaf. And at first I thought, is this me? And I suddenly realised we were both shaking like a leaf. And I thought how fantastic that this man can feel what I, as a very naive, inexperienced youngster was feeling, the same terror. And that remained with me always: his vulnerability never diminished; he was always terrified.'

Or Stravinsky. When he famously said of *Le Sacre du Printemps* (*The Rite of Spring*), 'I had no rules to guide me. I was the vessel through which the *Sacre* flowed', he was well aware he was charting an entirely new territory for music as he and his amanuensis Robert Craft described to me. Or Shostakovich who thought – no, who *believed* – according to his widow Iryna, her voice trembling and on the edge of tears as she told me, that for most of his life he was about to be taken out and shot, like so many of his close friends had been, for having apparently 'offended' the regime and Stalin in particular.

Or Wagner, by all accounts a despicable little man who nonetheless overshadowed the entire nineteenth century world of classical music. Anti-Semitic, arrogant, intolerant, dishonest, a philanderer; there is not much to be said in his favour, except that he did write some of the most influential music ever composed, but, again, at considerable personal cost. A wanted criminal, a bankrupt, a fugitive, a felon, but all for art, he would say. Again, what courage to keep fighting when all seemed lost – repeatedly.

We know that none of these people were saints. All had deep personal flaws; indeed, almost certainly some would be described as thoroughly reprehensible human beings, not the kind of people you would want to call your friends, despite their fame, real and imagined. But as Nadia Boulanger, the great French teacher and musicologist, explained to me when I asked her why on earth Stravinsky had come to her for 'lessons' in the early 1920s in Paris, after having already written three of his greatest hits – *The Firebird, Petrushka* and *The Rite of Spring*: 'When a man comes with a vision,' she said, 'all we can do is try to go where he leads. We could not make the journey ourselves because we do not know the path. Nor do we have the courage for such a journey. So all we can do is follow.'

What we must also never underestimate is the fearsome cost that such courage usually entails. Margot Fonteyn, one of the most used and abused dancers in the entire history of ballet, although crippled with arthritis, was still 'dancing' at the age of sixty-seven because her 'employer', the Royal Ballet at Covent Garden, knew that with her name on the programme, they could sell every seat in the house. The fact that she died in a decrepit farmhouse in Panama, which I filmed, that had only a corrugated tin roof, no phone, no running water and no electricity; dying of cancer but somehow surviving on cornflakes, and that her body was then dumped in an unmarked pauper's grave – this all seems to escape many biographers, especially those working for the BBC Music department, as it 'tarnishes' our image of the great dancer. I would argue that, on the contrary, such details enhance and enrich our admiration for her astonishing achievements.

As for Maria Callas, her short career was entirely destroyed by a greedy, selfish Greek shipping magnate who 'collected' her as he had collected glamorous women all over the world (it was rumoured he had paid $10,000 dollars for a night with Eva Peron), and then persuaded Callas that they were to be married, thus wrecking her previous marriage. In fact, he gave her nothing – no jewels, no money, nothing.

Her trusted producer, Franco Zeffirelli, described to me: 'Nothing. Just half a cargo boat, which sank, along with the career of the greatest singing actress of the twentieth century.'

And think of Benjamin Britten. Not just that he was homosexual at a time when in England it was illegal, with prison a constant threat. Not just that he was a conscientious objector in the Second World War and was frequently branded a coward. Not just that with his weak heart, he was constantly ill – probably mostly psychosomatic. 'He spent an awful lot of time in hospital,' a close family friend told me, 'suffering from one disease, one illness, after another. Everything he's written has the subject of pain in it somewhere, doesn't it?' the friend added. 'So if we suffer the pain we do in listening to some of his music, imagine what it must have cost him to write it? It was the *pain* of being alive.'

Jack Charlton said a wise thing when I was interviewing him about Bobby Moore, the only English captain to lift the football World Cup. 'You know,' he said wistfully. 'Bobby Moore was one of us, one of the team. But he wasn't like us.' If ever there was a simple description of genius, that's it. One of us, but not like us.

So, if they are not like us, what is my role in all of this? First, to remember my encounters with these extraordinary people and many others like them, and to remember also the fights I had with various executives or commissioning editors in television who, for the most part, contributed little and were sometimes collectively ignorant, ill-informed and quite often illiterate. And yet they have, for the blink of an eye, power, in that they have money and access to the airwaves. I made one film with Ken Russell, *Isadora,* of which, although it was in most senses Ken's film, I am inordinately proud. Although that was our sole collaboration, we remained good friends until his dying day. One Saturday morning, not having spoken to him for maybe a couple of years, he telephoned to ask if I could remember the name of the commissioning editor for Music and Arts programmes for Central Television, an ITV company, in the autumn of 1977. 'Ummm...?' I replied. 'Come on,' he said, 'you of all people have cause to remember who that person was, the commissioning editor, et cetera, et cetera.' I really did wrack my brains, but could not for the life of me remember his or her name. I told Ken that, if necessary, I could check back in my diaries to see if that would help. I could hear that Ken was becoming increasingly impatient, so, eventually, I apologised and told Ken I could not remember, and to be perfectly honest I didn't really care. 'Precisely,' he chortled down the phone. 'No-one can remember his or her name, and what's more no-one cares. They have been completely forgotten, and you and I were making films ten years before this person existed, and we are still making films ten years after this 'person' has disappeared into oblivion.'

Secondly, allow me to quote Shostakovich in words written for him by the playwright David Rudkin in my film *Testimony*, about Shostakovich – Shostakovich whom we can now see as almost a lone voice, an agonisingly truthful and eloquent voice, describing Soviet Russia under the horrors of Stalin. Shostakovich was denounced by the Kremlin (again) in January 1948 for having apparently mocked the regime with his Ninth Symphony, which quoted, according to his chief persecutor, Comrade Zhdanov, 'a Yankee sergeant whistling.' Zhdanov and his henchman Khrennikov, about whom much more later, had then torn up the manuscript of his Ninth Symphony in front of him and then danced a *gopak* on the fragments.

Shostakovich was forced to reply, publicly, before a thousand of his colleagues. As Rudkin put it: 'Maybe I fall too much beneath my own private shadow,' Shostakovich said, 'and fail to speak, openly and plainly, to the living, and with objectivity? Then, yes, I fail. Fail by the standards of the highest art, which are the only standards. So I am grateful that you rebuke me. To be sure.'

'To reach the people: that is the question. But how is it done? I expect to receive instruction from you. I will study it with deep interest.'

But how *is* it done? That has always been my dilemma. How is it that I manage to persuade these great people, many reluctant ever to give interviews, to open their hearts to me, by comparison a nonentity? Is it my happy smiling face? Somehow, I doubt it. Is it my refusal to be bound by meaningless schedules and some preconceived 'agenda' imposed on me by those moronic commissioning editors? Possibly. For me, an interview has no time constraints, no editorialising, no obligations to anyone other than to the subject him or herself. Is it the knowledge that my films will have no 'narration' – no preening and self-regarding 'fearless frontline reporter' mumbling garbage and telling you what to think – only the subject themselves, speaking for themselves? Is it my patience, my willingness to wait and wait and wait again while my subject becomes clear about what they wish to say? Is it the simple fact that in all my films I am interested only in content, in my subject's courage, never in style? What is it that these people want to tell me; not what I want them to tell me? That is all there is; nothing more.

The strange thing is, that I never intended to get involved in film or television. While at university, the height of my ambition was to be a minor, and probably not particularly good, academic. But this was changed by a friend, several years older than me, Patrick Garland, who later went on to become a distinguished theatre and film producer. 'What was I planning to do in the long summer vacation?' he asked. The previous year I had packed butter in the basement of a branch of Sainsburys; that is, the butter would arrive in enormous blocks, and my job was to cut the block into one-pound squares, wrap it and send it upstairs to the shop to be sold. I confess, I was brilliant at it.

'I have a more interesting suggestion,' said my friend. He had just joined the BBC and was being sent to Salzburg to make a documentary about its international Festival. Ironically, I too was to make a film about the Salzburg Festival some forty years later. I spoke a little German and knew the city quite well, so this seemed an opportunity not to be missed. My job would be to hump the film equipment around to wherever it was needed, and film equipment in the early sixties was heavy and cumbersome. Never mind, I thought. This sounded much more fun than packing butter.

On about the third day on location in Salzburg, Patrick said he needed the equipment 'up there', in the castle on the Mönchsberg mountain (more of a large hill, in truth) which dominates Salzburg. 'No problem,' I replied. 'By 8 o'clock in the morning please,' he said. 'No problem,' I said. He did not say why it was needed there, or what it was he was going to film. But, dutifully, I hauled the equipment up to the castle in time and slumped, exhausted, in the small room where he had said it was required.

I was still catching my breath when in marched a muscular giant of a man who strode over to me and said aggressively, 'And who are you?' Mercifully, I recognised him as I mumbled my name. It was Oskar Kokoschka, the expressionist painter and erstwhile lover of Gustav Mahler's widow, Alma. He was soon followed by the film crew and numerous students who began setting up their easels, and I realised that we were about to film a master class given by one of most famous painters alive. But what were they about to paint or sketch? Within a few yards of where I was slumped was their subject. The most beautiful, completely naked, girl I had ever seen. It was a Damascene moment in my life, because I can remember thinking: Oscar Kokoschka, a beautiful naked girl, and I'm being paid for this! To hell with any feeble ambition to be a second-rate academic. This was the life for me – a life in film and television.

'To reach the people: that is the question. But how is it done?' I hope to provide a few clues in writing this book. As Captain Vere remarks at the end of Britten's opera *Billy Budd*, 'I was lost on an infinite sea, but I've sighted a sail in the storm, the far-shining sail, and I'm content. I've seen where she's bound for. There's a land where she'll anchor… for ever.' The Squire in Bergman's *The Seventh Seal,* which has had a profound effect on me throughout my life, put it even more succinctly: 'Feel the immense triumph in that last moment when you can still roll your eyes and wriggle your toes.'

Chapter 1

Cambridge

Arriving at university, I had hoped it would be the best of times; in many ways it turned out to be the worst of times. A little lad from Lowestoft Grammar school, I had no idea, for instance, about 'eating in hall' – as far as I recall, I had never eaten with anyone except my godparents, who had brought me up. I didn't possess a tie, and was too poor to own a suit. I had never even shared a room with anyone except my younger brother. The year I 'came up' (the social implications of that still thunder across the years), the intake at my college was about a hundred, of which no more than a handful were from other than a public school. Thus, the entire language and manners and rules which I was expected to understand and conform to were mysterious, alien even. I was made to feel isolated, unwanted and definitely unwashed. And when the student in the next room to me committed suicide towards the end of my first term, I was not surprised. The image of his coffin being taken down the staircase haunts me to this day. It is a scene which has appeared in one form or another in many of my films.

Far from being helped, it seemed to me then that the college authorities ignored those who simply did not fit in, especially when it was discovered that I had no interest in rowing or rugger. By chance, I was lucky in my room-mate, with whom I am still in touch sixty-five years later, and also in meeting a fellow grammar school lad (Trevor Nunn, Downing College) who galvanised in me a hitherto little-realised interest in the theatre. Eventually I rose, by default I still believe, to become president of the Shakespearean Marlowe Society, in which I had some local success and which, in its turn, persuaded me that the BBC held the key to my future. That is not a place I would recommend even to my worst enemy now, but at the time, the mid-sixties, it seemed a place of opportunity. However, it took three attempts to secure an interview at the University Appointments Board to enquire how I might join. I was told of a scheme called the 'General Traineeship', the purpose of which was to 'train' the future management of the BBC. 'Unfortunately,' he said, 'we (I never discovered to whom the 'we' referred) don't think you are suitable material, so we cannot recommend you.' 'All I want is the forms to fill in,' I told him, probably belligerently. 'Alas,' he said, 'We've run out' – clearly a lie. Of course, I then got the forms direct from the BBC. I did apply, and was one of seven chosen from over 4,000 applicants

I was 'saved', if that's the right word, by a bizarre series of coincidences. At the 'Freshers Fair', at which all freshmen and women are harangued into joining every conceivable club, or political party, or ego-soothing 'leisure pursuit', I was intrigued by the ten reasons given on a roneoed pamphlet for joining the Conservative Association, this notwithstanding an early visit to the Union where I had been sickened by the vulgar bombast of a man calling himself The President, one Leon Brittan. Item 10 on the pamphlet concerned the difficulties between 'Town & Gown' and advised that all good Conservatives should do their bit to smooth over potential ill-feelings. It said (and I have it still): 'Take out the girl from Woolworth's'. So I did – a blonde, bouffanted bombshell called Christine, whose taffeta dresses would have made her an instant star on 'Come Dancing'. I stayed loyal to her during all my years as an undergraduate.

I did find one senior friend in the college: the then Master, the distinguished constitutional lawyer Sir Ivor Jennings. For reasons which I never figured out, except possibly that he, too, had been to a grammar school, he took to me, and not merely because I was a promising scholar. More, perhaps, that he took to Christine, and it became a condition of my being invited to any college function that I bring her, although her dresses and raucous laughter caused shock-horror among the Dons and their mousy wives. For this, at least, I have cause to be grateful to the Conservatives.

And Christine it was who insisted that I take her to the première of a film about a new 'group' called The Beatles. At the time, my only knowledge of music was Beethoven's Fifth, although I was not sure what the 'Fifth' referred to. I went to the press conference before the première at the old Regal Cinema representing *Varsity*, the University student newspaper. After the usual asinine questions, and during the ensuing melee, I was accosted by one of the group's guitarists, who asked what I did. 'I'm a student,' I replied. 'Of what?' he asked. 'Moral Sciences,' which I tried to explain had nothing to do with morals and even less with science.

Understandably he thought this hilarious. Would I show him round the University that afternoon? 'No,' I replied; he/we would be mobbed. Very well, he would come in disguise. And when I met him later, outside his hotel, he was sporting a long beard and a dirty mackintosh. I took him to the Wren Library, King's Chapel and so on; mercifully, he abandoned his 'disguise'. In fact, no-one troubled us. 'Call me when you come to London,' he said on parting. I did, three years later. We met again, despite his being by then world-famous, and John Lennon became one of my best friends and greatly influenced the films I began to make subsequently.

So what is the moral of this tale? In retrospect, it would appear that the college prepared me for nothing. It did what it interpreted as its duty, but neglected what for me were more fundamental needs. My tutor, an engineer called Ernst Frankl, had the wisdom to suggest that I attend whatever lectures I wanted, not necessarily those associated with Moral Sciences. I did, and heard, among many others, Frank Leavis on the English novel and Jack Plumb on eighteenth-century British history. Of course, the times they were a-changin'. The intake year before me had been obliged to do National Service. And the acceptance of non-public school students, I was told, had badly affected the social mores of college life, although I am appalled by the apparent timidity of the present lot. And as to whether the inclusion of women students has enlightened the sex lives of the inmates, I doubt it.

Despite refusing to turn up for any 'graduation ceremony' for either degree, I hold no bitterness towards the college. Being there has not damaged my career. It was irrelevant. Much later, a friend was offered an honour by Her Majesty The Queen. He could not resist replying, 'Which Empire do you have in mind?' It seemed equally irrelevant. The years at Trinity Hall were, for me, wasted years – except for one thing. The friendships I made then have stayed with me throughout, and the loyalty that resulted has become the cornerstone of all that I have managed to achieve since. Such friendship is priceless and irreplaceable. Sadly, realising that she could not follow me to London after graduation, Christine was my one casualty. I regret it to this day.

I once worked in the summer vacation as a bus conductor. My driver, an asthmatic, disillusioned, book-devourer from a council estate off the Hills Road, referring to my student life which he regarded with envy, told me, 'Never forget. This is not a rehearsal for life. This is life itself.' I never forgot, but it was not something I was taught at Trinity Hall. Perhaps it should have been.

Chapter 2

Ken Russell

After University, I did join the BBC as a general trainee, effectively a scholarship scheme. Before my interview at the BBC, I was given a sound piece of advice. 'Wear something garish', I was told, 'and mug up on some unlikely topic rather than books or films.' I dutifully wore a bright yellow tie, and on the train up to London learnt an entire page of *The Racing World*. So when asked about my 'special interest', I recited this same page, which happened to be about greyhound racing, a topic in which I had no interest whatsoever. Years later, I read the report on my interview. It said, 'Knows about greyhound racing; should do very well in the sports department.'

But also during the interviews, I had made it plain that if they were to take me, I would like to work with Ken Russell. I had seen his film about Elgar and also the film about Bartok, both of which I had thought were extraordinary. Whoever had made these films, I realised, had a distinct visual intelligence at work.

One of the people who interviewed me was Huw Wheldon, then Head of Documentaries. But on my first day at the BBC, I was sent to Broadcasting House to read listeners' letters on *Woman's Hour*. Live on air – on Day One! Somehow, at the end of Day One, I managed to get Huw Wheldon on the phone and said, 'I've not spent years at a university in order to read letters on *Woman's Hour*.' He told me to come and see him the following day.

So I went to see him. 'Yes, yes,' he remembered my request to work for Ken Russell, but for now he was going to send me to Radio Nottingham for six weeks. 'What for?' I asked. 'Well, I think you will find out,' he replied. Eventually I came to admire and adore him. But at that point I was so angry, I almost resigned.

Off I went. This was 1964, long before the days of real local radio. Radio Nottingham consisted of a retired army colonel and his dog. The colonel was drunk every day after two o'clock, which was when he showed up in the office. In fact, it turned out to be a stroke of genius on Huw Wheldon's part, because by Day Three, up in Nottingham, I was doing everything. I'm out there with a microphone interviewing; I'm editing the tapes; I'm trying to figure out news stories, and how to transmit these back to London. I was a one-man local radio station. After six weeks, I was brought back from exile and finally went to work for Ken Russell. Huw Wheldon had told me, 'You will never get a better grounding.' And he was absolutely right. I had, incidentally, bought and read during my exile the entire works of that other citizen of Nottingham, D.H. Lawrence, books which I still have today.

So by the time I was let loose on Ken Russell I did 'know' a little bit - not much, but I had the beginnings of a technical grounding. The film that Russell was preparing was his portrait of the dancer Isadora Duncan. I even had the temerity to suggest a totally unknown actress called Vivian Pickles for the lead role. I had seen her at the Royal Court and suggested her to Ken. But my role, as Ken explained it to me, was very simple. The difficulty was that a couple of Egyptian entrepreneurs, the Hakim Brothers, owned all the rights to *My Life*, Isadora's autobiography. Therefore, my primary job was to go to the newspaper archive of the British Library and find contemporary references reported in the papers for every one of Isadora's exploits that we might want to include in the film.

My second job, he told me, was to get permission to use some of the more important locations. For instance, when Isadora had begun an affair with Paris Singer, of Singer sewing machine fame, he owned a large mansion, Oldway House, which he had remodelled on the Palace of Versailles especially for her, in Paignton. Paignton!? We would need to film there, so off I went to Paignton, only to discover that the house was now the main offices of Paignton Town Council. I had to persuade the entire council to move out for the week that we needed to film there. Here I was, less than three months in the job, on £15 per week, and I knew that Russell would never take no for an answer. Reader, I succeeded.

If craziness was the order of the day, perhaps my proudest achievement was to organise a jazz band to sit on top of the hearse containing the coffins of Isadora's two children, who had accidentally drowned in the Seine. Look closely, and you will see several members of what would become the Monty Python comedy troupe atop the hearse – uncredited, of course.

Filming is always full of hazards. In one particular scene, where we were on Dartmoor and had got lost in the fog, everything had gone wrong. The scene was supposed to take place in Siberia, where Isadora was on tour with her Russian lover, Yesenin. The fog had come down unexpectedly; some of the extras had vanished, as well as the actors playing Isadora and her manager, presumably eaten by the Baskerville Hound; the antique period car we were using for the film had ceased to function; the camera had jammed. So the scene in the script where Isadora, in frustration, throws her letters to the wind, was unfilmable. Or so we thought. I was immediately cast as Isadora's manager; Russell himself was the chauffeur trying to get the car going, and the assistant cameraman was tasked with throwing the letters in the air. The end result looks spectacular in the finished film, but what you can't hear is Russell absolutely losing his temper and shouting and screaming at everybody in sight. Looking at me, he said, 'How do they expect me to make films when I surrounded by fucking amateurs?' Then he paused, and said, 'No, fucking beginners!' Then there was a long pause and then, pointing at Sally, his new but devoted production secretary, 'And,' he said ominously, 'fucking half-timers!' The implication was that here was Ken Russell, an icon already within the BBC and elsewhere, yet so Mickey Mouse was the BBC's organisation that all his immediate team were either in short trousers or straight from school. We were all trying to do our best, and he knew that, but he felt he wasn't being given the kind of support he deserved. Huw Wheldon would have absolutely denied that, but the fact was that all those ground-breaking films of Ken's were made for peanuts. I remember the budget on *Isadora* was £13,500, and that included being on location for five and a half weeks. It was a lesson in how to use your minimal resources to the maximum advantage that I never forgot.

When you got to know him, however, you began to realise that Ken was enormously grateful for anything that anyone did for him. We all worked round the clock, most of us finishing up sick, to make sure he had what he needed to make his film. At one point, he wanted to upgrade my credit, but that was not allowed by the BBC, as I was only a 'general trainee'. When the film was edited, Huw Wheldon asked to see it, as was his right. A screening was arranged in the East Tower of the old Television Centre. It's a powerful film, and very emotional at the end. And Wheldon was an emotional Welshman; at the end of the film there were tears in his eyes. There was a very long pause, then he turned round to Ken and said, 'You boys. You boys clearly had a wonderful time making this film, I can see that. And it's a wonderful film. But there's a couple of scenes…' One scene, in particular, I remember was the scene with the children drowning in the Seine, although it had actually been shot in Egham Ponds. Huw said, 'Ken, I'm really not sure what you *meant* by that scene.' Ken exploded, 'If you can't fucking understand…! You've supported me in the past!' I was cowering. Wheldon, after all, was the boss. But Huw didn't bat an eyelid and said, 'There's this other scene I'm not sure…blah, blah, blah'. Then he said, 'But I can see you've had a wonderful time. It's a wonderful film. Thank you so much. It will be one great triumph.' And off he went.

There was a long pause. Then Ken looked at me, and said, 'You know, the bastard's right. I think we never really got that right. Now what can we do about it?'

Again, another lesson learned. How to be a good producer, not the interfering, focus group-orientated busybody beloved of today's television. A few months later, I inherited a film about Benjamin Britten. Whereupon Ken exploded again. I had betrayed him! I had let him down! He'd taught me everything! He'd befriended me! I was a lost child living in London and he'd welcomed me to his house - which, indeed, he had. With Ken, it was always personal, a personal commitment he required from people whether they were an actor or a technician. And provided he sensed that this personal commitment was there and that it was real and genuine, it didn't matter if they were completely incompetent. He'd probably tell you so. What mattered to him was that you'd live and die for his film. He was unbelievably generous, and genuinely concerned about your welfare. He suspected I had nowhere permanent to live, having just emerged from Cambridge, and he worried about that. I was always being asked round to dinner, or even taken out to dinner. He became the rock on which I began to build my career. I felt more secure about what I was trying to do because I had lived in his pocket for about six months. He wanted me to get involved in every stage of the film process, to see how it was done. So, in truth, I was given a six-month masterclass from a master, another lesson I never forgot.

Ken also taught me that music in a film must be part of the narrative drive of that film and not mere decoration. Above all, that no detail is too insignificant. To be prepared is everything; not that it excludes improvisation. But to have a secure foundation, an idea that propels the film, is all that counts. It's not the cleverness of the editing or even the style. Certainly not the silly fringe haircuts or theatrical cloaks. Content is everything. What are you trying to say, and when you know the answer, saying it clearly. 'Mean what you say, and say what you mean', as he told me repeatedly.

I need make no apology for Ken Russell's career, but I think it was the case that the more he felt he was being ignored, the more desperate he became to make his mark. As a result, several of his films are riddled with excess, almost always unnecessarily so. One of his biggest supporters was Norman Swallow in Granada Television, who had previously been the head of Omnibus at the BBC and had, with Humphrey Burton, then Head of Music and Arts, commissioned one of Russell's finest films, about the life of Debussy. Swallow was a Mancunian and he was determined that Russell should fulfil his dream of making films about the Lakeland poets, Wordsworth and Coleridge, not least because Russell had by now bought an idyllic cottage in Borrowdale Valley. His subsequent film about Coleridge, *Clouds of Glory*, is among his very finest, and although Russell and I had not worked together since *Isadora*, we had remained close friends. He invited me to see a preview of his new film and then discuss it with him in his cottage in Borrowdale.

In the opening five minutes of the new film, Coleridge, in a quivering haze of opium addiction, blunders around desperately searching for a bottle of laudanum to drown his nightmares, toppling piles of books, smashing tables, destroying manuscripts, hurtling through the bric-a-brac of his existence. Ice cold, a voice bitterly intones the opening verses of *The Rime of the Ancient Mariner*: 'It is an Ancient Mariner, And he stoppeth one of three…' as we see the poem made flesh in one fantastic image after another, never a pause, until, alone, adrift on a boat in a storm, Coleridge (brilliantly played by David Hemmings) plunges the boat's anchor into his wife's breast, killing her as if she were the albatross of the poem. It is a sequence of such power and ferocity and majesty, set to the third movement of Vaughan Williams's Symphony No. 4, and later his 6th, 7th Symphonies and *Job*, with some Britten thrown in for good measure. Never again will we be able to think of Vaughan Williams's music as cow-pasture English countryside, or read *The Ancient Mariner* and tell our children that English poetry is nice and harmless. It is, I suspected, Russell's testament, a scream of rage and a reminder that, even if despised, he was just the best English film director we had.

'I am ready for the abuse,' Russell told me. He had read it all before. "A psychologist of the uglier emotions"; "ideas as pretentious as they are bizarre"; "threads of all the foulest ditches and sewers of human despair". 'These have been some of the more kindly reviews I have had in recent years,' he told me. 'You can only be hurt for so long. It's a waste of time trying to answer. I'm sure the film critics hope that, by writing such things, I'll give up making films. It may come as a nasty surprise to them, but I intend to go on until I drop. The only thing to do is ignore them and get on with your life and your work.' Another lesson for me, I thought.

'The trouble is that people expect my films about composers, for instance, to be like paragraphs in Grove's *Dictionary of Music,*' he told me. 'Yet these same people will see and admire a Picasso portrait of Brigitte Bardot which looks nothing like her. Films are images, choreography, not words with pictures. You remember a good film by the vividness of its imagery, not the eloquence of its dialogue. Film echoes thought; it is just as elliptical and as rich as thought. The problem is, however, that film is still encumbered with Victorian-style photography, by its need to seem literal, by the commercial limitations contained in the idea of a 'film script' wherein everything has to be explicit. Film is in its infancy. It is an exploration, a celebration of the imagination: not a restriction, a barrier or a weapon. One achieves this freedom through discipline, of course, and knowledge of one's craft. But that, finally, is what it's all about. Film is freedom.'

Yet another lesson for me.

Not surprisingly, Russell commanded unqualified admiration from the actors he worked with. David Hemmings, who played Coleridge, told me he had 'never taken such chances before, never dared let himself go with such freedom'. I tracked down Richard Chamberlain, who had played Tchaikovsky in *The Music Lovers*. 'He is not an actor's director', he told me, 'in the sense that he gives you specific instructions. But he creates a tension, a charge of electricity, which brings out your best.' David Warner delivered (in his view) his best film role as Wordsworth. 'I was exhausted but completely exhilarated,' he told me. Michael Caine thought Russell was one of the greatest directors in the world; Vanessa Redgrave, who ravished the screen as a besotted nun in Russell's film *The Devils* told me simply that 'Russell's work is some of the best ever done in cinema.' And Robert Powell, who portrayed Mahler in the film of the same name added, 'He asks a lot from you, but he gives you so much in return.' And Glenda Jackson, who spoke so movingly a few years later at Russell's funeral, said, 'He made me believe *anything* was possible.'

'Critics always say that I must hate my subjects because I endow them with such hateful qualities, making them vulgar or obscene or full of bad taste. But I love my subjects, just as I love my work,' Russell told me. 'Hatred is much too wearing. I want people to see what I have seen, right or wrong, to share my understanding and *love* of Coleridge. It is not meant to be the whole truth and nothing but the truth, but of my response at a particular moment, my interpretation of another's vision. Making films is so utterly exhausting that only *love* and excitement for what one has seen and known in a painting or a sculpture or a piece of music can sustain you. Especially love.'

Ken Russell's work cottage in the Lake District, where we chatted into the night clearly sustained him, just as his new baby daughter (his seventh child) warmed him. He is alone, and knows it. Of late, he has had to acknowledge this loneliness as never before. His marriage to his first wife, Shirley, had gone awry; his new wife, Vivian, did seem to bring him some comfort. But his agony is the uncertainty of his future, 'like a bird before a gale', as Huw Wheldon had once described him, 'powerless to affect its destiny'. 'I feel I am a foreigner, in exile,' Russell told me, a little sadly. 'When I am in London, the people there seem furtive, dressed up for effect, as if in a nightmare. No one, nothing, seems real. Here in the Lakes, with the constantly moving skies, I feel I am in touch with the elements of our existence. Somewhere, I'm told, a few appreciative souls still like my work, somewhere, beyond this valley.'

Tragically, not long after our reunion, he split from Vivian, who demanded the cottage in the Lake District as part of the marriage settlement. His dream gone, he was once again a bird before the gale. Two further wives followed, and another child. In spite of a foray into Hollywood, his films became shorter, more desperate, and often shot on primitive camera phones because no-one would finance him. Melvyn Bragg, a long-time collaborator and screenwriter for *Clouds of Glory* and *Women in Love*, Russell's Oscar-winning feature film, continued to support him on *The South Bank Show*, but, as Bragg told me. 'At one point when Ken was absolutely desperate for work because he had no money, I commissioned a film about Bruckner. Nothing seemed to be happening, so one day I went to the film editing room and found Ken more or less slumped, completely drunk, and making no sense whatsoever. This was a bad period for him, a very bad period of drunkenness, but also despair.'

In the end, Ken Russell probably opened the eyes and ears – including my own – like no other British film maker: from Vaughan Williams to Benjamin Britten, from Bax and Butterworth to Bliss and Frank Bridge. I owe Ken Russell all, and much besides, from Isadora onwards. I, too, live among the hills and valleys, but of Cornwall. I, too, have been constantly attacked for vulgarity. His preoccupations have become mine over the years. 'Too many people think that films are frivolous things,' he said despondently. 'Well, they are my life. I bought my first movie projector when I was nine, and during the war cycled thirty miles every week to Salisbury to see the latest release. Although I am told my work is in large part autobiographical, I feel I am too mixed up with myself to see myself clearly. Images, places, memories, dreams, my preoccupation with death, a revolt against the living death of modern man, for whom death and pain have been anaesthetised, the ritualistic celebration which is Catholicism – yes, I know these things appear over and over. But a film about myself would be very boring. Just me, sitting in a room, playing a lot of records. Not much point in any of that.'

The bewildering fury of Russell's film on Coleridge, however, told a different story. In Coleridge's own words:

'I pass, like night, from land to land;
I have strange power of speech;
That moment that his face I see,
I know the man that must hear me:
To him my tale I teach.

He went like one that hath been stunned,
And is of sense forlorn:
A sadder and a wiser man,
He rose the morrow morn.'

Chapter 3

Alice

My involvement in Jonathan Miller's film of *Alice in Wonderland* was tortured and tortuous.

Having survived Ken Russell and his film *Isadora*, on which I had acted as location fixer, casting director, 2nd unit director, music supervisor and general factotum, none of which I remotely regretted, I was once again summoned by Huw Wheldon, by now Managing Director of Television at the BBC. He told me of Jonathan Miller's plan to make a substantial film of the Lewis Carroll story. 'I think he will need a producer who understands how such a film is made,' Wheldon told me. 'He will need a safe pair of hands, since I'm not too sure Jonathan should be let loose on such a large-scale project without help, and help from someone who has done it before and will be able to deal with him.' I learned later from Russell's unpublished diaries that he had told Wheldon he considered me to be the best 'producer' he had ever had, and that it was 'monstrous' of Wheldon to take me away from him. Considering that Russell had had loyal 'producer support' from both Wheldon and Humphrey Burton, I have always thought this to have been somewhat of an exaggeration.

I should make it clear that most of the ideas permeating the film of *Alice* were Jonathan's; my involvement, or at least that was the intention, was to be purely on the production side – in effect, the film's producer. As such, my first (successful) move was to introduce Miller to Dick Bush, who had been the cameraman on *Isadora* and later on Russell's film about Coleridge, *Clouds of Glory*. I told Miller that I considered Bush the best there was in the BBC, notwithstanding his involvement in some obscure cult called The Plymouth Brethren, a fact which greatly amused Miller.

Although at that time BBC Television was transmitted entirely in black and white, both Bush and I tried to persuade Miller to shoot the film in colour (the physical medium was, after all, celluloid), but to no avail. I was sent off to find the locations and make some suggestions as to casting. As I greatly admired Wilfred Brambell, for instance, having met him during the filming of *A Hard Day's Night*, though more lately he was known almost exclusively as the wizened father in *Steptoe and Son*, I suggested him for the part of the White Rabbit. I also brought in Eric Idle, long before Monty Python made him famous, and found Anne-Marie Mallik who played Alice. In fact, my hardest job had been to persuade her parents – a distinguished Indian lawyer father and a very prim upper-middle-class mother – that the experience would greatly benefit their daughter's education. The rest of the cast involved many stars who would later feature in my own work, from Peter Sellers to Sir John Gielgud, from Peter Cook to John Bird and Michael Redgrave.

Inevitably, I asked Miller if he had given any thought to the music that might be needed for the film. He said, 'Oh, I know so little about music, and you seem to know a bit about it. Why don't you organise some concerts for us to go to. I'll pay, but you arrange it.' A rather strange request, I thought, but I was happy to oblige. 'Oh, and by the way,' he added, 'if you can, get a box in whatever concert you find, so that I can sit at the back and read a book in the event that I need some stimulation.' It so happened that the first concert I came across was being given by someone I knew (the Beatles connection again) and for whose concert I already had a ticket. It was at the Festival Hall; the soloist was the great sitar player, Ravi Shankar. 'Oh well,' said Miller, 'If you insist. But please come and pick me up at my home and we'll go together so that I don't get lost.'

The evening duly came. When I picked Miller up as planned, I was not surprised to see that he was clutching a pile of books, loosely tied together by a purple ribbon. Every time we stopped at some traffic lights, I noticed that he slid down in the passenger seat at the front of the car. I apologised for what I thought must be my erratic driving, but then I realised it was because he didn't want to be recognised. Eventually, we took our places in a box at the Festival Hall, and – just as he said he would – Miller sat at the back, rather obviously reading one of his books, I thought.

Anyone who has ever been to a sitar concert will know that the first several minutes are taken with the sitar and tabla players 'tuning up', and after the applause as Shankar and Alla Rakhar entered the stage, this is precisely what happened. After a few minutes, however, I felt a hand on my shoulder and Miller saying breathlessly, 'That's it. That's the sound I need. Genius. Thank you.' And then he fled into the night with me running after him, trying to explain that the concert hadn't started yet. The following day I went to see Shankar and told him about the film. Would he agree to provide the music? I think he had no idea who Miller was, but on my assurance that it would be a bona fide project he agreed. Many months later, he and Rakhar duly arrived in Dubbing Theatre X of the East Tower in the old BBC Television Centre to improvise the music to the by then partly edited film.

Imagine my horror, therefore, when I read the following in a *Life Magazine* interview published to coincide with the film's transmission as a 'Wednesday Play' on 28 December 1966: 'When I first began to visualise the Lewis Carroll story, I saw immediately that since it had been written in the Indian Summer of Empire (1865), only the sound of India could provide the musical background.' I would be the first to admit that Miller's instinct, as in so many things, had been spot on, but to justify or to rationalise it in this way seemed to me entirely specious.

Later, Miller and I fell out completely, and I was rapidly demoted down the credits. Wheldon even told me that Miller would have preferred that I was not credited at all. Wheldon had refused the request. Miller even went so far as to include in my 'Annual Report' (the BBC had such things in those days) that I was someone not to be trusted; 'wild and uncontrollable', was the phrase he used, apparently. I can offer two reasons: the first, gossip, the second, fact. Part of my job was to organise all the actors for the extras and small parts. There was a particularly beautiful Russian girl who appeared in rather more scenes than perhaps she should have. She told me that Miller had made it clear to her that he required a little TLC, but she had rebuffed him, not least because she and I were already involved in a brief but passionate affair. Miller, I assume, was less than pleased to be usurped by this upstart Palmer. Forty years later, Anne-Marie, now Mrs Huxstep, a banker and mother of four children, confirmed this to be so.

The second reason was rather more serious. When I saw the first rough-cut of the film, having watched all the rushes day after day as they were being filmed, I was greatly disappointed by the result. I told Miller unequivocally that either he or his editor (Pam Bosworth) had not made the best of the material, and that the editing was often clumsy, frequently diminishing rather than enhancing the power of the images that Dick Bush, the cameraman, had created. I was ordered from the viewing room and never spoken to again. The only positive result was that I vowed that thereafter, I would always edit my own films if I was ever given the chance to work again.

Chapter 4

Britten

In fact, it wasn't long before a golden opportunity came knocking – literally. My first solo film, *Britten and His Festival*, however, I inherited quite by chance. Benjamin Britten was apparently extremely reluctant to be filmed. A previous twelve-minute profile made by John Schlesinger for Huw Wheldon's *Monitor* had displeased Britten, although no-one had ever been able to figure out why. He had made various BBC studio recordings, most notably a folk song recital with Peter Pears, a visit to the BBC's Riverside Studios to record a Mozart piano quartet (since lost) and a ninety-minute studio-based 1963 *Monitor* special called *Britten at 50* which included movements from the *Sinfonia da Requiem* and the then brand-new *War Requiem*.

But with the forthcoming opening of the new concert hall at Snape in 1967, renewed efforts were made to persuade Britten to agree to a full-length portrait on location in Aldeburgh. Thanks to the influence of his trusted record producer, John Culshaw, and his friend Humphrey Burton, then head of Music and Arts at the BBC – both of them later to become among my closest professional colleagues and an enormous influence on me and my work – Britten agreed. I was rescued from my post-Miller disgrace and hired as Humphrey Burton's tea boy.

Then everything went pear-shaped. The week before we were due to start filming, Humphrey got fired by the BBC because it had been leaked to the *London Evening Standard* that he and others from the BBC, including Frank Muir, were about to set up the first *commercial* ITV station in London: London Weekend. This was seen, principally by Huw Wheldon, as a terrible act of betrayal (Humphrey was being groomed to take over BBC Television when Wheldon retired), and Burton was shown the door.

I was forgotten in the turmoil; or, rather, what the BBC saw as an important film in its arts coverage about Britain's greatest living composer was forgotten. But not for long. I was nervously awaiting instructions in my hotel in Aldeburgh, looking out across the North Sea – curiously calm that day, I thought. At that time there were no phones in our rooms, so there came a 'knock knock' on the door, with the manager saying there was a phone call for me in reception. It was Humphrey Burton telling me what had happened, but I was to stay put and await developments. Back to my room. 'Knock knock' again, with the manager saying there was another phone call for me in reception. Huw Wheldon, not only Managing Director of BBC Programmes at that time but also a distinguished military commander from the Second World War, Military Cross no less, was ringing me to say not to panic. 'The cavalry are coming!' he said with that unforgettable Welsh bravado and enthusiasm with which he imbued everyone. Back to my room.

'Knock knock' again, with the manager saying there was yet another phone call for me in reception. I replied that I didn't care who it was, I was not answering any more phone calls. 'Oh, I think you'll want to take this one,' he said, 'It's Mr Britten.' 'Don't worry,' said Britten. 'We've heard the news. Please come up and have tea and let's discuss it.'

I had obviously already met him when planning the film with Humphrey Burton. But to be summoned in this way was not my idea of a quiet life. But, as I had little choice, off I went to tea in The Red House, his home. Britten made the tea; Peter Pears cut the cake. I recall being so nervous that I don't think I uttered a word, while the two of them fussed about and kept telling me not to worry. *They* would get me through it. What I most remember, however, is the two of them giggling throughout the tea like silly schoolchildren. And so began a journey which, for me, has been undoubtedly one of the most important of my life: my association with one of the greatest composers of our time.

Years later, after Britten had died, when Pears asked me to make a semi-official biographical film about Britten, later to be called *A Time There Was*, I asked him if he recalled our first tea together and why he and Britten seemed to me to be having a giggling fit. Oh yes, he said, he remembered very well. 'You see,' he went on, 'we never really wanted to make that film. Then Humphrey got fired, and we were left with you.

And we guessed that you hadn't the faintest notion how to set about making the film, so the result would be that we could do precisely what we wanted – if anything! How wrong we were,' he added with a smile. 'Ben loved the film, as did I, and we were very proud to welcome you into our "family", as it were.'

Eventually, I made five films with or about Britten, including a film of his opera *Death in Venice,* made at his request almost, on location in Venice. This continued association came about partly because of a chance meeting with a formidable woman called Sue Phipps, who was Peter Pears's niece but also the manager and general factotum of the two of them. My first encounter with Sue was, in fact, being told off by her during the making of that first film in 1967, for trying to abscond with a rather beautiful member of the Kodaly Girls Choir, who were singing at the Aldeburgh Festival that year. 'Much too young for you,' was Sue's stern admonishment. I was later told that she had recounted this escapade to her uncle Peter, who had thought it highly amusing. But, clearly, I was in the doghouse.

To say that she then guided me through the difficulties of filming Ben and Peter, not to mention the grumpy Sviatoslav Richter (the great Russian pianist who loathed being filmed) would be an understatement. For example, in spite of repeated requests from me and Britten himself, Richter had refused to be filmed, point-blank, until Sue came up with a master plan of deception and deceit. 'You must be absolutely ready at 3pm on the stage of Snape Concert Hall', she told me, 'and I will arrange for Ben to bring Richter over for a "rehearsal". And I will tell Ben that he must simply "guide" Richter to the piano come what may.' Which is precisely what happened, with a wonderful resulting sequence of Britten and Richter playing the last movement of Mozart's *Sonata for Two Pianos in D Major,* with Richter constantly trying to upstage Britten by slowing down and speeding up the tempo to throw Britten off course in revenge, almost, for this act of deception. Britten was far too wonderful a pianist himself to be fazed by this, but at the end of the filming, if looks could kill, the glare I got from Richter when he realised he had been outmanoeuvred would have shrivelled me into a speck of dust.

And it was Sue who initiated that second major portrait I made of Britten, called *A Time There Was,* not long after he had died. Make a film about the love affair between Ben and Peter, she told me. But when I broached this with Peter, his eyes welled up and he asked, 'Will we get away with it?' After all, the legalisation of homosexuality between consenting adults was only just over ten years old. 'We will,' I said. And we did.

Both of these early films achieved some modest success; the 1967 portrait was the first BBC film ever to be networked in the USA, and the second won the first of my three Italia Prizes. But I knew in my heart that they were only sketches of what should have been. So as 2013 approached, with the hundredth anniversary of Britten's birth on the horizon, Sue challenged me again. Over a long day at her home in Suffolk, she kept prodding me: think what the *War Requiem* is really about; or *Owen Wingrave*; or *The Ballad of Heroes*; and the *Cello Symphony*; and *Turn of the Screw*; above all, *Nocturne* and its explosive climax 'Sleep No More!' 'Ben's music is about pain, above all else,' she said, 'his and the world's as he saw it. Make a film about that and I will help you. It won't make you popular, because all those who think Britten's music is primarily just brilliant decoration will be deeply offended.'

And so we did. The extended interview she gave me for that film, looking glamorous as always, seemed to me at the time, and since, worth a thousand books. She understood Britten's deeply troubled genius better than anyone. I tried to make a film not only worthy of him but also of her. She came to the première at the Barbican in London. She cried; actually, she wept. I nervously asked if she thought Ben would have been offended by the violence of the film and its relentlessly harsh message. She said little, except that she was certain Ben would have known that here was the truth about him, at last.

But to return to that initial tea party in 1967. Britten's and Pears's instincts had, in fact, been spot on. I really had very little idea what I was doing. For example, I wanted to film one of the movements from *A Ceremony of Carols,* the closing section of which consisted of alternating chords from the harp and the boys' choir. I discovered in the editing that I had not filmed a sufficient number of chords, either from the choir or the harp. Easy, I thought. I'll just cut out a couple of bars. After all, the music does tend to repeat itself at that moment.

I then forgot about it until the first screening, which was held in the old BBC studios in Lime Grove, hosted, of course, by Huw Wheldon. I sat between Britten and Pears. The film (celluloid, in those days) was already running when I suddenly remembered my 'cut'. What was I to do? Try and distract Britten at the crucial moment? Cough loudly? I was in such a panic that the 'cut' had been and gone before I could do anything.

At the lunch afterwards, Britten was very gracious about the film, and I breathed a heavy sigh of relief. He hadn't noticed, I thought.

Came the moment after lunch that Britten climbed into the limousine at the door of the BBC; Pears hugged me and told me to come back to Aldeburgh soon. Britten embraced me warmly, and began to climb into the car. Just at the very last moment, he turned back to me and said, with a big smile, 'You know, I'm not sure if it isn't better without those extra bars.'

'I believe that the artist must be consciously a human being,' Britten recalled several years later. 'He is part of society and he should not lock himself up in an ivory tower. I think he has a duty to pay towards his fellow creatures. It is not only a duty; I feel it's a pleasure too. I want to have my music used. I would much rather - this seems perhaps a silly thing to say - but I would rather have my music used than write masterpieces which were not used.'

'But everything he's written has the subject of pain in it somewhere, doesn't it?' Sue Phipps asked me. 'The *pain* of being alive. But he also had physical pain, a lot of physical pain. One wonders why he had to go through that. You'd have thought that psychological and spiritual pain would have been enough. He was always ill. He spent an awful lot of time in hospital, suffering from one disease after another, which was extremely difficult for doctors to deal with because it was probably what most people would nowadays call psychosomatic. Somebody suggested that he should go off to a psychoanalyst - probably been the best thing he could do - and he was absolutely furious. 'You expect me to ruin my gift? I'd never be able to write music again if I'm psychoanalysed.' That was the end of that. So if we experience the pain we do in listening to some of his music, imagine what it must have cost him to write it.'

Not quite the image of Benjamin Britten I was expecting, nor that perceived by the general public and, particularly, by those buffoonish and smug BBC radio and television commentators who infest the airwaves.

To begin with, the revolutionary and pacifist tendencies in Britten were never far from the surface, which feelings culminated, of course, in the incomparable *War Requiem*. 'We were very much to the Left of politics,' Peter Pears told me. 'But the dividing line really came with the violence; Ben and I were very early signatories to the Peace Pledge. One of his earliest works was the *Ballad of Heroes*, which appealed for strong action against militarism. Sadly, it had very few performances. I don't remember crowds of pacifists walking around London singing it,' Pears said with a laugh. 'So I'm afraid in that way it wasn't what you might call a great success.'

But when, years later, the BBC, no less, decided to commission an opera specifically for television, the resulting work, although judged a failure at the time, was *Owen Wingrave*. 'Here was the great chance,' Donald Mitchell, Britten's latter-day publisher, explained to me, 'to use television, which Ben himself did not care for, to reach a huge world-wide audience, to speak out as best he could for the need for peace to replace the violence of the world in which we all lived.'

And for me this was encapsulated in Wingrave's first great aria, sung while he is watching the troops in manoeuvres in Hyde Park.

'False plumes and pride, obedience
that ends in destruction and murder...
And, to the Royal murderers, whose mean thrones
Are brought by crimes of treachery and gore...
They cajole with gold,
And promises of fame, the thoughtless youth
Already crushed with servitude; he knows
His wretchedness too late...
Look to thyself, priest, conqueror, or prince!
Whether thy trade is falsehood...'

Again, not quite the Benjamin Britten of popular imagination.

But what was he really like as a man? Again, all my memories are quite at odds with the customary image. Yes, he could be vicious, stingy, unforgiving, and his career was littered with those who were cast aside when perhaps he felt they were no longer useful to him. The worst case, perhaps, was Stephen Reiss, who had since 1948 slaved endlessly with the creation of the burgeoning Aldeburgh Festival, moving chairs (literally), arranging rehearsals, soothing temperaments. Britten admired him so greatly that his opera *Midsummer Night's Dream* is dedicated to Stephen Reiss and his wife, a rare honour. But then came the building of the new concert hall at Snape, itself a major undertaking requiring more expert management, and Reiss was suddenly dropped, persona non grata. No-one knew why, but Reiss was devastated and never recovered, dying a few years later from a heart attack and a broken spirit.

I, too, suffered from a similar rebuke. During the opening ceremony by Queen Elizabeth of the new Snape Concert Hall in 1967, the Duke of Edinburgh had casually asked me, in an affectionate tone, 'What has the old man written for the gala concert?' When I recounted this remark in my regular column I then wrote for the *Observer* newspaper, Britten (I was told) was beside himself with fury against the Duke, and me for repeating the remark. 'OLD!?' he exploded. Britten was fifty-three at the time. One of Britten's earliest champions had been Desmond Shaw-Taylor, the music critic of *The Sunday Times*. After the television première of *Owen Wingrave*, Shaw-Taylor ventured to suggest in his newspaper that perhaps the work was not best suited for television. Desmond showed me Britten's response. He had torn Shaw-Taylor's modest review into shreds with a note saying that he was never, ever, to come to Aldeburgh again.

Meeting Britten and Pears was like meeting a pair of prep school masters. Britten always seemed to wear the same knitted tie. Both of them dressed extremely respectably. 'You'd never get Ben lolling around in a kaftan, would you?' the counter-tenor James Bowman told me. For years, they had the same housekeeper, Miss Nellie Hudson, for whom they actually had built a little cottage in the grounds of their home, The Red House, in Aldeburgh. 'They were home cooking lovers,' she told me with pride. 'But when Mr Pears came home from singing abroad, he'd bring a continental recipe for me to do. He was more into food than Mr Britten. Mr Pears would say, "Well, Mr Britten liked nursery food, you know, he likes his nice milk pudding." I said, "Yes, but he likes it nice. Nice creamy milk pudding." And Mr Britten liked spotted dog. You'd never have to stint with anything. But Mr Britten had to be careful, because he hadn't got a strong inside like Mr Pears had. Oh, and they were always clean, very clean. Mr Britten was always in and out of the bath. Oh Lord, yes, they were very clean people.'

'I remember going for dinner one evening with Peter and Ben and some friend of Peter's, who Ben plainly didn't terribly like,' James Bowman remembered, 'so I think I was there as a sort of foil. Mrs Hudson kept coming in and banging down dishes in front of us with "here's your dinner". But it was all very domestic. Ben sat there, and we almost had to spoon-feed him. He sat at the head of the table like a little boy. He never put his hands on the table; they were always under the table.'

'He couldn't bear dirt,' Sue Phipps told me. 'He had to know where everything was and everything had to look just so. The difference between the two of them became quite obvious when you thought about catching trains at railway stations. Ben liked to be there two days beforehand, but Peter liked to jump onto the train as it was leaving the station. They were two halves of a whole,' Sue Phipps recalled. 'Peter was the feminine side and Ben was the masculine side. In any relationship like that it tends to be the woman who looks after the man.'

'And Peter was much more aware of the necessity for comfort, for a mattress to absorb the shocks. So there were so many aspects of their relationship which made life easier for Ben, not just the working relationship, but also a wonderful kind of tenderness. He understood about Ben and his friendship with boys; I think he approved of it, actually. But he cherished him enormously. There were moments, of course, when Peter had his own needs and went off, sometimes even with women, not for a very deep relationship, but he did enjoy the company of women and from time to time Ben got a bit jealous of that. But on the whole, all Ben's needs took precedence over Peter's. Until they reached the concert platform. And then when Ben got so upset and so worried about going onto the stage, it began to destroy Peter's nerves altogether and sometimes he shouted at Ben and said, 'For goodness sake pull yourself together. I can't go on to this platform and sing if you go on like this.'

I asked Peter about their homosexuality. 'The word "gay" was not in Ben's vocabulary,' Peter said casually, 'I mean, there was a streak of the puritan in Ben, decent behaviour, decent manners, all part of a fine life. Gracious living, if you like. But "the gay life" he resented, and we thought it was an absurd title to give a movement which was so full of difficulties and tensions and troubles. No doubt, one would have become reconciled to that description eventually, because everyone else uses it. And it's certainly a pleasanter-sounding word than "homosexual".' Tearfully, he added, 'It was established very early that we were passionately devoted and close, and that that was it. It wasn't superhuman, no. But there was very, very little that disturbed our relationship, and I was terribly conscious of his faith in me. I like to think that I returned that as warmly as he gave it. But I can't ever feel that I could reach his particular extraordinary quality of trust and faith and love.'

Michael Berkeley, himself a composer and son of another composer, Lennox Berkeley, was also Britten's godson. 'As a godfather,' Berkeley told me, 'Britten was better than any I've ever known and certainly better than I've ever been. I would get postcards and letters from all over Europe. There would always be five or ten pounds enclosed, and obviously at Christmas and birthdays. I think he would have liked children. I think he even talked to my mother about that. He wanted to adopt. He identified with children. It wasn't that he wanted to interfere with them; he was childlike in that way. But all of his insecurities meant that he understood what being a child was like, especially in an adult world, and so he was much less well-equipped to deal with adults.'

'He was also a complete hoarder,' Colin Matthews, Britten's latter-day musical assistant told me. 'After Ben died we've been able to recreate the garden of The Red House because he kept all the receipts for plants he had bought, year in, year out. We also know how much he paid for virtually every item of furniture in the house because he kept all the receipts and bills.'

Of course it was impossible – and it would have been impertinent – to ask Britten himself about 'being a composer', although, to my astonishment, he did venture some thoughts on the matter one afternoon when, trembling, I asked him about his daily schedule. I think it helped, and amused him, when I pointed out that while he had been born in Lowestoft on the east coast of England, I, too, had spent part of my youth there at the local grammar school. And although his parents' house had been at the 'posh' end of town, mine had definitely been at the poorer end of this fishing community.

'I don't really work very much,' he said jokingly. 'I do the bulk of my work away from the paper; when walking, when driving cars, in trains; not in aeroplanes, which I don't enjoy so much. Then, when the music is fixed in my head, I go to the paper and work out more precisely the details. I like working to an exact timetable. I often thank my stars that I had a rather conventional upbringing, that I went to a rather strict school where one was made to work and I can, without much difficulty, sit down at eight-thirty or nine o'clock in the morning and work straight through the morning until lunchtime. I don't say I always enjoy the work at that time, but it isn't a great struggle to do so each day. I find actually the day divides up quite naturally into three or four periods – the morning as I said, when I work, then lunchtime, then in the afternoon letters or, rather more importantly, I go for a walk when I plan out what I'm going to write in the next week at my desk. I then come back after tea up to my studio here and work, say, through to dinner time, about eight o'clock. After dinner I usually find I'm too sleepy, too exhausted to do much more than to read a little bit and then go to bed rather early. But, I admit, as I get older it is becoming more and more difficult to satisfy my ear that I have found the right notes to express my ideas.'

Simple, really.

The truth was slightly more 'serious'. As Colin Matthews explained to me, 'He did write at extraordinary speed. I mean, once he'd got the idea of the work in his head, he wrote with enormous facility and very rarely got stuck. I mean, there are letters and diary entries saying, "I've got hopeless stuck." Well, for Britten that meant a couple of hours or perhaps an afternoon when he couldn't get going. Not like with others who might have a six-month block. There were very few works of his that had any "blocks". It's absolutely staggering. He would give himself something less than six months to write a whole opera with the performance scheduled and completion of the full score mapped out clearly before him.'

'He didn't compose at a piano, as people so often imagine,' his copyist Rosamond Strode explained to me. 'That's the Hollywood notion of a composer. He worked in his head first, endlessly, and then at his desk. And he was terribly insistent that it was desk work was the bit that mattered. And then he'd play over what he had written. But he didn't do it at the piano; he'd play over what he'd done sitting at his desk to see that his ears were satisfied.' Imogen Holst, the daughter of Gustav, and another of Britten's musical assistants, agreed. 'Working for him was very exhausting, especially because of the speed with which he himself worked. It was quite incredible. When I used to tell people that he could do thirty pages of his full score in one day they thought I was lying.'

While at Cambridge, I had sung, badly, in the University Church choir. The organist was a distinguished musician, not least because he had only one arm. Douglas Fox could drive a car, although his manner of driving was often quite scary. He knew I could drive. One day he asked me if I could drive him over to Coventry to hear a new work by Benjamin Britten in the new Cathedral. I agreed, and so found myself at the world première of the *War Requiem*, 30 May 1962, part of the Consecration Festival Celebrations of the new Cathedral – the old cathedral having been bombed during the War in 1941. It was a chill and drizzly evening, and although the performance was due to begin at eight o'clock prompt, as it was being broadcast live on the BBC, the Cathedral authorities had decided to admit us all though only one door, so there was a long queue of people trying to get in on time. And if you listen to the recording of the broadcast, for a good ten minutes after the announcer has introduced the programme, all you hear is the shuffling of the audience trying to get to their seats. Ironically, in the BBC Archives is a letter from a listener expressing gratitude for these moments of comparative silence before the performance began, which had allowed her to 'gather her thoughts in appropriate contemplation' of what was to come.

And what was to come would never be forgotten by anyone who was there. A myth grew up that either the composer, or the cathedral authorities, had requested that no applause was to take place, before or after. This was nonsense. When we finally got to our seats, we applauded as the soloists and conductors (there were two: Meredith Davies, conducting the large orchestra, and Britten himself, the smaller chamber orchestra) took their places. But at the end there was total silence. We felt as if we had been run over by a truck. We could not speak. The emotional impact of this new work that obviously none of us had heard before was overwhelming. I was in tears. I could not speak to my one-armed organist Douglas Fox for some hours afterwards. I was sitting about halfway back in the nave, and when the music stopped I could see that such was the silence that none of the soloists or conductors knew quite what to do. Eventually, I saw Meredith Davies step down from his podium, walk across to Britten, take him by the arm and lead him off, backstage. Years later I asked Davies what had then happened. He said he had begun to say to Britten words to the effect that the performance had not gone too badly, only for Britten to put up his hand and, believing that because of the silence the whole event had been a failure, say grumpily, 'Well, at least the idea was good!'

In fact, as I learned when I got to know Britten later, the 'event' had nearly been a total disaster. It's quite clear from the correspondence that both the Cathedral and the Festival committee thought that Britten would treat this commission as a great honour and do it for nothing. Britten was quite caustic in his comments about that, effectively saying, Would they expect a cleaner to come and work for nothing?

But because the Consecration Festival was so important to the *Diocese* of Coventry, the Festival committee had decided that the chorus for the Festival should be made up of a mixture of nine local choirs. Anybody who wanted to sing could sing, including those who couldn't read music. Therefore, many of the choir members would be attempting a work that was completely out of their comfort zone. With rehearsal time limited, the initial rehearsals couldn't have amounted to much more than note bashing. It was almost as if they were trying to teach people who couldn't read music to sing from memory. So, when Britten arrived for the first full rehearsal in April, one month before the première, he had apparently said, 'This is not going to happen,' and wanted to cancel the performance.

Worse was to come. Because this was a brand-new building, out of concern regarding the loads that would be exerted on the new floor, the

Cathedral authorities had refused permission for any tiered staging for the chorus to be erected. This meant that many of the choir, certainly those at the back, couldn't see the conductor, and he couldn't see them.

But the other major problem, as Dietrich Fischer-Dieskau, the baritone soloist at the première told me, was that they had all been led to believe that the acoustics in the new building were 'wonderful'. However, Britten said (according to Fischer-Dieskau), they were 'absolutely pernicious'. Very few people in the orchestra or the choir, let alone the soloists, could hear what was going on. Added to all this, Britten himself was not well. He was suffering from bursitis. He'd had surgery for piles earlier in the year and was certainly not at his best.

Naturally, it was always anticipated that Britten would conduct the première himself. But because of the horror of the rehearsals, he had lost his nerve, and according to Peter Pears had decided that he couldn't conduct the whole thing himself. Panic ensued. I still have the original programme for that famous night in May, and it shows Britten conducting the main orchestra with Meredith Davis, who'd been training the choirs, conducting the chamber orchestra. They decided, or I think Peter Pears forced Britten, to swap their roles as conductors.

And the final insult, was that Britten had always wanted the three soloists to represent three different countries which had suffered most in the Second World War. Peter Pears, who was obviously English; the baritone Dietrich Fischer-Dieskau, who was German; and because of Britten's friendship with the cellist Rostropovich, Galina Vishnevskaya, star of the Bolshoi and wife of Rostropovich, would sing the soprano part. And she was Russian. Again, all hell broke out.

It is usually said by way of an excuse that it had been too late to organise a visa for Vishnevskaya. That was a lie, simply because she was already in London singing *Aida* in Covent Garden. In fact, she was told in words of one syllable by the Russian Embassy in London that she was not, not now or ever, to appear on stage with a *German*! The official note read (Galina showed me):

> *'The government refuses you permission to appear on the same stage as a German. We would not want to see a Soviet Russian girl side by side with a German, Fischer-Dieskau. It is forbidden and politically unacceptable.'*

Vishnevskaya's name still appeared in the official programme book, although in fact the soprano role was sung that night by Heather Harper.

The success of the *War Requiem*, especially after the release the following year of its double-LP recording, selling over 300,000 copies in the first three months alone, took Britten by surprise. 'He felt he couldn't play the role of the nation's composer,' Colin Matthews told me, 'which is what he'd suddenly been turned into.' 'He wanted to be cherished. He wasn't to be revered,' Sue Phipps added. 'But I think he would have said, "Oh, it isn't myself, it's my music." But he and his music were one and the same thing really. Part of him was very touched and very pleased. I wouldn't say he ever took it for granted, because he didn't. But he was very happy that he was recognised. Collecting various awards was always a bit embarrassing. Going to the Palace and hobnobbing with people who hadn't the faintest idea why he was there.'

Last word again to Sue who, while weeping after seeing my final film about Britten, *Nocturne*, reminded me of our first encounter on the beach at Aldeburgh all those years earlier. 'She's much too young for you,' she had said, admonishing me for my bad behaviour and thus beginning my incredible journey close to the one of greatest composers of our time. 'That he was born during the last year before the First World War, and grew up and was a young man in the Second World War, and then began to express everything that was happening and going on in the world. What would he be saying now if he were still alive? He did come at exactly the right moment in order to be able to say what he had to say, and I think we can go on listening to his music forever and still not get the whole message.'

One footnote: I chose to conclude my first film, *Benjamin Britten and his Festival* (a truly inspired title!), using the great fugue at the end of the *Young Person's Guide to the Orchestra*. This was partly because of an hilarious story that his trusted record producer, John Culshaw, had told me while we were filming. The previous year, Britten had recorded the piece with the London Symphony Orchestra. The recording had gone well (after all, Britten was also an accomplished conductor) until it came to the final fugue. For whatever reason, it had proved difficult to hold together, and after several attempts Britten was getting increasingly tetchy. So Culshaw decided it was time for a break, and that they should all have another attempt 'after tea'.

When the orchestra reassembled, Britten gave the cue for the closing moments of the percussion variation leading into the finale, and then set off conducting the fugue at a noticeably much quicker pace than they had previously rehearsed. Culshaw feared the worst. Osian Ellis, the harp player, told me himself that he had panicked as his part in the fugue was not easy, even at a slower pace. Somehow, though, they all survived together right through to the end. As the last chord faded away, Britten paused, eventually just shrugged and gave out the broadest of grins. See what you can do when you try, he seemed to be saying. This recording was broadcast one afternoon on Radio 3 by Humphrey Carpenter, Britten's first biographer and a very fine broadcaster. When the fugue came to an end, there were at least ten seconds of complete silence, to the extent that I thought my radio had ceased to function. Eventually Humphrey's voice said simply, 'That, ladies and gentlemen, is pure genius.'

Chapter 5

Peter Sellers

Soon after the modest success of my first film about Benjamin Britten, I was approached to make a profile with or about the actor Peter Sellers, whom I had met during the filming of *Alice in Wonderland*. The film I then made in 1970 was originally banned by the BBC; then re-cut; then pillaged without acknowledgement by all who followed making films about Peter Sellers; then plagiarised at length by one of his biographers, again without any acknowledgement; then publicly derided by Sellers himself on the Michael Parkinson chat show. Then he denied he had ever done such a thing, and then said that it was the only film that ever came close to understanding him - all of which caused me to leave the BBC in disgust that they had never made any attempt to defend me.

The initial problem was that I had made a film about a famous comedian which wasn't remotely funny. Although the film had no narration and certainly no cack-handed, squawking 'presenter', it was interspersed with excerpts from a long interview I did with Sellers' former fellow 'Goon', Spike Milligan. Here are some of those excerpts: 'Sellers was a circus freak, or sideshow, or psychiatric specimen. Peter had such a large area of unexplored emotionalism within him in which he could drown. He's always on the edge of ferment, of tears, of hysteria. The actual business of living has made him afraid.' Or again, 'He thinks, "Wherever I am, it's boring." Can you imagine the agony of that? If he hadn't made it financially, I think he would have killed himself.' Sellers sat with me and his agent, Dennis Selinger, as we screened the film for the first time. He cried a lot and kept saying, 'Oh God. He's got it right.' At no point did he ask me to remove anything that Spike had said. It seemed as if I had opened a veritable can of worms.

Nonetheless, in retrospect, working with Sellers was pure joy, always entertaining, but sometimes breath-taking in what he confessed. 'I *want* to be happy,' he told me, 'I'd like to be happy, very much. I'd like very much to be happy.' It was actually the ubiquitous Dennis Selinger, Peter's agent, who had suggested that I make a portrait of his star client, who was becoming increasingly exasperated at being called a clown rather than a serious actor. It was not the only time that Selinger pushed me in a direction I was not expecting. He was the one who also suggested, some years later, Ben Kingsley as Shostakovich.

'I go to parties,' Peter told me, 'and people hang around with their mouths open saying, "Any second he is going to arrive." The only reason I do sometimes go to these parties is in the hope that it will quench the thirst of all those people who want to see you, because that's what your agent says. You arrive there – all the photographers in the world, all the press agents in the world – "This is your town baby, you can buy it." Then an odd thing happens. They shake hands with you, look at you closely in the eyes for a few seconds, and then their eyes wander over your shoulder to see who else is coming into the room. Or somebody will lurch over and say, "Do us one of those funny things you do in the films." "What funny things?" "Oh, I don't know. I saw you do a funny thing in a film once." I find that I've been disappointed so many times in people that I've become, not bitter, but I tend to approach people warily, in case they're going to clobber me. I find I've been clobbered a lot.'

Considering Sellers made over eighty films in his career, garnering three Academy Award nominations – some great, like *Dr Strangelove* and *I'm All Right Jack*; some infamous, like the apparently endless series of *Pink Panther* films as Inspector Jacques Clouseau; some which made him a fortune, like *The Millionairess*, with Sophia Loren; some terrible, which lost him a fortune because he had invested in them, like *The Fiendish Plot of Dr Fu Manchu* – it's hard to believe he had suffered for his art. But it became increasingly clear as we worked together that he had.

When asked, Stanley Kubrick could not recall why he had cast Sellers as Clare Quilty in his version of Nabokov's novel *Lolita*, but his performance as a mentally unbalanced TV writer with multiple personalities was perhaps a clue to what was to come. 'First there was Hitler,' Spike Milligan told me, 'who loved Wagner, children, flowers and sunsets, and then he goes and murders six million Jews. Peter can't work off his madness; it's all bottled up inside him. Peter's biggest rage is that he can't be violent, like Hitler. But don't mistake him. He's full of rage, the rage of a murderer.'

'When I stare in a mirror, all I see is one of the awfully strange brigade of pudding faces who melt into the crowd,' Sellers told me, 'I hate seeing myself. I'm not pleased with what I see in the mirror. I'm just disgusted.'

I followed him while he was making a feature film called *The Magic Christian*, directed by his friend and frequent collaborator Joe McGrath and also starring Ringo Starr. It tells of Guy Grand (Sellers), who, being fabulously wealthy, can buy or bribe or do whatever he wants. For instance, he throws thousands of pound notes into a pool of excrement, inviting passers-by to jump in and help themselves which, of course, they do. Spike was of the view that *The Magic Christian* gave him the chance to express what he felt about the human race in a commercial film. 'The whole thing could have been written *about* Peter, instead of *for* him,' he explained. 'I've always been aware of the power of money,' Peter told me, 'They wave it in front of you to get you to do things. In fact, you can buy anyone in the film industry, and I mean anybody – including myself.'

For Peter, however, it was not always so. For some years, he struggled to be accepted for what he believed he was: a serious actor with a gift for impersonation. After the war, he set up a review show in London, which was a combination of music (he played the drums) and impressions. But even *The Goon Show* – which had initially made him famous, albeit only on the radio – was not quite what it seemed. 'We *had* to create *The Goon Show*,' Spike told me. 'It was a fantasy world where you could make the characters do what you wanted because you were writing the script. You always win. You can't get arrested in a fantasy world unless you want to. For anyone who found reality a bug, like Peter did, *The Goon Show* was pure therapy.' Sellers played four main characters – Major Bloodnok, Hercules Grytpype-Thynne, Bluebottle, and Henry Crun – and seventeen minor ones. Starting with 370,000 listeners, the BBC show eventually reached up to seven million people in Britain and was described by one newspaper as 'probably the most influential comedy show of all time'.

Characters like Neddie Seegoon, played by Harry Secombe, could be struck, beaten, burnt, boiled, drowned, clubbed, nailed to a cross – and Peter would love it. For him, the characters were real and came alive. 'Every official that had ever ignored Peter,' Spike continued, 'was now being made to pay not only for his own idiocy but for all those idiots in all of Peter's past life. Idiot producers who had ruined wonderful material; idiot managers who told him he couldn't act; idiot BBC officials who treated him like a naughty boy. They were the enemy and had to be destroyed, or Peter couldn't survive. He thinks he's the only clean man in a leper colony.'

He was born Richard Henry Sellers in 1925 to a well-off family in Southsea, a suburb of Portsmouth. His parents, Agnes Doreen 'Peg' (Marks) and William 'Bill' Sellers, worked in an acting company run by his grandmother. His father was Protestant and his mother was Jewish (of both Ashkenazi and Sephardi background). His parents' first child had died at birth, so Sellers was probably spoiled during his early years. He enlisted in the Royal Air Force and served during the Second World War II. Peg was to become a dominant force in his life. She sacrificed her responsibility to her husband and made Peter the head of the household. Any time of the day or night, he would call out, 'Peg, Peg' and she'd drop everything and come running. Weeping, he told me, 'I remember when my mother died. Even though I had children alive, she was my last close relative. I felt a great feeling of loneliness; I just couldn't pick up the phone and speak to her any more. I felt that a lot.'

Most of us miss our mothers, or some relative whom we think of as our mother figure. But in Peter's case, it became acute. Every day when we were together, over six months, there would be some reference to his mother. 'He is still a child, running away from his mother, who keeps looking back, seeing how far he can go before she stops him,' Spike told me. "How far can I get away," he's saying, "and still be safe?"'

His second wife, Britt Ekland, he married eleven days after he met her – no wonder it didn't last, people said. He wanted the security his mother had given him, and naturally he thought it must come through marriage. He was always trying to replace the security of his mother, but that security was a dream. It bore no relation to the real world where people are hard. The real world, full of obligations and liabilities, was like a violent attack on his warm glowing mother-son relationship, and it hacked him to pieces. 'I'm continually searching for a perfect woman. I keep reading of great women behind great men. They mother you, they are great in bed, they are like a sister. They're not there when you don't want to see them, they are there when you want to see them. I'll find one, one of these days.'

Knowing this, I found it increasingly difficult to reconcile the inner turmoil of the man I was dealing with day after day with his endless stream of invention and very funny stories. For instance, he needed to go to New York for a conference with his American agent, Harvey Orkin. So we sailed away on the maiden voyage of the Cunard's pride and joy: the liner *Queen Elizabeth 2*, on 2 May 1969. Peter was a guest of honour, and it didn't take him long (following dinner at the Captain's Table) to stage an improvised sketch on the bridge. Dressed in a captain's hat, and standing alongside the real Captain, Bill Warwick, and intercut with the ship apparently ploughing through the Atlantic, Sellers is seen staring into the distance as the ship and saying, 'Don't like it at all. What do you think?' Whereupon the real Captain agrees and says, 'No, don't like it at all.'

'What shall we do? Tell the passengers?'

'Not sure,' says the real Captain.

'Fact is', says Sellers, 'we're still in dry dock.'

We then discover that in fact the ship is being propelled by sixty topless ladies, rowing like hell under the lash of Raquel Welch. Mad? Definitely.

Upon arriving in New York, the meeting with Harvey Orkin, his agent, went as follows: 'Peter', said Orkin. 'Your career needs saving. So we're going to build you up to where you never should have been.' Sellers is naturally excited by this prospect. 'And then?' he tentatively enquires.

'Nothing,' replies Orkin. 'You vanish, for five years.'

'And then what happens?' asks Sellers, now clearly worried.

'We're going to wine you and dine you, and…'

'What?' says Sellers, now becoming more excited.

'Nothing,' replies Orkin. 'You vanish for another five years.'

All of which is delivered with a complete straight face, for my (and my film's) benefit. Sellers on a roll was unstoppable.

One day, we were filming a scene from *The Magic Christian* in which Guy Grand has paid Hamlet (played by Laurence Harvey) to perform 'To be or not to be' as a striptease act. Whether this was in the original script by Terry Southern, I know not. But suddenly, out of left field, emerges Sellers as a BBC (who else?) reporter, clutching a hand microphone and babbling (for my benefit), 'This is Nudbolt Thules, reporting on behalf of BBC News to explain the significance of what we are about to see – that is, sex in Shakespeare. In the opening soliloquy of *Richard III*, for example, Shakespeare does mean that Richard's sexual member is rather small and therefore misshapen, and he needs to have an erection to *strut* before the wanton ambling nymph. And in 'To be or not to be, that is the question', he means to ask, is he homosexual or is he not? Only the viewers can decide.'

Of course this completely improvised speech, which was definitely *not* in the Southern script, had the entire film crew in helpless laughter and quite ruined Laurence Harvey's grand entrance.

Stanley Kubrick recalled that it was always best to allow room for Sellers to improvise - ironically, something which ran contrary to Kubrick's normal tightly controlled filming. The famous scene in *Dr Strangelove* (written also in part by Terry Southern) where one of Sellers' three characters, the bluff RAF Group Captain Mandrake, has rumbled what the lunatic USAF base commander, Brigadier General Jack Ripper, has done: that is, let loose the bombers under his command to blow the Soviet Union to smithereens with nuclear weapons. Mandrake decides he must call the White House with this rather important news. Unfortunately, he is under arrest as an 'uncertified alien', so he has to beg the Marine guarding him for permission to make the phone call, only to discover he has no coins for the phone box. Kubrick recalled that he was not sure what Sellers would do, so set up his cameras with wide-angle lenses just in case something crazy happened. Sellers notices that the phone booth was next to a Coca-Cola dispensing machine, so he grabs the Marine's gun and shoots at the machine and out tumble buckets of coins for the phone call. The Marine then says, 'You'll have to answer to the Coca-Cola company for this.' The film crew were so convulsed with laughter that for a while they forgot to turn off the cameras. Inevitably that scene stayed in the finished film, a tribute to Kubrick having recognised Sellers' genius for improvisation.

A darker side emerged when we went skiing together in Zermatt, under the shadow of the Matterhorn. Peter asked to go out alone, but we could film him from a distance. The image of a black-suited Sellers against the white of the snow, trying to ski all alone on the lower slopes of that mountain, has haunted me ever since. 'Sellers sees himself as a desert island,' Spike Milligan told me. 'To try and know him is like going to a desert island. And in the middle of the island is a lake, and in the middle of that another desert island. He's that lonely. He's desperate to be happy, successful, wanted, happily married. He's desperate not to destroy his past. It's all desperation. He *is* desperation. He wants to be accepted as normal, and he knows he's not. The real Peter Sellers will have vanished long before anyone gets too close. Perhaps the enigma is more real than the man himself.'

Milligan appeared only once in live theatre with Sellers, although in fact even then they were never on stage at the same time. The play was *Son of Oblomov*, which opened on 2 December 1964 at the Comedy Theatre in the West End. It ran there for 559 performances. Milligan spent much of the play in bed with the diminutive Joan Greenwood, who had been a famous film star in many of the great Ealing comedies of the 1950s, including most noticeably *Kind Hearts and Coronets.* The following April, Queen Elizabeth II and her family attended as part of her thirty-ninth birthday celebration. Just after the curtain rose, a group of four latecomers attempted to slink to their seats directly in front of the Royal Family. Milligan immediately shouted, 'Turn up the house lights! Start everything again!' He pointed to the blushing foursome and cried, 'That's cost you your knighthood!'

Then, noticing that Peter Sellers was seated between Prince Charles and Princess Margaret, Milligan asked in a loud voice, 'Is there a Sellers in the house?' Sellers immediately shouted, 'Yes!' Milligan then launched into a vaudeville routine with Sellers about Prince Philip's suspenders, with Sellers participating from his seat with the royals. This culminated in Milligan giving a high-kick, lobbing one of his bedroom slippers at Sellers, only just missing Prince Philip's head. Once back in bed with co-star Joan Greenwood, Milligan spent the rest of the performance poking fun at the Queen for bringing her son to such a racy play. The performance ran forty-five minutes over its schedule. Prince Charles reportedly saw the play five times.

Milligan, however, had a different view of Sellers on stage. 'Peter is a freak, not a genius. Which makes him even more unique. His ability to reproduce another character is so startling, he must have some kind of misshapenness within him. Once, I was on stage with him – I think at the Camden Theatre recording *The Goon Show* – and he came on each night as a different character. As I looked at him, it wasn't Peter at all. Will he turn up tonight, emotionally? All you could do is watch him. Meeting him was like interviewing a ghost. You have to keep watching him because there's often a complete difference between what Peter says and the emotion of him. He often just repeats statements he's read about himself to prevent you from getting closer to him. Peter feasts off people – he finds himself so totally boring that he's got to escape from himself and find refuge and security in another personality – that's the only form of communication left open to him. He could become every living breathing thing; his gift of impersonation was so incredible. I sometimes think he left a copy of himself at home, because the version he saw in the mirror was ageing and ordinary. Faceless.'

Sellers was obsessed by gadgets of all kinds, as he demonstrated for me - 16mm movie cameras on which he documented hours of his private life; hi-fi sound systems which he often discarded or gave away within hours of acquiring them; cars fitted with televisions; cars which he bought on a whim in the morning and disposed of that same afternoon; cooking utensils, even though he couldn't cook; primitive mobile phones which he couldn't work satisfactorily so dumped them in the bin; and stills cameras. He even took fashion photos for *Vogue* magazine. He defined photography for me as the art of loneliness in pursuit of the lonely. 'The only things that didn't let him down were his gadgets,' Spike Milligan suggested. 'He had to surround himself with material gadgets to make him forget he is alone. The films, the salary, the fact that he'd gone a long way from Southsea where he was born; a long way from touring with his parents; vaudeville acts, the RAF, India, Germany; six weeks at The Windmill theatre, seven years with *The Goon Show*, three children, plays, pantomimes - yet it seemed to him it had all come to nothing.'

In fact, his world came crashing down during the filming of *Kiss Me Stupid*, directed by Billy Wilder and starring Kim Novak and Dean Martin, when he had the first of a series of heart attacks on the night of 5 April 1964, before having sex (he claimed) with his new wife, Britt Ekland. Sellers had inhaled amyl nitrite (poppers) as a sexual stimulant in his search for 'the ultimate orgasm'. He suffered a series of eight heart attacks over the next three hours and was despatched to the Cedars of Lebanon Hospital in Los Angeles. Wilder, with whom Sellers had already quarrelled several times, was unsympathetic about the heart attacks, saying that 'you have to have a heart before you can have an attack.'

'If you have several heart attacks in a row, and the supply of blood has stopped for two minutes,' Sellers told me, 'I think something must happen. They did tell me I'd suffered no brain damage at all. I'm pretty sure deep down - and this is something only I know - that was not true. I come across periods of blankness and loss of memory. But I do remember one thing clearly: a feeling that I might expire but I wouldn't actually die. I remember there being a large strong outstretched arm, pulling me. I knew that as long as I hung on, I wouldn't die.'

Recover he did. Divorced Britt Ekland. Married Wife No. 3, a model called Miranda Quarry, who had accompanied him on the QE2 voyage, at the Caxton Hall, Westminster, she wearing a gypsy dress and accompanied by her two Pekinese dogs. That marriage didn't last either, and another heart attack precipitated a fourth and final marriage to a young actress called Lynne Frederick. 'He never had a hearth, a home,' his son Michael told me. 'He never put a kettle on and made a cup of tea. He'd never sit round a fireplace, all those primitive tribal things that give each of us a sense of orderliness. They seemed to be denied him. He *had* no fireplace.'

Throughout the six months of our filming together, he had constantly talked about his 'boat', at that time moored off Mallorca. And that this should be the climax of our film. 'I know the crew. They know me,' he told me, his eyes positively glazed as he spoke. 'They don't bother me. They keep out of my way. I can run the boat myself, the *Victoria Maria*. You're not stuck in one place. You get out to sea and there's nobody there. Vast expanses of blue. When it's lovely weather. I know nothing nicer than being at sea on a yacht, putting into ports when you want to put in, getting off when you want to get off, eating on board, swimming – it's the ultimate luxury. If you said to me, "What is the most material luxury you have in your life?" I would say my boat.'

And so a visit was arranged. We all flew out to Mallorca together: Sellers, his batman Bert Mortimer, the small film crew and me. When we arrived at Mallorca airport, I volunteered to gather all the luggage and transport it down to the dock so Peter could set off in advance without having to bother with all the arrangements. But when we arrived at the dock, Peter and the boat had vanished. Gone into the Mediterranean. We decided to wait, and did so for three days wondering what to do. Eventually, Bert reappeared full of reassurance; Peter had just 'forgotten' that we were following on behind. Then we managed to get a couple of days of glorious filming, until he decided he must return to London for some important business meetings, which we knew was not true. 'When he arrived at the boat,' Spike said, 'he thought: Well, there's the moon; there's the stars; so what happens now? I've seen the stars before, I've seen the ocean, I've heard the music, I know the tune – what else is there? Nothing else? Let's all go back to London. Like everything else in his life, faced with the reality of something, he had no choice but to run away. This constant journeying of his. He's like a panther in a cage, pacing backwards and forwards for eternity. He daren't stand still because he'd sink and drown in his own tears, so he has to keep going although he knows he has nowhere to go. The yacht; his home; all a dream.'

So, what to make of this extraordinary man? 'Peter will never be at peace, never be happy. That's why he's devoted to the past,' Spike concluded. 'He needs the past to bolster up the present before he can even look into the future. Even bad memories are inverted into good ones – if they were in the past, they were wrapped up and finished with; he came through that period and had survived, and he gets an illusion of security. He cries for yesterday and this made him very lonely.'

Sellers struggled with depression and mental insecurities throughout his life. In later life, his behaviour on and off film sets became more erratic and compulsive, and he frequently clashed with his directors and co-stars, especially in the mid-1970s when his physical and mental health, together with his continuing alcohol and drug problems, were at their worst. He never fully recovered from that 1964 heart attack because he refused to take any prescribed heart medications and instead consulted with 'psychic healers'. As a result, his heart condition continued to slowly deteriorate until, on 20 March 1977, he barely survived another major heart attack and had a pacemaker surgically implanted to regulate his heartbeat, although he complained this caused him further mental and physical discomfort. However, he refused to slow down his work schedule or consider heart surgery, which might have extended his life by several years.

Sellers was scheduled to have a reunion dinner in London on 25 July 1980 with his *Goon Show* partners, Spike Milligan and Harry Secombe. However, at around midday on 22 July, Sellers collapsed in his Dorchester Hotel room from another massive heart attack and fell into a coma. Despite the best medical attention, he died in a London hospital just after midnight on July 24, 1980. He was only fifty-four. He was survived by his fourth wife, Lynne Frederick, who later married David Frost, and three children: Michael, Sarah and Victoria. At the time of his death, he was scheduled to undergo angiography in Los Angeles to see if he would be eligible for heart surgery.

He had once been invited to appear on *The Muppets* television show as Peter Sellers, the great comic actor. But, he had replied to Kermit the Frog, 'That, you see, my dear Kermit, would be altogether impossible. I could never be myself. Because you see, there is no me. I do not exist… There used to be a me, but I had it surgically removed.'

The greatest comic actor since Charlie Chaplin? Possibly. But at what a cost. Spike Milligan when asked to comment on his friend's death, referring to the grand reunion that the Goons had planned, said simply, 'Anything to avoid paying for dinner.'

Chapter 6

Frank Zappa

On the wall of my office in front of me is a plaque titled 'The Six Stages of Production'. It reads:

1. Wild Enthusiasm

I first met Frank Zappa in a dingy basement in New York's Greenwich Village. Wiry, with a black goatee and wild black eyes, he was determined to make me understand that rock 'n' roll was not what it seemed; indeed, that it was so pathetically misrepresented by the media of the day that its social and political aspirations had been drowned in a bathtub of frothy coffee.

The film I had made earlier that year, called *All My Loving*, had been considered so controversial by the BBC ('harmful to youth', I was told) that it had been planned to show it after *The Epilogue*, that is, after television for the day had officially ceased, which it usually did at around eleven o'clock in the evening. David Attenborough, then Director of Programmes for BBC Television, wrote an internal memo stating that the film would only be broadcast over his dead body. Fortunately, neither half of his assertion turned out to be true.

Two months later, Zappa had called me to say he had been 'impressed by the courage of your film' and would I be interested in helping him with a project of his own. I think by 'courage', he meant that I had given airtime to Jimi Hendrix, The Who, Cream, Eric Burdon, not to mention Zappa and his group, The Mothers of Invention, all formidable musicians who had previously either not appeared on BBC television, or else had been ridiculed. My film, *All My Loving*, he said, had treated them and many others with seriousness, both musically and culturally.

What was the project?

2. Total Confusion

When we met, Zappa gave me 'the script' of his project - 300 pages, some handwritten, some paste-ups, some incomprehensible, a few lyrics, and a frequent use of the word 'penis'. *Ah*, I said. He wanted me to 'visualise' it, he said. *Ah*, I said. To create the atmosphere of life on the road of a touring rock 'n' roll band. *Ah*, I said. When do we shoot, I asked? In a couple of months' time, he said. Do we have a cast, I asked? No, he said, apart from various musicians from his band including Mark Volman and Howard Kaylan, also known as The Turtles. The cast, he said, that's your job. *Ah*, I said. The opening line on page 1 of 'the script' read: 'If you were forced by a crazy person to insert a mysterious imported lamp into the reproductive orifice of a lady harpist, would you do it?'

Ah.

I soon discovered something of what had happened to his 'project' up to that point. Zappa had approached his record company, United Artists Records, to persuade their parent company, United Artists Films, to finance a feature film to be called *200 Motels* about the trials and tribulations and misery (and sex) of life on the road - groupies, boredom, drugs, boredom, crappy motels, boredom, and...boredom. Songs would include: *Half a Dozen Provocative Squats, Shove it Right In, Dental Hygiene Dilemma, A Nun Suit Painted on some Old Boxes*, and... *Penis Dimension*. Not surprisingly, United Artists had...hesitated. Zappa then said he would use his next record advance to finance the film if United Artists would agree to distribute. Okay, they had said, but they needed a 'safe pair of hands' whom they knew to direct. Enter Muggins, and a production company was formed called - what else? - Bizarre Productions.

3. Utter Despair

On the positive side, I learned that Pinewood Studios had been booked (for ten days, a little short for a full-length feature) and knew that

Zappa was no mug as a musician. His lyrics might be full of absurd provocations, not to say squats, but having studied with Varèse (or so he claimed) he was eminently capable of writing in full score, or, at least, filling the pages with a great number of dots and squiggles. Whether they added up to anything more than the sums of their parts, remained a matter of debate. Anyhow, they needed an orchestra. Your job, he said.

So the Royal Philharmonic, with whom I had worked before, was volunteered, although I somehow failed to mention to them that they would be seen throughout the film in a prison camp called 'The Centreville Recreational Facility', with the percussionists dressed as Nazi guards. But it *was* Pinewood Studios, I kept repeating. They were mightily impressed by that. As was a brilliant trumpet player and brass band conductor I had come across called Gary Howarth, later a most distinguished orchestral conductor called Elgar Howarth.

Zappa wanted 'serious' musicians involved, he said. Enter John Williams, the great classical guitarist. There was to be 'dancing'. Enter Gillian Lynne, another old friend, later to become rich as the co-creator of *Cats*. I called up every crazy rock 'n' roller I could think of who owed me a favour; enter Ringo Starr (disguised in the film as Frank Zappa) and Keith Moon, the drummer with The Who, who had appeared in my film *All My Loving*. Zappa's score required a choir. Enter the Monteverdi Choir – although they have always denied they had anything whatsoever to do with it, partly through fear of what their eminent conductor and founder John Eliot Gardiner might do to *them* if he ever found out. 'We need class actors,' Zappa told me. Enter Wilfred Brambell (*Steptoe and Son* and *Alice in Wonderland*) and Theodore Bikel, sometime folk singer and Captain von Trapp in the original stage production of *The Sound of Music*. He was to play Rance Muhammitz, disguised as a TV announcer named Dave. You work it out. The problem was that there was no real script I could give them.

4. Search for the Guilty

Now comes the interesting part. Zappa's idea – to portray what life was really like on the road – was a good one. Having survived several rock 'n' roll tours myself, with Hendrix, Uriah Heep and others, I knew that the madness which shook the headlines: 'Group trashes hotel with motorbikes', or 'Group floods dining room with broken beer bottles', was only half the story. The physical slog of night after night, in venues hundreds of miles apart (especially in the States), in rubbishy motels, with dysfunctional equipment, little or no time for sound checks, screaming jailbait all over you, thieves and hoodlums frequently stealing the group's instruments hours before a gig but then 'offering' to find them again for a not inconsiderable fee (or should that be ransom?); this was the real half of the story, and it went some way to explaining the consolations of sex and drugs. Zappa's ambition was to write this large upon the silver screen.

But how to do that, and at very short notice, and with a budget that today wouldn't even pay for the wigs? Film, the 35mm variety, was out, economically; plus there simply wouldn't be time. I told Zappa that the only hope was to try and shoot it on colour video. He was sceptical; United Artists were not to be told. I was sure they would cancel the whole thing at the very mention of the word 'video' and blame...me. My view, however, was that video was relatively quick, cheap and, most important of all, it might give us the chance to experiment with the technology which, although in its infancy – some would have said pre-infancy – seemed to me to have possibilities. If it failed, well, Zappa could always blame...me.

But, I argued, Zappa wanted to show, visually, the effect of hallucinatory drugs, for instance. To achieve this optically, using film, was of course possible, but it would be exceedingly slow and expensive, and then might not result in something sufficiently bizarre. It should be remembered that this was over fifty years ago, when the wonders of Industrial Light & Magic were unknown and Peter Jackson was not long out of his cradle. Digital pictures and *Jurassic Park* were still in a galaxy far, far away and not even heading in our direction.

5. Persecution of the Innocent

There was a second problem, or, rather, a second set of problems. Once we had our colour video tape, could we edit it? Don't forget that the first *analogue* colour video recorder (of two-inch tape, long since abandoned as a format) had only arrived in the BBC in late 1968, and although it could in theory be edited by physically cutting the tape with a splicer and then sticking the bits together with Sellotape, the edit could not be guaranteed. Sometimes it would play; sometimes it wouldn't. But, given the complexity of the proposed ten-day shoot, editing was going to be essential; it would have been impossible to record the estimated ninety minutes as if 'live'. Last problem: how many cinemas were equipped to show videotape on a large screen? None.

Therefore, somehow, the unedited tape had to be transferred to film. Obvious, but that had never been done before. Black and white television had sometimes been 'telerecorded' onto 16mm film, but the quality was poor and would never stand up to examination on the big screen. Laser scanning, nowadays an essential tool of the trade, was not yet even a flicker in the imagination of George Lucas.

By an incredible chance, I was grumbling about this latest problem with a friend who worked at the Technicolor laboratories. 'Simple,' he said. 'Remember that the television picture has three colour signals: red, blue and green? Well, so does the old three-strip Technicolor method of neg. & print.' Incredibly again, he found an old disused Technicolor camera, and if we could find a way to isolate the three television signals he said, bingo, we could transfer everything to three-strip 35mm film and thus solve the editing and distribution problems.

Despite the old camera making a noise like a disgruntled tractor as it pulled the three strips of negative film though its rusting sprockets, it worked. And if the finished film has any merit, it is precisely this: it showed the way forward for more-or-less every special effects film which followed. Of course, today's digital wonders, as, for example, in *Master and Commander*, are as related to *200 Motels* as the Concorde was to Leonardo's flying machine. But, at the time, we all believed we had seen the future, and it worked. How innocent we were.

6. Promotion of the Incompetent

Zappa frequently remarked during the frenzied ten days of shooting in Pinewood that he felt truly humbled to sit in its dining room surrounded by the photos and memories of the many great films that had been made in those studios. Zappa is dead now, but I would want to suggest that he, too, had made a small contribution to the pioneering spirit that has always been the hallmark of Pinewood.

A few years later I met David Lean, a true Pinewood veteran. Whereas I wanted to ask him about *Lawrence of Arabia* and the rest, all he wanted to talk about was *200 Motels* and how it had been done. Astonishing to me that he had seen it at all; but his interest in the film was a truly humbling experience.

Two footnotes: first, sometime in the mid-nineties, I was in Westwood in Hollywood. I happened to pass by a tiny cinema which probably only held six men and a dog. There on the billboard it said: '*200 Motels*, now in its 20th year. Rated R.' The film has gone on to be a cult film with a huge international following. Lurch back now to the mid-seventies for the second footnote. Zappa had wanted to perform *200 Motels* at the Royal Albert Hall. The performance had been cancelled at short notice by the management of the hall because, they said, of the obscene nature of the content. Zappa had sued the management for breach of contract, and the matter had finished up in the High Court. I had been called as a so-called expert witness. Did I really think, the Judge asked me, that a piece which included 'homosexual material' was suitable for performance in 'the home of the Proms'(*sic*)? It so happened that Britten's great opera, *Death in Venice*, about the homosexual love between the writer Aschenbach and his obsession for a boy called Tadzio, had been performed the previous year in the Proms. When I mentioned this, the Judge asked, 'And who wrote that?' 'Benjamin Britten,' I replied. 'And how do you spell that?' the Judge said.

Chapter 7

Leonard Cohen

My film about Leonard Cohen's 1972 European tour, *Bird on a Wire,* also has a complicated history.

Let me clear up one or two complete misconceptions - or, I might want to say, deliberate misrepresentations. I was asked to make the film by Marty Machat, who was Cohen's long-time manager right up until Machat's death in 1988. It was essentially his initiative, at least in part because he feared Leonard might never tour again thereafter. Mercifully, this did not turn out to be the case, but Machat's concern was understandable, given that at the time Cohen had frequently asserted a) that he did not enjoy touring, saying it exhausted him for no good purpose; b) that he hated having to repeat the same old songs night after night like a performing parrot, claiming he was rendering them meaningless by endless repetition; c) that he believed he was a poor performer on stage, crippled by a feeble voice; and d) that, as his first three albums had sold indifferently, he thought he might not have an audience. Also, although he did not know it at the time, Cohen's record company was threatening not to renew his contract.

All of this he explained to me when, in October 1971, we gathered to discuss the film in Machat's office in New York, although we had actually met before, backstage at the Isle of Wight Festival the previous year. Machat told me privately that he needed the film, because his client no longer wanted to tour and probably did not have a record deal, which in the commercial world of the early seventies was financial suicide. Cohen was resigned to a film being made about the European tour planned for the following year, however, because he hoped it might just bring him to a wider audience. I say 'resigned' because he was less than enthusiastic, especially when I said a condition of my becoming involved was that I would require total access to whatever I thought would be necessary for a stimulating and, I hoped, positive, film. Luckily, I had brought with me a copy of one of his early books of poems. 'Oh, so you know I am a poet,' he said. 'Of course,' I said, 'That was how I first came across you.'

He then made a series of conditions of his own: he didn't want a simple 'tour film'; he did not want to be portrayed as a sentimental folk singer of love songs about his latest girlfriend, Suzanne or Marianne or whoever; and, most importantly, he wanted me to make it clear that many of his songs had a political (with a small 'p') edge. I agreed, and then very reluctantly he agreed, and Machat said he would pay for the film himself so that Leonard would not be burdened with the expense.

Cohen kept his word, and I was given complete access and encouraged to interpret the material collected in any way I thought desirable. I also said my instinct was that it would be pointless recording all of the songs for every single concert, so we agreed that although I would be there for all twenty concerts, I would record the music on only four or five occasions to be agreed. And, as I felt very strongly that his poetry was a key to understanding the man, I also suggested that we film him reading several of the poems. With this he readily agreed. Indeed, so pleased was he with this idea that he even composed a poem especially for me, and wrote it out by hand and signed it in the frontispiece of my copy of his book *The Energy of Slaves.*

And maybe what is valuable about the film today is not only that it contains seventeen of Cohen's greatest songs performed by him in his prime (and it was nonsense of him to say he had no voice), but it also has a real feel for the rough and tumble and difficulties of life on the road. I know of few other films where the backstage confusion comes so vividly to life, with Cohen apparently taking no notice whatsoever of the camera. And don't forget, this film was shot in 1972, with slow celluloid colour stock, which required a lot of light to get any decent exposure at all. Had we been armed with today's digital technology, we would have been virtually invisible. But I doubt if today we would be allowed such access. Given that at that time Cohen had no record deal, there were no clueless PR people, no clueless record executives, no excessive management – just his stage crew and his band and my film crew of four; in all, about twenty people.

With a budget of around $35,000, the filming schedule went ahead as planned and, as I am my own editor, the rough-cut of the film was delivered about a month after the tour had finished. I've read that according to Bob Johnston, the keyboard player of Cohen's band and Bob Dylan's erstwhile record producer, many of the sound tapes were lost during the filming. Sorry, Bob; that's nonsense. The BBC asked to see the rough-cut and bought the film on the spot. Machat would have recouped three-quarters of his investment in one go. Alas, Cohen told me he thought the film was 'too confrontational', and worried that he often appeared 'exhausted, even wasted'. While the latter is undoubtedly true, I believed he was wrong about the film being 'too confrontational'.

However, my regard for him as a poet, a performer and a person had grown hugely during the film, so I wanted to give him the benefit of the doubt. Machat asked me to make available all the raw material (the 'rushes' or 'dailies'), and 'they would see what they could do.' What I did not know at the time, was that my assistant editor had told them he could do a whole lot better than I. Nine months and hundreds of thousands of dollars later (now of Cohen's money), a second version of the film was ready. I was told it was shown to the BBC, who turned it down flat saying 'it was a mess'. I now have a copy of their letter.

I was also told by Machat that he had refused to pay for the re-editing, thinking that it was now Cohen's responsibility. Version 2 had a brief theatrical outing, shown for one night only at the Rainbow Theatre in north London, 5 July 1974, almost two years after I had delivered the original version. I was not invited to see the revised version, was not at the Rainbow, and only saw it for the first time thirty-five years later. Had I seen it then, I would have insisted my name be removed, because although it contains about half of my original film, the structure had been destroyed, the musical editing was crass beyond belief, and the whole purpose of the film (which I shall come to in a moment) had been lost. When I read later that Cohen had only agreed to promote the film 'through gritted teeth', I think I can understand why.

The 'film' then apparently disappeared. Stupidly, I had never kept a copy of the original version for myself. Subsequently, in every biography of Cohen that appeared, I read totally misleading information about the film – and incidentally, not a single one of those biographers had ever bothered to consult me. I read that I had made a film about Tom Jones, which is why I was 'chosen'. I have never even met Tom Jones. I read that the film was Bob Johnston's idea. Simply untrue. One recent biographer even got the title of the film wrong and also the date of its filming. And so on, and so on.

Then, in late 2009, 294 rolls of film were discovered in a warehouse in Hollywood, many in rusted-up cans that sometimes had to be hammered open, and returned to their 'present owner', Machat's son, Stephen, via shenanigans so tortuous they read like a B-movie plot. These cans were then shipped to me in twenty-five enormous boxes by, of all people, Frank Zappa's manager. At first I believed that nothing could be salvaged. The cans did not contain the negative (still lost); some of the prints were in black and white; and much of it had been cut to pieces and/or scratched beyond use. But when one day I knocked over a box by accident and found most of my original sound dubbing tracks, I knew we had a hope of putting the jigsaw back together.

Taking full advantage of the latest digital technology, we began to rescue the material fragment by fragment, slowly and painstakingly, polishing every tiny fragment, first by hand, then electronically, then digitising the result. In all the finished picture comprises almost 3,000 such fragments. It took months and months, and probably cost more than the original filming, and although by no means perfect, it is now very close now to the original.

On balance, it did not *look* too bad, but it did *sound* wonderful. I was invited to show the film during the Toronto Film Festival in 2010 (Cohen was, after all, Canadian), and later to introduce it and explain some of the background at the Hot Docs festival, also in Montreal. A few days before my intended visit, the organiser of the festival rang me to ask if they could have a second screening, so great had been the demand for tickets. Before the first screening, I introduced the film with some of the anecdotes above. But before the second screening, I was loitering in the foyer of the cinema when a woman came up to me and poked me in the ribs, saying I had ruined her love of Leonard Cohen. Why so, I asked? Had she seen the film the previous evening? She had, she said. 'And I went home and put those same songs we heard in the film on my record player, and by comparison they are TERRIBLE.' Whereupon she gave me a kiss and disappeared. So, yes, I would want to say that many of the recordings of the songs in the film are far superior, certainly more moving, than their equivalent on either the original vinyl LPs or their later remastering onto CDs. We hear Cohen's voice in his prime, and not the old groaner of later years.

Above all, I believe that what we achieved was very close to the spirit of the original, and the finished film, *Bird On A Wire*, went on to win numerous international prizes. I know that Leonard saw the resurrected version we delivered; we had taken care to keep him informed.

He sent me a brief note which said simply, 'I'm glad the problem has gone away.'

He could not have been more wrong. Cohen's present management threatened to sue me, claiming I did not 'own' the material. Worse, Stephen Machat, without telling me, had signed a contract with Sony Music (Cohen's new record company) for many thousands of dollars (I have a copy of that fraudulent contract), claiming that the 'new' version was entirely his own work, for which he had paid himself. This was a lie. He never contributed a penny to the restoration, and was never seen in the cutting room, not even for a courtesy visit.

Which brings me back to the original purpose – my original purpose – in making the film. Yes, the songs are haunting, and unforgettably so. The poetry, now restored, having been deleted in Version 2 by persons unknown, is special. But so is the man. Cohen objected in the original film to scenes of a riot during a concert in Tel Aviv. I wanted those scenes because they showed Cohen's power over an audience, not by him shouting, but simply by his presence. Authority doesn't really describe it; transparent goodness is probably closer.

> 'Who by Fire?' he sings.
> 'And who by avalanche
> Who by powder
> Who for his greed
> Who for his hunger
> And who shall I say is calling?'

So my film also demonstrated Cohen's profound belief that it is a poet's responsibility to address the problems of the world – the political problems – and not shirk them. In this, he is a true brother of Bob Dylan. Yes, his songs – like those of Dylan – are riddled with personal details, but like all great art they transcend these and make them relevant and more universal. Just look at the lyrics for *The Story of Isaac*. They begin with references to a father appearing 'when I was nine years old'. Cohen's father had died when he was only nine. But that's not what the poem or the song is about. It is about those 'who would sacrifice one generation on behalf of another', as Cohen says in the film.

That belief in the responsibility of the poet, tough and uncompromising though it is, was the centre of my film, so woefully laid to waste by those who had attempted to destroy what we had done.

Chapter 8

Miss World

The late sixties in England were a time of considerable social unrest. Witness the trial at the Old Bailey of *OZ* magazine, accused of 'corrupting the morals of the young' – a trial in which I was involved. Witness the shadow of the Vietnam War, with riots in Grosvenor Square and elsewhere. Witness the Troubles in Northern Ireland becoming ever more bloody.

Nonetheless, every November the British people showed where their more important concerns were focussed, when twenty million of them tuned in to watch the annual Miss World beauty contest. 'People watch,' Eric D. Morley, the founding father of this particular beauty contest, told me, 'because they believe something is going to happen. It's an event. On top of that, the girls benefit. Nobody asks them to take part in the contest. They go in for it themselves. They *want* to travel, they *want* to show off their beauty. And who's exploiting them when all the money goes to charity? Where do you get all these accusations of exploitation from?'

It was a typically pugnacious question from the man who had invented the Miss World contest in 1950 and, with his wife, had remained its brilliant organiser ever since.

When our paths first crossed, Morley was managing director of a large British entertainments conglomerate, Mecca, as well as chairman of about forty of its subsidiary companies – dance halls, off-street betting shops, bingo chains. Although already in his fifties, Morley was always at his desk by eight in the morning, six days a week. He worked a fourteen-hour day and believed in profit-sharing for his employees long before such an idea became fashionable in Mrs Thatcher's Britain. He was also the president of Variety Club International, the major showbiz charity to which all British entertainers subscribed. Raised in the East End of London and now a father of five, he was an orphan. His mother and stepfather had died within a month of each other when he was only ten. Before then, he had not even known his name was Morley, having used his stepfather's name of Roney and thereby acquired the nickname 'Macaroni'.

Morley insisted that the real power behind the throne in the Miss World Contest was his wife, Julia. 'My husband fusses so,' she told me. 'In fact, we try to keep it a family affair. My brother runs the press office. Another brother organises the girls' itinerary – after all, over a hundred girls are in London for almost two weeks. So we have to take them to the theatre, to the ballet, to lunch in the House of Commons, down the river to Greenwich and to Hampton Court, as well as an evening of music hall. It's all quite exhausting, and that's before the actual contest begins. There is no place in the world where so many countries can get together for twelve days, live under the same roof and share the same itinerary, twenty-four hours a day for two solid weeks. It's just like a mini-United Nations. Throughout the year, we're in touch with over a hundred countries, and the worst part for us is having to select just one person who is going to win the title of Miss World. But that's the name of the game, and you've got to accept it.'

Julia Morley also told me, 'The thing is, you are representing your country. You want your country to have a good name. So you have got to go along with everything the organisers of the contest tell you to do. When they ask you to stand for photographs, I don't expect the press to be considerate. You have to give yourself.'

'I used to notice that the most beautiful girls didn't automatically win,' the first-ever Miss United Kingdom told me. 'And since, in 1958, I wasn't one of the most beautiful ones, that was for sure, I had to try and find out why. Because I *wanted* some of that pie. I realised that little local girls didn't really have much of a chance, irrespective of their natural talents, because they hadn't learned the tricks of the trade – how to talk, how to smile, when *not* to smile. So I planned every single move I made. I even made a miniature catwalk in my bedroom and practiced walking up and down it, as well as twisting round to best advantage. You have to know how to keep up that smile forever. You have to be ladylike; you have to be an ambassadress. You don't have to enjoy yourself so much as do the right thing, say the right thing, at the right time...'

But Miss Canada told me, 'If we were being treated merely as objects, all they would do is put us in bathing suits and parade us up and down on stage and that would be that. But they look into us more deeply than that. They look into our minds...'

The British representative for the Miss World contest was chosen through a series of lesser events such as Miss Widnes Bay, Miss Lower Slaughter, and, thence, Miss England. The Morleys suggested that I meet the present Miss England, which I did, over tea, at the Ritz Hotel. 'I was elected Miss Vulcan, aged only eighteen,' she told me excitedly. 'Naturally, after that I wouldn't give up,' she added. 'Well, would you, after you'd paraded in hot pants before a coach load of rugby players and won a bottle of champagne? I've still got it. The champagne, that is. I did the circuit after that, and eventually won Miss Manchester North and £25. I won Miss England at the third attempt, and after that, well, it had to be full time, didn't it? Last week I opened a petrol station. Can you imagine? I charged them £100, which I thought was cheap at the price. I had an evening out with the managing director of some firm in Nottingham, can't remember his name, I'm afraid, and got another hundred for that. I designed my own Miss England outfit, by the way. A bowler hat, pin-striped waistcoat, collar, tie and short shorts. Oh yes, and a copy of *The Times* with the Queen on the front cover reproduced on my...backside. Rather cute, don't you think?'

'It's important for me to feel that I'm achieving something,' she babbled on. 'There can be very few girls in my profession who have achieved as much as I have. That's why I think the judging at some of these contests is a bit hasty. The so-called 'personality' interview is a joke. "What are your hobbies?" they ask. Well, if I say modelling or something, they're all going to pull a face and think "How boring!" So I have to think of something else frightfully original, like car maintenance, and hope they don't ask me another. I never see any point of winking at any of the judges, do you? It's a pity more people in high places don't seem to care what I do. It's not the glamour of the job which attracts me, but the feeling that I'm contributing something. I only live for this week and the next, don't you? Otherwise one wouldn't know where one was. I'm really quite old-fashioned and no-one has ever asked me to do anything, you know, anything, well, not quite nice. It's the aurora, really. One has to preserve it.'

The Morleys had given me permission to film the entire Miss World contest with no restrictions, '...as long as it is done in good taste. You see,' Julia Morley told me confidentially, 'the press are bastards. I know they have a job to do, but they always miss the *atmosphere* of the hotel at which the girls stay.' I promise to pay due attention to the 'atmosphere'. The entire first floor of the hotel has been taken over by the Miss World organisation. The lifts have been fixed so that the first floor is by-passed; the service elevator has been taken out of commission; the fire escape is brightly lit by quartz lights and watched by the all-seeing TV security cameras; a team of karate experts patrol the hotel. The press are kept to one room, on the ground floor, where the strongest drink on offer is orange juice.

Seen Miss India? one camera-toting journalist asks me.

Coo-er!

Will we have Miss Israel down for a photo, d'you think?

Ask her to wear something a bit short, know what I mean?

Tell her to wear nothing, shouts another.

Miss Belgium's up to 12 to 1, says another.

And Miss Holland's coming up too. Coo-er!

'I prefer the Miss Universe Contest,' Miss Austria tells me. 'There, they treat you like a person. Here, they treat you like babies. Everybody seems to think that if you're beautiful, you have to be silly.'

The press insist on a group photograph, so some of the contestants dressed in short gymslips are persuaded to pose outside the hotel in the freezing cold. (The contest is held in November). According to the rules, all contestants are required to bring a one-piece swimsuit, an evening dress and their national costume. Which one is the gymslip, I wonder? In fact, the paparazzi barrage begins the moment the contestants step off their planes, and since most international flights arrive in London before breakfast, it is reasonable to assume that most of the girls are not looking their best. The day I filmed at Heathrow Airport, the official welcoming party was a Mr Ray Labargue, a bingo hall manager from South London. 'Good god, look at the luggage,' he told me as Miss New Zealand popped up behind a mountain of suitcases. 'Greece is late,' he adds. 'Must have broken down somewhere. I've been hanging onto Guam so as to marry her up with Madagascar, in a London-bound taxi that is, but Korea seems to have disappeared.' 'Get your leg up dearie,' shouts a photographer. 'Come on. Be a sport. Get your leg higher. HIGH-ER.'

'I'm used to this sort of garbage,' Alfred Patricelli, the USA sponsor, informed me. 'I've been in the business forty-one years. You expect it in any kind of sport.'

The cultural tours of London organised for the girls are certainly well-intentioned. Hampton Court can look lovely in the rain; St Paul's

Cathedral is misnamed Westminster Cathedral as described in the official 'Miss World guide'; Miss Thailand particularly enjoyed the Old Time Music Hall, as she speaks no English. Lunch with the Variety Club, at which each girl had to stand on her allocated table to be auctioned – for charity of course – especially pleased Miss Canada. 'They expect you to be smiling and waving and friendly all the time,' she told me. 'If you want that title, you have to go to hospitals and kiss little children on the cheek and try to cheer them up. I go to big VIP lunches and meet movie actors. In this job, you get to meet very important people.'

Day Six is a Sunday, and the morning is set aside for press photos. 'You just stand there and people walk round you,' Miss Hong Kong told me. 'They look at your badge to see where you come from, then they look at your face, then they write things about you. You feel like a prize cow, especially when the bookies start assessing your chances.' 'Holland's coming up, ain't she?'someone shouts.

By Sunday evening, however, the serious business of the beauty contest begins. Traditionally, the contest is held in London's Royal Albert Hall, an enormous, circular concert hall, built between 1867 and 1871 by Queen Victoria to commemorate her husband, Prince Albert. 'The thing is,' the girls are told by Eric Morley's nephew, 'this place is round.' Morley himself organises the rehearsals, every step of which he has planned precisely. 'Walk five paces forward,' shouts Morley to the first girl. 'Look straight at the camera (the whole event is to be televised), counting 2,3,4,5. Then turn toward the next camera. Pause. Count 2, 3, 4, 5. No, no, no. This camera HERE! Move faster, dear. You are behind time. Move faster! Allez oop. 2, 3, 4. SMILE. Look toward that camera. STOP!! That was a disaster! How can you do this to me? The number of times…'. Morley takes everything personally. The girls, many of whom do not understand a word Morley is saying, look concerned.

'A German photographer once made an offer of £5,000', Morley told me later, 'to anyone who could find evidence of rigging or association with girls. But they dug and dug and could find nothing. We're always accused of favouring Miss United Kingdom,' Morley went on, 'but we never had a Miss United Kingdom winner for the first eleven years. But then, as soon as we did, all hell broke loose. Don't forget we are partners in a great enterprise that is held completely in aid of children's charities, which has raised over a million pounds in its first twenty years.'

Backstage at the Albert Hall, THINGS ARE GETTING TENSE. 'Chewing gum is left on your seat before you sit down,' Miss Jersey explained. 'Last night I had my seat *pinched*. It was all neatly arranged with my national costume, but when I came back it had all been removed. Someone else was in my place. Charming, I thought.' Miss Jersey had brought twelve swimming costumes from which to choose the one she should wear. 'But I don't really like any of them,' she told me.

'The secret, when you go out there in front of the cameras,' Morley's nephew explains to the girls, 'is relax!' (Cue simultaneous translation of 'relax' into many languages by the girls' chaperones. No-one speaks Korean. Miss Korea, therefore, understands nothing, but she does keep on smiling). 'If you go out there with tense shoulders,' Morley's nephew continues, 'you will look tense on the screen. So before you get onto the stage, think of something stupid. Pretend the camera is your boyfriend. Or your mother.'

The day before the actual contest is frantic. 'My name is Pye...P.Y.E., Press Officer. So far there have been two bomb scares and one attempted abduction,' he explains to me. 'Miss Denmark has complained of a peeping Tom, but most of the other girls think she did it as a publicity stunt.'

The actual contest is straightforward. First, before an invited audience, the girls parade in their national costume. The judges are not there, although they do see a video of the parade. On the following night, the girls parade in evening dress and then in swimming costumes. Fifteen finalists are chosen by the judges, and these are interviewed to reveal their 'personalities'. The judges are not chosen until the last possible minute to avoid any charge of favouritism, and only they are responsible for selecting the seven finalists. 'Miss United Kingdom always gets into the last seven,' Miss Jersey told me. 'So does Miss USA, because the Morleys need her sponsorship and Patricelli, the American sponsor, has been in the business longer than *anyone*. Because of sympathy for Israel, Miss Israel was almost certain. And if they pick Miss South Africa, who is very beautiful (and white), they would have to pick Miss Africa South, who is black. So all the remaining girls are having to compete for two or three places in the last seven. Now, is that fair?' Miss Jersey asked me.

Backstage, Miss Hong Kong is having a quick slug from a hip-flask. 'I hope I do okay,' she tells me. 'If not, they'll stone me when I get back home.'

'I'm Sandy,' Miss Canada says, trembling all over. 'Just me. Just a little- town girl, from a little farming community; about ten thousand people. Everyone works for one big company there, including my dad. Just a quiet little town. Only one murder in two hundred years. I feel a bit numb.'

12 to 1 Miss UK, says one of the journalists.

14 to 1 USA.

15 to 1 the field.

Miss Holland has come in, hasn't she?

I just want to go home, says Miss Denmark.

15 to 1 the field.

Miss Japan is chosen for the last seven. Suddenly it is realised that Miss Japan speaks no English. Mrs Morley insists that Miss Japan's chaperone accompany her onstage for the 'personality' interview. Everyone is shouting, shrieking. Miss South Africa, also in the last seven, looks bemused. Miss Jersey (not in the last seven) says it's because Miss South Africa is too stupid to understand what is happening. Miss Japan totters out onto the stage in very high heels.

'Didn't you hear the uproar backstage when the winner was announced?' Miss Ireland asked me later. 'Well, we all expected Miss United Kingdom to be in the last five, but not the winner. I don't want to talk about it. It's too upsetting.' Alfred Patricelli, whose girl (Miss USA) had come fifth, collected ten thousand dollars from a betting shop; he'd guessed the right result. The winner was Helen Morgan, previously Miss United Kingdom, previously Miss Wales.

'Is your son here?' a reporter asked the new Miss World in the scramble immediately after the crowning. Her son? 'No, he is not,' she replies. 'Where is he? And are you married?' asks the reporter. 'Please don't talk about her son,' Mrs Morley interjects fiercely. 'The son has nothing to do with this at all.' Ah, but he has, and one could see immediately where the conversation was leading.

Five days later, pursued by those who wanted to know about her son, Miss Morgan collapsed and was immediately taken into the protective custody… of a newspaper. Other newspapers outbid each other with rival tittle-tattle about the unmarried mum now crowned Miss World. Morley is personally threatened by the feminist brigade; his house is under siege; his children are hounded. Miss Morgan is forced to resign. Mrs Morley also collapses, but announces bravely that she will carry on, as will Miss South Africa, now appointed Miss World. 'There are no skeletons in *my* cupboard,' Miss South Africa announces. Miss Morgan is told, by the press, that she is to be named in a divorce case initiated by the wife of the man whose child she bore. One headline read: '"It was a dirty trick," says the now ex-Miss World's mother.'

Morley had complained to me furiously about the lies that newspapers told about the Miss World contest. He now also complained to me furiously about the lies I was telling about him - well, if not lies, at least distortions. He did his best to prevent the film from being shown. To this day it has never been broadcast in the UK as I had originally finished it. The Helen Morgan incident was not the first time the Miss World contest had run into trouble. The previous year's winner, Marjorie Wallace, had been forced to quit because of a public affair with the singer Tom Jones, a married man.

'It was a complete party,' Miss Honduras told me after the contest was over. 'Here I am now, sitting with nothing to do. The party's over. But I have no regrets about having come.' Miss South Africa, Anneline Kriel, the eventual 'winner', later married the entertainment and casino magnate Sol Kerzner, who built the notorious Sun City.

But I always wondered what became of 'Sandy' - Miss Canada, Sandra Campbell, from that small farming community of Leamington, Ontario. Later, I learned, she became a huge television personality in Sydney, Australia, and later a marketing executive with a major American corporation. She was only sixty-three when she died.

14 to 1 the field.

Chapter 9

Orson Welles

It all started with a fan letter. While at University, I had little interest in films. But there was a strange little cinema down a dark passage just off the Market Square, to which I was taken one night – an experience that really did change my life. It only held about thirty people, was called (inevitably) The Arts Cinema, and showed films back-projected – that is, the projector was behind the screen and sometimes not properly aligned. But its specialty was 'foreign language films', shown sometimes without subtitles.

Within a month I had seen Fellini's *8½* and *The Trial* by Orson Welles, and, above all, Bergman's *The Seventh Seal* and *Wild Strawberries*, both of which haunt me even until today.

Years later, I came to know Bergman a little through his brilliant and long-time stage designer, Gören Wassberg, who designed various opera productions of mine around Europe. Bergman told me, 'Never forget, it is the face, the face, that tells you everything about a character.' And who could forget Welles's 'entrance' in the film *The Third Man*, his face, half-lit, appearing out of the shadows of a doorway? I was so astonished by his film of Kafka's novel *The Trial* that, after my first screening, I went to every subsequent one in the days that followed. Its use of abstract imagery and music unnerved me to such an extent that, although I had no idea how to contact him, I immediately penned a fan letter to the great man.

A few years later, when I had joined the BBC, my mentor Huw Wheldon told me he knew how to contact Welles (he had produced a series with Welles called *Sketchbooks*) and so off my letter went, not really in the expectation of any reply. To my astonishment therefore, not more than six months later, came a telephone message. 'I am in Spain, in a dreadful film, and bored,' the unmistakable voice said. 'Come immediately and let's discuss the music.' And so here I was, in the desert above Almeria, watching Welles endure playing Colonel Cascorro in a sort-of Western directed by Giulio Petroni called *Tepepa* or *Blood and Guns*. At our first encounter, Welles said, 'I hate the film; I hate the director and I hate my co-star, whose name I can't remember. But I need the money to complete a bit more of my own film of *Don Quixote*. You'll stay with me, of course. The film's producer has provided me with a villa right on the sea. There's plenty of room.' Even in the context of such a miserable film, it was the face, his face, that transfixed me. Bergman was absolutely right.

I had intended to stay for just the day to ask Welles from where had he 'discovered' *The Trial*'s later-to-be-very-famous theme tune, known as the Adagio by Albinoni. 'Nonsense, my boy,' he said. 'We have *a lot* to talk about.' And talk we did, for a week. To this day, I have no idea why he suddenly decided to open himself to someone he had never met before. But for a week I was given a master class in film making, fourteen years before Alan Yentob claimed to have filmed his 'exclusive interview' with Welles.

Was Welles really bored, and that's why he wanted to talk? Or frustrated? Or was he responding to a need to unburden himself? I have no idea. But I was the beneficiary, that's for certain. He was the perfect host, and knew everything there was to know about the fresh fish caught off the coast on which we feasted every night. Why me? Or perhaps that should be: lucky me.

When Welles made *Citizen Kane* in 1941, he was the first director to be given total control – he's never had it since, he told me. But what had turned the enfant terrible of fifty years ago, into the grand old man of the cinema who pines for politics and prefers to talk of anything but films? In 1960, Orson Welles had begun work on a film that remained uncompleted. His interpretation of Cervantes's masterpiece, *Don Quixote*, had never reached completion, he said, just as his ambition to become President of the United States had always bedeviled him. Welles told me that the unknown Spanish actor cast in the role of Quixote had sent a message recently to Akim Tamiroff, Welles's Sancho Panza. 'My dearest friend,' he wrote, 'please write to your dearest friend and ask him when we shoot some more. I fear lest I may be dead before the task is finished.'

'I know I should have been in politics,' he told me that first evening overlooking the Mediterranean. 'I was seduced away from it. Because I love the movies. It's like someone travelling along a highway who stops, sees a beautiful girl standing at an inn door, and never goes further. I just fell in love with this ridiculous medium.' Asked if he regretted that seduction, Welles, staring grimly into the distance, replied, 'Certainly. Certainly. A film is a dream. A dream that is vulgar, stupid, dull and shapeless; it is perhaps a nightmare.' And so, his imagination filled with such dreams, Welles has for these past endless years – just like Don Quixote – 'roamed the whole world, armed cap-a-pie and mounted on his steed, in quest of adventure, redressing all manner of grievances and exposing himself to danger on all occasions'.

The boy Welles was a phenomenon. He could read fluently by the age of two, and at seven could recite by heart any speech from *King Lear*. Long before he was ten, he was adapting Shakespeare for modern dress production and had written several plays of his own. At eleven, he wrote an elaborate 8,000-word analysis of Nietzsche's *Thus Spake Zarathustra*.

His mother was – among other things – a champion rifle shot, a passionate but oft-imprisoned suffragist, and a concert pianist; she was also a friend of Ravel and Stravinsky, and young Orson frequently conducted local ensembles and played the violin in their presence. His father, a wealthy industrialist, deserted the home when Orson was five. So began a journey that for him, he told me, is still continuing.

'When my mother died, two years later, I joined up again with my father and the two of us travelled round the world – to Berlin, Budapest, Australia and Peking. By signing my name on chits for everyone's drinks at the bar,' he says, 'I was able to cause universal happiness.' And when his father died, Welles, by now broke, set sail for Dublin, taking with him all his possessions – in a sack.

He had landed at Galway in 1937, where, with his last remaining dollars, he bought a horse and cart in which he toured Ireland as an itinerant 'painter of landscapes'. He was so poor that he slept in local monasteries, usually in an empty coffin. When he eventually arrived in Dublin, he succeeded in persuading Micheál Mac Liammóir, the boss of the famous Gate Theatre, that he, Welles, was a leading star on Broadway and wouldn't mind helping out in Dublin to pass away his vacation. Or so the story went. He laughed uproariously as he remembered this, especially as Mac Liammóir appears to have invented the story.

His 'local success' took him back to America, where, in 1938, he founded the Mercury Theatre, which was to become one of the most influential of all American theatre companies. His all-Negro version of

Macbeth gave him a certain notoriety; and his subsequent presentation of H. G. Wells's *War of the Worlds* as a genuine radio news commentary about a supposedly real invasion from Mars, made him the most talked-about upstart in American public life.

As Welles described it, monsters as tall as skyscrapers and armed with death rays were pounding up the New Jersey turnpike. Thousands fled into the streets - many suffering heart attacks. 'We warn the people,' Welles announced, 'to evacuate New York City as the Martians approach.' In Indianapolis, a woman ran screaming into a church where evening service was being held and shouted, 'New York has been destroyed. It's the end of the world. Go home and prepare to die.' The National Guard in New Jersey was mobilised. Gas masks were distributed hurriedly in the New York suburbs. Cars piled high with all that could be salvaged from the impending holocaust rushed headlong into the countryside. Again, a huge chortle from Welles as he described this to me.

Neither the public indignation which followed Welles's inevitable 'exposure' as a con man, nor H.G. Welles's eloquent complaint to the Columbia Broadcasting System (CBS), could now impair the progress of our knight errant. RKO offered him a film contract in Hollywood, giving him unprecedented control over the product, as well as 25 per cent of its gross receipts and an advance of £20,000 on the contract.

The result - said Welles at the time - was 'the greatest film ever made'. The critics were not quite so sure. They preferred to call it '*one of* the greatest films ever made'. Although Welles denies to this day that *Citizen Kane* was a parody of the life of the newspaper tycoon William Randolph Hearst ('Kane would have liked to have seen a film of his life - but not Hearst; he didn't have enough style'), Hearst was none too convinced. He offered RKO £300,000 - the cost of making the film - to burn it before it was released.

RKO refused, so Hearst, in the columns of his fifty or so newspapers, threatened to attack the entire American movie business. He made sure that RKO could get no circuit bookings for the film, since Warner Bros, Loews and Paramount all relied heavily on Hearst papers as advertising outlets. Eventually RKO had to hire independent local halls in New York and Los Angeles to get the film shown at all.

Thus, financially, Welles's first film was a disaster. The fact that, had he dropped dead then and there at the age of twenty-six his name would still have been immortal, was of little or no concern to the big business men who ran the film studios, he told me.

His next film, *The Magnificent Ambersons*, was re-edited behind his back by Robert Wise (who later directed the films of both *West Side Story* and *The Sound of Music*). Welles, naturally, was furious at Wise's duplicity and rubbished him publicly as a consequence. However, on rewatching the 1961 film of *West Side Story* (which composer and lyricist Bernstein and Sondheim hated), I was reminded that Wise also won Oscars for directing both films! Although Welles made two more films for Hollywood, he was finished as far as the film studios were concerned. He left, saying, 'Hollywood is a golden suburb for golf addicts, gardeners and men of mediocrity. I belong to none of these categories.'

Since then he has gone wherever the work is - which is mostly in Europe. He is always poor, he told me, but always busy. He has acted in fifty plays and forty films. He made *Macbeth* at a cost of £75,000 in only twenty-three days, 'to encourage other film makers to tackle difficult subjects at greater speeds,' he assured me. He had completed only six other films, often financing them himself in whole or in part with money earned from his acting. He had been married three times; for his second wife, Rita Hayworth, he bought a vast area of land in California as a wedding present at a cost of only a few dollars. 'Miss Hayworth built a house and decorated it but then complained that it was too lonely,' he told me with a smile. An agent then leased the house to Henry Miller and Welles - who had never visited it - sold it for a profit of only $80. The area of land was called Big Sur and today is one of the most valuable plots on the California coast, worth millions of dollars.

His third wife, Paola, and his twelve-year-old daughter now inhabit a wood-beamed, white stucco country house outside Madrid, he told me. As Paola is a Countess, this has made him a Count, he added with a chuckle; so at the local country club he is listed as Count di Girfalco. He considered taking up French citizenship, thus making it easier to raise government money for his Franco-Italian film productions. But he likes Spain because he has friends there who don't want to talk about his films. His Paris address is secret, as is his London home - 'and if I ever phone you in the future, it will be from a call box,' he said, with a grin.

In spite of the continuing hostility of the studios, he told me, he has gone on preparing film scripts.in readiness for his hoped-for return. Among these were *Heart of Darkness* by Conrad (his favourite); adaptations of Tolstoy's *War and Peace*; Dostoevsky's *Crime and Punishment*;

Pirandello's *Henry IV*; Rostand's *Cyrano de Bergerac; Moby Dick;* James Joyce's *Ulysses; Around the World in 80 Days;* a modern-dress version of *Julius Caesar; Salome; The Odyssey; The Iliad,* and dozens of others which he just listed off as he picked the bones out of the sea bass he had ordered. 'I've been given the use of my tools exactly ten times in twenty-five years,' he said. 'Just once, my own editing of a film has been the version put into release, and, excepting my Shakespearean experiments, I have only twice been given any voice at all as to the "level" of my subject matter.'

'Orson Welles,' wrote Jean Cocteau, 'is a kind of giant with a child-like face, a tree filled with birds and shadows, a dog who has snapped his chain and lies in the flowerbeds; an active idler, a wise fool, isolation surrounded by humanity, a student who dozes in class, a strategist who pretends to be drunk when he wants to be left in peace.'

'I don't suppose I shall be remembered for anything,' Welles said to me ruefully. 'But I don't think about me or my work in those terms. Just as it is vulgar to work for the sake of money, so it is vulgar to work for the sake of posterity.'

'The trouble with Orson Welles,' said Huw Wheldon, who after all had guided me to Welles, 'is that most people think he is no longer fashionable.' 'Let us drink,' says Gregory Arkadin, the hero of Welles's seventh film, *Confidential Report,* 'to those who, as Shakespeare had it, can to themselves be true...no matter what their nature may be.'

For Welles, as for Don Quixote, there was never a more apposite and ultimately more destructive remark.

'In this last year alone,' he told me, 'I've been in Romania, Yugoslavia, Southern California, Miami, Chicago, Spain, Germany, Paris, Mexico. Now think of all the things that are happening in those countries this year. And what life means to people in those countries. What changes their life. What makes art possible – if indeed art is even necessary, which has yet to be proven. It's the nature of politics and what politics makes of life that are important. And it is the quality of human life that politics makes possible which should concern us above everything else. That is why I work and why I am concerned. Politics is much more interesting than anything else, it seems to me, because it is the direct stuff of destiny.' A lesson I did not forget from my master class.

'When I was young, there was a big effort – largely instigated by Mr Roosevelt – to get me to run for senator,' he went on. 'The fact that I was an independent radical made it very difficult to find the right state, but eventually it was decided that if I were to run at all, it had better be in my home state of Wisconsin. But again, it was thought that a Democrat, any Democrat, wouldn't have much chance of winning because so much money had been put into the Republican candidate's campaign. So I declined, feeling that if I was to run at all, I might as well be certain that I would win. They tried to persuade me that I had a good chance, but I declined. And that's a decision I'll have on my conscience all the rest of my life, because the man who did run and did win was Joe McCarthy. And if I had run and had beaten him, there would have been no McCarthyism in America and a whole decade of American politics would have been different.'

'I like the perils of responsibility,' he said, ordering another bottle of white wine. 'I like to be the one on whom it all depends. I like to take the chance; I'm that kind of gambler.' (Another lesson for me?) 'So I know I have the motives and the instincts that make a political leader. But now, as a frustrated political leader, I have found I suppose some sort of place as a film director. A director is, after all, an imitation leader, an ersatz man. He is necessary for the length of time it takes to make a film. And that's why my political itch finds itself satisfied in my present vocation; in some way, for the length of shooting time, I feel that I am necessary.'

Again, was he telling me this for my own benefit? I felt he was.

'Some people want to be loved and some to be worshipped. 1 just need to feel that, at least within a certain framework, I am essential. Had I been a senator, I might not have been any more essential than I am now, but I might have been more effective. As it is, I have to content myself with movies, and were it not for the fact that the invention of the moving picture was a moment of historic importance equivalent to the invention of movable type, I would have despaired long since. For the first time in the history of the world, a creative artist is now given the opportunity, and lately through television, to address millions of people.'

Even if not directed at me, I had begun to feel he thought it should be.

'I can see a great revolution coming in America. A revolution to the right, if you can call that a revolution. A movement of great violence and a repudiation of a great many basic democratic processes. And following that, because of the existence of a new, almost apolitical, radicalism among the young, there will be a second revolution, a true revolution, a revolution of the barricades. America is in for some very rough years. And exciting ones. It's gonna shake the fat cats until there's nothing left for them to sit on.'

Of course, on that sunlit evening in Spain in 1968, he was not to know that Trump would come to power and move to destroy democracy.

'It seems to me, however,' (he was clearly now in full flow) 'that art should stay clear of politics if it becomes propaganda. I'm interested in politics, but not in art as propaganda. Nonetheless, I believe that films, while not turning their backs on fiction, should also not be of the "Here's the truth; here is life" school. They should be full of opinions, expressing the personality and ideas of their creator. Film is a very personal thing, much more than the theater, because the film is a dead thing, a ribbon of celluloid, like the paper on which one writes a poem. Theatre is a collective experience; cinema, film, is the work of one single person – the director. And the camera is, therefore, much more than a recording apparatus. It is a medium via which messages reach us from another world, a world that is not ours but which brings us to the heart of a great secret. Here magic begins, when you realise that a film, besides being a ribbon of celluloid, is also a ribbon of dreams.

'Thus, I try to keep the screen as rich as possible, an illusion of life that fades very quickly when the texture is thin. But I feel no affection for my old films. I have no favourites. I don't go to premières. I've rarely seen a film of my own with an audience. It's torture to sit in a movie house and watch the mechanical repetition of your own work; a work that can never be altered, never improved.

'I hate to look in the mirror, except when I shave. I can't bear to hear myself on the tape recorder and never look at the rushes of my films except when I have to because I'm directing them. It's not because I hate myself, but because I find I'm more self-confident if I don't look into the subject too closely. My self- confidence – such as it is – is based on a sort of happy ignorance; the minute I look rather sharply into the question of my voice, my face, my intentions, or anything else about me, I find too much to criticise. I actually prefer to remain blissfully self-confident, even if that means being ignorant.

'I'm also totally ignorant of the market. I don't go to enough movies to talk knowledgeably about them, and if I'm asked, it becomes embarrassing, because I either sound off bluffing, or I'm plain scurrilous. Having once been a reporter myself, I know the guy is in need of a good quote, otherwise he'll be out of a job. So I instinctively feel, for instance, that Jean-Luc Godard must be a great director because people say so. But I've never seen anything of his that I like, though I imagine I will if I go enough. I'm also oppressed by the weight of books that are written about movies. I'm only interested in the stuff itself, and I just wish a few other people were too. It makes me sad. It's like a conversation about making love. I think you either make love or you don't, but you don't talk about it. There's really nothing that talking can add to the experience. And so I have bad press relations, because people want me to talk about my movies, but I haven't got anything to say. I just growl about, like a bear in a cage, and so get indifferent reviews. Ask me about something I'm interested in. And there are a million things I'm interested in - painting, bull fighting, magic, food and, of course, politics. Probably the best political movie would be made by somebody who thinks that all politicians are crooks, and I don't. To me, politics remains the most fascinating thing in the world and it is my deepest regret that I missed my chance. I have also a great love and respect for religion. But I also have a great love and respect for atheism. What I hate is agnosticism - people who do not choose. And I firmly believe that we have to choose in the modern world between the morality of the Law and the morality of basic justice. I would prefer to let a murderer go free than let the police arrest him by mistake. If my films have any kind of common motive, I suppose that is it.'

By now the sun had set. But Welles had not, could not, would not. My master class was at full pitch. Welles's world, he explained, is divided into predators and victims. This is never more clearly expressed than in *Confidential Report* when the chief character, Gregory Arkadin, continually describes everyone as scorpions or frogs. I had long thought that Arkadin is one of Welles's most formidable and important creations. Welles had adapted the film script for. *Confidential Report* from a novel he himself had written in 1953. Arkadin is a profiteer, an opportunist, a parasite, a man who lives on the decay of the world. A scorpion. And yet he is the hero of the film, the person upon whom it all depends. Like Welles himself, I wondered as we finally agreed that night was upon us and maybe we should resume the following morning, after his day's 'work' as some obscure Mexican general was done.

That night I could not sleep, and not because of the excess of wine that we had consumed. It came to me in a flash that probably all of Welles's film heroes were, in fact, anti-heroes, grotesque monsters, above the Law, nocturnal wanderers in search of their identities, and obsessed by that search. They are nearly all Manichean, unscrupulous, damned. Quinlan in *Touch of Evil* dies in the slime of a river bank, just as Harry Lime had died in the sewers of Vienna. Iago is incarcerated in a cage above the Cyprian rocks and Arkadin throws himself out of his private plane. Macbeth is butchered as if in a slaughter house, and the battle scene from *Chimes at Midnight*, with its mangled brains, its decapitated limbs, its screams and pick-axed skulls, must be among the most horrifying scenes ever to have reached the commercial cinema.

Welles's screen is filled with images of cruelty. Othello lies in a swoon after listening to Iago's accusation against his wife, his eyes cast upwards in terror at the gulls croaking above in the summer sky, his mouth dragged open, frozen in a silent scream of agony. Welles seems to have taken as his motto in this, as in nearly all his other films, the line of Macbeth: that what we are watching 'is a tale told by an idiot, full of sound and fury, signifying nothing'. And because it signifies nothing, the tales he has told in all his films involve those who might seem to be above the Law.

But no man is above the Law. And nowhere is this more clearly spelled out than in the prologue to his film of *The Trial*, the cause of my original fan letter. 'Before the Law,' says the narrator, 'there stands a Guard. A man, Joseph K., comes from the country begging admittance to the Law. But the Guard cannot admit him… For years he waits. Everything he has he gives away. Eventually, on the threshold of death, he asks the Guard one final question: "How is it then that in all these years, no one else has ever come here seeking admittance?" The Guard then tells him, "This door was intended only for you - and now I'm going to close it." It has been said that the logic of this story is the logic of a dream - or of a nightmare.'

Joseph K. is guilty, because he is part of the human condition. Welles had freely adapted the story from Kafka, an adaptation which caused nearly all the British critics to shriek that Welles had, once more, tampered with the classics. Since, as he reminded me later, *The Trial* is the only film apart from *Citizen Kane* to have emerged in the form that he, Welles, had intended, the critics had felt doubly justified in their tiny squawkings. What they forget - as they had also done when similarly attacking Welles's film of *Othello* when Verdi and Boito had already been mucking about with the original - was that the published edition of *The Trial* was not by Kafka anyway, but Max Brod, who had made his own arrangement of Kafka's chapters. Welles had rearranged the chapters again and substantially changed the end. Kafka had ended with K. crying out as the knife was pushed venomously into his heart and twisted twice: '"Like a dog". It was as if he meant the shame of it to outlive him.' This apparent defeatism was too much for Welles. He makes K. shout defiantly, after his murderers had refused to knife him themselves, 'You'll have to do it.' They throw sticks of dynamite at him, and K. laughs insanely as he grabs the explosives.

The following morning, watching Welles become increasingly irritated by the director of his Mexican epic, I began to realise that I still had a hundred questions I needed to ask. He couldn't wait for the lunch break, and in this sense neither could I. More fish, and his favourite desert: *Îles flottantes*, and a lot of it. It was a blistering, brilliant, sunny day in Southern Spain. But, troubled by my thoughts overnight, I quoted him Shakespeare's Sonnet 43:

> When most I wink, then do mine eyes best see
> For all the day they view things unrespected,
> But when I sleep, in dreams I look on thee
> And, darkly bright, are bright in dark directed.

'Yes,' he said, gleefully. 'My film *Touch of Evil* was all shot at night. So was most of *Macbeth*. The malevolent power of shadows, of nightmares, of horror, I exploited to the last drop.' Interestingly enough, I observed, his very first screenplay had been of Conrad's *Heart of Darkness*, the hero of which, Kurtz, cries out as he dies, 'The horror, the horror'. '*Chimes at Midnight* we deliberately shot in the poor light of winter,' he added. 'And I use mirrors to distort and distend.' In *The Lady from Shanghai*, O'Hara, the hero, finds himself in Luna Park – a funfair – and wanders into the Crazy House Hall of Mirrors. The eye watches huge close-ups mingle with the fragmented, twisted images in the mirrors, which suggest O'Hara's mental and physical instability. Elsa, his mistress, and Bannister, her husband, also come to the Crazy House looking to kill O'Hara. As they all begin to shoot it out, the mirrors are smashed into further fragments; but every time a mirror disintegrates, it carries with it the face of Elsa (played, incidentally by Welles's second wife, Rita Hayworth). It is not only the body of the woman that perishes, but the idea, the allegory of woman.

'More *Îles flottantes*? You must; it's so good here.'

I wanted to know more about his total mastery of the soundtrack. Welles, ignoring the pleas of an assistant director on the Mexican epic that he should return to the film set '*immediately*', said he was the first to realise that the cinema should not adhere to the theatrical fallacy that people invariably wait for one person to finish a speech before being interrupted. Thus, in his films, several people often seem to be talking at the same time; one piece of dialogue will continue while the scene changes behind them. Welles was also the first to use reverse-tapes and electronically-created sound effects, both much used now in pop music.

Welles's enormous virtuosity has been put in the service of the de Sade dictum that 'in a criminal world, one must be a criminal'. As Leland says in *Citizen Kane*, 'We can get Kane out of our minds, but not Kane's dreams.' 'The phenomena on the screen,' Welles tells me, 'are the phenomena of the soul.

John Ford was my teacher, although my own style has nothing to do with his. But Ford's *Stagecoach* was my movie textbook. Before I made *Kane*, I ran it over forty times, making myself totally familiar with the routine and the techniques and the equipment, meanwhile ignoring the technicians who, then as now, always say that things just cannot be done.'

During *Citizen Kane*, Welles developed with his lighting cameraman, Gregg Toland, a system of closed sets – that is, sets which always have a 'roof' – thus giving the lighting a grey, claustrophobic quality. With his insistence on deep-focus photography, he also gave each scene a three-dimensional texture; you are invited in to watch whatever interests you in the scene, since the celluloid image now takes on the full range and depth of the human eye. Thus the characters gain in ambiguity, because the significance of each movement of the action is not arbitrarily stressed by artificial camera techniques. Also, this sudden depth of vision allowed Welles to emphasise how much his characters were dwarfed and influenced by their surroundings.

There is a shot in *Citizen Kane* which begins on the face of Kane's mistress and protégé, Susan, as she prepares to sing in rehearsal on the stage of an enormous opera house. The camera moves slowly upwards and upwards, still keeping Susan and everything else in perfect focus. Eventually, it reaches the topmost catwalk above the curtains, where two technicians who have been watching Susan (still in focus, but by now minute) look at each other and express their disapproval of her with a shrug. Susan's feeble voice, and the boredom with which it and she are greeted, are interpreted perfectly in that one simple camera movement.

Welles was also the first to realise the effectiveness of newsreel – genuine or faked – in the pursuit of authenticity. At *Citizen Kane*'s first showing in Italy, the ruse was so successful that the audience booed the projection box because they thought the photography was of such poor quality.

And so on, and so on. The catalogue of Welles's technical genius would fill several volumes. 'I have dragged my myth around with me,' he tells me as lunch finally comes to an end. 'Or, rather, it is my myth that has dragged around me.'

After the filming was finished for the day, Welles wanted to continue with this theme of the myths told about him. 'The most damaging myth', he said, 'has been that I overspend. I'm extravagant with my own money, but not with other people's.' He says, 'But I know how each of these myths started. When I was still filming *The Magnificent Ambersons*, Nelson Rockefeller and Jock Whitney asked me to head a film expedition to South America. This was tied up with a 1941 semi-diplomatic mission initiated by Mr Roosevelt in the interests of the Good Neighbour policy. I was to shoot, among other things, a giant Technicolor documentary about a carnival in Rio. No script, no story-line, just a budget of a million dollars. The rushes must have looked very mysterious to those executives who'd never heard of the project. "Just a lot of coloured people," said one studio executive, "playing their drums and jumping up and down in the streets."'

'Meanwhile, there had been a great shake-up in RKO. Rockefeller's men were out, and the new lot wanted to make a plausible case against the mismanagement of the old administration. My million-dollar caper in Rio – without even a shooting script – made a perfect target. I've never managed to live that one down.'

The accusation 'wild and uncontrollable', although not directed at me, seemed very familiar.

There are myths about Welles's carelessness over the completion of his films, that he forgets about the editing, the dubbing and the printing. There are myths about his extravagance with resources. 'In fact,' he told me, 'the reverse is true. I am a businessman. If I were a painter, I might have to starve a little, but I would find paper or canvas or a wall on which to express myself. Being a film maker in the commercial world, I need a million dollars to make a film. You *have* to be a business man to handle a million dollars. I remember sitting at a meeting of cinéastes with Jean Cocteau and Rene Clair, and we were regarded as being cynical because we refused to talk about anything but what films cost.'

As to the technicalities of film making, he reminds, 'No one can pretend to be a film director unless he does his own editing.' (Again, a lesson for me). He supervised the editing of *The.Trial* himself, working daily for three months, eighteen hours a day. 'I plan every shot, then throw all the plans out. The images have to be discovered in the course of work or else they are cold and lack life. And the images are welded together in the editing. For my style, my vision of the cinema, montage is not *an* aspect, it is *the* aspect… the images themselves are not sufficient. They are very important, but they are only images. The essential thing is the duration of each image, and what follows each image. Not the meaning of each image – that is up to you – but the image itself. I search for an exact rhythm between one frame and the next. It's a question of ear; the editing is the moment when the film comes to terms with the *hearing*.'

Again, this seemed awfully familiar in my own experience.

Probably, of all film-makers, Welles is the most resourceful, always improvising to avoid disaster. When the producer went bankrupt during the shooting of *Othello,* and there was no money to hire the costumes for the scene in which Roderigo is murdered, 'I shot the entire sequence in a Turkish bath – no need of any costumes.' When money ran out during the sound dubbing of *The Trial,* Welles himself voiced no fewer than eleven of the speaking parts, quite apart from his own role of Hastler. More than anyone else, it was Welles and his very resourcefulness that smashed the Hollywood machine. Hollywood had taken an awesome revenge. The last twenty minutes of *The Magnificent Ambersons* were scripted, directed and edited by someone else as we have seen – but still issued under Welles's name.

Welles would often scrape together an hilarious hotch-potch of international talent to make his films. *Chimes at Midnight* had a French camera crew, he told me, a Sicilian prince as executive producer, a Mexican bullfighter as first assistant and, as second unit director, a Spaniard by the name of Jesus Franco. He couldn't afford an arranger for the musical soundtrack, so Welles did it himself.

He still practises magic, 'to pay for the groceries', as he put it. He used to delight in sawing Rita Hayworth in half on stage, and once, in Las Vegas, for an extra special fee, he combined the woman-sawing trick with a recitation of Lear's last speech to Cordelia.

Back at his hotel/palazzo, he showed me his favourite 'toy': a small portable gramophone on which he 'keeps a check on the classics', and a reduced but essential library of Shakespeare – his 'staff of life' – Cervantes, Conrad, Evelyn Waugh, Montaigne, Raymond Chandler, Gogol, Dickens, Colette and Plato. He comforts himself with the thought that 'the greatest danger for an artist is to find himself in a comfortable position', but one suspects he no longer believes it.

Recently, he had been invited by his friend Frank Sinatra to appear on the latter's American television show. Sinatra wanted him to sing a song by Anthony Newley. Welles, in need of cash, took singing lessons. He sang. And as a result, the Hollywood studios have decided to offer him various films – as a director. It was the ultimate irony.

'I don't blame them,' he tells me. 'The people who give out the jobs are the leaders of an industry; and the people who think film is an art have to smuggle in the idea, like contraband. And as to my being persona non grata, well, there are now only four restaurants in the world that won't have me. Actors aren't allowed in these anyway. That's how it should be. If actors were more separated, they wouldn't become what they have become: just another part of the boring middle class.'

As our time together drew to a close, I realised, even if I had not known it before, that to be confronted by this six foot three inches and twenty-one stone of him, is to have known a legend, and not one legend but many. To judge Welles as Kenneth Tynan, a now distrusted London critic, did by saying that he's grown fat spreading himself thin, is far too easy. He clearly loved life, and he was not ashamed to admit it. His curious mixture of barbarism, cunning, childishness and poetic genius had driven him on in a manner that Don Quixote would have understood. 'I might have been the Senator from Wisconsin,' he says reluctantly. 'Wouldn't be very necessary. Who knows? I don't really think that I'm necessary to films, or necessary to anything. But, given a certain task, and a certain assignment, then one wants to be necessary within that context. There are so many things I might have been; I was even a part-time picador. Teaching – what a wonderful thing that would be. How I'd love to be a teacher. Who wouldn't?' Says Don Quixote: "My dear Sancho, Dulcinea and I have been considering my career as a teacher."'

As far as *Don Quixote* is concerned, Welles assured me he has only ten minutes to go – that final sequence. He's shot it all so far in black and white and now is determined to complete it in colour – 'so that it will sell'. Shooting had actually started in 1955, although Welles had previously been planning it for six years. It was originally intended for American television, but he now hoped to see it in the cinema. Don Quixote is played by Francisco Rieguera, an unknown Spanish actor and Doré's etching come to life; Sancho Panza is Akim Tamiroff. Neither has been paid a penny since they started. 'It really will be the greatest film ever made,' Tamiroff told me later, 'Or the worst.' Much of it has been improvised; Welles is linking the film with a commentary and dialogue – all spoken by him, of course.

'My Don Quixote and Sancho Panza are exactly and traditionally drawn from Cervantes,' Welles explained to me, 'but nonetheless contemporary.' Through their eyes, we see the modern world as Welles sees it: cruel, despotic, hedonistic and foolish. The film is a panorama of fashionable morality and trend-setting fashion. In sentiment, if not in fact, he hoped it will be as near to autobiography as it can be, without being explicitly so. The Don has ambitions - romantic, political, idealistic and religious - all of them frustrated, all of them disappointed. He wanders far from the home which he loves but which satisfied him not, far from the friends and colleagues for whom he worked but who trusted him not.

Welles - for whom bitterness is, I suspect, much akin to love - once declared on his passport form that when he was dead, his coffin was to be delivered to the undermentioned personage, whom he nominated as President Dwight D. Eisenhower. 'I so wanted to die during his administration, so that my dead body would suddenly come between Ike and his TV in that White House drawing room.' But die he did not, Instead, during that administration, he made the most distressing and yet the most symptomatic and, I believe, autobiographical of all his films: *Confidential Report*. Certainly, Arkadin is a remarkable amalgam of all Welles's hero-figures - odious, vicious, egotistical and sly. During a party at his castle, Arkadin tells some of his guests a fable. A scorpion, who could not swim, approached the bank of a stream and begged a frog there to carry him on his back to the other side. The frog complained that the scorpion would sting him. But the scorpion replied that this was impossible because he himself would then drown with the frog. So the pair set out across the stream. Halfway over, the frog felt a piercing pain in his back. The scorpion had stung him. 'Is that logical?' he cried. 'No, it is not,' answered the scorpion as they submerged together, 'but I can't help it. It's my nature.'

As I get up to leave, Welles takes my arm and, like the Ancient Mariner, says of Arkadin, 'He is a man who declares himself in the face of the world. I am as I am. Take it or leave it. Such a man has a sort of tragic dignity. And after all, it is a question of dignity, all this, and of verve and of courage. But it doesn't justify him.' And then, quoting from his masterpiece, he added, with infinite sadness, I thought, 'Yes, the days we have seen, Master Swallow, as the chimes ring out at midnight.'

I thank Welles for his time, his patience, and say feebly what an honour it has been. 'Don't forget, Arkadin created himself in a corrupted world,' Welles says finally. 'He doesn't try to better that world, because like Don Quixote – maybe like the President of the United States – he cannot. Like the rest of us, he is a prisoner of it. And so, like many of us, Quixote and I have sacrificed our own lives in the protection of artistic freedom and truth. Make sure you don't do the same,' he said with a chuckle.

'Oh, and if you get a call from a phone box when you're back in England, in all likelihood it will be me!'

Chapter 10

Laughing All the Way to the Bank

Few films have given me so much fun as the back-to-back profiles I made about Liberace and Hugh Hefner. Both characters were to some extent figures of ridicule, but, as I learnt, the truth was totally different and both have been cruelly portrayed by those who were just after a quick laugh. In Liberace's case, he was grotesquely misrepresented by Michael Douglas in a 2013 film which caused deep offence to anyone who actually knew him; and in Hefner's case, his carcase has been crawled over by so many feminists and proto-feminists that the real man has become unrecognisable.

When Liberace was named top of the bill at the Royal Variety Show in 1972, more than an eyebrow or two were raised in surprise. At that time, Liberace was commonly believed dead or, at least, to have faded into benign legend and obscurity. Perhaps his inclusion was yet another example of the dubious tastes of those entrepreneurs responsible for that annual charity event. However, by general agreement from audience and critics alike, Liberace stole the show, dwarfing the remainder of the three-and-a-half-hour *fest* with his showmanship, his musicianship and his one-upmanship. By comparison, Elton John, for example, was seen for what he was at that time: insignificant. As a musician, that is. I was there, and I was hooked.

Over the following three months, at his invitation, I visited Liberace's three homes in Hollywood and Palm Springs, drove in his thirteen cars, was bitten by his nine dogs, played on his nineteen pianos and had been exhausted by his boundless energy. At first, I admit, I found myself just a little deterred by his effete and almost vulgar public reputation. But I have to report that of all the pop or entertainment stars I have filmed, then and since, and whose reputations I have tried to understand (many would say ruin) from Frank Zappa to Jack Bruce, in retrospect, Liberace seems to me to be among the more amazing.

Contrary to gossip, he was neither lonely nor oppressed by his mother. His taste was controlled, even demure. He was not unnecessarily extravagant, nor was he extravagantly mean. Nor was he discontented or bitter or perverse. Nor was he retired, or even semi-retired, as many believed. As a money-spinner, he out-grossed at that time almost everyone else in pop and was among the top ten of all American 'showbiz' entertainers. He worked non-stop throughout the year except for Christmas, when he gave parties.

I filmed him in Warwick, Rhode Island during the end of his 1972 season. Not exactly the centre of the universe, but possessing a large enough catchment area to sustain at that time, for example, five performances of the concert version of *Jesus Christ, Superstar.* By comparison, Liberace gave fifteen performances, each one sold out, and his personal take-home pay for those two weeks' work before moving on to the next sold-out auditorium – after all expenses had been paid, including manager, hotel bills and his 20-piece band – was around a quarter of a million dollars; in today's values, probably fifteen million dollars. And in case one thought he was only 'big' in America, consider this: when discussing the marketing possibilities of my film, his manager gave me a list of the countries to which the then most recent Liberace television series (made in 1969) had been sold – 103 in total.

Compare this obvious success with an article published at the time in the *Daily Mirror* and written by its then-feared columnist, 'Cassandra'.

> 'He is the summit of sex – the pinnacle of masculine, feminine, and neuter. Everything that he, she and it can ever want. I spoke to sad but kindly men on this newspaper who have met every celebrity coming from America for the past 30 years,' 'Cassandra' (real name William Connor) wrote. 'They say that this deadly, winking, sniggering, snuggling, chromium-plated, scent-impregnated, luminous, quivering, giggling, fruit-flavoured, mincing, ice-covered heap of mother love has had the biggest reception and impact on London since Charlie Chaplin arrived at the same station, Waterloo, on September 12, 1921. This appalling man – and I use the word appalling in no other than

> its true sense of terrifying – has hit this country in a way that is as violent as Churchill receiving the cheers on V-E Day.
>
> 'He reeks with emetic language that can only make grown men long for a quiet corner, an aspidistra, a handkerchief, and the old heave-ho. Without doubt, he is the biggest sentimental vomit of all time. Slobbering over his mother, winking at his brother, and counting the cash at every second, this superb piece of calculating candy-floss has an answer for every situation.
>
> 'There must be something wrong with us that our teenagers longing for sex and our middle-aged matrons fed up with sex, alike should fall for such a sugary mountain of jingling claptrap wrapped up in such a preposterous clown.'

Not surprisingly – although reluctantly – he told me, Liberace had sued for libel and been awarded £8,000 in damages which, characteristically, he gave to charity. During the trial, the defendants' counsel had cross-examined Liberace about various alleged excesses. Liberace, angry, had replied that if he was as absurd as counsel was suggesting, then he wished the court to know that he was crying all the way to the bank. The jury laughed, and, effectively, the case was won.

Having given birth to such an oft-quoted phrase, he went on to use it with devastating effect (and justification) during his stage show. As he introduced one number, for example, he would turn to his audience and say with a smile, 'You remember that bank I cried all the way to? I bought it.' Then, after a pause, as if to rub salt in, he would look round and add, 'I kinda like this place.' If one remembers that in his prime Liberace sold more LPs than any other comparable recording artist, one might pause to reflect upon the serious financial power of the jest. Oh yes; and as I soon discovered when making the film, he could also play the piano rather more skilfully, in fact, than most of his detractors liked to admit, although he was acutely aware of his technical limitations. During his act on stage, he would rattle off Chopin mazurkas and preludes as if they were beginner's exercises. The review that pleased him most was one written after a San Francisco concert: 'Liberace is no Rubinstein. But neither is Rubinstein a Liberace.'

His mother, a vigorous eighty when I met her in 1972, lived in his Hollywood house. Brother George, as Liberace described him, was a successful bandleader in Sacramento, California, and well-loved by one Governor Ronald Reagan. Another brother had died many years earlier. According to Liberace, the dead brother had promised to be a better musician than either of his brothers. Sister Angie was then already a grandmother. Neither she nor George appeared to show the slightest trace of jealousy of their more famous younger brother.

I'm sorry if that sounds disingenuous, but that's exactly the way it was. Their father had been a penniless Italian immigrant from a village near Naples; Mom was Polish/German. Both were musically inclined, according to Liberace; Signor Liberace had been an accomplished French horn player. Liberace Junior had started young, he told me. At four he was apparently already an accomplished pianist; at seven and a half he had won a scholarship to the Wisconsin College of Music in his home town, Milwaukee, and had made his professional debut with the Chicago Symphony Orchestra when just nine.

The scholarship had lasted for seventeen years, during which he had developed, among other things, a passion for the cinema. One day, he went to see a film about the life of Chopin, in which the composer/pianist was never shown playing the piano unless he was dressed exotically and surrounded by candelabra. If that's good enough for Chopin, the budding Liberace had observed, that's good enough for me. Subsequently, his audience never allowed him to drop what had begun as a self-deprecating gimmick. His manager told me that one year, in the late 1950s, Liberace had tried to give up his elaborate costumes, so great was the cost of maintaining them. But his audience had boycotted all his performances until the costumes reappeared. 'His income dropped 800,000 dollars in *one* year,' the manager told me in awe.

But, like many other artists brought up in America in the 1930s, Liberace had initially found work hard to get. He had worked in supper clubs to supplement his earnings, playing the classics to handfuls of society ladies in upstairs rooms. At first, he had hated doing what he saw as a prostitution, not to say waste, of his talent. But, to his surprise, he discovered that what he had hated more was receiving a standing ovation from such gatherings and then walking home 'a nonentity'. That anonymity had irritated him, and he resolved to overcome it.

The advent of television in 1950s America had provided him with exactly the right opportunity. With his ease of smile, apparently secure family life and by now extensive piano repertoire, he was precisely the kind of comfortable, reassuring performer that was needed in the Eisenhower years. On television, he appeared warm without being patronising; above all, he seemed sincere. He really wanted to please the man on the street, and the man on the street knew it. So, from being an unknown, Liberace – and his family – became almost overnight members of a world-wide family of 20 to 30 million. In the only terms that really mattered to him, Liberace had arrived.

Having arrived, he was scrupulous in ensuring that his presence would always be welcomed. He became a distant but accessible rich relation, who visited occasionally, distributing bounty, but who then withdrew to his own faintly legendary existence. Stories about his eccentricities became a source of envy and wonderment. Liberace was always careful to fulfil this role – at first, one suspects, from a sense of duty, commercial or otherwise, but later totally from conviction.

His homes *were* like museums. He formed a trust to preserve after his death (he hoped) the objects he had bought or acquired. His pianos, for example, included one built at the time of Chopin that he had lovingly restored; a piano/organ dating from the 1920s that looked much like any other grand piano but was able, by means of various levers and knobs, to sound like either a piano *or* an organ; a piano-roll piano for which he had cut his own piano rolls on an old machine he had unearthed in a junk shop; a double-keyboard piano that worked much like a double-keyed harpsichord, in that you could lock each manual together in various octave couplings; a theatre organ that could play castanets, triangle and bass drum, as well as bird sounds; and miniature pianos in gold, silver, china, glass, string, pewter, onyx and plastic. I lost count of them; there must have been several thousand.

The master bedroom in Liberace's Palm Springs house was piled to its barrel roof with mid-nineteenth-century furniture, each piece polished and restored, collectively worth a fortune. One item, an ornate desk once belonging to Tsar Nicholas II, was insured for a quarter of a million dollars – maybe eight to ten million dollars in today's value.

Indeed, Liberace's various houses reflected his mania for restoration. His Hollywood house, built in the 1920s by Rudy Vallee, for instance, had been a boarded-up shack reputed to be haunted when Liberace had acquired it in the early 1960s. When I visited it, it still retained a curious magnificence, despite being surrounded outdoors by green carpeting in place of grass, and an open-air garden capable of being heated in winter to 70 degrees Fahrenheit by means of radiators concealed in every tree.

His Palm Springs house, a deserted Spanish convent called 'The Cloisters', had been similarly derelict when he had bought it. When I first met him, Liberace had also become interested in saving the great early twentieth-century mansions in Newport, Rhode Island, once the weekend 'cottages' of the Vanderbilts, the Rockefellers and the Astors which had featured in *The Great Gatsby*. The treasures of American architecture, he argued, were being laid to waste through neglect or carelessness. Someone had to rescue them, he told me. A Roman Catholic, Liberace built a shrine to St Anthony in his Palm Springs house, which he then filled with relics saved from destroyed churches.

At first sight, perhaps, these houses seemed filled with exactly the junk that you might have expected a Liberace to collect. Whatever is crass or silly, you can be sure to find it: a piano-shaped desk in his study, a piano-shaped bar in his guest house; piano keys on the freezer; piano keys all over the barbecue spit; even a piano-shaped nut grinder. The piano-shaped swimming pool had gone ages ago, he told me sadly. It had begun to look like a public pond, he said, because of all the sightseers. Quite apart from all this piano-ism, there did seem to be an abundance of tat. Winking electrified candles everywhere. Plastic beads and chandeliers. Reproduction Canalettos - and this from someone who could probably have bought several originals. Cheap coloured glass you could find in any car-boot sale around the world.

But having confirmed all one's prejudices about Liberace, one would suddenly notice in a wall cupboard the size of my sitting room some Georgian silver coffee pots. Not one, or even two, but dozens. And cut-glass and crystal. Enough to fill several Aspreys. In fact, Liberace had once owned an antique shop, but he had soon discovered he was a much better buyer than he was a seller. Having acquired objects for his shop, he never wanted to part with them, he told me. In fact, much of the furniture for his Palm Springs house had come with a museum he had bought in Florida.

What made the whole fantastic collection tolerable, however, was Liberace's attitude towards these possessions. One day, while filming, he showed me with pride what he described as the largest onyx table 'in existence'. It must have been all of ten feet long and five feet wide and clearly weighed a ton. Its price, he said, was beyond estimation. Later, the cameraman asked if he could rest some equipment on this table. 'Sure,' said Liberace. 'Go right ahead.' Minutes later, and there was a most resounding bang. The table had cracked across the middle from the extra weight. 'Oh well,' giggled Liberace, 'I now possess the largest onyx table in existence - that is also cracked.' He never mentioned the subject again.

Of course, this antique collecting - and he did little else when on tour except speed to the nearest antique shops and ship back to

Hollywood whatever had taken his fancy – was only part of his carefully cultivated 'legend'. Almost every other aspect of his career had been equally extraordinary. On one occasion, he had been kidnapped and held for ransom in Cuba. On another, he had been left to drown in the Mediterranean. He had written a best-selling cook book and was – as I was frequently to discover – an excellent gourmet cook.

On yet another occasion, he had very nearly died from carbon tetrachloride poisoning, and had been told by a team of eight doctors that he had only weeks to live. He had summoned his business manager and told him to calculate how much hard cash he would have left in the bank once his will had been executed. Three-quarters of a million dollars was the reply. So Liberace had proceeded to spend three-quarters of a million dollars in two weeks – not on himself, because he reckoned he was a lost cause, but on his friends and family. He had bought them cars and motorcycles, diamonds and silver. He had even bought a house for somebody. Luckily, he recovered in time to celebrate Christmas with his friends and their new toys. Now, as then, he had no regret about what he had done.

If it all sounds too good to be true, nonetheless it *is* true. He gave away more money than he kept because, as he said, you can be just as happy with one million dollars as you can with two. His mother had added, 'My boy, you can only wear one coat at a time.' Not that such advice ever limited his wardrobe. In his Hollywood house, he kept approximately 200 shirts, 300 pairs of trousers or sports slacks and 400 pairs of shoes. He had the whole lot duplicated for his Palm Springs house and claimed he had worn them all.

Liberace's costumes were made by one of Hollywood's old-time movie costumiers who had clothed some of the all-time greats: Fairbanks Snr., Gable, Valentino. 'Sometimes I look at all these clothes,' he told me with a chuckle, 'and I can hardly believe it myself.' He grinned, adding, 'My clothes may look funny, but they're making me the money.' and then he roared with laughter at the absurdity of the rhyme.

'I suppose as long as I remain a bachelor,' Liberace once told me cheerfully, 'people are going to ask me why I never married. Most of my fans don't know that my parents divorced – my father is still alive, although I don't see him much. I came close to marriage two or three times and was engaged once for quite a long spell. But it never worked out. I usually reply to questions about marriage or dating – and it's not meant to be facetious – that I admire my brother George. He is happily married – for the fifth time.'

The nearest he came to suggesting anything but the obvious motivation for his work was when I asked him whether he had any regrets about not continuing his classical music career. Gesturing towards the crowd waiting to greet him outside his caravan, he said, 'Compared to this, I think being a concert pianist would have been quite lonely.' The remark had not been intended as a psychological insight, merely a casual reflection. 'Possibly my biggest achievement,' he added, 'is that I am one of the most recognisable and waved-at persons in the world. And I love it. As long as they love me, I love them.'

This reciprocal affection was genuine and absolute. Without it, Liberace would undoubtedly have ceased to be. But with it, he found constant satisfaction. His act, the epitome of that much-maligned quality, 'professionalism', was well over two hours long - simply because he enjoyed it. When he got on the stage, he just did not want to come off. And his audience - at times seeming like a statistically-selected rent-a-crowd and not just the middle-aged mums that one might have expected - just loved it too. Liberace inspired great loyalty in them, as well as in his personal staff (his manager, Seymour Heller, was with him for almost his entire professional life, as was his musical director). Happiness would be the key word, were it not so distrusted and despised. But how else could you describe the quality of a man who maintained that it was easier for the facial muscles to smile than frown?

Oh yes; and although some 'idiot' (his term) had once made him change his name to Walter Buster Keys because he was told his own name was unpronounceable, the maestro had quickly changed it back again to its original, which was Władziu Valentino Liberace.

Liberace died on 7 February 1987, at his Palm Springs house, with his sister Angie by his bed. He was only sixty-seven. The death certificate said he had died of cardiac arrest, due to congestive heart failure brought on by sub-acute encephalopathy. Seymour Heller attributed Liberace's obvious weight loss in the months before his death to a 'watermelon diet'. In fact, he had been in ill health, with emphysema from his daily smoking, as well as heart and liver troubles, since 1985. Most likely, he eventually died of complications relating to AIDS, having been diagnosed as HIV positive two years earlier.

Liberace is buried in Forest Lawns Cemetery, Los Angeles, next to his brother George and his mother. Ironically, their graves are only a few yards from where Tony Richardson had filmed some of his 1965 Evelyn Waugh black comedy *The Loved One*, starring Liberace as a funeral salesman. For me, Liberace was a man who was often naively generous, endlessly courteous, and a privilege to have known.

His last years, however, were clouded by tragedy, some of it of his own making. He had repeatedly denied his homosexuality, not least because he believed it would be bad for business. And, of course, this was some years before being homosexual was accepted in the wider community as being 'normal'. In 1982, Scott Thorson, Liberace's twenty-four-year-old bodyguard, limo driver and alleged live-in boyfriend of five years, had sued the pianist for $113 million in palimony after an acrimonious split. Yet again, Liberace publicly denied that he was homosexual and insisted that Thorson had never been his lover, although in a bizarre twist he admitted he had paid for Thorson to have plastic surgery so that the two might look more like each other (like father and son perhaps?). In 1984, most of Thorson's claim was dismissed, although he received a $95,000 settlement. Thorson said that his lawsuit was legitimate because it was primarily based on his right to Liberace's property as his lover. Thorson later said in his book, *Behind the Candelabra – My Life with Liberace,* published after Liberace died, that he had settled because 'I did not want to fight it out with a dying man.'

The resulting film, starring Michael Douglas as Liberace and Matt Damon as Thorson, was a grotesque misrepresentation of the man I knew. For instance, I never saw Liberace quaffing champagne in his spa pool with Thorson; I never saw him 'mince' across any room; in his daily domestic life he was almost aggressively heterosexual. The tragedy was that, as Liberace had often told me, he had wanted children of his own (maybe his dogs were a substitute) and that perhaps, in Thorson, he had found a 'solution' to that want. He had certainly hoped that Scott would inherit his estate and all therein. But it seems that Scott had betrayed that trust. And, partly as a result of Thorson's influence, Liberace had also dismissed his long-suffering manager of almost forty years, Seymour Heller, declaring that Thorson could do a better job and that, in any case, Heller had been leaking money over the years into his own pocket. Heller was so distressed by the unjust accusation that he died not long thereafter (his widow claimed, of a broken heart).

Many of the artefacts that he had assiduously collected over the years were left in trust to a Liberace Museum in Las Vegas, the city of many of his triumphs. A considerable sum of money also helped to establish the Liberace Foundation, whose avowed intent was to encourage young musicians with various scholarships to assist their studies. The Foundation continued for a few years, although with no-one to administer it, it enjoyed little success. The museum closed in October 2010 due to 'lack of business', resulting in the subsequent dispersal of his treasured possessions – that is, those that had not 'disappeared' in the interim.

It was whilst filming Liberace one afternoon in Hollywood in the mid-seventies that he showed me an invitation he had received to one of Hugh Hefner's regular Sunday afternoon parties in the grounds of *his* Hollywood house – later called the Playboy Mansion. 'Why don't we go together?' Liberace had suggested. Which brought me face to face with the sex-mad monster of repute, Hugh Marston Hefner. And what a shock that was. Courteous, polite, self-deprecating, generous, witty, gregarious…I was astounded. Where was the man of ridicule? Where were the 'Bunnies' with their absurd, corset-pinched costumes and fluffy tails? Where was the orgy?

On the contrary, after I had been introduced by Liberace, Hefner himself insisted on showing me round what he called his 'property'. He was like a little kid, showing off his new toys with justifiable pride.

'I really wasn't looking for a house when I stumbled onto this place,' he told me. 'I had an apartment up above our office building on Sunset Boulevard where the Playboy Club is located. But as so much of my personal and the professional life overlaps, a house seemed in order, and when I stumbled on this place rather by accident, it was too good to pass up.'

'But the back yard was a kind of a special problem,' he told me, skipping along the immaculately trimmed lawn, 'because with all the lovely grounds, we discovered the place had no pool and no tennis court. So the first order of business was to put in both, and that turned out to be a blessing because we were able to do something kind of special. The aim here was to not screw up what we already had in the way of a very European feeling. Obviously, a traditional-shaped Hollywood pool wouldn't do the trick, so we tried to put the pool in a setting with rocks and waterfalls that would complement what we already had and continue that kind of special other-world feeling. In truth, these six acres, only a block and a half from Sunset Boulevard, seems like it's in the middle of Europe or maybe on another planet. It's a little bit of a Shangri-La for me.'

Then he showed me a pool in which mostly Japanese carp were swimming. 'It's a very unromantic description for a very exotic-looking fish,' he said with a laugh. By now, a white cockatoo had perched on Hefner's shoulder. 'The whole interest in animals really goes back to my childhood and even, I think, a return in middle age to some of those interests again.' He seemed unstoppable in his enthusiasm for his menagerie. 'But I never was much of a bird fancier before this guy (the cockatoo was now determinedly biting Hefner's shoulder). He's like a dog, demanding attention.' And now a brown chimpanzee has appeared and was also wanting attention. 'The marvellous thing, which I couldn't have believed when we put the place together, was that all the animals would stay and the birds would stay on the grounds and wouldn't hassle somersaults around each other.' Another chimp appeared, or was it a monkey? 'Yogi has learned to drink from the bottle.' And now a small pony wandered into view, clearly intrigued by my camera.

Without pausing for breath, Hefner continued, 'Prairie still has to be fed,' referring to the monkey. 'Oh yeah, come here sugar. He's obviously the spoilt one and he needs a great deal of affection, don't you? Peek a boo...peek a boo, want a banana, eh? Oh yeah. There's a nice banana. These are a pair of doves (now perched on his head) born on the property. The original pair were given to me by (his then girlfriend) Barbi on Valentine's Day and these are their offspring. It turns out love birds deserve their names; they seem to reproduce as fast as rabbits.'

'I did have a happy childhood; I did have an emotionally secure childhood. My Dad came from very poor farmstock and we were raised during the Depression. So he put at the top of the list of school report priorities: "Earning a living for the family." So while it was a happy home, he was absent from it a good deal. He had to work early in the day and didn't come home until late at night.'

By now our guided tour had reached the main swimming pool where, admittedly, a couple of young ladies were lounging topless. But Hefner ignored them.

'The idea was to create the illusion that the pool was really just an extension of the ponds where the fish are swimming. Obviously the water is not the same, because it's blocked by a large stone underneath the stone bridge which we are now crossing, so that it *appears* to continue as one. And then we made waterfalls for the pool cascading from what appears to be a man-made mountain in the middle, but actually is a cave...which I'll now show you. The water in here is all heated to about 82 degrees, and at the back of the cave we have a series of jacuzzis. It turns out that this has proved to be for some reason the most popular spot of all!'

At which remark he lets out an uproarious laugh. 'That's something due I think to the emphasis that everybody is putting on health these days!'

And this is Hugh Hefner, master pornographer, entirely responsible for the collapse of Western civilisation?

It was Barbi Benton who had convinced him to buy the house located in Holmby Hills, Los Angeles, near Beverly Hills. From the 1970s onward, the mansion had become the location of lavish parties held every Sunday afternoon, which were always attended by celebrities and socialites, today including Liberace. The house was enormous, Hollywood-style, over two-thousand square metres and best described as 'Gothic-Tudor'. It had been designed by Arthur R. Kelly in 1927 for Arthur Letts Jr., son of The New York Broadway department store founder Arthur Letts. It had a two-storey Great Hall with twenty-two-foot ceilings and staircases leading directly from the entrance to the second floor; a catering kitchen (with walk-in refrigerator and freezer) with twenty-four-hour food service; a butler's pantry; a Regency era-inspired dining room and adjacent, breakfast-oriented Mediterranean Room (alternatively known as the 'Med Room'); a vast wine cellar (with a Prohibition era-style secret door); a library frequently utilised as a backgammon/Monopoly-oriented gaming space; a living room with a built-in pipe organ that increasingly functioned also as a dedicated screening room replete with film projection facilities (this was before the era of video) for showing first-release movies during Sunday evening buffet dinners. The house also contained six full bathrooms and two half-bathrooms, some of which were en-suite. I only know this because Hefner told me so himself. The house was later used as a location for the film *Beverly Hills Cop II* and Quentin Tarrantino's 2019 epic, *Once Upon a Time in Hollywood*

In the grounds, Hefner planted a citrus orchard as well as two forests of tree ferns and redwoods; the latter was ultimately developed with nearly a mile of walkways. He also built an aviary featuring an array of birds, lizards and exotic flora alongside tropical aquaria. He also had constructed various greenhouses which housed a collection of rare orchids, plus one of the only private licensed zoos in the United States, which included several primate enclosures. These, Hefner explained to me, had been installed to rankle members of the adjacent Los Angeles Country Club, which had refused to admit him.

Hefner eventually lived there for forty-seven years, but when we arrived to film him, he had only just moved in. The house was always called the Playboy Mansion West, because his original house and workspace had been in Chicago near where he had been born (more of that in a minute.) Hefner gave me full run of both properties; no doors were ever closed. Plus, access to the plane in which he used to commute between Chicago and Beverly Hills, his McDonnell Douglas DC-9 known as the 'Black Bunny'.

I'm sure there was a darker side to this bouncing young chap proudly showing me his new house, or at least so we have been told relentlessly by ex-girlfriends, ex-Bunnies, ex-wives, ex-drug addicts, ex-employees; all of whom crave their moment in the sun. Yes, he loved sex, and frequently; but who does not? Yes, he lived a life of boundless pleasure limited only by the need to work. And work he did, twenty-four hours a day, creating and editing his magazine, managing his ever-increasing number of clubs and hotels, defending his lifestyle against all comers, including those who took his money (his magazine, *Playboy,* paid excessive amounts for articles and photographs – not all of them nude) but then attacked him.

A childlike exuberance just seemed to flow from Hefner. By now, we had adjourned to his bedroom, complete with its circular bed which he could rotate so that it faced whichever way took his fancy He was unstoppable. 'I had been interested since childhood in writing, cartooning and things related to magazine editing. Indeed, I started newspapers in both grammar school and high school. And I started drawing in a number of scrapbooks which I still have (and which he then showed me), story projects such as a cartoon adventure of the life and times of myself and my friends. And when I was in my teens I was also very busy writing plays, short stories, mysteries, science fiction, novels, songs…

I think my grammar school paper is still going today. Tea?

'When we started the magazine *Playboy* we had no money at all, and I mean literally no money. I doubt that any major magazine in our time has ever been started with as little initial investment. My own investment in *Playboy* was $600, all of it borrowed. The entire enterprise is now valued [in 1973] at something around $200 million.

'I consider myself very lucky, for all the obvious reasons, but also for reasons that run a good deal deeper. I think anybody is fortunate if they're able to do successfully what they really enjoy doing and get satisfaction out of it. And obviously, in my case, my own success has come about in ways that a great many other men are able to relate to. I live the kind of existence surrounded by beautiful things, female and materialistic, that make life very pleasant. But I also consider myself lucky not because these are the projection of other people's fantasies, but because they are a projection of my own. So for me the magazine became a kind of handbook for a whole way of life.'

Not for the first (or last) time I was finding it difficult to reconcile the public image of a sex-crazed monster with the man who sitting in front of me, albeit on his bed, albeit in his regular dress of pyjamas (silk, admittedly), albeit in his house of wonders where one could find a Picasso or a Miro or a Hockney on the walls.

'The real essence of *Playboy* was trying to put not just sex, but the whole notion of play and pleasure, back into the American concept of living. And that proved to be a little more revolutionary than I realised when I started. Our notion was that a total man ought to have a part of his life that could properly described as a 'playboy attitude', of putting play and pleasure back into a lifestyle that hitherto had been dominated by a puritan, work-orientated, anti-sexual, anti-sensual attitude. Americans knew very well how to earn money, but not very much how to enjoy it. I believed, and I still believe, that legally and culturally our society, and much of the Western world, and for that matter much of the Eastern world, is still suffering from really deep-seated sexual repression, and we are still a long way from throwing off the chains of superstition and bondage.'

He wanted me to see his original Playboy Mansion in Chicago from where his empire had first been launched, and so I was despatched on the Black Bunny back east to the Windy City and told to report back when I returned on what I had found. Again, nothing fully prepared me for what I discovered. Located at 1340 North State Parkway, the Chicago House had been the headquarters for Playboy Enterprises and the epicentre of the 'Playboy lifestyle'. The mansion had secret underground tunnels connecting it to nearby buildings, which apparently allowed celebrities and guests to come and go discreetly.

Built in 1899, the Mansion was a pastiche of Gothic Revival architecture, 'in the French style' as the Chicago Tribune put it at the time. It had an indoor pool, complete with a waterfall and grotto which had a secluded nook adjacent to the pool designated as the 'Woo Grotto'. It 'could only be entered by swimming through a waterfall softly splashing between the thatched huts and fake palm trees', I was told by one of Hefner's secretaries, whom he had ordered to show me whatever I wished. A secret button in the floor above 'lifted a trap door above the Woo Grotto' so that couples canoodling below on the grotto's plastic cushions would suddenly find a square hole above, rimmed by grinning faces.

Other basement 'facilities' included a six-car garage, steam rooms, a tanning room and an exercise/game room. The first two storeys of the house were dominated by a large ballroom in which Hefner held his weekly Friday parties for his friends and many of the company's staff. It was also used for major fundraisers for political and charitable causes, and served as a de facto office for corporate and editorial meetings, which often lasted in excess of twenty-four hours. I know; I endured one of them. There was also a twenty-four-hour restaurant kitchen, and a top-floor dormitory for Bunnies employed at the Chicago Playboy Club in the city and 'distinguished guests' such as me. In fact, no sooner had I arrived from Los Angeles than there was a polite knock on my door, where I was confronted by a very pretty Bunny who asked me whether I would 'like to go normal or go gourmet'? Alas, she was referring only to supper.

Located on the second floor of the building was Hefner's personal suite, to which I was also given full access. It was connected to a Roman bath, described for me as an 'elaborate bathing/sleeping area' designed for group sex sessions. It contained 'baroque gold spigots and faucets that sprayed and showered' alongside 'a tub with chest-high water' and a mirrored alcove with an early and mink-covered waterbed. Hefner's suite was dominated by his round, rotating/vibrating bed, from which he claimed much of his creative work was done.

I have to admit that I was not denied access to any of the above; indeed, was made to feel completely welcome by all of his staff. The last laugh was on me, perhaps, when I noticed on the front door of the Mansion a brass plate, apparently given to Hefner by Auguste Spectorsky, known as 'Spec', the magazine's long-time influential editorial director, with the Latin inscription *Si Non Oscillas, Noli Tintinnare* ('If you don't swing, don't ring').

Back in Los Angeles, Hefner quizzed me on my reactions to the Chicago Mansion. I had been dazzled, was all I could say. He seemed pleased by this and went on, 'We give an enormous amount of money to prison reform, drug reform, abortion reform, the elimination of black discrimination [when we spoke the last Ku Klux Klan march in Washington had taken place only a decade before] and paying for legal counsel – for instance, in getting a young man out of prison where he had been condemned for *10 years* for having had oral sex with a girl.'

'I consider myself a rather moral man. In fact, a highly moral man in what I consider to be the true sense of morality in its broadest social and Freudian sense. Obscenity, like beauty, is very much in the eye of the beholder. And the real obscenity for me, of course, has got nothing to do with sex. The real obscenity is killing, is war, is bigotry – that's obscene. It's a very sick society that wants to censor images of the act of love, even if explicit. But images of killing and hate are perfectly permissible.'

Okay, I accept that a lot of this was special pleading, and as the years went by I was aware of all the allegations of sexual and drug-related depravity that were laid at Hefner's door, even a murder. The apparent suicide of Hefner's assistant Bobbie Arnstein, who had been our guide in Chicago; then the high-profile death in September 1973 of Adrienne Pollack – a twenty-three-year-old Bunny and former dormitory resident who had reportedly served as Arnstein's deputy in proffering recreational drugs for guests and orgy participants at the Chicago Mansion; the subsequent collapse of his hotel chain and gaming clubs; and even the barbed attacks from his widow Crystal.

Hefner died in 2017, aged 91, and was buried in Westwood Memorial Park immediately to the left of Marilyn Monroe, whose photograph he had printed on the cover of the very first *Playboy* magazine in December 1953. Crystal told *The Guardian* that, 'Hef was on the extreme side of narcissism' and 'I had to play mind games to survive.'

It's Sunday afternoon again, and Hefner (all his friends call him 'Hef', so maybe I could now join that club) and I are once again wandering around the grounds of his Los Angeles property. 'It's amazing,' he tells me, 'how an environment can change a person's life and really open them up. I'm enjoying the outdoor life now more than the indoor life, and I've always, always been an indoor guy. I think that I am considerably different than the person that most people read about when they read about *Playboy* and the man who created it. Whenever you read a negative piece, it's partly a reflection of our own distorted focus on society and that writer's values and prejudices. Working for *Playboy* is for most of our key people a labour of love and something we believe in.'

He pauses and points to a tree house in the distance. 'I don't think you can see clearly, but up through the tree over there is a little house about half way up that redwood; that's where the monkeys live. There's a rope that hangs down where they come whenever they're looking for food. For me, I confess all this still has a very real dream-like quality about it. The boy is father to the man.'

Two footnotes. In 1965, *Playboy* had bought the lease on one of Chicago's most famous skyscrapers, the Palmolive building, for its headquarters. Some years after, the Chicago Daily News published a roster called 'The 62 Best People in Chicago'. It claimed to list all those who were making notable contributions to Chicago, whether because of ancestry, corporate rank or recent accomplishment. Hugh Marston Hefner, the most successful entrepreneur Chicago had produced in the previous fifty years, was not included.

And, finally, after the film was shown on television in the United States and elsewhere, I received the following letter.

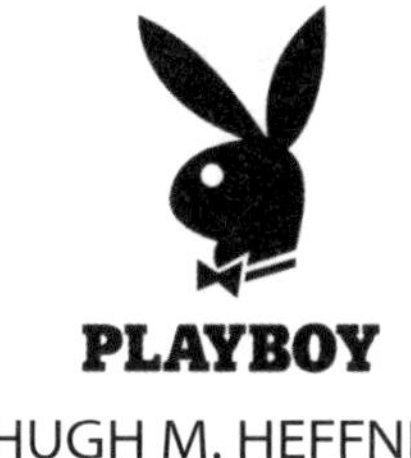

PLAYBOY

HUGH M. HEFFNER
Editor-Publisher

December 26th 1973

Dear Tony,
I've just finished screening your completed documentary on *Playboy*, and I must say you have done a remarkable job. This is the first film ever done on us that manages to convey anything of the human beings behind the enterprise.

I am extremely pleased with what you have accomplished and especially pleased that you have managed to humanize the man behind *Playboy* in a way that I never thought possible.

Let me also take this opportunity to wish you a happy holiday season and all the best for the coming year. Anytime you are in Los Angeles, feel free to come over. You'd always be welcome.

Hef

Chapter 11

Led Zeppelin

I had known Jimmy Page from the days when he played with the Yardbirds, as had Cream's Eric Clapton later. I would not say that we were friends, but we certainly knew each other. And I had in fact written the first-ever review of his new band, Led Zeppelin, in my column in *The Observer* in June 1969. 'They describe their sound as "contemporary blues",' I wrote. 'Their ice-cold musical discipline gives each song a barbaric splendor, an edgy fascination which rumbles round the imagination long after its title is forgotten.'

I was, however, a little surprised when Peter Grant, their bullish manager, who had previously been involved with the Yardbirds, called me early in 1975 asking if I would like to go on tour with the group on what might be their last-ever tour of the United States (it wasn't, as it happens), starting mid-March in Hampton, followed by Seattle, Vancouver, San Diego and onwards. Why me? Because the lads, and especially Jimmy Page, get very bored on tour, he said, and it would be great to have someone around with whom they could chat intelligently and who was not interested in their drugs, sex lives or any similar rock 'n' roll gossip. 'These are educated young men,' Grant said. 'Maybe you could educate them some more.' And with that he laughed uproariously.

Statistics, especially about pop/rock groups, are always misleading. With Led Zeppelin, statistics were more-or-less irrelevant – except that they were truly astonishing. In May 1975, they gave five London concerts at Earls Court, total capacity of around 85,000, and this following their twenty-six-city U.S. tour, total number of seats sold in excess of 700,000. No rock group in history, including The Beatles, no entertainer, no film star, no opera singer had ever attracted such an audience. Most groups were content to fill Madison Square Gardens in New York (capacity around 20,000) for one night, maybe two. Led Zeppelin's American promoters reckoned they could have filled it for a month.

Even more bewildering were the group's record sales. In six years, six LPs. No one knows exactly how many had been sold. One reasonable estimate was 14 million. The latest, in 1975, was a double album called *Physical Graffiti*; it had entered all the American charts at number three, the highest recorded entry for any album. Its advance sale of $15 million was without precedent at that time. One New York shop reported selling upwards of 300 copies per hour, outselling the Rolling Stones 11 to 1. And this without any of the usual trappings of publicity – no group photos, no television or radio appearances, no 'singles', no PR department of any kind.

That they were English; that they were the biggest commercial success story in rock of all time; that they were musicians of phenomenal capabilities – not for them the one- hour performance preceded by novelty acts, but three and a half hours of intensive and exhausting music-making; that they released albums often without even printing their name on the cover (it is barely decipherable on the sleeve of album No. 6); that they were each soft-spoken, articulate, intelligent, withdrawn and to an extent largely unknown as individuals, was to their credit. In my erstwhile role as a music critic for *The Observer*, I had rated them the best rock 'n' roll band of the 1970s, and certainly the most musically accomplished since Cream and The Beatles. Compared with them, the Donny Osmonds and all their proclaimed teeny-bopperism were rubbish – and they still are, a mere flicker on the smiling face of popular music. As was the pretentious claptrap of David Bowie and the like. As Robert Plant, Zeppelin's singer, told me, 'If only Kidderminster could see me now!' And here I was, about to be on tour with them, and thrust into the middle of the mayhem.

The initial ride from New York to Washington was my idea of luxury travel. We left the Plaza Hotel on Fifth Avenue at around five. It was freezing, but the convoy of black limousines made the journey easy. As was always the case when they travelled, Led Zeppelin had a flashing police escort. Swiftly then to Newark Airport, chatting en route with the group's improbable manager, thirty-nine-year-old Peter Grant, well over six foot and twenty stone.

In the last six years and innumerable concerts, Grant told me he had missed only five, all when he was seriously ill. In the rock business he was considered fearsome. Certainly, he had revolutionised, almost singlehandedly, rock 'n' roll management. Before his time, groups would perform for either a straight fee or an advance against about 50 per cent of the gate. Frequently this resulted in groups returning from the States after months of coast-to-coast touring literally penniless – The Who were a prime example. Grant stopped all that. As he told me, he informed any promoter that Zeppelin would only play for 90 per cent of the proceeds. Everyone told him he was crazy. But he got it, and that was now the standard deal for all his artists. Grant smiles, with obvious satisfaction.

We arrived at Newark Airport. It was raining. Zeppelin's plane looked sleek and menacing in the gathering dark. It was an enormous Boeing 720, dark blue and speckled with stars. Almost as imposing as the President's Air Force One, the name 'Led Zeppelin' gleaming along the fuselage, the group called it The Starship. 'It makes Hefner's Bunny plane look like a toy,' says Grant, beaming with delight because his wife (who teaches ballet at her own school in Sussex) had just telephoned to say that her pupils had come first, third and fourth in some national dancing championship. 'I love my job,' he says, as he rolls up the ramp onto the plane, 'but it's not my idea of glamour.' He wears eight chunky turquoise rings, all Navajo antiques. 'A bit garish, isn't it?' he says in a broad Cockney drawl, flapping his hand round the plane's interior.

Like the rest of the group, Grant detests flying. Illegitimate, a stagehand at the Croydon Empire, a runner for Reuters, a bouncer at the famous (in the late 1950s) 2i's Coffee Bar, a mini-bus driver, a film double for Robert Morley, a trainee chef, Frank Ifield's driver, an amateur wrestler called Marcio Alassio, tour manager for the Everly Brothers, multimillionaire, and now principal architect of Led Zeppelin's commercial success; he sits Buddha-like astride *his* aeroplane, scratching a straggly, unkempt beard, in torn jeans, off-the-peg jacket with patched elbows, a 20p shirt from an Oxfam shop, old boots and a Davy Crockett hat given him by Plant. In short, a concerned father who worries excessively and endlessly about his two children.

Grant told me he had a particular aversion to album bootleggers. He was once seen out in the audience at a German Zeppelin concert, snatching the tapes from a bootlegger's machine and tearing them up. A policeman called to the scene, although armed with a gun and an Alsatian dog, took one look at Grant's enormous bulk and threatening expression and walked away. Not surprisingly, Grant was also often called upon to break up squabbles between members of the band, keeping the peace with a bellowed cry of 'Shut up and go to sleep!' He was a father-figure to the exuberant young men of Led Zeppelin as they rampaged first class around the world.

On one occasion, at New Orleans airport, a bunch of American sailors were seen giving Jimmy Page a hard time, jeering at his hippie clothes and long hair. Grant picked up one of the sailors and demanded, 'What's your problem, Popeye?'

To Grant, the band were always 'the boys'; despite his gruff demeanour he regarded them very much as his family. Supporters of the band were given warm and friendly treatment. Critics were regarded as enemies, to be thrown into the nearest swimming pool. Above all, everyone agreed that the qualities Grant most appreciated were honesty and loyalty. He was much loved and admired by all who knew the man behind the image. Elvis Presley once berated his band for not playing well enough in front of 'Mr Grant', who was out in the audience.

Back at Newark Airport, the group straggle on board for the forty-five minute journey to Washington: Plant, six foot, grinning ear to ear, bounding along with irrepressible enthusiasm, pumping everyone by the hand, shouting hello, looking fit to run a mile and suntanned enough to win Mr America. John Paul Jones, the keyboard and bass player, sliding into a leather chair, opening the backgammon board and not saying much to anyone except 'It's only rock 'n' roll'. John Bonham, percussion, roaring in (expletives deleted), loud, bulky, tough, his Midlands accent slicing through the restrained politeness of the others. Last of all, shuffling, apologetic for being late, delicate, fragile almost, Jimmy Page, lead guitarist, founder of Led Zeppelin – in his own world legendary, more respected even than Eric Clapton, more prolifically inventive than any rock/blues guitarist then working, wearing an 'Elvis on Tour' badge and looking as if he has been without sleep for several days. He has also been ill. Could be from malnutrition, although more probably a leftover from the glandular fever which struck him some years earlier.

Hostesses flit about during the flight offering caviare, smoked salmon and all manner of drink. Page drinks tea. So does Plant, laced with honey and lemon. Plant, the lemon squeeze kid. Page is ruefully examining his fingers – one of them was almost crushed in a train door just before the tour. 'I almost became the hottest nine-fingered guitarist in the business,' he smiled.

Arrival at Washington, and the usual police-escorted, sirens-wailing motorcade. Plant has heard that President Ford's daughter wanted to come to the concert that night but Dad wouldn't let her because the following day was school. Hurtling down the freeway, cars fleeing left and right, swoosh into the back door of the concert hall, metal doors clanging firmly shut behind us to keep out the fans. Inside, backstage, only the distant roar of the audience.

Unhurriedly, the group unpacks and prepares. The ritual has begun. Jones lies on a bench, gazing blankly at the ceiling. Page wanders around clutching a British Airways travelling bag out of which come neatly folded, although torn, satin trousers, a pair of shoes and one sock. 'Oh dear. What a dilemma,' he says half-mockingly. Plant is still drinking tea, complaining of the cold. 'Can't we do a summer season?' he asks. Everyone ignores him. Bonham, or Bonzo to Led Zeppelin aficionados, speeds noisily back and forth into the lavatory – he too has been ill, with diarrhoea, since the tour started. Endless potions and tinctures have not cured him. There's muttered talk of hiring a doctor, permanently. Apart from that, an ethereal calm.

Zeppelin carried with them a staff of forty-four, including numerous and armed security guards. The road crew, led by designer Ian Knight, had been together for four years. His resources were considerable: 150 lights, including three krypton laser beams and a 'Led Zeppelin' neon sign; five lighting towers which can be raised or lowered electrically; smoke machines, thunder puffs; a total of 310,000 watts. In addition, there was a computerised sound system, programmed with digital delay, which could stir up feedback, howl round, repeater patterns and synchronised sound; a total of 70,000 watts capable of being heard over a mile away.

And then, suddenly, BANG. On stage. Twenty-six thousand fans erupt in cheers. Even from my standpoint on the side of the stage, their performance is overwhelming – and that in a medium which finds superlatives necessary and predictable. There was no theatre like it, no action painting which approached the constantly fluctuating patterns of light and sound which this lethal combination of talent managed to unleash. If the Beatles had dragged popular music from the inanities of middle-class, middle-aged, business-orientated pap, then Led Zeppelin had propelled rock 'n' roll into the forefront of artistic achievement in the mid-1970s. As Page winds himself up into one chilling display of guitar virtuosity after another; as Plant struts and preens and peacocks the stage, wild hair ringleted, shirt flapping, breast glistening; as Jones focusses hard on organ, piano, moog and bass guitar, the joy of improvising again and again around Page's rollicking gymnastics evident in his face; Bonham pounds and pounds his battery of drums and gongs, ferociously following where the others lead, urging, cursing, shattering any suspicion of musical complacency.

As Page told me later, 'For me, the music of the streets has been returned from whence it came. Ours is the folk music of a technological age. A sub-culture. So, as an event, the group is only as good as its audience.' And they were very, very good. 'Can you think of another song, any song, for which, when its first chord is played, an entire audience of twenty-thousand will rise spontaneously to its feet, not just to cheer or clap hands, but in acknowledgement of an event that is crucial for all of them?' I could not answer that, but such was undoubtedly the case as Page began a gentle, seductive, haunting, longing, lonely song: 'There's a lady who's sure, all that glitters is gold. And she's buying a stairway to heaven...'

The following day I spent time with John Paul Jones (born John Baldwin; the name change was suggested to him by none other than Andrew Loog Oldham, the notorious first manager of the Rolling Stones. Oldham had seen a poster for a 1959 film, *John Paul Jones,* in France). He's been playing the piano since he was six, Jones told me. His father, who had vamped for silent movies, had a particular talent for playing Rachmaninoff. John Paul Jones preferred Debussy's *Préludes,* Book II, and Ravel. With his dad on piano and himself on bass, Jones had toured the hunt balls, bar mitzvahs, belly-dance parlours, US bases, and a residency at the Isle of Wight Yacht Club. Eventually, he graduated into the London sessions circuit, primarily as an arranger. His most notable work, he thought, was for the Rolling Stones album *Their Satanic Majesties Request,* although he had also arranged for Lulu and Herman's Hermits. 'I was arranging fifty or sixty things a month and it was starting to kill me.' He had even thought of applying for a job as choirmaster at Westminster Cathedral.

Jones had met Page while backing Donovan's *Hurdy Gurdy Man* album, and some years later had read that Page was forming a new group. His wife had urged him to telephone, which he did. 'It's a very pleasant way of making money, all this rock 'n' roll stuff,' he told me. 'A superstar? No, I've no idea what that is. I'll tell you one thing, though. When we first came together, we were each of us determined that, whatever happened musically, we were not going to blow it because of bad management. Success? Oh well, I suppose I view that with some curiosity. But I'd much rather be at home with my wife and children (then he had three daughters – eight, seven and three). I've been married nine years; my wife is my best friend. I get hell for going on tour. Once I had all the time in the world and no money. Now I have the money, but no time!'

Their next concert on the tour was at New York's Madison Square Garden which, like any vast auditorium, could be dangerous and frightening. At an earlier concert there, Grant's security men had confiscated three revolvers and twenty knives. As we arrive, late, the police escort fails to stop a long-haired youth smashing the window of Page's limousine: 'Jimmy, Jimmy! Jesus Christ is here!' Grant pours out of the Cadillac. The police, truncheons raised, advance on the kid. Page also jumps out: 'Please, please don't hit him.' The motorcade then flows under the familiar metal doors, which slam shut behind us.

When the group had assembled for their first concert way back on Boxing Day 1968 in Copenhagen, Bonham – whose father had been a carpenter – had never travelled on an airplane. But now, in 1975, he told me proudly that he owned twelve dozen pedigree cows, eighty sheep and actively farmed one hundred acres in Worcestershire. His sole ambition, he said, was to win a rosette for his bulls. His friends now called him the 'car dealer' because he once collected twenty-one cars in twelve months, including four Rolls, three Bentleys, a Maserati, and assorted Aston Martins.

Plant had told Page about Bonham. He said he was not popular because he played too loud. Grant had to send forty telegrams – Bonham was not on the phone -- before the recalcitrant drummer replied. He wasn't interested, he said. He was getting £40 a week, steady.

At the end of the concert at Madison Square Gardens, the group are raced from the hall in an attempt to get away before anyone realises they have left. Outside, someone has tried to steal one of the group's limousines; garbage cans have been set on fire to prevent the group's escape.

About two weeks later, upon hearing the news at six o'clock in the morning that the tickets to the Boston concert that they had been queuing up to buy had sold out, two thousand disappointed fans had smashed up the venue in frustration, causing an estimated $75,000 worth of damage. Consequently, the Boston concert was cancelled.

Tales of violence have always surrounded the pop and rock world. Some are true, but most are exaggerated by the media for cheap thrills. Few observers have taken time out to consider the utter boredom of life on the road. Admittedly, in their time, Led Zeppelin, who were frequently described as barbarians, have contributed to the collective fund of hotel-wrecking stories. They utterly deny having thrashed a naked girl with a live octopus. Actually, it was a dead shark, Plant told me non-committally. But what else can a group do after a concert, he said, with the energy level being at full charge? The accumulated tensions of touring plus the quiet desperation of suddenly having nothing to do in the middle of the night sometimes erupts into senseless hooliganism, he admitted. 'You can't just go to bed with a cup of hot chocolate,' Bonham explained to me, pained that I should have failed to comprehend.

One particularly vengeful night cost Grant $3,000. 'Oh, that's nothing,' the hotel manager said. 'Not half as much damage as was caused by a recent Methodist Convention and they didn't reimburse me a cent. Anyway,' said the manager, 'I quite understand. The rooms are very, very boring. I often feel like tearing the place apart myself.' Grant smiled, slowly, and brought out another $5,000. 'Have one on me,' he said. Whereupon the manager smirked, and then proceeded to demolish the room. Bed linen, television set, fixtures; all were hurled about indiscriminately.

'I really enjoyed that,' said the manager afterwards. 'Thank you.'

Grant had known Page since Jimmy was fifteen. 'When I took over the management of the Yardbirds', Grant explained to me, 'I was advised to get rid of Pagey, their lead guitarist. He was a trouble-maker, I was told, and I soon found out why. The Yardbirds had recently appeared in Antonioni's film *Blow-Up*, recorded its title song, toured the States as a support act for the Rolling Stones, done their own US tour for five weeks, and had exactly £112 to show for it. Someone had ripped them off mightily. Pagey vowed it would never happen to him again.'

When the Yardbirds had eventually split up in 1968, Page retained the copyright on the name, almost by way of revenge against the record company that he was convinced had also ripped him off. Page told Grant about Jones and of their session work together, suggesting that he and Jones might form the basis of a new group. Later, when Page and Grant were walking along Oxford Street, they met a longtime colleague who told them strange tales of a physical explosion in Birmingham called Robert Plant. The two travelled north and were greeted at the door of some seedy club by a rough, rug-headed kern whom they took to be the bouncer. But when they saw the same man on stage, they both realised they were watching potentially the most startling singer/performer since Elvis. He was more venomous than Jagger and with a voice of stinging range and power. 'It unnerved me, just to listen,' Page told me. 'It still does, like a primeval wail.' And so Plant joined the band.

Next was Bonham, and finally Jones was signed up. Then Grant did a deal with Atlantic Records in New York which set the pattern for all his future transactions. Atlantic had blithely announced that they wanted the new band because it included Jimmy Page. 'But you don't know my price,' Grant had replied. They soon found out, and were persuaded to part with the largest royalty ever negotiated for a group of musicians whose 'group' hardly existed yet. No one knows exactly how much it was, but it is said to be five times larger than the first royalty paid to The Beatles. Their first album cost £1,782 to produce, including the cover. It grossed $7 million within weeks. Keith Moon of The Who had suggested the name; he thought they would go down like a lead balloon, or even a Lead Zeppelin, ha, ha. 'Led just looked better than Lead,' he said, 'which Americans would inevitably pronounce as "Leed"'.

Back in England, however, the group was ignored. No one would book them, except as a supporting act. Grant was forced to try Scandinavia. Even after the successful release of their first album in the States, no-one wanted to book them there either, but for a different reason. No other group could be persuaded to follow them, or precede them. They joined up eventually with the Woody Herman band and performed on the same bill as them at the Fillmore East in New York, 30 May 1969. This is where I first saw them, following which I wrote my original review in the *Observer*. Woody Herman, who was scheduled to play second, was crushed into oblivion and never appeared. Led Zeppelin played for over four hours, including five encores. They eventually stopped only because they had simply run out of material. The saga had begun.

Since that beginning, Led Zeppelin have grossed at least $30 million per year from 1970 to 1975, at least a billion dollars in today's value. For several years after 1969, Grant would often keep the group off the road, sometimes for as long as eighteen months, until he judged the moment was exactly right for a spectacular return.

The concert in San Diego was planned as one such 'spectacular return' during the 1975 tour. Bonzo was ill again and had to stop at several gas station lavatories en route to the airport. The new travelling doctor, hot from Yale Medical School, produced a medicine chest of bottles. All seemed useless.

Grant was wearing a Japanese smock and a Spanish matador's hat. Wearing both would look absurd on anyone else, except on Grant. Again, the race from the airport to the Sports Arena, sirens blasting, car doors resolutely locked. Plant, who writes most of the group's lyrics, gangly and awake, a lifetime Wolves football supporter, does his imitation of Wolves star and Northern Ireland striker Derek Dougan to keep everyone amused. For such a titanic performer on stage, he is ludicrously polite off. He lives for the day, he told me, 'as long as it is functioning'.

Like Bonham, Plant also lived on a farm at that time. His was a working mountain sheep farm between Worcestershire and Shropshire that he 'maintained with finesse'. Spending time alone with him proved difficult. He insisted on doing handstands and generally prancing about while talking. He was apt to trot out the clichéd reply to what was, most probably, a clichéd question. 'I want to slap apathy in the face before it becomes too big a wart.' Ah. 'I'm proud of what we've done, of what we represent. We are a diversion, which I believe to be artistically valid. So let's all go to the revolution, but who knows the way?' Ah, indeed.

After six years at King Edward VI Grammar School in Stourbridge, close to Birmingham, he finished up earning £2 a week 'making tea for a seedy old man who was supposed to be teaching me chartered accountancy'.

He hated it and left. He had already sung in the backs of pubs while studying for his O-levels, so he had little difficulty in forming various small bands such as The Crawling King Snake, all named after old blues tunes. But his performances found little acceptance in Birmingham, where he became known as 'the wild man of the blues from the Black Country'. He moved south to 'Middle Earth', the now-defunct cellar club in Covent Garden, where much of what subsequently became known as underground rock was developing. There, Plant developed the heaving swagger of his voice, by turns mellifluous and shrill, accusatory, pleading and sweet – a devastating instrument, his by chance and not by suffering – arguably the first white voice that had the measure of the blues at a time when the tradition of blues 'shouting' was dying.

'It's not a voice you can practice with,' he told me. Once, he was a Mod and had gone to the beaches at Margate with other Mods to fight the Rockers. Then he was a Rocker, and then a beatnik. He told me he read Sartre, Camus and Kafka. Then he became a rock star with a steel constitution and a 'curved smile'. Like other rock superstars, he confessed, he wastes thousands on silly cars.

Yet his command of an audience is uncanny. I have seen him rouse a docile mob of 20,000 to a thundering, quivering mass. 'We're laying it on the line,' he told me, 'the audience knows we are trying to communicate a fulfilled ideal. Doesn't anyone remember laughter?' *Ah.*

It was six in the evening in Los Angeles, California. There was to be no concert that night; the last was two days ago. Page has eyed me suspiciously although politely since I arrived. At other times, he appeared so preoccupied that I need not have existed.

Fellow musicians rate Page one of the finest guitarists. His technique may lack the effortless charm of Eric Clapton; may lack brutal wizardry of one of rock music's heroes, Jimi Hendrix. His songs may not equal the agonised self-pity of Bob Dylan, nor his compositions equal the formal brilliance of Benjamin Britten, about both of whom he speaks very knowledgeably. But his grasp of both the limitations and possibilities of his music is formidable. When he was first voted the Number One guitarist by various rock magazines, he was genuinely surprised. 'I'm not really much of a guitarist, am I?' he asked me.

Having persuaded Page's armed guard (seated constantly outside his room) that I was genuine, I was allowed to knock at the door. After a long pause, a voice within said quietly, 'Who is it?' I told him and he let me in. Gone was the flashing majesty of his appearance on stage, fast as a cat. Instead, a thin, almost inaudible, ghost of a man, like a choirboy, dog-tired but smiling. He had been awake non-stop since the last concert forty-eight hours ago. 'I thought something was coming through,' he said, waving his hands towards his guitar sunk into a chair. 'But, well, I suppose there have been too many interruptions.' He wanders about his darkened room, disconsolate, exhausted, alone. 'I've compared notes with other writers and artists,' he tells me defensively, 'to see what time of day is most productive. Writers seem to thrive on schedules. Poets, or composers like me, just go at it. I've lost all concept of time long ago. I hate my music being described as rock 'n' roll. 'Pop' as a name is also ridiculous. They're both a long way from the truth. What we play is street music, folk music, and that's why we refuse to get involved with the media. If what we are saying has any truth, then people in the street will know.'

He hadn't started playing until he was fifteen – he was only thirty-one when we talked. An only child, the son of a personnel manager, he grew up in Heston next to London's Heathrow airport. He remembers distinctly the event that changed his life. He had heard Chuck Berry singing *No Money Down* and knew (correctly) that in its own primitive and naive manner it touched a profound social nerve. No money down, live now and pay later: the whole gaudy never-had-it-so-good, 'I'm alright, Jack', trashy post-war materialism was caught in that one song.

Page had begun playing anywhere and everywhere, been interviewed on television by Huw Wheldon, and by the time he was twenty had become the youngest - and probably also the best - session guitarist in London. He had worked with P.J. Proby, The Who and the Rolling Stones. He had played at the famous Marquee Club off Oxford Street, and at the equally famous jazz and blues club on Eel Pie Island in West London. He had done a stint of one-night gigs around the country until, finally, he had collapsed with fatigue. He also cut a solo single called *She Just Satisfies.* It was rubbish, he told me. As had been his work as a session player, he now thought. In the end he had had no idea what he was doing or why. Eventually he joined the Yardbirds, initially as a replacement bass player, and the rest we know.

Well, not quite. He told me he would like to fill his house with pre-Raphaelite paintings (he eventually did just that in the famous 'Tower House' in Kensington), but for the moment he couldn't afford to do so because he still pays 98% in taxes on song writing royalties. 'I keep meeting people in the States who can't afford to come back to England,' he says with a wry grin. 'But I hope to stick it out in England until a compromise comes along.'

At this point, he is the only Zeppelin who is not married. 'I once told a friend, I'm just looking for an angel with a broken wing, one who couldn't fly away.' Death threats are frequent. He worries about the whole pace of being on the road, of constantly having to live up to his image, whatever that is. When he returns home, he can't eat or sleep or relax in any way for days, often weeks, he tells me.

And what of his music? Stylistically, it was a tour de force, borrowing from Bo Diddley, the Stones, Cream, Burt Bacharach and Kool and the Gang: A fusion of jazz, rock, blues and flamenco. It was persuasive and snarling, whether acoustic or electric. It was deceptively facile, yet almost never overblown. It relied heavily on the blues for its emotional strength, yet had expanded the electric vocabulary of that ill-used idiom while remaining firmly locked within it. A song like *Stairway to Heaven* is characteristic. It begins softly, with acoustic guitar playing a quiet, aching snatch of melody. The singer begins gently with one of the most simple of themes. Gradually, but inevitably, the sound develops over ten minutes into a massive climax, the bass and drums providing an elemental roar from which the guitar (now electric) and singer tear a raging, hurting song.

Not all Led Zeppelin's songs are based on this pattern, but there are a sufficient number to recognise this as the group's signature. Again, it is the multiplicity of cross references which made the music arresting, almost as if the band were summing up rock 'n' roll and yet also re-fashioning many of its conflicting elements into a new sound which had the possibility, thereby, of extended development. One heard snatches of Beatles chord progression, the miasmic, tortured blues lines of Leadbelly, the rhythmic brutality of Pete Townshend. Yet the whole was different from the parts. At the time it was the 'hardest' sound you were likely to find on disc, never distorted but always relentless. What is more, it was beautifully fashioned.

And what of Jimmy Page, the group's composer and producer? Of all those working in the pop milieu at that time, he was the master craftsman. Groups like Cream discovered that pop (or rock, or whatever cliché you choose) was possessed of considerable instrumental capabilities. The question remained of what to do with those capabilities. Page recognised that the answer was simple: craftmanship.

There is no difference, essentially, between a Led Zeppelin song like *In My Time of Dying,* with its moaning guitar, extended and improvised vocal line, all lasting for over twelve minutes, and an early Chuck Berry or Presley number like *Baby, Let's Play House.* Except for one thing: The Led Zeppelin song is better constructed, better played and better recorded.

Page also understood the importance of ensemble playing. That may sound a little obvious, but for years the self-indulgent egocentricity of pop stars prevented them from hearing one another. Group after group split up 'because they could no longer hear each other', he tells me. In choosing Jones, Bonham and Plant, Page was lucky enough to have discovered three musicians with self-awareness comparable to his own. There were bands whose sound was less crude, and perhaps more 'tasteful'. There was no band at that time, however, whose constant ability to produce harmonies and counterpoint on which to hang their improvisations was so sophisticated. It made them impossible to copy, as many discovered.

Page told me of one occasion some years back when, as the group entered, the entire audience of some 25,000 lit matches or candles or lighters and stood in silent recognition of a sound, an achievement, that they felt spoke eloquently for them and their longings and their disappointments. The sight of those flickering beacons, says Page, stopped him dead in his tracks. It was, he recalls, 'a moment of true magic'.

I think we talked that evening for around three to four hours, his hands fluttering bird-like in the darkness. Time, he told me, ceased when they performed on stage. They had tried frequently to cut down their performances to around two hours or so, but it always crept back to well over three.

As Page drew me further and further into his world, time slipped away with equal grace. I often think of him now, perched high up in his Hollywood hotel, curtains shut, film projector standing idle, records stacked untidily on the floor, guitar in his hands, waiting – as he says – for something to come through. Occasionally, the silence is interrupted by the need to move on to the next city, the next concert. Food is brought in; the armed guard ever watchful; the telephone more or less permanently off the hook; the television blank. That he is probably worth a fortune is clearly meaningless to him, except insofar as it pays for his privacy. He has the isolation and discipline of a monk. By remaining calm at the centre of a disintegrating culture, he felt he could provide an example for its future development. If we needed heroes, then rather Jimmy Page than political buffoons or licensed jesters or sporting apes or absurd television 'personalities'. Much rather the shy, nervous, steely youth whose songs inspired a generation.

The audience is letting off fire crackers as the group huddles at the side of a specially built sixty-foot-wide platform. Page is shaking like a leaf – literally. The Astrodome near Washington is long enough to take two jumbo jets end to end with a couple more either side. The racket is unbelievable. 'This is ridiculous,' says Bonham, visibly sweating. 'Ladies and Gentlemen: Led Zeppelin…'

It couldn't have lasted; it never does. Witness the Beatles' demise. Three hundred million records sold is no mean achievment. John Bonham died on 25 September 1980, aged thirty-two. He was discovered unresponsive in his hotel room by John Paul Jones. A coroner later found that Bonham had taken forty shots of vodka in twelve hours. His death was ruled an accident and it was determined that he had choked on his own vomit. The band did not have the heart to continue and had disbanded. In a 4 December 1980 press statement they stated that, 'We wish it to be known that the loss of our dear friend, and the deep sense of undivided harmony felt by ourselves and our manager, have led us to decide that we could not continue as we were.' The statement was signed simply 'Led Zeppelin'.

There was the occasional reunion of the remaining three members – for example, at Live Aid. Both Jones and Plant later resumed solo careers, with Plant successfully teaming up with Alison Krauss, an American bluegrass country singer, fiddler and music producer, and Jones developing his career as a serious composer receiving commissions from such as the distinguished mezzo-soprano Sarah Connolly. Jimmy Page cured himself of any cocaine addiction and became a recluse in spite of rare appearances, for example, at the Beijing Olympic Games closing ceremony. From the early 1970s to the early 1990s, he owned Boleskine House, the former residence of occultist Aleister Crowley. He later resided in Sonning, Berkshire, in Deanery Garden, a house designed by Edwin Lutyens, and, more recently, in Tower House, which was built by the architect and designer William Burges between 1875 and 1881, described as 'the most complete example of a medieval secular interior produced by the Gothic Revival, and the last'. Page, an admirer of Burges and of the Pre-Raphaelites with whom Burges was closely aligned, commented in a BBC interview in 2004, 'I am still finding things 20 years after being there – a little beetle on the wall or something like that. It's Burges' attention to detail that is so fascinating.' Tower House is now almost a living museum dedicated to the Pre-Raphaelites.

As for Peter Grant; marital problems, diabetes, cocaine addiction and the death of Led Zeppelin drummer John Bonham all took their toll on Grant's health. After the official breakup of Led Zeppelin in 1980, he virtually retired from the music business to his private estate in East Sussex. Towards the end of his life he, too, conquered his cocaine addiction and lost a significant amount of weight. He sold his estate and moved to nearby Eastbourne, where he was offered, but turned down, the civic position of local magistrate for the town council. In 1992, he appeared as a cardinal in the film *Carry On Columbus*. In his remaining years, Grant became a keynote speaker at music management conferences, where he was lauded and saluted by modern industry professionals. He died of a heart attack November 1995. Coincidentally, his funeral was held on the fifteenth anniversary of Led Zeppelin's official breakup. Phil Everly from the Everly Brothers, paid tribute: 'Without his efforts, musicians often had no careers. He was the first to make sure the artists came first and that we got paid, and paid properly.'

And for the privilege of being invited to tour with Grant's greatest invention, I am forever grateful.

Chapter 12

John Lennon and All You Need is Love

It all started with a chance encounter with John Lennon on the streets of New York in the early seventies. 'Doing anything useful?' he asked, with his customary directness. Over a *delicious* lunch of brown rice, the plot was hatched. 'There will be no escape,' Lennon warned, laughingly, as we mapped out one of the most foolhardy ideas yet devised by man: nothing less than the entire history and development of (American) popular music. 'It's what's needed,' he kept telling me, 'Something that pieces together all the various elements that have gone into making what rock 'n' roll is today: country, jazz, blues, ragtime, the music hall, soul – it should be easy!'

Lennon had been my mentor once before – indeed long since before – when I had first met him in Cambridge in November 1963. At that time, there was a lunchtime press conference at the old Regal Cinema for a newish group performing in Cambridge that night, The Beatles, which I was urged to attend by my then-girlfriend Christine. I went there representing the University student newspaper *Varsity*. After the official press conference had broken up, everyone was milling around and I had a tap on my shoulder and heard a voice say, 'Why didn't you ask any questions?' It was Lennon. I said, 'Because the so-called press conference had been the usual mumbo-jumbo of silly questions and even sillier replies from the group.' 'And what do you do?' my interlocutor asked.

'I'm a student.'

'What of?' he asked.

'Something called Moral Sciences.'

'Well, that sounds pretty silly to me,' he said.

And indeed it was, especially when I explained it had nothing to do with morals and even less to do with science. As I was a student, he said, would I show him around the University that afternoon? I think he imagined the University was one big campus rather than a disparate collection of colleges. At first I refused, saying that it was not my idea of fun being mobbed, as undoubtedly he would be. 'How about if I come in disguise?' he asked.

Having had my bluff called, I felt I could not refuse, so I dutifully showed up at Lennon's hotel that afternoon, to be confronted by a man in a false beard, an enormous fedora hat, and the dirtiest raincoat I had ever seen. We both laughed. Shed of his 'disguise', I managed to get him into the great chapel of King's College, and more importantly, as it turned out, the Wren Library at Trinity College, where he took down book after book from the shelves, despite my pleading with him in a whisper to be more respectful, fearing that otherwise my University career might be over before it had begun. I realised later that, for Lennon, 'books' meant 'education', which he felt had been denied him by his involvement in the crazed world of rock 'n' roll.

Eventually, it was time for him to report for duty as a member of The Beatles to prepare for that evening's performance. And as we parted, he thrust into my hand a piece of paper on which was a telephone number, saying he would not be able to see me after the concert because, for security reasons, the group would leave rapidly by the back door immediately they finished performing.

'Call me when you come to London,' he said.

'I'm not coming to London,' I replied, rather plaintively.

Almost three years later, I still had that piece of paper. By now, I was working at the BBC. Although when we had met at the Regal Cinema, The Beatles were already well established, having had two number one hits, by 1966 they were intergalactic. Still, nothing ventured, nothing gained. Believing that the number probably no longer existed, I dialled it anyway and was astonished – first, that it rang at all, and second, that someone answered. But I could tell from the tone of the girl's voice on the other end that I was the 400th person who had telephoned that morning saying that 'John Lennon said to call.' In response to her expression of doubt, I replied, 'Well, he did, and here is my number.' To my further astonishment, half an hour later I got a reply. The voice introduced himself as Derek Taylor. He was The Beatles' long-suffering PR man and close friend. I stood up, shocked. Taylor said he had a message for me from John. I gulped, thinking that message might be along the lines of 'Who the hell are you?' and/or 'Why don't you f**k off?' Nervously, I eventually asked what was the message. Taylor replied, 'John wants to know why it has taken you two years to call him back.' Lunch – brown rice, of course – was arranged, and so began an unlikely friendship.

At the lunch he complained to me that many of the great musicians he admired simply could find no place on a BBC dominated by *Top of the Pops, Juke Box Jury* and gyrating nubiles – musicians such as Hendrix, Eric Burdon, The Who, Frank Zappa, Pink Floyd and Cream – none of whom, at that time, had ever been seen on BBC television. 'I had a duty,' Lennon had told me then, 'to find a way to get them onto the television screen, by fair means or foul.' He would make the introductions to the various artists; I would make a film about them. And meanwhile, he suggested a title for the as-yet non-existent film: *All My Loving.*

The BBC hated the resulting film. David Attenborough, then Director of Television and since a good friend, famously wrote an internal memo apparently saying 'over (his) dead body would the film ever be shown'. After six months 'on the shelf', it was rescued, if that's the word, by John Culshaw, newly appointed Head of Music and previously Benjamin Britten's trusted record producer at DECCA. What a lucky encounter in Aldeburgh that now turned out to be!

Under pressure from Culshaw, it was eventually proposed that the film be screened after *The Epilogue,* in late October 1968. Paul Fox, then Controller of BBC1, suggested a compromise. 'I'll trade you two f***s for three pisses,' he said, and thus the film was shown. Mrs Whitehouse, a housewife from Nuneaton in Warwickshire and self-appointed guardian of the nation's morals from her front sitting-room, sued.

Before the film was broadcast, I arranged a private screening for Lennon who, after all, had originally kicked the film into life. He asked me what I thought the public reaction would be. I said I believed that the popular press, the 'red tops', would praise the film since it included many of their pop music heroes, but the serious press, the 'broadsheets', would attack the film as being pretentious hogwash. 'Wrong,' he said, and bet me £5 that the reaction would be the reverse. The popular press rubbished the film. Richard Williams wrote in *Melody Maker,* 'the film was an awful hash up'. But the serious press wrote reams about its 'true meaning'. Critic James Thomas wrote, 'It was a psychedelic experience which ten years from now will be seen as the definitive document of its time. How often does television make you sit on the edge of your chair?'

Stuart Hood, a former Controller of Programmes at BBC Television, writing in *The Spectator,* said he had 'no doubt that wherever the film is shown it will win professional acclaim. Remarkable for its virtuosity, its impact is inescapable. No wonder it has been the subject of passionate argument in the corridors of the BBC for months.' *The Telegraph* wrote that 'It was absolutely chilling.' *The Observer*: 'It said more about pop music than a year of Top of the Pops.' *The New Statesman*: 'Brilliant and frightening.'

McCartney sent me a telegram of congratulations. Lennon considered me 'an ally for the cause'. As he wrote to me, 'We have smashed down the door of the BBC, and rock 'n' roll on television will never be the same again.'

In that at least, he was right, although he never paid me my £5. More or less every sequence of *All My Loving* has been stolen and used in other films, usually without attribution, and even on its fifth screening a few years ago on BBC Four, it provoked a row. Interestingly, the film was first shown in the BBC's Omnibus slot, normally reserved for the 'high arts'. In fact, the week after *All My Loving* was screened, Omnibus showed a film about the sculptor Henry Moore. Omnibus also showed my film of *Cream Farewell Concert.* So the notion that 'high art' and 'low art' (both despicable terms) could be shown and acknowledged side by side and each treated with the same respect, was clear two years before Melvyn Bragg claimed to have 'invented' this notion on his *South Bank Show.*

The reaction to *All My Loving* did not affect my relationship with the Beatles, and I became the only person not directly involved with them to write liner notes for one of their albums. In my role as a music critic for the *Observer* newspaper, I reviewed their 1968 'white' double album, beginning: 'If there is still any doubt that Lennon and McCartney are the greatest song writers since Schubert…', a remark which, although I went on to justify, was greeted with derision by all except the Editor of *The Observer,* David Astor. He thought it apposite, despite 'outraged of Tunbridge Wells' declaring how dare this upstart Palmer compare 'trash with genius'. Today, such a musical comparison would pass completely unnoticed because of its essential truth, and again, it was two years before Melvyn Bragg claimed such comparisons as his own. I owe Melvyn an enormous amount; he commissioned sixteen films from me as an independent producer, more than from anyone else.

But in breaking down the barriers between 'high art' and 'low art', he merely followed the pioneering work of others.

So here am I in New York, four years after *All My Loving*, and, thanks to my chance encounter with Lennon, once again gorging on brown rice (what else?), thinking the unthinkable: nothing less than the entire history and development of (American) popular music. I realised that my ignorance of the subject was matched only by my stupidity in attempting such a task. Lennon's justification was simple. At that time, the early 70s, there was a fashion on television for thirteen-part series (thirteen weeks being a quarter of the scheduling year). The most famous of such were Kenneth Clark's *Civilisation;* Bronowski's *The Ascent of Man;* and David Attenborough's first nature series *Life on Earth.* So why not a series about arguably one of the most important strands in twentieth-century culture: the rise and rise of popular music? It was an argument difficult to deny.

Lennon also suggested a solution for its structure: 'Get some of those clever people to write down why such-and-such a subject is important to them. Use that as a starter. Ragtime, blues, music hall, jazz, the musical and so on. Oh, and if you need a good title, how about *All You Need is Love*?' Lennon laughed; clearly he thought that was good joke. 'That's what it's all about anyway,' he went on as he swept out of the restaurant door, 'or rather the lack of it. Cheerio….and have fun!'

Money. That's what such a vast project needed first, since something on this scale was not going to be cheap. Enter Paul Fox again, now boss of Yorkshire Television. He brought in Cyril Bennett, his equivalent at London Weekend Television, whose new Controller of Entertainment was one Michael Grade. 'Tell us what you have in mind,' said the Three Wise Men. 'Well…' I waffled. 'Oh yes?' said Bennett. By this time I had mapped out individual episodes on the blues, jazz, ragtime, country, The Beatles, glitter rock…in all, I said, about sixteen episodes. Their eyes glazed over. I could see them thinking, 'Man's an idiot.' 'Are you seriously asking for SIXTEEN hours of prime time television?' 'Yes, why not?' I replied.

Grade thought his uncle, Lord (Bernie) Delfont, might be willing to fund it. Fast forward to a meeting with Delfont, the tap-dancing impresario who ran every end-of-the-pier show in the country as well as EMI and the annual Royal Variety Show. I reminded Delfont that the Royal Variety Show had recently featured Liberace, about whom I had made a film. 'My boy,' he said in between cigar puffs, 'it will be a pleasure.' Had Lennon, The Beatles being EMI's No.1 Artist, let it be known that the proposed series had his approval? I never found out, although George Martin, The Beatles' renowned record producer, told me years later that he had been told by the management to give me whatever I needed.

Delfont also pointed me towards a company called Theatre Projects, in which he had a stake, and its leader Richard Pilbrow. 'A *theatre* company?' I asked. (Pilbrow had been responsible for designing much of the stage machinery of the new National Theatre.) 'Yes,' said Delfont. 'You need a helping hand!'

And so, under Pilbrow's guidance, I wrote to 'those clever people' asking them for 2,000 words on what their particular area of expertise meant to them - George Melly on the blues; Leonard Feather, the great jazz historian; Paul Oliver on the history of the blues; Jack Good; Humphrey Lyttelton; The Beatles' long-time press officer, Derek Taylor; Stephen Sondheim on the musical; Nik Cohn; Charlie Gillett; Rudi Blesh on ragtime...These were not to be the 'scripts' of the films, I explained, but a reference point from which I could begin my journey. Together with a brilliant sergeant major, Paul Medlicott - who subsequently became (another coincidence) chairman of the BBC Symphony Chorus, thus providing me with one of the best sequences of my film about Vaughan Williams, *A Sea Symphony* - we set about making lists of every artist we could think of who should be included if humanly possible. The episode on swing, for example, we thought *must* include Benny Goodman, Artie Shaw, Cab Calloway, Ella Fitzgerald, Woody Herman, Frank Sinatra, Bing Crosby, Lionel Hampton and...well, that would do for a start.

Eventually we had a list of nearly 500 artists. The military campaign was about to begin. The astonishing thing is that, thanks to Medlicott's organisational genius, we filmed nearly all of them.

We criss-crossed the United States - north, south, east and west. We travelled to West Africa and up into the Sahara; to the lakes around Salzburg for the origins of operetta; to Coventry Cathedral and Mike Oldfield's hideaway on the Welsh borders; to Liverpool and Northern Ireland where, surrounded by men with ArmaLite rifles, we filmed IRA and Provo songs while 'the Troubles' raged outside. We drove for hours into the Navajo desert to film Bo Diddley, who had threatened to shoot anyone who was white. We played Russian roulette with Phil Spector, and sat dumbfounded while Brian Epstein's mother spoke for the first and only time (in tears) about her beloved son. We toured Harlem with John Hammond, who had discovered Billie Holiday, and saw the grim poverty that she and many black performers like her had had to endure. We stood with Sam Phillips in the tiny studio where he had first recorded Elvis Presley. At his insistence, and in spite of his tracheotomy, we interviewed Richard Rodgers about his fantastic partnerships with Oscar Hammerstein and Dick Hart. We heard Earl 'Fatha' Hines patiently explain that he was 'a tool' of Al Capone. Eric Clapton played a heart-rending version of *Layla*; Lonnie Donegan delivered 'the performance of a lifetime' (he told me) of *Rock Island Line*; Leonard Cohen reading angry political poems from within East Berlin, in the shadow of the Berlin Wall; Roy Rogers and Dale Evans; Bill Wyman, also in tears, describing the funeral of Brian Jones; Tina Turner; Pete Seeger telling what it was like to be mocked and spat at for his 'communist sympathies'; McCartney, accompanying himself on acoustic guitar, singing - for the first time in public - *Yesterday*. 'I felt I wanted to do something special for you,' he said, recalling with gratitude that the notorious comparison I had made in *The Observer* between him and Schubert, mocked at the time, 1968, but long since proved to be correct. I hope I have been able to repay in some small measure a fraction of the colossal debt we owe to him, and to Lennon, my demanding mentor.

Looking back, over fifty years later, I can see there is much I omitted or forgot or didn't fully understand. I think that was inevitable, especially as I had less than £1 million and only five months in which to film. The entire series of (eventually) seventeen films was completed in less than a year. My biggest omission came towards the end when, having finished filming but not yet finished editing, punk rock, in the shape of the Sex Pistols and The Damned, burst upon the scene. I begged for more money and more time and an eighteenth episode, but these were refused. The series was already scheduled on television around the world, and I don't think Bernie Delfont cared much for Sid Vicious. You can see why. But what strikes me now is how lucky we were to get to so many people (and places) that were gone in a very short time thereafter. The ninety-year-old pianist Eubie Blake remembering talking to and playing with Scott Joplin; the ninety-four-year-old Irving Caesar and the hundred-year-old Irving Berlin; Yip Harburg (*Brother, Can You Spare A Dime*) and Hoagy Carmichael (*Up a Lazy River*) re-living the thirties; Roosevelt Sykes remembering his slave parents; Liberace on Elvis - all gone now, as are many of the places that have such resonance in the story. Sam Phillips' studio is now a parking lot. New Orleans and its seedy jazz clubs, vanished. Historic Memphis and

Beale Street, so crucial in the story of ragtime and the blues, bulldozed. The Cavern, gone. The Grand Ole Opry, now a theme park.

While filming, I did have the occasional glimpse that what we were doing might have lasting significance. For example, I obviously knew who Muddy Waters was, if only because Mick Jagger constantly mentioned his name, but we simply couldn't find him. And then, while filming in Chicago, I noticed he was playing in a club on the West Side. Somehow, my assistant, the indefatigable Annunziata Asquith, managed to find a phone number and we spoke. 'Sure,' he said, 'Come on over', after I had mumbled an explanation of what we were doing. Fearing that Waters' reputation was such that the club would likely be packed, we arrived very early to set up our primitive equipment (oh, if only I had had the compact digital equipment now at my disposal! This was slow colour film, which needed mountains of lights, was cumbersome, inefficient - and slow!). It would not be true to say that there were more people in my crew than in the audience, but that is what it felt like. Here was one of the most iconic figures in the history of rock 'n' roll, but at this time (1975) he was more or less forgotten. The same for B.B. King, who couldn't stop thanking me for having taken the trouble to seek him out and film him. Likewise, Dizzy Gillespie. And most astonishing of all, Jerry Lee Lewis, whom we found playing in a Holiday Inn on a side stage as guests were checking in to that dump of a hotel.

I think now that what persuaded so many great artists to take part was simply this: we were obviously treating them with the respect they deserved, not only as artists but as human beings, and that had just not happened to most of them before. It had nothing to do with money - we paid them only a pittance, and always the same amount, regardless of their 'status' (Lennon's idea again). Partly, this was a consequence of us travelling to them, and not summoning them to a studio. Partly, I believe, they trusted me not to kow-tow to focus groups or illiterate television 'commissioning editors', nor reduce what they had to say to 'sound-bites', nor resort to the absurd and destructive fashion of snap-snappy editing so that no-one could remember a word anyone has said. Apart from anything else, that was - and it remains - insulting to the audience.

I believe that what they had to say, then and now, *is* important, and it *is* important we take note, because their story is a crucial part of the social history of the twentieth century - in the United States and Europe, at least; only part of that history, maybe, but a significant part, and that is what each film endeavours to illustrate. I once filmed Aaron Copland, the great American composer, who said to me, 'In a hundred years' time, when people want to know what it was like to be alive and well and living in the 1960s in the United States, they won't be listening to my music. They will be listening to The Beatles.' Not entirely true, perhaps, but he has a point. Pete Seeger, the authentic voice of protest, wrote to me to say that 'the colossal emotional, intellectual and historical range (of the series) is breathtaking.' And even Bing Crosby noted that I 'had gathered together a priceless archive; and the editing is truly outstanding.'

Perhaps the real contribution that the series made was to demonstrate that it was possible to make extended studies of 'popular music' without frightening the horses, and television executives in particular. Once again, as Lennon said, we had knocked down the door and paved the way for others.

Popular music is now big business. But that business depends on the creative talents of a group of remarkable individuals, who have borne witness to the world in which they found themselves. The story of popular music, therefore, is of the struggle by these individuals to survive the demands of an avaricious, thieving and capricious industry.

My films are a celebration of those individuals and their struggle.

One footnote. When I brought the finished films back to the Three Wise Men, there was some discussion about the best time to schedule the films. A glint came into Cyril Bennett's eye – 'Saturday evening at 10.30,' he pronounced. My heart sank. 'But that's right opposite *Match of the Day*,' I protested. 'Precisely,' said Bennett. 'We intend to blast them off the screen.' Mad, I thought, but at least I should be grateful for seventeen hours of networked ITV. After week six – that is, well before we had got to the juicier episodes with The Beatles, the Stones and so on – for the first (and sadly, the last) time, a Jeroboam of vintage Bollinger arrived at my house with a note from Bennett: 'We did it. We buried them!'

One final footnote. When we eventually brought out the entire series in a glossy CD box-set, our American distributors insisted that we do a 'title check' – that is, to obtain legal certainty that there were no restrictions on the use of the title, *All You Need Is Love*. I argued that the phrase was by now common parlance, and surely there could be no possible restrictions on its use. Lennon, who had told me to use the title, was by now very dead so he could not be appealed to. But, as the lawyers for the US distributors were very insistent, we proceeded to check. The first thing that was a surprise, was that the Beatles themselves had never copyrighted or even trademarked the title. But, unfortunately, two organisations had: one was a brothel in Amsterdam, and the other, a manufacturer of risqué ladies' underwear in Hong Kong. We proceeded to use the title without further discussion.

Chapter 13

Callas

In the late 60s and early 70s, the *London Evening Standard* had a remarkable arts and music editor called Sydney Edwards, remarkable not simply because he wrote intelligently, but also because he claimed to be a Cockney who liked to give the impression he was uneducated and knew no-one. The very reverse was true. Later, the Evening Standard Theatre Awards would be named in his honour when he suddenly died only a few years after our 'mystery adventure'.

One day in early 1974, Edwards called me and asked in his unmistakable accent what was I doing the following day, and did I have a passport?

'Why?' I asked.

'Can't tell you, Tone. It's a secret.'

He then arranged to pick me up the following morning and we sped off to Heathrow Airport.

'Where are we going, Sydney?' I enquired nervously.

'Can't tell you, Tone. It's a secret.'

When we boarded the plane for Paris, at least I knew our destination.

'Why are we going to Paris, Sydney?'

'Can't tell you, Tone. It's a secret.'

Now we are in a taxi toward the centre of Paris, and we pulled up outside a rather grand mansion in avenue Georges Mandel.

'Who are we going to meet?' I asked, ever more anxious.

'Can't tell you, Tone. It's a secret.'

Up in the lift; Edwards was obviously expected.

Push the doorbell, and there stood Maria Callas.

My jaw fell through the floor. She looked relaxed and glamorous and greeted Sydney with some affection, and was introduced to me; I stammered something – I can't remember what.

We were invited in for tea, which Maria's maid had prepared. While Maria went to another room, Sydney whispered that it was a bit like having tea with the Queen (Elizabeth). When she stands, the 'audience' is over and you must leave. The polite way of saying 'Time to go'. But Maria was forever standing, sitting and standing again. I did not know what to do. Consequently, I was also forever standing up as if to go. 'What's the matter with you, young man?' she said, with a laugh.

It then became apparent that when Sydney had met Callas after her farewell concert at London's Festival Hall the previous year (26 November 1973), she had asked him if he had any suggestions as to what she might do after the tour was finished. Although she was still in the middle of a worldwide twenty-six-concert series of 'farewell concerts', she felt she would need 'to do something' – anything – to prevent her getting bored. Sydney must have suggested, 'Why not a documentary about your life?' Although she had made a good film with Pasolini, *Medea*, it had not been a happy experience and she was reluctant to contemplate another film. Sydney had obviously persuaded her that he knew the right person, and she had agreed to meet.

She asked me what would the filming entail. 'Just an interview,' I said. 'Maybe a long interview, and I could build the film from there.' Although Sydney had hinted that the most time we could expect with her at that first meeting was an hour at best, I was surprised when she suddenly announced that it would be best to continue the conversation over supper, and she would arrange the restaurant. Not only that, but when we arrived there, she insisted on ordering the food. What I remember is that our plates were piled high with delicious food, but Maria's plate seemed to have no more than a lettuce leaf. 'Oh, that looks delicious. May I try it?' she said, pointing at something on my plate. 'Oh, and *that* looks delicious,' she said pointing at something on Sydney's plate. 'May I try it?' In the end I think she ate most of our food – well, not quite. But then came the ice cream dessert. She obviously adored ice cream, so no chance that our ice cream would be pillaged; her helping was enormous. Her last secretary, Nadia Stancioff, later confirmed this behaviour was characteristic, and told me a very similar story of the two of them having supper.

The upshot of all this (and we didn't actually escape until around 2am the following morning) was that Maria agreed to do the interview and a date was arranged. In retrospect, following the initial interview, I can now see that she was very lonely and desperate to work. In fact, I later came to realise that she was probably among the loneliest people I had ever met - extraordinarily so, given her worldwide fame and adoration by zillions of fans. As the great tenor Guiseppe Di Stefano, who had accompanied Maria on that farewell concert tour, told me, 'The first thing she said to me after our reunion was, "Caro Pipo. Every day is one day less."'

Sadly, after that first interview and in spite of continuing her farewell concert tour in North America and finally Japan, she became sick - and increasingly so - with the result that I decided to wait and hope for some improvement. Sadly, this never happened. Her slow decline mercifully came to an end when on 16 September 16 1977, members of Maria's staff found her collapsed on her bathroom floor. A doctor was called, but Maria was dead minutes later. She was only fifty-three years old.

I was now under some pressure to complete my film, but I was prevented from doing so when a Greek woman called Madame Vasso Devetzi appeared, claiming that Maria had left her entire possessions to her, providing a piece of paper with Maria Callas's signature on it to prove it. Devetzi was a pianist who, it became apparent later, had insinuated herself into Maria's confidence to the extent that she had even taken charge of organising the prescriptions for Maria's sleeping pills, a move her immediate staff had objected to. But, with her dominant personality, it appeared that Devetzi had more or less taken over control of the entire Callas household. Maria had become addicted to the various pills that Devetzi had organised. Later, I was told that she would regularly flatter Maria and that, because her health was declining, Maria either did not care or was unaware of what was happening to her.

When the doctor who had attended the dead body asked who the next of kin was, Devetzi replied, 'There is no next of kin. I am Madame Callas's executor.' Neither of these statements was true, not least because Maria's mother and sister were still alive. After the funeral at the Greek Orthodox church, the coffin had been placed in the hearse, ostensibly to be taken for a private burial, but the hearse had actually taken it to a crematorium.

This hasty decision, apparently planned by Devetzi, raised yet more serious questions, because no one had been consulted. Cremation was very unusual for anyone of the Greek Orthodox faith. Doctors later doubted that Maria had died of a heart attack, as had initially been believed, but with no autopsy conducted her death was shrouded in mystery. Franco Zeffirelli, the renowned operatic and theatre director and Maria's close friend, told me he always believed she had been poisoned.

Other vultures now appeared on the scene. Maria's first husband, an Italian businessman called Meneghini, now stated that their divorce was invalid because it had been granted only in Italy, not in Greece, although she was Greek. He claimed he was therefore entitled to her estate. After legal wrangling and bickering with Devetzi, Meneghini settled for half of the estate, with the rest going to the 'Maria Callas Foundation', a spurious and phony scheme devised by Devetzi. In the end, it is thought that Devetzi deceived the Callas family by stealing two million dollars from the so-called Foundation.

Into this mayhem now entered EMI, the record company. They 'owned' an exclusive and worldwide contract on Callas's voice, and so collected all the royalties from Callas's numerous best-selling LPs. Indeed, EMI's lawyer Charles Rodier told me that the revenue from these royalties was so colossal that they kept the entire company afloat financially. EMI led the charge, saying that Devetzi's 'paper inheritance' was a forgery. They refused to part with one cent of the royalties. Rodier, who had already granted me permission to use Callas's recordings in my film, advised me to wait while this whole mess was resolved.

I think Rodier imagined it would be only a matter of months. In fact, the legal wrangling went on for almost six years. One day Rodier telephoned me to say it seemed as if a final resolution was at hand, and could I help by visiting Devetzi in Paris and charming her. It so happened that I had been planning to drive to Bayreuth in Germany to attend the annual Wagner Festival, so a stop-over in Paris would be a welcome break in the journey. I duly arrived at Avenue Georges Mandel – for tea! Devetzi was most solicitous. She said she was happy that all the quarrels had been resolved, and she wished me luck with completing my film. Feeling I had done my duty, I drove on to Bayreuth, arriving at my hotel well past midnight, only to find a message from Charles Rodier asking me to call him *urgently*. Tomorrow morning, I thought, would be sufficient.

The following day I awoke to find a second message from Rodier, marked 'Urgent Urgent'. When I spoke to him on the hotel phone (and this was long before the days of mobile phones), all he said was, 'What did you do?'

'Well, I was charm itself,' I began.

'Yes, but what did you *do*?' he asked again.

'Well,' I began again…

'Don't you know?' he said. 'She died last night! So, what did you *do*? Poison the tea!?'

'Now get on with the film,' Rodier said. And so I did. And what a journey of discovery that turned out to be. It was every bit as dramatic and messy as the mayhem after Callas's death. I realised early on that I was not making a film about a great opera singer who was also a woman in trouble. Rather, it was a film about a woman who was in a hell of a mess who, by the way, was also a great opera singer. It was the woman herself who gripped my imagination. I interviewed Zeffirelli and Giuseppe Di Stefano. I found singers such as Arda Mandikian and Zoe Vlachopoulos, who had known her in Athens immediately after the Second World War before her international career had begun. I even found the first conductor she had ever worked with during the war, Maestro Leonidas Zoras. I found her last secretary, Nadia Stancioff, and the bass singer who had 'discovered' her 'great big ugly voice' (his description), Nicola Rossi-Lemeni. And Madam Biki, her original costumier in Milan, as well as many other contemporaries, such as Carlo Maria Giulini, who had conducted some of her earliest triumphs at La Scala opera house in Milan.

Gradually there emerged a story never told before - although many times since by film makers and biographers who never met her - of how a Greek shipping tycoon named Aristotle Onassis had effectively destroyed her private life, and, more importantly, her career. She had been contentedly married to her first (and only) husband, Battista Meneghini, when she had developed a passion for Onassis. According to Callas's biographer, John Ardoin, Onassis was a thoroughly disreputable character. He 'collected' women. He was rumoured to have paid $10,000 for a night with Eva Peron. He was desperate to be accepted in Monte Carlo, the domain of Prince Rainier and Grace Kelly. However, knowing of his seedy reputation, they would have nothing to do with him. Until, that is, he turned up with Maria Callas on his arm, which opened all the doors. Zeffirelli told me the only thing he ever gave her was 'half a boat; no jewels, no money, nothing; and eventually the boat sank'.

Maria was actually born in Manhattan, not Greece, on 2 December 1923 in a hospital in Washington Heights, on the Upper West Side, and christened Maria Cecilia Sophia Anna Kalogeropoulou. The father had had a pharmacy in Greece, but not having had much success, had taken his wife, Litsa, and his first daughter, Jackie, to the United States. And there he changed the name from Kalogeropoulos, which he felt was difficult for an American to pronounce, first to Kalos, then Callas. Litsa was so convinced that her new child would be a boy, that her disappointment at the birth of another daughter, Maria, was so great that she refused even to look at her new baby for several days.

But when Maria was thirteen, Litsa decided she had had enough of her husband - they were later divorced - and in 1937 removed both daughters back to Athens. There, they lived in some poverty at No. 61 Patission Street. 'For years, she wore baggy drab clothes,' Nadia Stancioff told me. 'Her mother always made dark little dresses with white collars. And when I met Maria's sister Jackie, I said, "How is it that you were always so beautifully dressed and so elegant, and your sister always looked like a rag doll?" "Well," Jackie said, "a lot of the clothes were made by their mother, but Maria didn't have the figure to wear them, and so she always looked dumpy."'

'My sister was slim and beautiful and friendly, and my mother always preferred her,' Maria recalled. 'I was the ugly duckling, fat and clumsy and unpopular. It is a cruel thing to make a child feel ugly and unwanted... I'll never forgive her for taking my childhood away. During all the years I should have been playing and growing up, I was singing to make some money. Everything I did for them was mostly good and everything they did to me was mostly bad.'

'Dumpy' was probably an understatement. Nicola Rescigno, the American-Italian who conducted Callas's US première in 1955 at the Lyric Opera in Chicago, in what was to become one of her most famous roles, as Norma in the opera by Bellini, told me, 'Maria was not born a beautiful woman. Maria was fat, obese, ungraceful. When you realise the type of body she started out with in life, which was like that of a pachyderm, you would be amazed at how the ugly duckling eventually turned into a swan.' Zeffirelli agreed. 'She was an extremely ballsy lady. Everything was immense: big eyes, big mouth, big teeth, big nose, and rather hairy. Big bust. I was impressed. She looked like the Statue of Liberty.'

Life in wartime Athens under Nazi occupation was not easy. Arda Mandikian, an Armenian soprano for whom Britten later created the role of the ghost Miss Jessel in his opera *Turn of the Screw* (Britten was said to have remarked that no matter who sings the role, they all sound like Arda), was a fellow student with Callas at the Conservartoire in

1941. She told me, 'It was a terrible time. Hunger; seeing people dying in the streets. If you had the money to get some sort of food you got it. If you didn't, you had to sell things. All your valuables had to be sold to the black marketeers to buy food. Maria was pushy in a way; she did what she had to do by 'befriending' various Nazi officers.' According to both Callas's husband, Meneghini, and her close friend, the mezzo-soprano Giulietta Simionato, Callas related to them that her mother had pressed her to 'go out with various men', mainly Italian and German soldiers, to bring home money and food during the Nazi occupation. Simionato was convinced that Callas 'had managed to remain untouched'. But Callas never forgave her mother for what she perceived to be a kind of prostitution which had been forced on her.

'We had to walk everywhere, because there was no transport whatsoever,' Arda Mandikian continued. 'Maria used to come four times a day to the Conservatoire for lessons from their distinguished vocal teacher, Madame Elvira di Hidalgo, quite a distance backwards and forwards on foot.'

'When she first came to Madame Hidalgo's class in 1939,' her fellow student Zoe Vlachopoulou recalled, 'she was a tall, fat, dark-haired girl with beautiful eyes and great self-assurance. Judging by her appearance, I did not think she would be able to sing. But when she opened her mouth, my own mouth fell right open. And Hidalgo was transfixed. Maria seemed to learn everything so quickly. By the end of her first term, she was speaking fluent Italian and French. She was obviously very clever.'

Callas made her professional debut in February 1941, in the small role of Beatrice in Franz von Suppé's *Boccaccio*. Another fellow soprano, Galatea Amaxopoulou, who sang in the chorus, later remembered that 'Even in rehearsal, Maria's fantastic performing ability had been obvious, and from then on, the rest of us started trying ways of preventing her from appearing.' At Hidalgo's insistence, the conductor Leonidas Zoras, then in charge of the Greek National Opera, which was temporarily housed in a cinema called The Palace, cast her in her first starring role in August 1942 as Marta in Eugen d'Albert's opera *Tiefland*. 'There was no electricity,' Zoras told me, 'so we used to sit at night with oil lamps. But every ten minutes, the lamps would go out, but Maria would insist on cleaning them and lighting them again. "We must rehearse, rehearse, rehearse", she would say.'

What effected the later transformation from duckling to swan were two things. First, she saw photos of Audrey Hepburn, then filming in *Roman Holiday*, and decided she had to look like her. And second, her businessman husband Meneghini introduced her to Elvira Leonardi Bouyeure, known professionally as Madam Biki, a notable Italian fashion designer and couturier of the postwar period based in Milan, with the instruction, 'Make her lots of clothes; make her look good.' 'Maria, being rather tight-fisted,' Madam Biki told me, 'would probably not have bothered. But Meneghini hoped that, from this transformation, a new Callas would emerge.'

'It was utterly amazing,' her biographer John Ardoin told me, 'but in a year she lost thirty-seven kilos. She was still a very young woman, so her flesh hung off her like an empty bag. She then went to tremendous efforts: gymnastics, massages, anything to absorb all this loose flesh. She never managed with the ankles. In fact, one of the reasons she never wanted to perform *Carmen* on stage was because she would have to show her feet and ankles in the dance, and she just did not want to do that.' And in a phrase that haunted me and would inspire the film I eventually made, Ardoin added, 'Maria "The Woman" now wanted to be the equal of Callas "The Artist" – but Maria "The Woman" paid a devastating cost for this attempt.'

But what of Callas 'The Artist'? During the preparations for her spectacular 1947 debut at the Arena of Verona in the Amilcare Ponchielli opera, *La Gioconda* (when she weighed almost a hundred kilogrammes), she met Tullio Serafin, the great Italian conductor. It seems he immediately understood her potential, her talent and her voice. She had been recommended by Rossi-Lemeni. 'Serafin used to call her *una grande vociaccia*,' Rossi-Lemeni told me. 'Vociaccia' is a little bit pejorative. It means an ugly voice; but *grande* means a big voice, a great voice; a great big ugly voice, in a way.' From here until her last appearances on stage as Tosca, in February 1964 at Covent Garden, and then as Norma at the Palais Garnier in Paris in Zeffirelli's famous productions, few artists have achieved such universal acclaim and adoration. Zeffirelli told me, 'She literally changed the face of opera. It was a recurrent joke among us, to divide the history of opera into eras. BC and AC. Before and after Callas.'

Graziella Sciutti, her fellow soprano and friend, added that 'She brought, finally, drama back to the opera. And what was meant by the origin of opera, when Monteverdi and all the Camarata Fiorentina invented this new art form. It was a *melodrama*, it was a *recita cantando*, which meant that you were performing as a singing actor. With the evolution of singing in the nineteenth century, however, the new composers all concentrated on 'bel canto' (beautiful singing), so little by little we lost in performances the strength of drama. It became just a beautiful sound exhibition. And that was a betrayal, as a matter of fact. Callas, with her sense of drama, brought opera back to its origins, of what it means.'

But again, at some cost. Graziella Sciutti remembered that once they 'were waiting to go on stage for Maria's last big aria. It was not the première, just one of the performances. And I saw she was in such a state of nerves that I went and said, "Maria, for God's sake, I mean think of the glory that you have." And she grabbed my arm, squeezed it hard, and said, "You know that every time I go out there, they are waiting to get me."'

Then along came Onassis. First he wrecked Maria's marriage. Yes, Meneghini had made himself unpopular with various promoters and Intendants of opera houses by demanding ever higher fees. But there is no doubt that Maria loved him and had benefitted from their relationship. As Rossi-Lemeni told me, 'I remember one time we were leaving for a tour of South America, to Buenos Aires. And she was crying like a child, leaving Meneghini in Genoa. It was maybe the only time when I saw Maria Callas really moved, really sincere, really caring for somebody. She was crying and she was desperate about leaving Meneghini, because Meneghini represented for her not only the husband; he was her father, her brother, the security that she found in life.'

Menghini himself showed me piles of letters from Maria. 'These are all Maria Callas letters, thousands. I have thousands of letters. Would you like to hear one? Let's see… "My dear adored one, at last I have got to my destination after the journey." These are letters overflowing with love; they contain love and very little else.'

'He was a very loving husband,' Graziella Sciutti told me. He adored her. And probably like all such adoration, he suffocated a lot in her, and because of this love, he made her make so many mistakes. Some unnecessary lawsuits, against newspapers, for instance. And he would sometimes get her excited backstage against a colleague. When you are under the pressure of a performance, when your nerves are under an enormous strain, when somebody comes and says, you know, 'This one did this', and 'That one has said', the person explodes. There is no other way. And sometimes he did that and made life very difficult for her.'

Their later divorce was disputed by both sides. Meneghini, as we have seen, claiming that because the divorce had only been granted in Italy and she was Greek, the divorce certificate was invalid. Callas claiming that although she had since become an American citizen, she had now decided to take back her Greek citizenship so that 'she could become a free woman. Because under Greek law, who is not married after 1946 in a Church, is not married. So right now I am a free woman and very happy to be so. That is why I had to give up my American citizenship unfortunately. You understand?' Well, not really.

The reality (if that is what it was) according to Zeffirelli, was that 'she was very, prim, and very moralistic. Also, because she was shy, she never had a real confrontation with a man. Never had a clash; I mean a big bang with a man, in spite of my discovering her once in a passionate embrace with Visconti. I worked for Visconti and he undoubtedly was the most important artistic influence as a director on her professional life. But the big bang never really happened until Onassis appeared. She didn't need the glamour; she had enough glamour. She didn't need the 'high society` because wherever she wanted to go she was welcome. People were laying their fur coats at her feet. She could have all that luxury except for this emotional and physical relationship that Onassis provided. He was the first man that gave her that, she told me. 'I'm at his mercy because I'm like a virgin who suddenly goes through that incredible planet of revelations, of a full physical life.' And for Onassis, 'It was a tremendous publicity coup for him. There's no way to deny it. She made him more famous and more respectable than he was. So he ended up being accepted in Monte Carlo fully. Perhaps he could have lived without that because he had enough money and enough power, but he wanted more. He wanted to be accepted.'

Besides being acutely shy, Maria was also incredibly vulnerable. 'I mean, I'm undefended,' she told John Ardoin. 'I've been undefended all my life. You might be, as I have found out, frequently misunderstood, hated, attacked. And I have not been able to fight back. And you have to sit back and take it in absolute silence. It hurts. You hate it, because it is unjust. The world is full of unjustness. But I'm a born fighter - not out of necessity, or not out of love of a fight, because I loathe fighting. I'm sick to the stomach after it. But if I have to defend myself, I have that much pride to say, well, there's no way out, go ahead and defend yourself. I thought if I became great, I would be able to have freedom, stability, the happiness to be able to perform better, under the best circumstances, under the best mental frame of mind. Well, it was a lie. It's not true. The more famous you become, the more difficult things are, Do I have freedom? In the press? If I can't justify myself, I can't live a normal life. It's a long and lonely life.'

Maybe she believed this new-found passion for Onassis would buy her the stability and confidence she craved.

Nadia Stancioff told me that Onassis had telephoned Maria in October 1968 from Greece to say he was coming to Paris in a day or so, and could they have dinner? Of course, she had said. 'But that night, she turned on the television to see news of the wedding of Onassis to Jacqueline Kennedy. This betrayal left Maria Callas inconsolable, despondent, grief stricken; she was heartbroken when she saw the news – on television! It was the first she had known about it. She retreated to her Parisian apartment and became reclusive to many of her friends, including me. Onassis, the love of her life, had deceived her.'

Within months, the Onassis/Kennedy marriage effectively collapsed. Onassis returned to Paris and, incredibly, Maria took him back, but the union was soon thwarted after Onassis's son was killed in a plane crash and the billionaire Onassis spiralled down into a great depression from which he never recovered. Now in hospital in Paris, Onassis was visited every day by Maria. Jacqueline Kennedy never went once. When Onassis died in 1975, Jackie Kennedy received $150 million from his estate, presumably as the result of a pre-nuptial agreement. Maria received nothing.

And so to those terrible final years. Her performance of *Tosca* at Covent Garden was, arguably, the greatest performance she ever gave – or, indeed, anyone has ever given. She poured her entire heart into that role: all her ambitions, disappointments, anxieties and longings into one heart-wrenching performance. Zeffirelli skilfully led her to the crucial moment when Tosca stabs her jailor and suitor Scarpia, maybe believing that it was Onassis that she was stabbing, and believing she was ridding herself of her obsession. Fanciful, maybe, but not impossible. Some commentators who should know better, especially those in an appalling 2025 BBC television documentary, claimed that at this point (1964) her voice was shot. This was based on some American crackpot theory that the wobble in her voice had been present from the beginning of her career. Hence she could only croak, '*Muori dannato! Muori! Muori! Muori!*' (Die accursed! Die! Die! Die!) as she stabs Scarpia. Well, maybe they should read the score, or listen to her singing the great aria that precedes it, '*Vissi d'arte, vissi d'amore*' ('I lived for art; I lived for love'), and ask themselves the true meaning of this aria.

Her subsequent Pasolini film, *Medea*, teaching at Juilliard, directing in Turin, and a worldwide tour did little to assuage her hurt, nor did the increasing attacks on her performances during that tour. In our devastating final interview, she said, 'Well, throughout my whole life I always thought I should never go on singing, because I never thought I was any good. I'm the first terrible critic of myself. But I really never said publicly that I would not be singing again. I said that to myself ten thousand times, but I really never officially declared that I would not sing anymore. I know I had created some bad habits. As a matter of fact, I think that on the whole I have improved of late. I had acquired what they call a wobble on the high notes, which is a pulsation, and I have managed to improve that. Now, during the remaining concerts on my tour, I will improve even more the whole status of the voice. Because there's nothing like the stage that can make you work properly.

'I don't read the criticisms because I know exactly what I do before anybody tells me. So I don't want to read them and disturb my peace of mind and my nerves. I feel better if I don't read criticism. It's better. Naturally, the voice is not what it used to be twenty years ago. Nobody pretends that. It's natural. The audience knows that; I know it. They can't just applaud the legend if you don't give them something to applaud. And after all, what is the legend? The public made me. What is a legend? I think I'm a very human, human being. If I wasn't human, I probably would have sung better.'

'She did see herself as Maria,' Nadia Stancioff told me, 'and there was this other being that was Callas. And she talked about Callas as "La Callas". She spoke of this other part of herself. And there was Maria, who was very charming, sometimes difficult, sometimes infuriating, sometimes coy, loveable, a wonderful friend. And then there was Callas, who was the woman on stage, who was the artiste. I remember, for instance, her listening to records – her own voice – when we were in Greece together on an island. And at the end of the record, she looked very sad, very pensive, and she said, "Callas will never sing that way again."'

Guiseppe Di Stefano, who had partnered her on that last fateful tour, told me that 'Maria Callas, throughout her life, showed that you can be the most successful person in your field, but still the most important thing is love, passion. So every woman who is a passionate woman feels sympathy for Maria. Because they realise that all this success meant very little. The most important thing is love. After such immense success she was crying, "I was horrible. I was horrid. I was no good." She was the kind of artiste who was never happy. People like this, they cannot be open, and they suffer. They don't want to show it, so they take pills. These pills, they were damaging her brain. She was taking three pills, then later she forgot she took three pills and took another three. She was falling on the floor, like she didn't want to fight anymore.'

'I really began to cry like a child,' Zeffirelli told me. 'I've seldom cried that much. I really couldn't stop. There was so much to regret, because I felt we had abandoned her. Perhaps if we had devoted more time, as friends, instead of taking for granted that she would solve her problems by herself. I realised that we had been unfair. Perhaps if we had been closer to this woman as a woman, given her a sense of life around her, she wouldn't have died. That was my deep, deep regret.'

Let Di Stephano have the last word, and he was in tears as he told me, 'In life, when you talk in public, you are all dressed-up, you know? You are ready to meet people, to talk. But when you are on stage and you sing, you are nude. You have to open your soul. Through your singing people get to know how you are made. When you are bored with something, you don't worry about it, you just get to hate it. That's why some artistes do not last forever; because they get bored. I mean, every night they have to repeat the same thing. But as a person, as a human being, you want to live, you want to enjoy life, you want to know. And a woman like Callas – she was born to live as a woman, a woman with a voice, not a voice with a woman. So her life was love, success as a woman. And that was the fight that she lost.'

Now, for me, every time I hear her voice and remember our brief acquaintance and the journey on which that meeting eventually took me, I also remember Sydney Edwards saying when I asked where this journey would take me,

'Can't tell you, Tone. It's a secret.'

Chapter 14

The Space Movie

The invitation to make a film about Apollo 11, the first successful landing on the moon, came to me out of the clear blue sky from NASA in mid-1977. I had no idea why they had asked me. All I was told, was that they needed a film to mark the tenth anniversary of that first landing on 20 July 1969.

I was invited to Washington and shown the mountain of film NASA had collected, from the very beginnings with John Glenn, the first astronaut to orbit the earth in February 1962, until the last Apollo mission, 17 December 1972. Use whatever I wanted, I was told.

And so, in the winter of 1977, the coldest winter in the eastern half of the United States for the past two hundred years, my trusted researcher Annunziata Asquith was despatched to Washington D.C. to begin systematically to comb through the hours of material put at my disposal and make notes of what I might need. She and I soon realised that very little, if any, of this spectacular visual material, now overly familiar through countless documentaries and feature films, had at this point ever been seen before.

I was also told that it was NASA's policy that I would not be allowed to interview any of the astronauts: but to compensate, I would be given access to all chit-chat between the astronauts and Ground Control. This, too, was beyond priceless. Here are a few examples:

Lift-off. We have a lift-off. Twenty-two minutes past the hour.
Lift-off on Apollo 11.
Okay. Everything's tickety-boo.
The Saturn V building up to 7.6 million pounds of thrust.

Let her rip.
Okay we're with you, I think we got all our marbles.

I don't know what happened, we had everything in the world drop out.
We've had a couple of cardiac arrests down here too.
There wasn't any time for that up here.

Hey, super double fantastic burn.
Little bit of shaking.
Okey-dokey. It's a nice ride up 'til now.
Down range 122 miles. Altitude 61 miles.

Apollo 11, this is Houston.
Something happened here…
What happened?
I don't know. There's a line that pulled off. What is that?
That's the heat flow you pulled off.
Well we understand that the cable came off its connector and we've got just the free end of the cable, is that right?
That's right.
Just take it easy, let's rest for a minute.
Can I have your heartbeat?
I've gone up to about 140.

Houston, the radar shows that our SPS helium pressure went to zero.
Be advised that our SPS helium pressure went to zero at lift-off.
The SPS helium pressure on board went to zero at lift-off, however at mission control centre we are reporting go here.

Velocity 10,000 feet per second.
We've had our problems here; I don't know what happened. I'm not sure we didn't get hit by lightning.
I think we need to do a little more all-weather testing.
Amen.

Looks like you're flying well up there, partner. The spacecraft looks good.
Oh, you betcha.
A super flying machine.
It looks kind of tinny to me.

Listening to all this, I realised immediately that I was being given the keys to a treasure house of wonders.

The story of Man's adventure to the moon, as far as the Americans were concerned, had really begun with President Kennedy in 1961. 'Now it is time to take longer strides,' he had said. 'Time for a great new American enterprise. Time for this nation to take a clearly leading role in space achievement. Which, in many ways, may hold the key to our future on Earth. The eyes of the world now look into space – to the Moon and to the planets beyond.

'But why, some say, the moon? Why choose this as our goal? And they may well ask, Why climb the highest mountain? Why fly the Atlantic? We choose to go to the moon. We choose to go to the moon because that challenge is one that we're willing to accept. Because that goal will serve to organise and measure the depth of our energies and skills.'

Provoked by the famous 'peep-peep' of Sputnik orbiting the earth over three years earlier, Wernher von Braun – the German-American scientist – addressing a Congressional committee had said, 'We have been told that the hammer and sickle flag has now been planted on the moon and we have no reason to doubt it.

I would not be at all surprised to be hearing a human voice from outer space that will have an unmistakable Russian accent.'

Worse was to come. On 12 April 1961, Cosmonaut Yuri Gagarin orbited the earth aboard his craft, Vostok 1. The United States had sent its congratulations. Then, on 6 August 1961, Cosmonaut Gherman Titov became the second man in space. He stayed in orbit for twenty-five hours and eighteen minutes. Two years later, Cosmonaut Valentina Tereshkova became the first woman in space. Her craft, Vostok 6, orbited for seventy hours and fifty minutes. The United States had sent its congratulations. No wonder Kennedy had made his stirring declaration. 'We have vowed that we shall not see [space] governed by a hostile flag of conquest, but by a banner of freedom and peace,' he had said. 'Those who came before us made certain that this country rode the first wave of the industrial revolution. The first waves of modern invention. And the first wave of nuclear power. And this generation does not intend to founder in the backwash of the coming age of space. We mean to be a part of it; we mean to lead it.'

But how the hell was I to organise all this extraordinary material into some sort of coherent film? Back in London, and desperately looking around for a solution, I met by chance an old friend, Richard Branson. He asked me if I could think of a film project that might interest his principal client, Mike Oldfield. As I was the only person ever to have successfully filmed the notoriously prickly Mike (for Episode 17 of *All You Need Is Love*) at Kington in Herefordshire, overlooking Hergest Ridge, Richard thought I had the best chance of emerging relatively unscathed from any such encounter. My admiration for Mike's genius was unbounded, a fact which for him was irrelevant - Mike was not susceptible to flattery of any kind!

I suggested to Richard that this proposed NASA film might be the answer, and in April 1978 I was sent to Mike's new house at Througham Slad Manor, in Gloucestershire, to discuss what might be possible. Despite being at his most confrontational, Mike seemed intrigued by the idea and said he would begin work as soon as I sent him some of the material, which I did soon thereafter. I figured that a year would give him sufficient time to compose a soundtrack to end all soundtracks. Meantime, I reported back to NASA that Mike Oldfield had agreed to write the music for the film. They were overjoyed, although I'm not too sure they knew who he was.

Much later, I learnt why the invitation had come to me. One of the NASA hierarchy had seen at least part of my history of American popular music, *All You Need Is Love*, and had reasoned that to have a film using their hitherto unseen and extraordinary footage accompanied by some modern rock 'n' roll and/or pop music might get the message through to as wide an audience as possible. Whether they had imagined The Beatles or Jimi Hendrix singing *Fly Me to the Moon*, I have no idea. But what they got was Mike Oldfield. And once Mike Oldfield was on board, Richard Branson and his cousin Simon Draper immediately said they would part-finance the film on behalf of their new company, Virgin Films.

As time passed, and with the tenth anniversary date getting ever closer, I was repeatedly assured both by Mike and Richard Branson that everything down in Gloucestershire was 'going well'. But, eventually, knowing that I had to deliver the finished film in time for its UK and US television transmissions, I insisted on hearing the music track, or at least the work in progress, and was duly invited again to Througham Slad. Mike seemed genuinely pleased to see me. He took me to his studio to listen to the results of his labours. He played me about seven minutes of music and asked if I approved. 'Of course,' I said. 'And the remaining eighty minutes?' 'Oh, I haven't done that yet,' he said.

It had taken him six months to write those seven minutes. Wonderful though they were, they were clearly not enough, and here I was, now only two months from the unmoveable deadline, with a BIG problem. Time to have another talk with Richard Branson. As always, Richard had a solution.

Part of the delay in Mike's finishing my soundtrack, he explained, was that he had wanted to complete what was to be his next LP (as they were in those days), provisionally titled *Incantations*. That, too, was unfinished, but Richard thought he could persuade Mike to let me use what I needed from this new composition, even though the final mix was far from complete. In addition, Richard had had recordings made of the orchestral versions of both *Tubular Bells* and *Hergest Ridge* (Mike's first two albums), which at that time had never been officially released, quite simply because Mike did not care for them. 'Leave it with me,' said Richard, with his customary unstoppable bonhomie.

And that is how I finally 'constructed' the music soundtrack for the film. I've always assumed that Mike approved, since we have remained friends ever since – quite an achievement I'm told, as far as Mike is concerned. In fact, his album *Incantations* was eventually released before our film was finished. And although I think he would not forgive me for saying so, I think the 'mix' we used was, in places, rather better.

His 're-edited' music track for the film, however, is remarkable, perfect in every way: evocative, powerful, an inspiring match for the images. And I'm sure that – plus, of course, the astonishing NASA footage and the sound of the astronauts chatting away in space – is what made the film so breath-taking. Virgin Films may have long gone, but together these elements made, and make, the film what it is: something rather special.

Also ringing in my ears as I began editing the film was President Johnson's speech immediately before the launch of Apollo 8, addressed to astronauts Frank Borman, James Lovell and William Anders. But it might equally have referred to Neil Armstrong, his co-pilot Edwin (Buzz) Aldrin and command module pilot Michael Collins, as they set off seven months later aboard Apollo 11, not only to the Moon, but to immortality.

Johnson had said, 'I had a memorandum a short time ago from the man who handled the Washington-Moscow hotline. And I thought you would be interested in a portion of that memorandum to the President. We asked them if they would be interested in being informed of the development of the Apollo programme. And the hotline personnel in Moscow responded enthusiastically and asked us to keep them posted. And here at the hotline in Washington, we relayed information in regard to the most important aspects of your flight. The Soviets were very solicitous about the welfare of you astronauts and expressed their great interest in the successive flights. Nearly five centuries ago, we heard stories of the New World for the first time. There is just no other comparison that we can make that's equal to what we feel today.'

What Armstrong and Aldrin must have felt as they finally approached the surface of the moon cannot be described adequately; in fact, it beggars belief, especially now knowing that Armstrong had actually brought the spaceship in to land… manually! The chit-chat between the astronauts and Ground Control, now made available to me by NASA, had an unbelievable tension.

> [Armstrong talking]: *"Thirty-five degrees. Seven hundred and fifty. Coming down at 321 now, 33 degrees. A hundred feet, down at 19. Five hundred and twenty feet down at three. Down at fifteen. Four hundred feet, down at nine. Fifteen down at two and a half. Three feet forward. Two twenty feet. Fifteen forward. Four and a half down. Five and a half down. Hundred feet, three and a half down. Nine forward. Five percent. Ninety-five. Seventy-five feet. Looking good now, and a half. Six forward. Down two and a half. Forward. Forward. Twenty feet down, two and a half. Thirty feet two and a half down. Six down. Four forward. Four forward. Five right. Okay, engine stopped."*
>
> [Ground control]: *We copy you down, Eagle.*
>
> [Armstrong]: *Houston, Tranquility base here. The Eagle has landed.*
>
> [Ground control]: *Roger Tranquility, we copy you on the ground. You've got a bunch of guys about to turn blue; we're breathing again. Thanks a lot.*

What unbelievable courage.

The film was duly completed in time for that tenth Anniversary, July 1979. Some years later, I was invited to a gala screening organised by NASA at the Egyptian Cinema in Hollywood. At first, I demurred, fearing that the poor quality of my film would be exposed by the state-of-the-art equipment in this renowned Hollywood cinema. But I was then told that I had to come. The guest speaker had requested it, and the guest speaker was none other than Buzz Aldrin, the second man to step onto the surface of the moon.

This is what he said introducing the film:

'It gives me enormous pleasure, and a thrill, to be able to introduce Tony Palmer's remarkable film about our space adventures. I say remarkable because at the time it was made, 1978/9, very little of the footage you are about to see had ever been seen in public, images which are now so familiar as to be truly iconic. But it was Tony who used them first, and we are very pleased that he did, even if he did construct the longest take-off in history! I still get a chill hearing some of the talk-back which, like the footage, NASA had provided for Tony to use. When the rocket takes off, boy is that a roller-coaster ride, bumpy as hell. So when you hear my voice saying "Little bit of shaking there", you'll know what I mean!

'We, the astronauts, knew nothing about how the film came about at the time, but we became very aware of its importance later on. You see, at that time, the Apollo missions had come to an end, way back in 1972, and I now realise that the bosses in NASA needed something to remind Congress and the President what an astonishing achievement had been made by all the Apollo missions, and therefore wasn't it worth investing in the Shuttle programme which was then stalling and in real need of lift-off, if I may call it that? The film helped to do the trick, and the rest is history, so thank you Tony for what you did.'

I was overcome with embarrassment, but at dinner afterwards, Buzz, now accompanied, I think, by his fifth wife, was generous indeed. Of course, I longed to ask him what it actually felt like being on the moon and staring back at our little blue planet, Earth. But fearing he must have been asked that question a thousand times, I hesitated. Meanwhile, my cloddish distributor had joined us for dinner and kept fiddling with his Blackberry, then the state-of-the art pocket computer. I kicked him firmly under the table and muttered 'Don't you realise who we are having dinner with!?' Grumpily, he plonked his Blackberry on the table. Seeing this, Buzz leaned over and said, 'Do you realise that there's more computer power in that tiny device than we had on the entire Apollo 11 mission?'

And that opened the floodgates. He couldn't stop talking.

'I'm often asked,' he began, 'whether I minded not being the first man to step upon the surface of the moon. Oddly enough, I was originally designated to be the first, but quite late on in the preparations, I was told it would be my co-pilot Neil Armstrong. Obviously, I was a little disappointed at first, but then I thought, Neil is probably a better pilot than me, so what the hell.'

In fact, they were both extremely experienced fighter pilots from the Korean War.

'And then, when we were coming in to land at Tranquillity Base,' Aldrin continued, 'we could see through the capsule's windows that the place was strewn with rather large boulders. You see, at that point the capsule was being guided by its on-board computer. And, seeing those boulders, Neil and I just looked at each other, and I'm sure both of us thought that if one of the legs on the LEM, the Lunar Module, touched down on one of those boulders, we might tip over and that would be that.

'Without saying a word, Neil leaned forward, switched off the computer, and piloted the craft home manually, and you can hear that on the sound track – "two feet forward, one foot to the left, picking up a bit of dust," and so on. After Neil had landed the LEM safely, I suddenly realised I couldn't see out of my visor. It had completely misted up with my sweat. So I flipped it open and looked over to Neil. Neil was utterly calm, and I knew at that moment that truly he was a much better pilot than me. And do you know? The incredible thing is that when we finally touched down, we only had precisely nine seconds of fuel left. What a man!'

Amen to that.

Apollo 11 landed on the Moon 20 July 1969. 'The Eagle has landed', astronaut Armstrong said. The next day, the *New York Times* published on its front page a poem it had commissioned earlier from the poet Archibald MacLeish to celebrate that first photograph taken of the tiny blue earth rising over the surface of the moon, an iconic image which had become known as 'Earthrise'. MacLeish's poem was a simple testament to Apollo's achievement and indicated what was, for him, the true purpose of exploration in space. I included it as the last words spoken in my film.

'For the first time in all of time,' MacLeish wrote, 'men have seen the Earth. Seen it not as continents or oceans from the little distance of a hundred miles or two or three, but seen it from the depths of space. The medieval notion of the Earth put man at the centre of everything. The nuclear notion of the Earth put him nowhere, beyond the range of reasoning and lost in absurdity and war. This latest notion may have other consequences. It may remake our image of mankind. No longer that victim off at the margins of reality, and no longer that preposterous figure at the centre. To see the Earth as it truly is, is to see ourselves as riders on the Earth together. Brothers who know now they are truly brothers.'

Chapter 15

Stravinsky

Not long after I joined the BBC, I received a phone call early one morning from someone I knew well – Robert Paterson, a distinguished agent and impresario in 1960s London, taking care of, among others, Marlene Dietrich and Duke Ellington. And also, as I was now to discover, Igor Stravinsky.

'Mr Stravinsky wants to meet you,' he said.

'Don't be silly,' I replied. 'He could not possibly know who I am.'

'No, this is serious,' said Paterson. 'Can you come to the Savoy where he is staying this afternoon?'

Well, no one on earth would resist having tea with one of the greatest composers of the twentieth century, so down I went to the Savoy Hotel, where I was ushered into the presence of the diminutive Maestro.

Although eighty-four years old and apparently being kept alive by blood transfusions, he had lost none of his prodigious energy and wicked sense of humour. He also had still not mastered the English language, in spite of having lived over twenty years in Hollywood with his second wife, Vera, and his American amanuensis, Robert Craft. He was courtesy itself, and he kept calling me 'Sir', to my intense embarrassment. 'Robert [Paterson] tells me you know John Lennon,' he said in his fractured English. 'If this is true, I should like to meet him,' he continued.

The request was so bizarre that I have often doubted since whether the conversation had actually taken place, but the other Robert [Craft] assured me later that it had. 'Of course,' I said, 'I will do my best.' Contacting Lennon was not a problem and whether the meeting ever did take place, I do not know, but it began a passing relationship with Stravinsky which I was later able to repay.

We met again the following year in New York and had dinner. As is normal practice in New York restaurants, the waiter immediately began to pour water into Stravinsky's glass, only to be stopped, with Stravinsky remarking (I think), 'Water is for defeat.' I was so tongue-tied that I dared not ask him what he meant, so the moment passed. A few years later, on 15 April 1971, I attended his Orthodox funeral at the Basilica of Santi Giovanni e Paolo in Venice, after which the coffin was taken by gondola to be buried amid the cypress trees and roses (and mosquitoes) on the island cemetery of San Michele, almost next to his erstwhile patron, Sergei Diaghilev. I was told later by Robert Craft that when they arrived at the burial site, it was discovered that the pit which had been dug was not long enough, so there were desperate attempts to dig out more soil to accommodate the coffin.

And so it was, that at the somewhat drunken 'wake' in Harry's Bar in Venice, the possibility of making a full-length biographical film was first raised by Craft. In the event, it took some years before this would come to fruition in the form of a three-hour documentary to mark the centenary of Stravinsky's birth in St Petersburg in 1882.

And not a moment too soon. I managed to interview many of those who had known him and still had clear memories of him: his great choreographers, Balanchine and Lifar; Vaslav Nijinsky's daughter, Kyra; the last two dancers alive who had actually performed in the 1913 Paris première of *The Rite of Spring*, Marie Rambert and Michel Petrov; Diaghilev's secretary, Boris Kochno; and of course Stravinsky's widow, the ninety-three year-old Vera Sudeikina, and his three surviving children by Ekaterina, his first wife: Théodore, Soulima and Milène. Within a few short years all of the people I interviewed were dead.

My introduction to the film, however, was less than straightforward. I was flown to New York and told I first had to discuss the conditions under which my film would be made with the family's long-time lawyer, Arnold Weissberger. Upon entering his office, he immediately said, 'Stand over there, up against that wall. I must take a Polaroid photo.' Having recovered, I asked him why he needed that. 'Because I have so many dummies come through my office door, I can never remember who they are. So I take a photo.' After a pause he went on, 'You realise this film is impossible. You have two warring camps. First the three children. Second, Robert Craft and Vera. Not only do they not speak to each other even when they are not suing each other, but if you include Craft in your film, you will never get the children. They hate him. Clearly, to tell the full story you need both, because Craft never met Stravinsky until the old man was in his sixties. So we thought we needed a complete idiot to attempt to round up both camps, and so we chose you. Okay?'

It was a challenge I could not resist. What I would subsequently discover was often the reverse of what I had expected.

If there is any musical work that can be said to have influenced much of the musical landscape of twentieth-century, it is, of course, Stravinsky's *The Rite of Spring*, first performed at the Théâtre des Champs-Élysées in Paris on 29 May 1913, as part of Sergei Diaghilev's Ballets Russes season. Despite the so-called *scandale* of the first night, later thought to have been engineered by Diaghilev, it was a huge success. 'But can you imagine the situation,' Nicholas Nabokov, cousin of the novelist Vladimir and himself a noted scholar, told me, 'that in 1917, when Stravinsky and his family had been exiled from Bolshevik Russia and had settled in Switzerland, my friends and I were actually collecting money for the Stravinsky family to survive? And this was the man who had already written three international best-sellers: *The Firebird*, *Petroushka*, and of course, *The Rite of Spring*. But because of the stupidity, first, of Tsarist Russia and then the Soviet Union, those works were not covered by copyright and Stravinsky never earned a penny. Can you imagine what he felt when he saw people like Ravel and Richard Strauss getting rich as a result of two or three works, and he, Stravinsky, having to struggle financially for most of his life?'

As far as *The Rite* was concerned, 'There are some pages which I like,' Stravinsky said. 'But there are dozens of pages to which I am absolutely indifferent.'

'The activity of composing is everything for me,' Stravinsky said once, fiercely. 'It is for what I live. I *like* to compose music, much more than the music itself. I am at ease in the difficulties of composing, even the difficulties. But I can wait. I can wait as an insect can wait. I am somebody who is waiting, all my life.'

Although born in Russia, and spending his summers in the estate of his wife's family in what is now Ukraine, Stravinsky had left for Paris in the footsteps of Diaghilev and the Ballet Russes in 1910. After 1910, he returned only twice to Russia; briefly in 1912 to clear up some family business, and in 1962 at the invitation of Khrushchev. In revenge, almost, the Russian authorities had 'discouraged' performances of Stravinsky's music in the Soviet Union, and not the least bizarre moment when making my film occurred when I sought permission to work in the pre-Glasnost Soviet Union of Comrade Brezhnev.

Permission for anything to do with any Russian musician, alive or dead, ultimately passed through the office of the General Secretary of the Composer's Union in Moscow, Tikhon Khrennikov. A meeting was duly arranged between me and Khrennikov over tea and sweetmeats. For over forty years, this bureaucrat (and sometime composer) had dominated Russian musical life. He it was, who had sat at Andrei Zhadnov's side as Shostakovich was publicly denounced and the manuscript of his Ninth Symphony torn up in front of him at a special congress in January 1948. Khrennikov had even (according to some reports) danced a sort of *gopak* on the torn manuscript. It was also Khrennikov who had advised the Politburo that Prokofiev's music was decadent and had thus made the composer's life a misery.

And he was the one who had made sure that Stravinsky's music was hardly performed throughout the Soviet Union.

At that first meeting, we sat together at a long table, without interpreters. Khrennikov, inevitably, sat at the head of the table. I cannot believe that he did not realise that I knew who he was and what he had been responsible for. Yet he sat beneath three portraits, to which he proudly pointed. To the left, Stravinsky; to the right, Prokofiev; and above him, Shostakovich.

Robert Craft told me that when Stravinsky was dying, or, at least, when he had convinced himself that he was dying, he had decided that the final act should not be played out in New York where he was then living, but on the shores of the lake of Geneva where he had spent many years after he had left Russia and where he had written some of his finest scores, from *Petroushka* to *Les Noces*. Craft had been sent on a recce, but had soon realised that Lake Geneva 1969 was not Lake Geneva of 1913. High-rise blocks and a general urban mess had transformed the village of Clarens, where Stravinsky had finished *The Rite of Spring* and where Tchaikovsky had once stayed, and had rendered the village unrecognisable and noisy. Craft decided it would be safer for the old man to stay on the other side of the lake, so that he could look across the water and remember the glories of his youth without disturbance. The Grand Hôtel at Evian Les Bains seemed perfect.

So off they went; Stravinsky, wife Vera, and Robert Craft, with the old man propped up in bed in his suite of the hotel, looking out over the lake, with a bottle of Chivas Regal whisky to one side and a bottle of Aigle (his favourite Swiss white wine) on the other, more or less waiting to die. According to Craft, they had not been there many days before an emissary arrived from the Soviet Embassy in Geneva, carrying a special message from Comrade Khrennikov. Stravinsky refused to receive the emissary, but Craft decided to find out exactly what they wanted. Yes, wasn't it terrible, said the emissary; all those years of neglect in the Soviet Union of Stravinsky's music (no mention of any official government ban). Stravinsky was, after all, the greatest *Russian* composer of our time (conveniently forgetting that, although born in Russia, Stravinsky had been a French citizen for nearly a decade, lived in Switzerland during what was arguably his most creative period, and had been an American citizen since 1945). Stravinsky was, probably, *the* creative composer of the twentieth century, if not the millennium (*pace* Shostakovich) according to the emissary, and in acknowledgement of his unique place in the affections of the Soviet people (*sic*), the emissary had been sent to offer Mr Stravinsky any medical facilities he required and an Aeroflot plane to take him back to the Motherland to take advantage of those facilities. It was, after all, his duty as a Russian to spend his last days in Mother Russia, and in recognition of his presence in Russia Stravinsky would be awarded two Heroes of the Soviet Union medals, three Orders of Lenin, *and* would be buried in the Kremlin wall. Craft must have looked shocked by this outrageous offer because, quick as a flash, the emissary added that of course if Mr Stravinsky preferred to die by the lake of Geneva, this they would respect. But they would still like the body back; the Aeroflot plane could wait, or return, as requested. However, if only his body was returned to the Soviet Union, only *one* Hero of the Soviet Union medal could be awarded, and only *one* Order of Lenin. *But,* he would still be buried in the Kremlin wall.

Craft told me that Stravinsky was in equal measure so amused and annoyed by this offer that he immediately improved in health and returned to New York, where he died a year later.

'Once – I don't know where it was,' Stravinsky told me, 'at one of the borders, I presented my passport. "What is your occupation?" said the customs officer. "It's written," I replied. "It says "composer of music?" "No, no," I replied. "Not a *composer* of music. I am an *inventor* of music. Invention is not forced; nobody forced me to invent. I could easily make commonplace music, which I know exists. It exists much more than good music. But commonplace music does not need to be invented."'

The 'inventor' had certainly grown up in a heady atmosphere. Even after over seventy years of Bolshevism, Leningrad/St Petersburg remained a magical place – not just because of its architectural grandeur, the result, perhaps, of the city having been 'invented' by Peter the Great at the beginning of the eighteenth century and constructed by families of Italian architects, notably the Rastrellis; not just because of its long association with artistic endeavour, from Pushkin to Dostoyevsky, from Tchaikovsky to Shostakovich; but principally because the sacred and the secular seem to jostle each other for centre stage, dependent on the one for the greater glory of the other. The finest cathedrals in all of Russia sit side by side with the finest palaces, and although widely different in ambition, strangely unified in architectural statement.

Little wonder to me, therefore, that Stravinsky was profoundly religious. At the end of the road in which he lived as a child was the most extraordinary church, Nikolsky Sobor, where he was baptised. To get to the Nikolsky, he had to pass the stage door of the Mariinsky Theatre (later called the Kirov, before returning to its original name), where his father had been a leading bass-baritone. 'Music praises God,' he told me as if it were self-evident. 'Music is as well or better able to praise him than the actual church building itself and all its decoration. I *believe* in the person of the Lord,' he said, stabbing his finger at me, '*and* in the person of the Devil.'

'Stravinsky was concerned in everything he did,' Nicholas Nabokov told me, 'with ritual and with belief, Christian belief. One cannot speak of him as a religious composer, however. But one can say that very few composers in the twentieth century have dealt with religious subjects as did Stravinsky.' The dedication of the great *Symphony of Psalms*, for example, is 'à la gloire de Dieu' ('to the glory of God'), a text which happened also to be inscribed over the door of the church in the square of Morges in Switzerland, where Stravinsky and his family were living at Maison Bernard at the time of the work's composition. And it is surely no accident that the first piece of music which Stravinsky admitted he had written was a setting of *The Lord's Prayer* in Latin, and the piece he was working on when he died was a setting of *The Lord's Prayer* – in Russian.

'My father was extremely faithful,' his second daughter, Milène, told me. 'He may not have gone to church very often, but he always had his icons around his bed, and before he went away on a trip he would always give us his blessing.' According to Soulima, his younger son, 'My parents took religion literally, which none of us four children really appreciated. I suppose it would have been alright had we been monks in a monastery. But praying together at home, in front of a few small icons, never seemed quite right.'

Even *Les Noces* (*The Wedding*), although it is full of the rumbustious high-jinks of a Russian village peasant wedding and is perhaps his most characteristically 'Russian' work, it is also – according to Stravinsky himself – 'a product of the Russian church. The sound of the priests chanting,' he told me, 'the ritual of the ceremony, these were constantly in my mind. As a result, invocations to the Virgin and the saints are heard throughout the piece.' Later, I asked Mrs Stravinsky if she recalled our dinner in New York where the maestro had refused a glass of water, saying that 'Water is defeat'. 'What did he mean by that?' I asked naively. 'No,' she replied, 'Water is for *the feet*!' – a reference to Christ washing his disciples' feet. I felt thoroughly chastened.

Nonetheless, the intensity of Stravinsky's religious passion seemed to contradict his most often quoted (or misquoted) aphorism about the nature of music itself. 'Music can express nothing,' he said. 'only itself. It can express itself eloquently, very eloquently. And in expressing itself, it creates forms. Musically speaking, purely musically speaking, there are rules, like rules in any game. Every game must have its rules; otherwise it is anarchy, which means nothing. I can be the worst of Communists in the world, but not an anarchist. Even the nicest anarchist.'

The intellectual Stravinsky, however, was frequently upended by Stravinsky the man. And all men reveal their true selves in marriage. 'My marriage had been decided by myself when I was very young,' he told me. 'I was going to marry my cousin, Yekatarina, the daughter of my mother's sister. In the Orthodox religion such a marriage was absolutely prohibited by the church, but I loved her from the beginning and so I married her.'

'She always understood whatever he had written or composed,' Soulima their son told me. 'She was the first to hear it. After all, she had been trained as a musician and played a little piano.'

'But as he became more and more successful as a composer, and was away from home more and more on his concert tours, my mother became very lonely. And soon we became aware that my father was leading a double life. He had his family, at home in Switzerland, and he had his mistress, Vera Soudeikina, with him on tour and in Paris where he had an apartment.'

'But my father suffered from this situation very much. I know,' Soulima told me with tears in his eyes. 'He had a passion and he could not cope with it. My mother made it possible for us to survive as a family, but for us children it was a tragedy, an inner tragedy. What could we have done? Turn our backs on our father? He was autocratic, very, but he was our father. Or go to our father and turn our backs on our mother, which would have been unthinkable.'

And then, in 1938, his elder daughter died from tuberculosis aged only twenty-four while Stravinsky was away with his mistress. 'I went to meet him at the station upon his return,' Milène told me. 'I had earlier sent him a telegram, telling him the bad news. My father said, "When the telegram arrived, I knew it. And when my child had died, I had *felt* it." He didn't cry, but he walked with his head down and wouldn't look at anyone. He wouldn't talk, and would go to his room and be silent and refuse to be disturbed. But this was nothing compared to a few months later, when my mother died from tuberculosis. It was March, I remember. The night had been very bad, and we could see what was coming. The nurse who was looking after my mother called us and said, "It is the end." My father was already there, just absolutely shaking with emotion and tears and beating the ground with his fists. I never saw him like that before. It was terrible to see.'

When I came to edit my film biography of Stravinsky, I intercut this part of his story with a performance of Aria II from Stravinsky's *Violin Concerto*. One particularly obnoxious little music critic said that, yet again, I had muddled the chronology, proving how ignorant I was. The critic had taken no notice of another anecdote in the documentary which explained the connection. I had interviewed the widow of Samuel Dushkin, the violinist to whom the *Violin Concerto* is dedicated and who had given its first performance in 1931. Dorothy Duskhin remembered that, during the early performances, when she had sat next to Stravinsky, every time Aria II (the third movement) was played, Stravinsky burst into tears. 'At first I believed it was my husband's performance,' Mrs Dushkin told me, 'but when Stravinsky always cried at this point in the music, I became very curious. Eventually, I summoned up enough courage to ask him what was the matter. And, after several glasses of whisky, he told me. He was trying to say sorry, he explained, to apologise to his wife, Yekatarina, for what he had done to her by leading a double life. He could never face saying it to her in person, so he had written it down in music.'

No wonder he wept, and no wonder Aria II is such an emotionally charged piece.

'I remember the day Cocteau died,' Robert Craft his amanuensis told me. 'Stravinsky couldn't speak. He cried. Gloom. Deep depression. Sorrow. He was a joyful man, one of the most truly happy spirits I have known. And he considered a saying of Kierkegaard to be a guiding principle in his life. Kierkegaard said to despair before God is a sin. Stravinsky believed that, passionately.' So much for music being unable to express anything other than itself.

Like all great creative artists that I have met, Stravinsky was also profoundly worldly, whatever his protestations to the contrary, and obsessed by the minutiae of day-to-day existence, including money. Craft maintained that the entire correspondence between Stravinsky and his greatest champion, Diaghilev, is dominated by squabbles about money. Before he left Russia, Craft told me, Stravinsky had owned a vodka distillery and several mortgages in the Ukraine. 'He loaned money. He was a usurer,' Craft said.

Nicholas Nabokov remembered that, above all else, Stravinsky was a hedonist. 'He loved all the pleasures of life,' he said. 'He loved to eat; he loved good wines, pretty girls.' Alexei Haieff, one of his pupils, told me he hated familiarity. 'If someone called him Igor, that would be the end. He would hate that man. He would remember his rudeness for years. "That awful upstart," he would say. "How dare he call me Igor?" He loved wine and whisky. Indeed, he liked his booze in any form and would often get slightly exhilarated. And he smoked!'

'He liked squares', Nijinsky's daughter Kyra told me, 'either in a chequered jacket or in chequered pants with a plain jacket that didn't match at all. He was like a dandy, but a caricature of a dandy. And he liked to give the impression of a school teacher at school with kids that were not behaving themselves. Very stern-looking; he liked to glare.'

'In spite of being a rigorously ritualistic, religious person, as ancient peoples often are,' Nabokov added, 'he also had an extraordinary sense of irony. *Everything* for him was really rather extraordinarily funny.' Including his own health. 'He was an appalling hypochondriac,' Craft told me, 'certainly for the last fifteen years of his life. True, he was often ill, and his health had often suffered as a result of set-backs in his creative life. After the riots during the first performance of *The Rite of Spring*, for example, he had caught typhus, almost as a reaction, and been very gravely ill. But he had colds all the time, for example. Like his mother, he had had tuberculosis, and had spent months in a sanatorium. He suffered from bleeding ulcers. He had crippling headaches. He had everything. He was kept alive in the end by constant blood transfusions. But he kept all his X-rays and studied them. Charts, medical diaries, statistics about his health; these fascinated him. Once, I remember, he took some radioactive capsules for an X-ray. "Now I am surely lighting up like a lightning bug," he said.'

'His briefcase was always packed,' Craft showed me, 'as if constantly ready to go. Playing cards, a transformer for his shaver, hundreds of erasers – he always said "I compose *avec la gomme*." A paper bloc with music lines so that he could scribble down musical ideas whenever they came to him, on airplanes or the back of hotel bills; an electrical pencil-sharpener which made a ghastly noise like a lawn mower; scraps of paper which could be posted into the scores later; various coloured inks so that he could quickly see his corrections; his own little comparative dictionary which dates back until the first decade of the twentieth century when he worked as the interpreter [German/Russian] for Hans Richter, the conductor and friend of Wagner; a book of cats! Did you know that the first place he usually made for in any new city he visited was not the concert hall, but the zoo? Even before the art gallery. He was often more curious about elephants, dogs, love-birds [at one point he had forty in his Hollywood home] and cats, than humans. He even kept a chicken farm behind his Hollywood house.

One of his very first commissions after he had settled in Hollywood in the 1940s had come from the great choreographer Balanchine, another exile, for a *Circus Polka* for the Ringling Brothers' Circus, to be performed by their troupe of elephants. At first he declined the offer, until he heard that the elephant's name was 'Modac'. But he misheard the name, and thought it was 'Medoc', one of his favourite wines, so he accepted the commission. This nineteenth-century gentleman (Stravinsky),' Craft told me, 'was so polite that he even shook 'hands' (or paws) with the baby elephant to whom the work is dedicated.'

Above all, in my brief acquaintance with him (an impression confirmed by Craft's long friendship with him), Stravinsky always seemed an immensely practical man, especially in matters relating to his art. 'My first efforts at composition,' he said, 'were trying to imitate the sound of a band I had heard at the Admiralty buildings on the banks of the river Neva in St. Petersburg. This I did by trying to pick out the intervals on the piano that I had heard. But I soon found other intervals which I liked better, so that already made me a composer!' What finally decided him, against parental opposition (they would have preferred him to be a lawyer), was a visit to the Mariinsky Theatre to see a performance of Glinka's *Ruslan and Ludmilla*. In the interval, he and his mother 'stepped from our box into the small foyer behind. Suddenly my mother said, "Igor, look, there's Tchaikovsky." I looked and saw a man with white hair and large shoulders. Tchaikovsky's death two weeks later affected me deeply, and seeing Tchaikovsky that night has remained fixed on the retina of my memory all my life.'

It's extraordinary to think that a man who saw Tchaikovsky was still composing *after* the Beatles had disbanded.

The practical side of Stravinsky's nature served him well when dealing with some of his more wayward collaborators. Nijinsky, for instance, who first danced *Petroushka* and had choreographed *The Rite of Spring*, was certainly wayward. 'My father didn't know from Adam how to go to a bank or cash a cheque,' Kyra Nijinsky told me. 'He had everything brought to him, and he was utterly dependent on Diaghilev for his meals and his massage. He was constantly supervised. By nature, my father was a very intuitive man. He never even took a year of harmony lessons, and never managed to read an orchestral score. He could not make head nor tail of it. Whereas Stravinsky was a brilliant, intellectual man, so a clash was inevitable.'

The clash came, inevitably, during the rehearsals for *The Rite of Spring*. First, as instructed by Nijinsky, the pianist played the score too slowly. 'The way Nijinsky was doing it,' Marie Rambert, who had danced in the first performance, told me, 'it would have lasted years. Stravinsky was in a terrible temper with him and Nijinsky was absolutely squashed. Stravinsky sat at the piano himself and played at frantic speed, banging on top of the piano and on anything else that came to hand to give us an idea of what he heard in his head.'

'It was Diaghilev,' Stravinsky told me, 'who had encouraged me to use such a huge orchestra. I'm not sure my orchestra would have been so large otherwise.'

I was guided by no system whatever,' Stravinsky said later. 'I had only my ear to help me. I heard, and I wrote what I heard.'

The first-night audience was less than pleased, as Marie Rambert remembered. 'Nijinsky sat on a high chair in the wings,' she recalled, 'visible to us the dancers, and shouting "Seven", "Eight", "Nine", trying to keep us in time. But then someone in the gallery of the theatre shouted "Un docteur!" as if we were all ill on stage. Someone else shouted "Un dentiste!" And then the noise was tremendous. Someone else cried "Deux dentistes". It was all a dreadful failure. But in our *corps de ballet* we were not surprised, because although the company was furious with the audience, we all hated the ballet. As dancers we loved to show off our beauty and graceful charms, but all that was banished and was considered ugly, ugly.'

Stravinsky's memories of the actual composition were rather more prosaic. 'I rented a room in Clarens by the lake of Geneva, to be alone,' he said. 'I worked from the beginning of the day until the end of the day. I didn't take naps; I just worked. I didn't even pay much attention to the five o'clock tea, and after dinner I worked again. And I remember I slept <u>very</u> well. And on the wall I wrote, 'In this room I am composing the *Sacre du Printemps,* Clarens, 1911, Igor Stravinsky.'

When the composition was finished, Diaghilev invited Stravinsky to Venice so that he could play over the score. 'I played him the first dance,' Stravinsky told me. 'Fifty-nine times the same chord. Diaghilev was a little surprised. I could see that he hadn't paid much attention to the rhythmical variations of the chords. So, after a pause, being a little embarrassed, perhaps annoyed, and not wishing to offend me, he asked me only one thing, which was very offending, "Will it last a very long time?" he asked. And I said, "'til the end, my dear, 'til the end." And he was silent, because he understood that the answer was serious.'

The same 'invincible will' (Craft's description) was displayed, but again in a thoroughly practical way, during his collaboration with Jean Cocteau as librettist for their opera-oratorio, *Oedipus Rex*. 'I had the idea to have a libretto in Latin,' Stravinsky said, 'to emphasise the ritualistic aspect of what we would see, frozen in time and space, implying some force greater than itself. So I told Cocteau that the libretto must be very banal, for a big public who understands nothing. And he composed for me a libretto which was Wagnerian! So I said, "This is not banal. This is Wagnerian! I need a much more simple libretto – a libretto for everybody. Nobody understands Wagnerian librettos. Not even Wagner." And he said, "My dear, pas d'inquietude; je vous faire une autre." Don't worry, I will make another. And he did, and it was a little less Wagnerian, so I said, "This is *still* Wagnerian." And he said, "My dear, it is a pleasure to work with you. I will make you a <u>third</u> libretto." And this he did, just like an Italian opera. Very banal. Which was just what I needed.'

Stravinsky had intended *Oedipus Rex* as a birthday present for Diaghilev, to celebrate twenty years of Diaghilev's company, Les Ballets Russes. The work was not a success with the audience. 'There was a big chill in the public,' Soulima told me. But who was this Diaghilev who had dominated the first twenty years of Stravinsky's career? He was, in fact, a distant cousin of Stravinsky's, 'a person of exceptional physical appearance,' Boris Kochno Diaghilev's secretary, told me. 'He was a head taller than the average, with a very strange personal beauty and, from the age of nineteen, a streak of white running through his brown hair. His role was that of a chess player. The people who surrounded him, his collaborators, were pawns, which he moved about on the chess board so that he, Diaghilev, always won.'

Certainly he paid his pawns very little, a cause of much annoyance to Stravinsky. Michel Pavlov, in the *corps de ballet* of the first performance of *The Rite of Spring*, told me that they were paid two francs per performance. 'We were always put in rooms on the ground floor of hotels, so that when the time came to leave, we could climb out through the windows and not pay the bills. Diaghilev *never* paid the bills.'

'Imagine my surprise,' Stravinsky said, 'when I had first received a telegram in St Petersburg from Diaghilev in Paris, asking me to write the music for his new ballet, *The Firebird*. I was his second choice, but still, it must have been a considerable risk as I had written no music of any consequence at this time. As far as I know, Diaghilev had only heard a short piece of mine in St. Petersburg called *Fireworks*. So I asked him how long did I have to complete for score for '*The Firebird*'. He replied, "Three months."'

As it turned out, the première of *The Firebird* in Paris in the spring of 1910, with Debussy, Proust, Ravel and Sarah Bernhardt – heavily veiled and in her wheelchair – in the audience, made Stravinsky an international star almost overnight.

When Diaghilev died, nineteen years later, 'It was the greatest shock my father had experienced until that time,' Stravinsky's elder son Théodore told me. 'He was in tears.' 'I was particularly saddened,' Stravinsky told me, 'because we had quarrelled over money yet again, and had deliberately avoided each other for the last six months. He was my closest friend, and his death marked for me the end of an era and was followed by years of wandering,' which did not end until Stravinsky settled in Hollywood, just off Sunset Strip, with his second wife, Vera Soudekina. Vera told me that soon after her husband had first arrived in America, he heard on the radio that the Japanese had attacked Pearl Harbour. He had immediately called the violinist Sam Dushkin, and said, 'But Sam, this is terrible. Where shall I go now?'

In fact, he stayed in Hollywood. He was no longer a nomad. The climate suited him, and he had a little house with a garden with his wife, whom he loved. In fact, he lived in that house longer than any other house he had ever lived in. He lived in a society of refugees: Aldous Huxley, Thomas Mann, Arnold Schoenberg. He lunched with the great American musicians of the day such as Benny Goodman and with various Hollywood moguls like Sam Goldwyn. He even made an arrangement of *The Star-Spangled Banner,* gave the manuscript to Mrs Roosevelt, played the piece in Boston not realising it was illegal to do so, got booed and was arrested. He became less formal, partly, I am sure, because Vera was very much a no-nonsense person. She was a painter and a part-time actress who had appeared in 1922 as the queen in Diaghilev's production of *The Sleeping Beauty* ballet in Paris, which was where she had first met Stravinsky. She had also opened a shop for fashionable and theatrical accessories called Tulavera with her friend, the dancer Aleksandra Danilova (Tula), and had created costumes for Les Ballets Russes. 'Diaghilev called me up and said, "Do you want to have dinner in an Italian restaurant?"' she told me. '"Bakst and Ravel will be there, and Stravinsky. Do you know him?"' "No," I said. "I will pick you up in ten minutes." So he came to the hotel and said, "You know, he's terribly moody today. So please be nice to him." And I was very, *very* nice to him!' Their relationship began soon after, as Soulima remembered, and they finally married eighteen months after the death in 1939 of Stravinsky's first wife, Yekatarina. In fact, Stravinsky was Vera's fourth husband. She continued to paint, held exhibitions around the world, and outlived her husband by eleven years.

Perhaps my strangest encounter during this whole journey had been with Diaghilev's last great choreographer, Serge Lifar. He wanted to be interviewed in the Palace Hotel in Montreux. Not because he himself lived there, but because he knew that Vladimir Nabokov had lived there and Lifar felt this venue would enhance his stature. We talked in French for a good two hours, until he came to the story of Diaghilev's death. Briefly, 'I had gone to Venice to see him. And over to the Lido. I looked up and there was Sergei Pavlovich leaning out of the hotel window, and I know immediately he was very sick. I immediately went back across the lagoon, and brought the best doctor I could find. But then, in my arms, on the night of August 29th, 1929, Sergei Pavlovich [pause] died!'

Whereupon I could see that tears were pouring down his cheeks. I waited for a long period, before thanking him for this most moving tribute.

The problem was, moving though the story had been, there was not a word of truth in it. Diaghilev had died on the 19th August of diabetes, and Lifar was definitely not there.

My problem was, what was to be done? As was my custom, my film had no narrator. If I left the story as it was, would that be condoning a falsehood? But his tears were unforgettable. What they showed was that even after fifty years the impact and memory of Diaghilev was so powerful that, in a real sense, he lived in Lifar's mind as if the world which they had all inhabited was still in the present.

And, of course, the most important magician in that circle was Stravinsky himself, 'discovered', as it were, by Diaghilev, who then commissioned his famous early works, including, obviously, *The Rite of Spring,* which truly changed the course of Western classical music. Stravinsky said repeatedly, 'I speak Russian. That you hear in my music. I *am* Russian.' It was as if there was nothing more to say about himself or his art. Throughout his life, and its many vicissitudes and apparent changes of direction, this Russianness burned through everything he did. It didn't explain everything, but it was the bedrock upon which all else was founded.

What a journey he travelled, and what an adventure of discovery I had experienced while retracing just a few of his footsteps.

Chapter 16

William Walton

Few composers have been more loved in their lifetime than William Walton. And the strange thing is that, despite an almost inevitable dip in his popularity following his death in 1983, here we are, in the twenty-first century, discovering once again the extraordinary power and richness of his music. His capacity to astonish and move us profoundly remains undiminished. In a soulless world, he confronts us repeatedly with our darkest fears, but also our most joyful aspirations. And in the end, that is why we love him.

My film was first broadcast as a *South Bank Show* on Easter Sunday 1981, and remains, as it was then, the only substantial film documentary on Walton. It had originally been offered to the BBC, but they had rejected it on the grounds that a long film about Walton 'would be of little interest to the general public' (*sic*). Eventually, it owed its existence to three people: Gillian Widdicombe, who introduced me to the Waltons; Michael Grade, who, as Director of Programmes for London Weekend Television, commissioned the film – he said it had appealed to him because of its 'subject matter', which he described as 'sun, fun and sex' (he was more accurate than he knew, as Laurence Olivier points out in the film). Grade later complained that I had under-estimated the importance of the Second Symphony by only including eight bars! In this, he was absolutely accurate, and I learnt never to under-estimate him again. Michael Grade: The best director-general the BBC never had the courage to appoint. And above all, Melvyn Bragg, who fought the moguls of ITV to make sure the film was shown exactly as I had made it – all one hour and forty minutes of it, and with only two short commercial breaks. That would never be allowed to happen today.

When originally shown, the film had some modest success, winning, among many other things, the Italia Prize. But it also had its critics, one of whom said that only I could transform one of the sunniest composers into a melancholic old grump.

I had been taken by Gillian Widdicombe, a music critic and rumoured biographer of Walton, to meet the composer at his house on Ischia in the Bay of Naples, and we had spent a very hot day discussing what it might be possible to film, given that Walton was, after all, almost eighty, and not quite in the best of health. He was, however, delightful, impish and anxious to please. Susana, Lady Walton, an irascible Argentinian on a good day, was, as ever, protective yet bouncily enthusiastic. Walton told me that when he had been knighted in 1948, he had written to Susana's father to say he had only accepted to make sure she could be addressed as 'Lady Walton'. The father, who had disapproved of the marriage, had replied, 'She was a lady long before she ever met you.' As she aged, Susana never appeared to 'shrink' in stature, simply because her hats grew ever more exotic, thus always giving the impression of remaining the same height. Nonetheless, she was only about five feet six inches and she delighted in confronting those somewhat taller than her, none more so than, in 1982, the then Controller of BBC Music Robert Ponsonby, well over six feet three inches. They chanced to meet at a BBC function late in 1980 when Robert cornered, or maybe that should be towered over, Susana and announced, 'Oh, Lady Walton. You'll be pleased to know that only this morning we have agreed to celebrate Sir William's eightieth birthday [in 1982] with performances of every single work that Sir William ever wrote, including some not previously published; First Night of the Proms, Last Night of the Proms…' 'Harrumph,' replied Lady Walton. 'But what are you going to do that's special?'

Later, when she disapproved of my draft of 'her' book, *Behind the Façade,* she threatened to kill me if I ever set foot on Ischia again.

Meanwhile, following my initial meeting with Sir William in happier times, as we had got up to leave, I remember saying to him something to the effect of,

'I look forward to—' (seeing him later in the summer). To my surprise, he suddenly replied, 'Death. That's what I'm looking forward to.' I realised that Walton must have thought I had asked what was *he* looking forward to. I sat down again immediately, and the conversation began again, although in a more sombre tone. What he explained to me in the following half an hour gave me a clue as to the real subject matter of my film (*pace* Michael Grade). I began to have the feeling that Walton considered much of his life's work to have been a waste, that much of what he'd done had been a failure, and that the end result of all his – but only, he said, to other people – immense achievements was a black hole, a nothingness from which there was no escape.

At first, I dismissed all this as special pleading from an old man who felt he had been forgotten, especially by the British musical establishment. But then I began to listen much more carefully to the music itself, and came to understand that this profound pessimism about the human condition – I don't believe 'melancholy' is anywhere near adequate – had been in Walton's music from the beginning. Listen in the film to *Drop, drop, slow tears,* a choral piece he had written while still at Oxford, aged only fifteen. Listen to the *Viola Concerto,* played in the film with heart-breaking sadness by Yehudi Menuhin. Listen to *Belshazzar's Feast* – 'By the waters of Babylon, There we sat down; yea, we wept…'. Listen to the *Cello Concerto,* composed on Ischia, at a time when most contemporary critics had written him off. Listen to his opera, *Troilus and Cressida,* perhaps not the masterpiece he had longed for, but still a work frequently overwhelming in its emotional intensity; a work still overlooked by the world's opera houses, but a work which contains aria after aria of pitiful grandeur, one of which gave me the title for my film: *At the Haunted End of the Day.*

Because, in the end, that's what my film was about: what we feel as human beings 'at the haunted end of the day'. I'm grateful – no, that's the wrong word; I have no words to describe what I went through when the great man came to London to see the finished film. There were many tears. Walton said he couldn't quite understand why there was so much fuss. 'My boy,' he told me, 'I've written far too much music. Do you really want to include so much?' There could never be too much William Walton, but for what there is, we are forever in his debt. And I hoped my film would go a little way to repaying the debt.

Two footnotes to this part of the story: First, I think this was Simon Rattle's first substantial contribution to television. In my view, it has never been bettered. No-one else could have captured the fury and bitterness of Walton's music so eloquently. Secondly, the irony was that, even in Walton's centenary year, 2002, such was the abnegation by today's broadcasters of nearly all responsibility for the arts on television, that this film would never have been commissioned. The film is too long, too depressing, and about someone who's dead. Unless, that is, it included a 'make-over' of Walton's garden shed – or perhaps a badly behaved poodle – and were introduced (or should that be traduced?) by the likes of the BBC's 'fearless front-line reporter' and Renaissance buffoon, the preening Clive Myrie.

Yes, but it's actually about someone who is alive in the hearts and imaginations of everyone who cares about the potential of music to make sense of an otherwise senseless existence. William Walton, through his music, gives us that hope and shows us, as Imogen Holst remarked, that 'music is a part of life that can't be done without.'

William became a wonderful friend, and I even persuaded him to take a small part in my Richard Burton/Charles Wood *Wagner* epic as Friedrich August II, Elector of Saxony and Wagner's employer in Dresden, who, much like Walton himself, didn't much care for Wagner and his preposterous claims to immortality. 'What's that dreadful noise?' the Elector (and Walton) declare in the film, reacting to some pompous little march Wagner had composed.

So when Walton died in 1984 I was understandably distressed, although, given the fragility of his health, not really surprised. I was determined to get to his funeral, wherever it was, whenever it was. But that was not quite as simple as it seemed.

Walton had died at his home on Ischia in the Bay of Naples over a week before, in the arms of his wife Susana, asking her not to leave him. But, having been brought up in the Church of England and wishing to be cremated, he had not reckoned with the curious laws of Italy. The nearest crematorium was six hundred miles to the *north*, outside Florence in Tuscany, and so the corpse had had to be transported by bumpy hearse, boat, train, and, eventually, by what looked like a dust-cart to its appointed gas oven. The irony of that last journey – north, when his entire life had been a long journey *south*wards from Oldham in Lancashire, via Oxford and the Sitwells and onwards to the Bay of Naples –would not have escaped him.

There was nothing unusual about the morning, I remember, other than its stillness. Not a leaf stirred. Mist shrouded the trees of Tuscany while a motley crew assembled for the funeral. The widow had come dressed in black mink – it was, after all, the chill end of March – and seemed, not for the first time, the life and soul of the party. From Rome had come a representative of the British Council, good cheer and good works sitting comfortably within his ample frame; from Ireland, a gentleman of uncertain origin (absent was his Finnish wife – his second, her third marriage, that is – but, I was assured, a very, very old family friend whom none present had ever met); from the BBC, a producer of distinction whose skill with the camera lens was to be tested when he insisted on a last photograph of the corpse before it disintegrated into a pile of ashes; from Fleet Street, a part-time journalist of unfortunate reputation who had laboured long and hard – for ten years, some said – on a biography of the deceased but had failed to produce a single word; the managing director of Walton's publishing company, about whom I had never heard the departed say a kindly word; and, lastly, the son of the man who had, over half a century earlier, 'discovered' him. Seven persons in all, including me, now gathered on a hill outside Florence to say farewell to the best-loved, best-respected – some would just say the best – English composer of his generation.

A Catholic country does not advertise its crematoria since, strictly speaking, the Canon Law does not admit of their existence. So we could have been forgiven had we got lost on the way, especially as the drive through scenes which reminded us of Leonardo and other Florentines – whose dates none of us could quite fix although we were all agreed they were ancient – was more beautiful than we had a right to expect this gruesome morning. Numerous signs assuring us that the cemetery was either '*Chiuso*' ('closed') or '*In Restauro*' ('under restoration') eventually led us to a squat brick pile whose only noticeable feature was a large chimney which poked obscenely at the sky. This was it, we were told. It proved impossible to enter, however, because the door had been entirely blocked by a gargantuan wreath sent by the British Performing Rights Society. A 'Death of Kings Wreath', ordered by phone, and more appropriate for a passing potentate than for a man who had praised them in song. Nonetheless, there it was. Again, ironic that this most vulgar display of public grief should have come from a society he had helped to found almost fifty years earlier, and which had then coined it from the extraordinary and on-going popularity of his music.

And so we stood, we seven, pathetically clutching our single roses hastily purchased that morning, dwarfed by this monster wreath. He would have been much amused. Such things always amused him; indeed, our loss that morning was not to hear his wicked laughter.

Well, if this was the place, it was as well that the living had not inspected the site the day before. Inside a tiled chamber, stood the oven. It was, or could have been, a reject from Auschwitz, and from memory (I've been there, also), I was certain it was. The same stench, and the same manufacturer. Its door lay open, lazily awaiting the next corpse. We all got the giggles, except the journalist who thought it was no laughing matter. In truth, even the widow thought that laughter was the only way to deal with this grotesque apparition. But - where was the corpse?

Up and down, up and down we walked, breathing deeply the Florentine air. Eventually, a search party was decided upon, but - with the exception of the widow - our collective knowledge of Italian was noticeable by its absence.

But the search party lacked leadership. Inactivity and immobility were its principal characteristics. And then, as if in answer to our prayers (not that there had been any), up chugged a dustcart and out jumped four burly, overall-clad workers, who proceeded to drag out from the rear a tin coffin, complete with name tag and number.

But where was the priest? Where were those black-suited attendants, the piped church music, those courtesies provided at English crematoria that give unfortunate mourners like us at least a modicum of comfort? Nowhere. This was it, and this was the place, and here we were, and there was the corpse. No point in complaining. In any case, there was no-one to complain to. Were *we* at fault, not having organised the priest, the choir, the prayers? It was, in any event, all too late. The workmen were already looking at their watches, anxious to move on, presumably to the next name and number of whatever it was that awaited them.

There followed a scene which would not be believed in fiction, let alone in fact. It seemed that because the body had been incarcerated in its tin coffin for over a week, transported by road, rail and sea - every mode of transport except the magic carpet - there was always the possibility of a mistake. Perhaps the wrong corpse? The Signora would understand. The souls of the departed must be guaranteed eternal rest, it was explained, and we wouldn't want to despatch a dear departed soul and son (or daughter) of Mother Church about whom we knew nothing. Whereas, of course, the late departed Signor Maestro being, well, not of Holy Mother Church, conflagration was in order...the Signora would understand. Whereupon the lady journalist demanded to see the decomposing corpse: one last look, she said, for history - for posterity at least. Very sensible, agreed one of the workmen. Whereupon we were ushered into the antechamber where lay the tin capsule - actually, we were assured it was of the finest zinc - in which, we were told and we hoped, lay our dead friend. The question was; how to open the zinc container? Blank faces and many Italian shrugs. The same workman, cigarette in the corner of his mouth, then produced what looked like a giant can-opener and proceed to hack away at the coffin.

Like the top of a tin of sardines, the zinc was slowly peeled back. Out of terror, we seven all held hands, except for the BBC producer who, sensing his moment of destiny, stepped forward to photograph the noble head of the discoloured, putrescent corpse. The journalist laid a flower in his hands (although I suspect Walton would have preferred the long-promised but never-written biography), and the widow confirmed that this was, indeed, her late husband. Whereupon we all rushed for the open air, and gulped it in now in desperate and grateful relief for having escaped that ghoulish moment. Then, from a comparatively safe distance, we all heard the oven being fired up, like the distant rumble of an atomic explosion. One would have preferred not to hear the firing, but so still was the air that every crackle of twig underfoot, every distant bleat of a bird, seemed to echo round the valley in a shout of protest against this final obscenity.

But the firing was only a prelude. Suddenly, from that erect chimney, belched forth a cloud of such black filth that our immediate reaction was to scatter in case of contamination. The widow grabbed my arm, and rather determinedly, marched me away from the inferno. I'm not sure now what she said; I'm not sure I would have remembered at the time; and I'm not even sure whether she was aware of the babble that emerged, such was the cathartic effect of the words. Words, words, so oft unspoken; so many opportunities lost; such damage inflicted. And yet, at the end, all they do is hide the silence. Or, on this occasion, shut out the terror. The son of the man who had discovered him came running, or, at least, came hurrying as fast as his bulk would allow. 'The ashes would be cool enough to be taken away in thirty minutes,' he announced triumphantly. We decided to wait.

Up and down, up and down. The cloud had thinned by now, but flecks of ash seemed to hang in the air like Christmas decorations looking for a tree. A white fleck, more solid than some, landed on the black forearm of the widow's mink. 'Ah, must be his little toe,' she said, with a twinkle. For once, even I could not laugh. Up and down, up and down. His publisher was trying to read the inscription on the Performing Rights wreath. As it had been sent by telephone, the accompanying message may have lost something in translation. Something about a composer called Wanton. He would have to tell them, back in London, of their mistake. The Irish friend muttered that maybe a stiff drink would help the proceedings. There was no-one present who disagreed.

Later, there only remained to plan the inevitable memorial service; a great occasion it would have to be, in Westminster Abbey. The urn containing the ashes would have to be taken back to Ischia in the Bay of Naples, to the garden he had helped fashion with his own hands. A creation, I do believe, that gave him more satisfaction than much of his music.

And so we departed, some back to London, others to the south. Upon reflection, there had been nothing sad about the occasion; a moment of bitterness, perhaps, when the widow had suddenly cried out, 'Oh God, why couldn't you have left him with me for one more summer? Now he will never see the agapanthus again or the lemon trees in bloom.' There was regret, certainly, that none of us had done all we could, in his lifetime, to reassure him that his life's work had been worthwhile. He had doubted it. I suspect he had always doubted it.

Indeed, that is how we met. To make that film for television about this life's work. 'My work?' he had enquired. 'Just a job,' he had said. 'Just a job.' I portrayed an old and disappointed man who, in the autumn of his life, constantly asked himself the same question, over and over. 'Was that all?' In striving to show the great humanity of the man, I believe that, despite my best efforts, I failed. I believe he knew it, although he never said so. I remembered again our first meeting when he had mistakenly heard what I had asked, 'Sir William. What are you most looking forward to?'

Echoing the Knight in Bergman's *The Seventh Seal*, he had replied: 'Death,' he said. 'Death'.

Chapter 17

John Osborne and Handel

My film about George Frederic Handel was originally shown in 1985 on British television, Channel Four, to commemorate the 300th anniversary of the birth of that honorary 'British' composer. It caused a predictable furore.

First, the script was written by John Osborne, a fictional construct using the language of the Bible as its template. Osborne? What the hell did he know about music? We called the film '*God Rot Tunbridge Wells* – a tale of woe and bloody-minded persistence'. 'A trashy comic strip' was among the more generous of reviews. Trevor Howard, in what turned out to be his last major film, was thought incoherent at best and absurd at worst. As for me; well, according to some television critics (who are mostly moronic, even illiterate), I had apparently returned to my bad old days of self-indulgent rock 'n' roll vulgarity, and had made a film full of anachronisms such as a wind-up gramophone, on which Handel played his 'recordings' (*sic*). I was nothing but a 'precocious irritant', wrote one. Osborne was amused (although not surprised) by all of this vitriol, especially when he was struck down with pneumonia and lugged off to a hospital in – yes, you guessed it – Tunbridge Wells. 'Mr Osborne,' he was told by a very sexy nurse (his description, as he related in *The Spectator*), 'this is punishment for having mocked our lovely town. How could you say "God Rot Tunbridge Wells"? Oh, naughty Mr Osborne.'

Only the music escaped criticism. The Australian conductor Sir Charles Mackerras (another honorary 'Brit') and his fiery cast – Emma Kirkby, James Bowman, Elizabeth Harwood, John Shirley-Quirk, Simon Preston, Anthony Rolfe-Johnson, Valerie Masterson, Andrei

Gavrilov and the indefatigable English Chamber Orchestra - were rightly praised for making Handel sound, well, like Handel: full of life and fury and not the usual syrupy stodge served up by a massed choir of thousands. Simon Preston, then organist at Westminster Abbey, had wanted me to use his choir. The Abbey authorities would not permit it, so we used them anyway but called them 'The Extremely Ancient Academy of Singers', and remarkable they were too.

And the result really does sound like one always felt Handel *should* sound like - strong, effervescent, and yet crystal clear.

And it was this quality that was spotted by Edward Greenfield, the long-serving and distinguished music critic of the *Guardian*, and from that moment the reviews did a complete volte-face. There was a steady realisation of what it was that Osborne had attempted: namely, strip away what felt like centuries of bad Handel performances (no names here, but Malcolm Sargent gets a swipe) and reveal a composer who had burst upon London like a tornado and had not only shaken the smugness of Georgian England to its roots, but also laid the foundations of an entirely different tradition of British music-making - bold, brassy and brilliant. And there was a growing understanding that the words that Osborne had put into Handel's mouth, although completely invented, had been derived from a clever reworking of those texts which Handel himself had used in his various operas and oratorios. Thus the King James Bible and Thomas Cranmer's *Book of Common Prayer*, two books Osborne held in reverential awe, came singing onto the screen in unforgettable resonance, with the gin-soaked and pickled voice of Trevor Howard relishing every last syllable. Howard was very hurt by the first reviews, but, luckily, he lived long enough to see the worm turn, although every worm that had passed itself off as a television critic he declared he would squash underfoot before he popped off.

And what of John Osborne? David Hare, in a lengthy interview he did for my 2003 film about Osborne, *'The Gift of Friendship'*, seemed to me to have got the man right. 'Osborne is the poet of failure,' Hare said, 'Failure is his subject. He's the poet of flop sweat. He's the man who writes about what it's like to wake in the middle of the night and to know you've failed and to feel that you're worthless and that you're not managing in anything you do, in your life, in your work, in your relationships with your friends, in your relationships with women. He looks failure straight in the face and he delivers you that feeling of failure, of not having managed to do what you hoped to do, either in relationships or in your own work.

'The number of people who want to take away from John Osborne what he achieved is limitless,' Hare went on. 'There seems to be no angle from which you cannot try to take away the fact that John did transform the British theatre in 1956, that everything was different afterwards, that he is the gatekeeper. And yet, somehow, people seem so bored with that idea, or it threatens them so much, or what he wrote still threatens them so much, that they will always try to attack that idea. They'll try to say he only wrote a couple of good plays and film scripts. "Yes, well, the autobiographies aren't bad." They will even try and strip him of his historic importance. But I don't see how you can. It's a fact. He changed what writing for British theatre and films could be.'

Nicol Williamson, who had starred as Bill Maitland in the première of Osborne's play *Inadmissible Evidence,* was in no doubt as to Osborne's greatness as a writer. 'For fifteen years,' he told me, 'Osborne was the greatest living English playwright. And in the words of Lear, I can say: mine eyes are not of the best, I'll you straight – but there's nothing wrong with my understanding. I speak from instinct and experience. I know that the words and the power and the brilliance of Osborne, to me, are the chronicled Shakespeare of his time. That's what they are.'

Why did everyone hate Osborne so much, therefore – part of which was reflected, I believe, in the reaction to our film about Handel? In his posturing, Osborne had often not ingratiated himself. His attack on what he perceived as English theatre in the 1950s had pulled no punches. 'There was a certain style of acting and performance and play and safety and timidity in every area, including design, that seemed to infect everything,' he told me. 'People didn't take it seriously. I mean, the novel was *the* thing that people took seriously in literature. Certainly not theatre or film. On the whole, they were run by very mediocre people.'

One day, when we were discussing the script for our proposed film about Handel, he read me some of the reviews which had greeted his first success, *Look Back In Anger.* 'The play has passages of good violent writing, but its total gesture is altogether inadequate,' he read. 'A scruffy and eloquent hater of class distinctions, sadly deserted by his adoring wife.' 'Something of a sadist and very much an exhibitionist, Jimmy Porter has married above himself, apparently out of spite against middle class respectability.' 'Back-street Hamlet talks bosh.' 'Audiences used to stand up and shout and say, "I'm taking my wife out of the theatre,"' Osborne told me. '"Take that horrible man off." And, "Why don't you hit him back?" That sort of thing. Which they still do, of course. And have done again in relation to our film about Handel.'

Had Osborne only himself to blame? In his famous 1961 open letter published in *Tribune*, he wrote: 'This is a letter of hate. It is for you, my countrymen. I mean those men of my country who have defiled it. The men with their manic fingers leading the sightless, feeble, betrayed body of my country to its death. You are its murderers, and there's little left in my own brain but the thoughts of murder for you. My hatred of you is almost the only constant satisfaction you have left me. My favourite fantasy is four minutes or so non-commercial viewing as you fry in your democratically elected hot seats in Westminster, preferably with your condoning democratic constituents. You have instructed me in my hatred for thirty years. You have perfected it and made it the blunt, obsolete instrument it is now. I only hope it will keep me going. I think it will. It may sustain me in the last few months. Till then, damn you, England, you're rotting now and quite soon you'll disappear. My hate will outrun you yet, if only for a few seconds. I wish it could be eternal. Your fellow countryman, John Osborne.'

He went further in a much-underestimated play, *Epitaph for George Dillon*. 'Listen, all I've ever got inside the theatre or out of it are raves of a microscopic minority and the open hostility of the rest,' Dillon says. 'I attract hostility. I seem to be on heat for it. Whenever I step out onto those boards, immediately, from the moment I show my face, I know I'm going to have to fight almost every person in that auditorium. Right from the stalls to the gallery, to the vestal virgins in the boxes. And my god, it's a gladiatorial combat. Me against them. Me and the mighty them. Well, sometimes I may win some of them over. Sometimes it's a half, maybe, sometimes a third, sometimes not even a quarter. But I do beat them down. I beat them down. And even in the hatred of the majority there's a kind of triumph, because I know that although they'd never admit it, that secretly they respect me.'

John Heilpern, Osborne's best biographer, reflected what I myself had come to think. 'What Osborne plugged into was the melancholy of his own soul,' Heilpern told me. 'I hope that doesn't sound pretentious because he was, essentially – for all his shit-stirring, for all his trouble-making, for all his fun – deep down a reflective, melancholy man, who had suffered because of it. And this is reflected in his heroes, including Georg Frederic Handel. His heroes are not satisfied people. They are people who cannot connect to life. They're people disappointed by lost opportunities or lost visions. Again it links to the idea of "England". There is a romantic strain of English life that looks to a lost Eden of England that may never have existed, but you still miss it. You may feel you were never entitled to it, but you feel there's something lost. And his heroes are like that. His heroes flail and fail in the pain of being alive today.'

And that is what we tried to reflect in our film about Handel, and in particular in Handel's music. As Osborne himself told me, 'I always respond to people and art and music which are simply honest, but very little is these days. Very few people in our trade, for example, are honest. They dissemble all the time and seek out respect. I've never done that. Been rather useless exercise if I had, 'cause I wouldn't have got it. I think today there's not much honesty in the behaviour of most people, and therefore in their art. Handel had it. Very rare. Everything's now so mealy-mouthed, isn't it? You can't say what people or art are really like. "D'you know, I find that terribly offensive," they say. Life *is* offensive for God's sake!'

'Think what has happened since I began writing. We have repudiated – and again it seems like some awful campaign – repudiated the Book of Common Prayer and the Bible, which is why I used that language for my script in our film. The Church of England has become so terrible and despicable in the way it has given in and become a branch of Butlins, which is what it is now with its happy-clappy guitars and hands raised to the skies in some meaningless gesture. So, when you go to church, it's no longer a question of being confronted with what you might really be and being chastened about it. Handel would have been horrified.'

Like most of my films, *God Rot Tunbridge Wells* cost peanuts – less than Miloš Forman (with whose 1984 film *Amadeus* our little effort was often compared) had spent on wigs, and it was largely financed by selling my grandmother and re-mortgaging my house. 'Why can't you do a <u>real</u> film', my accountant (since fired) had said, 'and make some proper money?'

In fact, the first money had come from someone claiming to be a relation: a Mr Alex Herbage. It was true that a distant great-aunt of mine called Anna Instone had been married to a Mr Julian Herbage (both were luminaries on the BBC Third Programme, as it then was), so I believed him. And when the first tranche of money arrived – £75,000, a not-inconsiderable sum – I began to believe him more. But when the second tranche did not arrive (and by now we had already started filming, with contracts signed, and so on), and, instead, two gentlemen from the Fraud Squad knocked on my door to inform me that Mr Herbage had been arrested for having silted away £250 million in the UK and the US on various nefarious investment schemes, I was somewhat taken aback. As far as I know, Herbage is still languishing in some prison here or in the United States, though I bear him no grudge, because without him the film might not have got off the ground. Anyway, the Fraud Squad informed me I was of no use to them, because I had written to thank Herbage for his generosity and had told him that there was a reasonable chance his investment in me and the film would prove profitable. His swindles had apparently consisted of taking money for 'investment', but then using it for his own purposes, something we all do but not on his scale, and he had unfortunately got found out – unlike the banks from whom I then had to borrow the balance of the budget at a very high rate of interest to complete the film. Gangsters all. Osborne would have signed up to that view immediately!

We were 'saved', if that is the word, by the aristocracy of England, and Osborne was certainly amused by that. The lady I then lived with, Annunziata Asquith, eldest daughter of the Earl of Oxford and Asquith, suggested I use her parents' manor as the location for Handel's Brook Street house. It was perfect. 'Ah,' said the Earl, 'well, why don't you also use Chatsworth House for one of the grand dinner scenes?' Perfect, except that the Duchess of Devonshire said that the candelabra which we had brought for the dinner table in the film were 'shoddy', so she promptly produced quantities of Devonshire silverware – and yes, it's the real thing that you see in the film. And there was the Duke of Buccleuch, and we used Drumlanrig House for one of the great houses that Handel visited as a boy. And what about the Earl of Shelburne? Bowood, his house near Chippenham, would be another possibility. Or the Duke of Rutland? Or the Palazzo Ruspoli in Cerveteri in Rome, where Handel had been a guest of Francesco Maria Ruspoli, who had named him *Kapellmeister*? Suddenly, I had a million dollars' worth of locations.

There was still the minor problem that some of Osborne's scenes called for vast crowds. 'Easy,' said my location manager. 'The Job Centre. Give them a bowl of rice and a pretty dress and they'll be as happy as sandboys, or girls.' And so they were, and thus the London of King George II is peopled by the unemployed of 1985, courtesy of various local Job Centres and a brilliant costume designer called John

Hibbs, who cobbled together over 500 costumes from odd bits and pieces that second-hand clothes shops had discarded.

And when it came to filming and recording some of the music, because Mackerras had insisted on recording the Royal Fireworks Music, for example, as it had been written – for a veritable battery of wind and brass instruments, not to mention twenty side-drums – how the hell were we going to assemble that number of period-looking instruments? 'Easy,' said the cameraman, 'use mirrors'. And so we did. No-one noticed, nor that the 'harpsichord' on which the deaf and almost-blind Handel doodles from time to time is actually a grand piano painted by Burne-Jones in 1890, almost 150 years after Handel had died. Ironically, the one person who did spot this was Andrew Lloyd-Webber, who had then tried to buy the piano. But these are mere details, and as Ken Russell had once said to me with tremendous glee. 'Facts? Those bastard critics want everything!' And Osborne would absolutely have subscribed to that.

Finally, I thought I should make some effort at authenticity by showing that Handel, although 'British', had actually been born in Halle, then still in East Germany. I was astonished by the speed with which we got permission to film there, given the paranoia of that Stasi-controlled regime. It was not without its difficulties (to remove a 'No Entry' sign screwed into the wall of Handel's birthplace took a 'government permit' from Berlin and a specially deployed military unit of twenty conscripts to unscrew four bolts), however, the filming there was a joy. It was only on the last day that my Stasi 'minder' told me why. It was realised "by his superiors" that I had worked with The Beatles, so they hoped by giving me permission to film in Halle, I would be able to persuade the lads to give some concerts in East Germany. I promised to pass the message on, although I felt obliged to tell him that John Lennon was no longer available, having been killed five years earlier.

Looking back over forty years later, I can quite see why the film – released eventually worldwide on DVD to ecstatic reviews – had caused the purists to wet their pants. It was not the first time (nor would it be the last) that John Osborne had taken aim at an icon of 'British' culture, and come up with an altogether radical view of a national treasure. Osborne portrayed him for what he really was: a man who stood with his chin out, chest puffed in a bull-like stance, defiantly his own man, just like Osborne himself. Mackerras adored the film, and for a time I was told he went around slightly misquoting one of Handel's speeches from the film. Handel/Osborne/Trevor Howard says, with appropriate insouciance: 'What have I done for the Georges of England!?' Mackerras said: 'What have we done for the Handels of England!?' Rescued them, great Sir. Rescued them.

After all, the title of the film comes from a letter Osborne claimed Handel had written after a visit to the Tunbridge Wells Ladies' Music Circle, which group had invited him to hear 'their *Messiah*' only months before he died. 'I always thought it was my *Messiah*', Handel had written back. Anyway, off he went and suffered it for the first hour, what with the massed choirs of Tunbridge Ladies and, no doubt, a scratchy orchestra. Back home in Brook Street, he wrote a furious letter describing the appalling occasion, finishing with the immortal line: 'so God Rot Tunbridge Wells'. It was an 'Up yours' to all those who had used and abused him throughout a long life of struggling against the pricks. With this sentiment, all of us – Osborne, Mackerras, Trevor Howard and not least myself – would most definitely agree.

Jimmy Porter, in Osborne's final play, of which I directed the première in the London West End, should perhaps have the last word (well, he always did, didn't he?), not least because he accurately reflects my own feelings. 'Hope falters,' says Porter, 'but never fawns or crowds, stands in line or even waves. Even in dread and noise, my youthful noise, tamed, timid and commonplace, it strains for a snatch of harmony. All of which is maybe as unclear to you as it is to me, as I say it. Barking. An old trumpet played upon, but not playing. Hearing, but only in the head.'

'But coherence isn't all. Coherence, like the intellect of your friends, conceals as much as is revealed to the lost like me, who contemplate the wreckage. To be alone and *not* demand the light? Words, stupid words. Language, that only is goodness, gaiety, unapproved, unlegislated, unscaled. That is alone life, triumph, victory and dominium.'

'I am foolish. I must remember to breathe when I speak,' and wriggle your toes, as the Squire says in *The Seventh Seal.*

Chapter 18

Vaughan Williams

Most of us have a schoolmaster who, even if only in retrospect, has had a profound impact on the ways in which our lives and careers developed. I had two. The first was my History Master, Eric Warne. I suspect now he was probably gay, because he clearly loved his pupils in much the same way as did Hector in Alan Bennett's *The History Boys*. In fact, when I first saw that play, I believed Hector was modelled on Eric Warne. Both came from Yorkshire, for instance. At Cambridge, I had the opportunity to attend all of the lectures given by, and sit at the feet (literally) of Jack Plumb - J.H. Plumb, the great authority on Georgian England (the era of Handel, of course) – although this was not the subject I was supposed to be studying. I think he got fed up with my staring at him throughout the lectures because he asked me one day who I was. When I confessed, he laughed and said that Warne, of whom he knew (Warne was a brilliant bridge player; had they both worked at Bletchley Park during the Second War?), must have been a good influence. When Eric retired, he gave me his book of lecture notes, which I now treasure. In his minuscule handwriting, he wrote as a preface: 'Never forget, history always repeats itself, but with increasing horror.'

The second was my music teacher, Denis Fielder, whom I encountered at my second grammar school, the Cambridgeshire High School. Olivia Newton-John's father had once been headmaster. At that point in my life, I was not remotely interested in music, so why Fielder tolerated me is beyond belief. I know he thought I was a fairly lousy pupil; despite his best efforts, I never did master the subtleties of the instrument he chose for me, the trombone. Like others, I suffered frequently from his waspish tongue and formidable temper, both at school and as 3rd trombonist in his beloved Cambridge Philharmonic, of which he was the conductor. Later, I began to understand the reasons for his wrath, and grasped that the important lesson he had taught me was: Never put up with second best; never tolerate unprofessional behaviour; never give less than a hundred per cent.

Together with Roger Waters of Pink Floyd and Tony Fell, long-time managing director of Boosey & Hawkes, the music publishers, I sometimes reminisced about how lucky we had been to suffer at the hands of Denis. 'Music is never just notes on a page,' he always said, 'and any composer who tells you so is hiding something. Always ask yourself what the composer is trying to tell you, whether about himself or the world he lives in, because you can be damn certain that he does have something to say and wants you to hear it!' And whenever my films, whether about Stravinsky or Britten or Walton, ran into trouble – and they usually did, from the likes of 'Outraged of Tunbridge Wells', I needed only to remind myself of Denis's demand: first satisfy myself that I was right. Always search out the man (or woman) who is the artist, not the artist who also happens to be a man (or woman). 'Why does Callas sing as she does?' I remember Denis asking me, long before I worked with her. 'Because she is a woman who is in trouble; a woman who happens to be singer, not a singer who happens to be a woman. It is human beings who make art, not machines,' he told me. I came to realise that his profound humanity came in part from Denis's experiences as a prisoner of war, about which he never spoke, but which I now see infused his whole outlook on teaching, on music, and therefore on art itself. Later, I hope I was able to repay a little of the debt I knew I owed him, by introducing him to some of those artists to whom he had, in effect, introduced me, such as Britten and Walton. When Walton met Denis, for example, Walton actually thanked him for *my* film. It was a tearful moment, because Walton's gratitude was directed at the rightful recipient.

And it was Denis who took me, aged seventeen, to the funeral in Westminster Abbey of Ralph Vaughan Williams, 19 September 1958. Why or how he had come to be invited, I have no idea, and sometimes I'm not even sure if I haven't imagined the whole expedition. But if it is only a dream, well, dreams are often more real than reality itself. I know I was there, even if only in spirit. And I know that from that moment eventually sprang the wish to make a full-length film about this extraordinary man by 2008, in time for the fiftieth anniversary of his death.

I struggled for years to persuade anyone to commission such a film. Yet, after my film had become an international success, numerous commissioning editors claimed they had commissioned it. Most of them lied, one in particular then at Channel Four. But that's what they do. Best of all, after hammering at the door of the BBC until my fists bled, I received the following letter from the then Head of Music and Arts:

> 'Dear Mr Plamer *(sic)*,
> Thank you for your enquiry about the composer Mr. V Williams.
>
> Having looked at our own activity via the lens of *find, play & share*, we came to the conclusion that a film about Mr Williams would be not be appropriate at this time. This is essentially because we are in the process of reconstructing the architecture of bbc.co.uk so as to increase findability, and to do that we need to maximise the routes in to content.
>
> We must establish the tools that allow shared behaviours, and so harness the power of our audience and the network to make our content more findable. We have decided to take a radically new approach to our production processes to dramatically increase the number of programmes we support at little or no resource cost, and therefore free resources for projects of real ambition whether they are programme related or native to the web.
>
> So given that this is the new vision for Vision, you will understand why a film about Mr V. Williams such as you have proposed does not fit our remit. But good luck with the project, and do let me know if Mr V. Williams has an important première in the future [he had died in 1958] as this findability might allow us to reconsider.
>
> Yours sincerely'

I was told later that the letter was. in fact, a hoax, penned by a disgruntled member of that department who wished to see the incumbent Head of Department junked. But in view of the steady destruction of a once highly esteemed corner-stone of the BBC, its Music and Arts Department, together with its remit to inform, educate and entertain, I can see why that person was disgruntled. God knows what he or she would make of it now. *The Traitors* music at The Proms? Fifty years of *Bohemian Rhapsody*? *Star Wars*? All profoundly second-rate. Nothing wrong with them in themselves, perhaps, but as part of 'the greatest classical music festival in the world', according to the BBC, and in place of dozens of other composers who can't get a look in? Presenter-led mashups of potted musical history which assume the audience is too stupid to follow any slightly complicated argument? Dramatised Mozart in slow motion? Endless repeats of fifty-year-old programmes, which even in their day were thought old-fashioned? The existence of the Proms, often remarkable in content, is always used as the excuse for the shoddy representation of classical music during the rest of the year. When Director-General Tony Hall arrived in 2013, he announced that 'music was in the DNA of the BBC', but then he did little to prove it. Gone are the days when classical music was celebrated for what it is: one of the finest creations of Western civilisation over the last 500 years.

Which brings me back to Vaughan Williams, whose nine symphonies were programmed at the Proms most years. Of course, he was not black, nor was he transgender, or female, or hosted by a mop-topped nonentity 'star', so no such boxes could be ticked on his CV. And he was thought somewhat old-fashioned, as was suggested in my hoax BBC letter above. But for me, he was a colossus who bestrode the English musical landscape in the twentieth century. Every aspect of musical life stood in his shadow. He kicked into life the National Youth Orchestra; what became The Arts Council; and what became the BBC's Third Programme, now Radio 3. He wrote music for some of the most iconic films of his day, including *Scott of the Antarctic.* He supported his fellow composers, for example Alan Bush, who was a strong and convinced Communist all his life. When the BBC said that as a consequence they were going to ban his music, Vaughan Williams told them if they did that, then they could do without *his* music. He would not allow any of it to be broadcast.

And when Michael Tippett was arrested as a conscientious objector, Vaughan Williams stood up for him at his trial and said, 'I don't believe in his opinions at all, but I believe in his right to have them.' Even more surprising, was an event at the 1936 Norwich Festival, where Vaughan Williams's choral suite, *Five Tudor Portraits,* was to have its first performance. In the same concert was also to be the first performance of the twenty-three-year old Benjamin Britten's song cycle *Our Hunting Fathers.* But the orchestra, the London Philharmonic, was having a rough time with the Britten score, making jokes about it and misbehaving as only orchestras can do. Apparently, Vaughan Williams became furious with them and said, 'Either you give this young man a chance and play his music properly, or I shall withdraw my own piece.'

'He was a seer, a visionary really,' Michael Kennedy, Vaughan Williams's biographer and amanuensis, told me. 'I don't believe that he would have entirely said the outlook for mankind was hopeless, but I think he feared it might be. What he wrote was increasingly preoccupied with questions of despair and death, but those questions had been there in his music from the very beginning.' I knew then this was a subject, and a man, who must command my attention.

So who was this man who had come to obsess me? Stephen Johnson, a notable and wise music critic, pointed me, I think, in the right direction, quite different from the absurd BBC documentaries (there are such) which portrayed Vaughan Williams as a semi-rustic, roly-poly figure leaning over the proverbial country gate muttering garbage. Johnson said that, for him, the quality that came over most remarkably about Vaughan Williams was his courage, and that rang a bell for me immediately.

'If you think about that pastoral idyll he celebrated in *The Lark Ascending*, clearly, there's an elegiac character,' Johnson told me. 'But I think it's an elegy for a vanished idea of the English countryside as Eden, as John Osborne had argued; that the pastoral life was one that would go on for ever and ever. I think Vaughan Williams maybe hoped that it would at first, but I think he became pretty sure that it wouldn't. That an irrevocable change was happening. And therefore there is a sense of him in his music contemplating the worst that might befall. The possibility that there is no meaning; that there is no answer; that there will be no vision in the moment of death which explains our life to us, no reconciliation with God. The unknown region maybe just emptiness or nothingness. This little life is rounded with something possibly even worse than a sleep.'

Ouch.

After all, *The Lark Ascending*, one of Vaughan Williams's most popular works, was written on a hill overlooking Margate as he watched boats being loaded with troops at the outset of the First World War, troops going off to be slaughtered. Is the music, in fact, a lament for them?

Just as had happened when I had made my film about Stravinsky, I managed to get to numerous rather elderly people who had known the composer before it was too late. Many were in their nineties and older; Roy Douglas, his copyist, was 104. Many were, sadly, dead within a year of my completing the film.

Vaughan Williams was born in 1872, the youngest of three children in the village of Down Ampney in Gloucestershire. His mother was the daughter of Josiah Wedgwood, the porcelain manufacturer, and a niece of Charles Darwin, and his father was the vicar of the parish church. 'Down Ampney is awful,' Belinda Norman-Butler, a family friend, great-granddaughter of Thackeray the novelist, and a mere hundred years old, told me. 'It's so flat. There's a very stark church; about 1850 I think. And as for the vicarage; an equally miserable house. It's all really pathetic. Dreadful. And there weren't any trees. Stark. It wasn't even a proper village. It was really too depressing. Apparently one day he asked his mother about Uncle Charles Darwin. 'What is all the fuss about?' She replied, "Well, you see, my dear, the Bible says that the world was created in seven days, and great uncle Charles thinks it took rather longer."'

When he was two, his father had died, and the family had to leave the vicarage and move to the Wedgwood family house in Leith Hill, near Dorking in Surrey, which became his home for the next forty years. He was educated at Charterhouse Public School. His Aunt Ettie, a Darwin, wrote to his mother to say, 'That foolish young man who will go on working at music when he's so hopelessly bad at it. He's been fiddling all this life [he was learning to play the viola] and still he can't play the simplest thing decently.'

Nonetheless, from Charterhouse Vaughan Williams was eventually sent off to the Royal College of Music, where he met a fellow pupil named Gustav Holst. 'They were different types of people altogether in personality,' Michael Kennedy told me, 'But the thing they obviously shared was a total honesty with each other and frankness. They showed each other their music and Holst would say, "This is rubbish" or "You ought to do this", and Vaughan Williams would say to him, "Something wrong there". They trusted each other implicitly.'

'Holst told me,' Vaughan Williams remembered, 'we have so much to contend with in England to escape the German influence in music, and there's no one to help us. Holst said, "Maybe we should go into training, as it were, to become truly English; so we mustn't get old for the next forty years because we have such a stiff job to do."' Even twenty years after Holst's death, Vaughan Williams still had a photograph of him in his bedroom. 'I felt lost without Holst to advise me,' he would say.

He even wrote to Elgar asking for lessons in orchestration. Lady Elgar replied that Sir Edward was too busy. 'In fact, the first time I had a conversation with Elgar was many years later,' Vaughan Williams later recalled, 'on the occasion of a performance of his *Cello Concerto*. He approached me and said, "I'm surprised, Dr. Vaughan Williams, that you care to listen to my vulgar stuff." He added that he wished us to be on Christian name terms and invited me to call him Teddy. This I could not do.'

After a spell at Cambridge University - he read history 'to get myself a proper education' - he went back to the Royal College to complete his musical education with the Professor of Composition, Sir Charles Villiers Stanford. 'Damnably ugly, me boy. Why do you write such things?' Stanford said. 'Because I like them.'

'But you can't like them. They're not music.'

He once showed Stanford a movement of a quartet which had caused him hours of agony in composing.

'All rot, me boy,' was Stanford's only comment.

He then got a job as an organist in South Lambeth, in London, in spite of having 'very large feet', according to David Willocks, organist and Director of Music at King's College Cambridge — and pupil, incidentally, of my erstwhile *War Requiem* companion, Douglas Fox. 'It was the only paid job I'd ever had,' Vaughan Williams remarked ruefully. 'In South Lambeth!'

'He was one of the best looking men I've ever known,' the ninety-two-year-old Simona Pakenham, historian, distant relative of Lord Longford and old family friend of Vaughan Williams, told me. 'So attractive. I remember a Christmas party once, and as I looked round the room I saw there were a lot of disconsolate looking groups of men talking to each other. And there was Ralph sitting on a sofa; at the back there were about five women leaning over him, two on either side of him, and another five sitting in front of him. All the males at the party were being completely ignored in favour of Ralph.'

'He loved dirty stories,' Michael Kennedy added. 'And he definitely loved female company. He loved good food and wine. He and I both loved rather slushy puddings, and I can remember once we had a lovely ice-creamy one and he said, 'It would be much better with this,' and he got some liqueur and poured it all over it. He was very fond of one of the London Steak Houses for a meal. And once a group of students came in who recognised him, I presume from the Royal College.

And they said, "Good evening."

"And where have you been?" he asked them.

And one of them said, "Oh, *only* to *Madam Butterfly*."

And he just looked at them and said, "When you can write a work" - and he probably didn't like Puccini all that much - but he said, "When you can write a work like that, then you can say, *'only' Madam Butterfly*."'

'I must say he shocked me more than once,' Belinda Norman-Butler told me. 'We were all brought up rather restrained, as it were. Once I was at the Festival Hall with him, and we were all having a cup of coffee when a very pretty young girl came by, and Uncle Ralph stopped her and said, "How's your love life going?" This sort of thing my father wouldn't have dreamt of saying in public.'

He dressed appallingly. 'Sort of farmer-like clothes,' remembered the eighty-nine-year-old Rachel Fardon, secretary of the Leith Hill Music Festival, of which Vaughan Williams was the founding father and conductor for over fifty years. 'He always had slippers, probably his bedroom slippers. If you didn't know who he was, you would mistake him as a farmer. In a way, we took him for granted, like a sort of Father Christmas. During the Second World War he was often found cleaning public lavatories in Dorking. We just saw this man shuffling about as he did, calling door to door collecting for the Red Cross. A penny a week. And then he would go out with the salvage collectors in torn jumpers and pork pie hat. He was the any-old-iron-man, collecting iron for the war effort. I must say, however, that sometimes he had a very bad temper. If things didn't go well in rehearsal, he lost his temper very badly. And on one occasion he lost his temper and shouted, "I've told you a hundred times never to watch me!"'

'He loved to travel on the London Underground,' Belinda Norman-Butler remembered. 'And I said, "You know, there are lots of people who would drive you. *I'd* drive you." And he said, "Well, it's so easy, Belinda. You could get along, you know, on the trains. And if I was driving, I would have to think about driving." I'm not sure he ever did drive very much, did he?' Eighty-year-old Robert Armstrong, Mrs Thatcher's Cabinet Secretary, told me that Vaughan Williams had decided to go to a rehearsal of some kind one morning, 'And we put him in a taxi to take him there, and made him swear to come back in a taxi. But he arrived back with a black eye, because he had decided to come back in the Underground and had slipped or fallen on the escalator, as a result of which he'd got a black eye. And somebody said, "How did you get that black eye, Ralph?" And he said, "Oh I had a spot of bother with an escalator."'

Not all composers have beautiful handwriting in their manuscripts as did Mozart or Shostakovich. Vaughan Williams's handwriting was truly appalling. The 104-year-old Roy Douglas, for years Vaughan Williams's long-suffering musical assistant and copyist, told me, 'It was bad even when he was very young, but it got worse and worse and worse and was completely indecipherable in the end. He occasionally sent postcards to friends, who would then ring me up to have them 'interpreted'. I have a feeling he was left-handed. In the 1880s, when he was born, and indeed in the 1920s when his career took off, you weren't allowed to write left-handed. I thought at one time I was perhaps the only person in the world who could read his music and his handwriting.'

'He also used to send me extraordinary letters,' Douglas went on. '"Dear Douglas," he wrote. "I have been foolish enough to write another symph. Could you undertake to vet and then copy the score? If in the course of this you have any improvements to suggest, I would receive them with becoming gratitude." Then a few months later he wrote, "Herewith FS, full score, and PFT arrangement of symph. Please, one: correct all actual errors of notes, etcetera. Two, correct all obvious errors of judgement" – who was I to do that? – "Three, all other cases which may be a matter of opinion but which you think are wrong, make a list. I shall value your opinion very much." Often he'd get a group of half a dozen people together, and I would then play the new symphony through on the piano. And then tea or coffee would be served, and he'd say, "What do you think of it? Is it all right? Is any of it worth keeping?"'

Although my film was never an attempt to make a linear, straightforward biography of a great man, there were three events which seemed to colour everything I was told. First, of course, it is well known that with Holst, Cecil Sharp and Maud Karpeles, he began to collect folk songs from Essex and Suffolk in particular. But, as Maud Karpeles pointed out, 'Their love of folksong was bound up with their love of England and the English countryside. But this was not just nostalgic romanticism. We believed that England's greatness lay in the future as well as in the past. And many of our songs which had come down to use through past generations, would live on in their own right as supreme works of art. Indeed, there are occasional moments when it's difficult to disentangle what is folk and what is Vaughan Williams. When he was asked whether a certain tune was his own or a folk tune, he replied, with a mischievous twinkle in his eye, "Well, it hasn't been collected yet."'

Second, was a strange meeting at his house in Barton Street, Westminster, when a hansom cab drove up to his door and a Mr Dearmer was announced. According to Vaughan Williams's own account, 'I knew his name as a parson who invited tramps to sleep in his drawing room, and I wondered whether he was going to ask me to do the same. But he had not come to me to talk about tramps. He came straight to the point and asked me to edit a new musical hymn book. I protested that I knew very little about hymns, but he told me that a committee of eight clerics between them had put down five pounds each for expenses and my part of the work would probably take two months.

'After thinking it over I decided to accept, only to find that the work occupied me two years. Contrary to my principles, I contributed a few tunes of my own, but with becoming modesty I attributed them to my old friend Mister Anon.'

Of course 'Mister Anon's' hymn tunes soon became universally known and loved; *For All The Saints, He Who Would Valiant Be,* to name only two. And the impact he had was made clear to me by the then Archbishop of Canterbury, Rowan Williams. 'At the end of the nineteenth century, there were quite a number of especially High Church Anglicans who were very dissatisfied with the philistinism of the Victorian era, as they saw it, in religious matters. They felt that religious music available to people was dull and sentimental. That somehow you had to fight your way through the Victorian undergrowth into a rather wider horizon, which for them meant relating to the Christian tradition before the Reformation. So what *The English Hymnal* did was make available straight away a great treasury of medieval music, beautifully arranged by Vaughan Williams. He understood his role as someone who was reviving and revitalising a native tradition. Turning things around from the situation where we were called a nation without music.'

'I think the Church of England has a huge amount to be thankful for,' added the Archbishop. 'I'm not sure if it's appropriate to canonise agnostics, but maybe for his contribution I think we owe him a great deal.'

The fury this new English Hymnal provoked surprised Vaughan Williams. The Times, 5 July 1907, wrote: 'The Archbishop of Canterbury states that after careful examination of the English Hymnal he feels bound to express his strong wish that it should *not* be adopted in any church in the diocese. His objection is that it contains hymns which appear to express doctrines contrary to the spirit and traditions of a Church of England.' The Bishop of Winchester wrote, 'It is greatly to be deplored that there have been admitted into this collection hymns containing invocations of the Blessed Virgin!'

All this came to fruition in one extraordinary month in 1910. In October came the première in Leeds of Vaughan Williams's First

Symphony, the choral *A Sea Symphony*: he, conducting on his thirtieth birthday, terrified of it, and being told by the timpanist, 'Don't worry about us, Mr Williams. Just give us a good four in a bar and we'll get you through it.' Miraculously, he effectively pulled together all he'd experienced so far – the great Anglo-Catholic church hymns, brilliant orchestration learnt especially from Ravel, and a celebration of England itself. The words were by the then relatively unknown American poet Walt Whitman, whose work had been recommended to him in the 1890s while still at Cambridge by a fellow student, Bertrand Russell. It is a profoundly passionate and spiritual work:

Swiftly I shrivel at the thought of God
At Nature and its wonders,
Time and Space and Death…

And a few weeks earlier, in Gloucester Cathedral, had come the première of a work with which he will forever be associated, the *Fantasia on a Theme by Thomas Tallis*. But what is this work really about? Glorious and uplifting spirituality? Stephen Johnson doesn't find it cosy or consoling at all. 'From the very first chords, those magical opening chords; they're almost a direct quotation from his cantata *Towards the Unknown Region*, which is about death. After all, how does the Tallis Hymn No 92 from Vaughan Williams's own English Hymnal on which the Fantasia is based begin?

"When rising from the bed of death
O'erwhelm'd with guilt and fear,
I see my Maker face to face,
O how shall I appear.
If yet while pardon may be found…"'

This was definitely not the Vaughan Williams who, leaning on a garden gate, mumbles banalities about folk songs – an image beloved of BBC documentary makers. We can now hear this music as a cry of pain, a warning of things to come.

And that was the third of the events I mentioned above: the First World War. Given his social background – Lord Bertrand Russell, Maynard Keynes, Darwin, Wedgewood, Virginia Woolf and the Bloomsburys – Vaughan Williams would surely have qualified for the officer class had he chosen. But no; he volunteered for the regular army. Luckily, his poor heath disqualified him as a front line soldier, and he was conscripted into the Ambulance Corps. As it turned out, however, the shock was profound. Can you imagine a man from his privileged background having to pick up bits of bodies, half a skull, a leg, an arm. He never spoke about his experiences in the war, I suspect because the effect on him had been so horrendous. Of his eight friends who had volunteered together, six were killed, including his fellow composer, George Butterworth. There's no doubt that the war left its ghastly and ghostly mark on all the music he wrote thereafter. The *Fantasia* is perhaps a lament, a cry of pain for the destruction of everything Vaughan Williams had believed in.

But there was another cry of pain, as I was slowly to discover. On 9 October 1897, three days before his twenty-fifth birthday, Ralph had married Adeline Fisher, in the parish church of Hove in Sussex. 'Everybody called her Aunt Adeline,' eighty-year-old Hervey Fisher, her great-nephew, recalled. 'She always seemed to be dressed in black. I don't remember any of her family dressing in gay colours. In my view the Fishers of that generation were a mad, although very distinguished family. One, Herbert, H.A.R., was Minister of Education in Lloyd George's cabinet and a great historian – an Order of Merit incidentally, just like Vaughan Williams himself. Another brother was Admiral of the Fleet. Another was Chairman of Barclays Bank. And Adeline's sister Florence was the daughter-in-law of Charles Darwin. Vaughan Williams's father, of course, had been a priest and the Fishers were also in the church. They were called 'Devines'. An awful lot of parsons. There was a Bishop of Salisbury, and at that time there were no less than five of his near relatives in the canonical pews of Salisbury Cathedral. The Fishers were also first cousins of the Vaughan family, one of whom, Dame Janet, became Principal of Somerville College in Oxford. And Adeline's niece, Mary, my great-aunt, was Principal of St Hilda's College. And if that was not enough, Adeline, who was also an amateur cellist, was also a cousin of the Stevens family, among whom was Virginia Woolf. They even looked alike.'

'I remember once being taken to see Virginia', the hundred-year-old Belinda Norman-Butler told me, 'and she looked at me for a long while, very pale and sad, and suddenly said, "Belinda. Do you love your parents?" Well, it's a very difficult question, especially if you're only seven, as I was.'

'They weren't like other people and said mostly nasty things about a lot of people,' Hervey Fisher told me. 'She once described my great-grandfather and his wife as being like "waxworks running in the sun". But they also had a way of always helping out when things went wrong. They wrote a booklet on *"How to Look After a Sick Room"*, with a whole chapter on "Crumbs in the Bed". How to get rid of crumbs from the bed!'

So this was the world that the young Vaughan Williams had now married into. It is clear that he was a very passionate man, so full of life, and by all accounts he was absolutely devoted to Adeline for almost fifty-four years of marriage. The tragedy was that for much of that time she was a cripple in a wheelchair. Vaughan Williams never admitted this in public, but that clearly must have crippled him in every other sense. Simona Pakenham said Adeline 'was more or less paralysed for nine tenths of their marriage. Poor darling, and he was so sweet to her. Carried her from room to room.'

'She was so very frail and disabled,' Lord Armstrong told me. 'And when they lived in Dorking, she couldn't really move from there. Even after a concert or an event in London he would walk the twenty-five miles back to Dorking to be with her.' And so her illness made Vaughan Williams withdraw from any active part of musical life. 'I think perhaps that finally broke him,' Simona Pakenham added. 'I mean, it was so awful because it went on and on. Of course if you live with an invalid, it's extremely taxing and trying, however many good helpers there are around. It probably wasn't even a marriage as we hope to understand it. And that's what seems to come out in the last symphonies for me, and also the earlier very angry Fourth Symphony. Is it rage against her, and his own, impotence? A cry of anguish that he is being stifled?'

In March 1938, at a traffic crossing, Vaughan Williams met the twenty-eight-year-old Ursula Wood, a poet who had been writing to him in the hope he would set to music a ballet scenario she'd written called, ironically, as it turned out, *The Bridal Day*. He was sixty-six at the time, and when Adeline finally died after the war they were married. Michael Kennedy doubted it had been love at first sight. 'He wasn't going to do anything to leave Adeline, and why should he? But how much Adeline knew, I don't know. There was certainly a pregnancy during the war, which Ursula had terminated. That was Ralph's. She told me so a long time ago. But I think she gave him whatever he had of happiness in his life. She always said, "I'm not a musician," but the amount she contributed to his life and, therefore, his creative life, is absolutely incalculable.'

And so on he went. An Eighth Symphony and, finally, a Ninth. As the ninety-five-year-old Ursula herself told me, 'Of course, Ralph was well aware that there were a lot of people who didn't like his work. This he knew was inevitable. It's a historical fact. Tastes change. And anyway, not everybody thinks alike. He became more and more aware of it toward the end of his life. And when his Ninth Symphony had some rather half-hearted, tepid, and really downright nasty notices, he said philosophically, "Well, they're probably fed up because I can still do it."'

But a few weeks after the première he died, and was buried in Westminster Abbey. It was not, in fact, a memorial service, as it has often been described, but the actual funeral service. The first for a commoner in Westminster Abbey for almost three hundred years. The last such funeral service, appropriately enough, had been for Henry Purcell, next to whom Vaughan Williams is now buried.

As the Archbishop Rowan Williams remarked later, 'I think there's an extraordinary deep spirituality in Vaughan Williams. It certainly isn't conventionally Christian, and I don't think he'd thank us for pretending that he was an orthodox believer. But I believe he recognised two things: that you couldn't understand the English musical tradition and English culture generally without the Christian church within it. And he recognised that religious music was something which articulated things that just were not articulated anywhere else.'

Stephen Johnson added, 'He knew there was something in religious experience. It wasn't just simply wish-fulfilment fantasy. That there was something about the human spirit here, even if there is no God. In his last works, Vaughan Williams is asking, Are we absolutely without hope? In *A Sea Symphony*, the soloists sing "Bathe me O God in Thee", "O Thou transcendent", "Sail forth. Steer for the deep waters". What if, when you get to the deep waters, you find only blackness? That is surely contained even in his early seminal works such as the *Tallis Fantasia*. And it went on throughout his creative life, mirroring the tragedy of his personal life. And finally, as he got older, he really did summon up the extraordinary courage to stare the truth of our existence in the face, even though it must have been acutely painful for him.'

My film was eventually commissioned by Channel FIVE, then known as the porn channel, in time for that fiftieth anniversary of Vaughan Williams's death in 2008. Although the commission had been for a fifty-five minute film, I was astonished when the channel agreed to show the entire film, almost two and a half hours long, and on New Year's Day in the afternoon. Press releases were prepared and approved, and we all went home for Christmas. Suddenly, between Christmas and New Year, an executive from FIVE called me to ask what had happened to my film? She had discovered that instead of it being programmed, as we had been told, for New Year's Day afternoon, it was now going to be transmitted at *9 o'clock in the morning* on New Year's Day, when, she assumed, most people would still be asleep. She, and I, were horrified. Later it was discovered that a 'scheduler', another disreputable tribe which plagues television, had thought that a long film about an obscure composer had no place on a popular channel like FIVE. Noticing that my film was almost the same length as the feature film *Last of The Pharaohs,* which had been originally scheduled for the morning slot, he had simply interchanged them. The last laugh was on him, however. Despite beginning at nine in the morning, my film achieved a record audience for FIVE that year. For the *Pharaohs* film, on the other hand, the audience was so low it could scarcely be measured. And the scheduler was never seen again.

'To suffer woes which hope thinks infinite; to forgive wrongs darker than death or night; To defy power which seems omnipotent. Neither to change, nor falter, nor repent. This is to be good, great and joyous, beautiful and free. This is alone Life, Joy, Empire and Victory.' Shelley's epitaph, used by Vaughan Williams as a prelude to his *Sinfonia Antartica,* was quoted at his funeral. I never met him, although by talking to his surviving, if elderly, close friends, I knew exactly what he meant, and felt that I had come to know him well. That's the adventure of making the films I do. Did I imagine I was at his funeral? Or was I really there? I do not know. But his music has guided me through this wretched existence and moved me profoundly. What Vaughan Williams represents is now as clear for me, as it was for Orson Welles as expressed in Shakespeare's Sonnet 43:

> '...when I sleep in dreams they look on thee,
> And darkly bright are bright in dark directed.'

Chapter 19

Wagner

It's four in the morning and the telephone rings. I should explain; the telephone is not by my left ear while I sleep, or attempt to, but several floors below in the rickety old farmhouse in the mountains where I always went to edit my films in peace and quiet. Brrr, brrr. God dammit. Don't they know it's my birthday?

Eventually, I stumble downstairs with the telephone still whining like a goat in labour. Yes?

'Sorry to disturb you,' says the voice, 'but I thought you should know the news.'

I recognise the voice; it's the producer of my film about Wagner which I'm struggling to edit, here in the mountains.

'I've just been telephoned myself by Harry Berens, the new chairman of our financiers. They've decided to cancel the whole film.'

I am now, suddenly, very wide awake.

'Cancel?'

'Yes, that's all he said. Cancel.'

I should explain. The film, titled *Wagner,* has as its leading players Richard Burton, Laurence Olivier, Vanessa Redgrave and John Gielgud; it has taken over seven months to film, in one hundred and fifty-three locations, in more or less every country of Europe; has been photographed by the triple Oscar winner Vittorio Storaro; has involved a massive logistical exercise with a technical crew drawn from nineteen different countries; has cost almost seven million pounds, of which ninety per cent has been expended with only the post production costs, editing, sound-mixing, final prints and so on still to come, and the whole thing is *CANCELLED*?

'Give me the bugger's phone number,' I yell down the phone. I knew I should not have seduced his wife.

'I'm sorry, I don't know his phone number,' the wretched producer complains. 'In any case, I think he rang from a phone box.'

'FROM A PHONE BOX?' I scream.

A cow starts mooing and clanking its infernal Swiss bell (I did say this was in the mountains). Clank. 'From a phone box?' I repeat sotto voce so as not to wake yet more cows. Clank. Clank. Too late. The whole herd is on the move. The last stampede. I know it. Actually, there are only six or seven cows, lumbering fat slobbering beasts who only want to clank and chew and couldn't give tuppence for Richard Burton or Richard Wagner, but it feels like more at this moment.

'Yes, Berens rang from a phone box to say the whole thing is cancelled. I did warn you. Being a City institution [London, that is], I was sure they were only interested in financing our film as some sort of complicated tax dodge. They never had any intention of seeing it through. Now that the film is almost finished and ready to go on sale, it's as if we have called their bluff. The *last* thing they want,' the producer said, 'is something they can *sell*, because if you have something you can sell, it will earn money, and if you've already written off the whole investment as a tax loss, you can't suddenly have it earning *money*!'

I refused to believe this nonsense. In any event, I have not spent almost seven years of my life struggling to get this film made only to have it all 'cancelled' from a phone box at four in the morning. Three years endlessly rewriting Charles Wood's script; another two years requesting, beseeching, begging and eventually borrowing the money to bring this eight-hour film to life; a further two years planning the great enterprise like a military campaign with the enemy waiting to shoot you down at every turn. Nor was I willing to see one of Richard Burton's finest screen performances go to waste; nor the golden moments in which Sir Laurence Olivier, Sir John Gielgud and Sir Ralph Richardson, the three great knights of the British stage appearing together on the silver screen for the first (and, as it turned out, the only) time; nor the frantic efforts of many hundreds of people to bring the film home on time and on budget. To have got all, or most, of the scenes safely filmed – in the can as it were – and all that remained was for the raw material to be edited and processed, and then to have it all cancelled, was absurd. But film making *is* absurd; it's not a profession for grown-ups, I had been repeatedly told. A profession peopled by children, who work hard and produce little, who profess to be interested in art but often cannot even spell the word.

The Wagner film had begun many years earlier over a drunken lunch in Düsseldorf with the composer's grandson. Wolfgang. The meeting had been arranged by John Culshaw, whom I had first met, albeit briefly, during the world première of Benjamin Britten's *War Requiem* and then later, when I worked as a tea-boy during his recording of Wagner's opera *Götterdämmerung* in the Sofiensaal in Vienna. Culshaw had been responsible for the first complete recording of Wagner's epic *The Ring*, subsequently acknowledged as being a revolutionary turning point in the development of recorded sound. With Sir Georg Solti and the Vienna Philharmonic Orchestra, Culshaw had advocated the simple proposition that a gramophone record should reflect the excitement of a live performance. In other words, Culshaw was committed to Wagner's own dictum, expressed in his will to his children and his children's children: *Make something new*!

When Culshaw later joined the BBC as Head of Music Television and rescued my film about pop music, *All My Loving*, our paths crossed again. 'Why not a film on Wagner?' he kept asking me. 'Because it is too vast,' I had replied, 'and no one will put up sufficient money to do it properly.' By 'properly', I meant on a wide screen, lots of music and a cast of thousands, and the BBC was not about to invest in an enterprise on that scale.

But now, almost a decade later, having had some minor success as an independent director, I felt confident enough to begin the ascent of Everest.

Wolfgang Wagner was one of the most direct and honourable men I have ever had to deal with. The fact that he spoke in short huffs and puffs and grunts in a Saxon dialect that was almost incomprehensible, even to his associates, did not detract from the force of his personality or the passion with which he could persuade you that you understood what he was talking about. 'Impossible, impossible!' he kept saying, as Culshaw and I told him of our plans. Actually, our 'plans' consisted of no more than informing him that we would shortly begin work on a script about his grandfather, and that it would be incredibly useful if he would agree to read it when it was finished and give us the benefit of his thoughts. After all, he *was* the composer's grandson; he had known his grandfather's only son, Siegfried; more, he had actually known his grandfather's widow, Cosima, who had personally known Ludwig of Bavaria, Nietzsche, von Bülow, Liszt and all the other incredible characters who had formed such an important part of Richard Wagner's life.

'Impossible, impossible!' Wolfgang kept repeating. 'You see, the difficulty is that if you were to tell the true story about my grandfather, no-one would believe you. Imagine. My grandfather is on the run – from his creditors, of course. He manages to find a boat at the port of Riga, and sets sail. A heavy fog comes down; the boat is lost. It drifts into a fjord, and Wagner hears the sound of horns echoing along the steep cliffs of the fjord. He writes down their call, which becomes the main theme of *The Flying Dutchman*. Fantastic, isn't it? But true, absolutely true. The trouble is that if you showed that as a scene from your film, you would be accused of exaggeration. Also, if my grandfather were alive today,' Wolfgang concluded, 'the only place in which he would be content – because it might give him the chance to realise all his dreams – would be Hollywood.'

And so, armed with this inspirational advice, Culshaw, Charles Wood and I began work on the script. Another piece of advice Wolfgang had given us would stand us in good stead as the years wore on. 'You will find', he had told us, 'that the world is full of Wagner experts. They can tell you exactly what my grandfather had for breakfast on the second Tuesday after the fourth Thursday of any month of the year, and even how long he had asked for the egg to be cooked. To this universal rule, however, there is one exception. Myself. The composer's grandson. I have no idea what he had for breakfast,' said Wolfgang, 'and nor do I care.'

Wolfgang eventually turned out to be a true friend of the project, correcting various factual mistakes we made as we went along, giving us permission to film in his grandfather's theatre in Bayreuth – the 'temporary structure' his grandfather had built of wood in 1875–76 and still standing, allowing us to read him the entire finished script, with Wood and myself reading all four hundred and sixty pages and playing all the parts. 'Just a moment,' said Wolfgang at one point. 'That bit is not correct. At least, I don't think so. Wait while I make a phone call.' Whereupon Wolfgang bounded over to a telephone and, after a short pause, said, 'Frau Liszt? Here is Herr Wagner…' Richard Wagner, of course, had married Liszt's daughter, so the present Frau Liszt was Wolfgang's cousin.

Wolfgang even allowed me to talk to his mother, the formidable Winifred, the friend of Hitler who, as a result of an unfortunate television film in which she had spoken admiringly of her relationship with Uncle Wolf, as young Adolf was known, was no longer on speaking terms with *any* members of her family, including her younger son. She had known Wagner's widow, Cosima, and this seemed to me another a vital link to the past.

Wolfgang, on the other hand, of whom there are various famous photos arm in arm with Uncle Wolf, quite cheerfully told me what he could remember. One particular occasion stuck in his mind. Uncle Wolf had been staying in Wahnfried, the Wagner family home at Bayreuth, during the summer of 1939. The following morning, Wolfgang and his elder brother Wieland had set off for school. About an hour later, they heard a mighty roar of trucks and motorcycles approaching and then surrounding the school, followed by a tremendous clatter of infantry with guns at the ready. Eventually, a senior officer marched into the little Bayreuth classroom, saluted a 'Heil Hitler' and asked Herr Wagner to stand up. The eleven- year-old Wolfgang had leapt to attention, no doubt scared out of his wits. The senior officer came over and removed all of Wolfgang's study books, which were later returned except for his geography book which, he now remembered, had contained an atlas that had been curiously defaced with little black squiggles all over Germany's eastern border with Poland. It was not until some years after, that Wolfgang realised his school atlas had been used by Hitler to plan the invasion of Poland. No wonder the schoolroom had been surrounded; it had contained state secrets of the most explosive kind!

The problem of casting our film proved almost as explosive. Vanessa Redgrave had always been first choice for the formidable Cosima, and I longed to persuade her to accept so that I could take her to Bayreuth and introduce her to Winifred.

I sent her a draft script. I sent flowers. I appealed by letter and telephone. All to no avail. She said she was too busy. Then, one Saturday afternoon, while I was watching a football match, I was summoned from the terraces over the intercom. My secretary had just received a phone call from Vanessa. Would I go round, now, for tea? The introductions were brief; *The Ride of the Valkyries* was rumbling away on a cassette player in the kitchen. 'I will do your part,' Vanessa said without any further small talk, 'but it will cost you a lot of money.' Before I could protest that ours was not exactly a big-budget film, she waved me down and went on: 'I need a million dollars. Nine hundred and fifty thousand for the party, and fifty thousand for me.' The party? Ah yes, the Workers Revolutionary Party, a Marxist organisation of which Vanessa and her clever brother Corin were co-chairs. I said I would think about her offer, and fled.

Persuading the beautiful Swiss actress Marthe Keller to take part was equally fraught. We met in a fashionable restaurant in London to discuss her role as Mathilde Wesendonck, Wagner's mistress and probable inspiration for *Tristan and Isolde*. I was in the middle of explaining a difficult scene (she said she had already read and approved the script) in which she is seen naked, wading through a glade in the forest. *A dream sequence*, I remember hearing myself say, when she suddenly leaned across the table and asked me if I would mind telephoning her apartment in Paris. 'Not at all,' I replied. 'You see,' she said, 'I left in a hurry that afternoon and had forgot to feed my two cats.'

'Oh, right,' I said. 'And who will answer the phone?'

'Oh, one of the cats,' she replied. 'Please tell them I'm very sorry and that there's plenty of food on the second shelf of the refrigerator.'

I don't think I dropped the spoon I was holding, but I must have looked puzzled, not to say surprised, because she was suddenly asking me if I was alright as I looked distinctly pale. Then she said, 'Here's the telephone number,' breezily thrusting a piece of paper at me, and I dutifully rose from the table and went off in search of a phone. I dialled the number, and…waited. Alas, there was no reply. The cats must have been sleeping, I thought, and returned to the table. Marthe smiled. I smiled. 'Fine, fine,' I mumbled. 'No problem.'

But Marthe was never one to forget a favour. Months later, we decided to film the nude scene with doubles, principally because Burton, although perfectly willing to be filmed nude, was worried that the camera would show the scars on his back resulting from a recent operation for a trapped nerve. In the event the scene, although shot with doubles, certainly looked as if it were Burton and Marthe Keller and it was, by general agreement, very powerful emotionally and psychologically. The music of *Tristan and Isolde* that accompanied the scene is, after all, some of the sexiest music ever written.

But when Marthe Keller saw the film, she blew a fuse. In fact, she blew every fuse in the building. 'The scene was disgusting and/or pornographic; she knew nothing of this,' she said (had she not read the script?), 'and it was all a cheap publicity stunt. To use doubles was also an insult to her craft and to her.' (Was she saying that the double's body was *more* beautiful than hers, or *less* beautiful? I never figured it out.) She threatened the film with a legal injunction unless this offensive scene was removed and all copies of the material destroyed. At that point in the production the men with the money were terrified of bad publicity, so they ordered me to cut the scene. Which I did, but naturally I kept copies of the material. After all, I was sure the cats had not been consulted, and they should at least be given the opportunity to voice their opinion.

By comparison, persuading Richard Burton had been easy, since the part of Richard Wagner, who could out-drink, out-talk, and out-wench any man alive (or, at least, so he boasted), was so akin to the mythical Richard Burton that eventually I was not quite sure who was playing whom. I have read various accounts of our first meeting, all by people who were not present: that he was variously drunk, naked, or incoherent. In fact, he was so polite (insisting on calling me Mr Palmer), stone-cold sober, and wearing curiously high-heeled white shoes. I remember I had a cold, and his then wife Susan insisted I drink a foul concoction she called raspberry juice: 'Don't worry,' Burton told me, 'I drink it all the time and look what it's done for me.'

'I shall look upon it all as a challenge,' he said as I left, little realising that the experience would change both our lives. During the filming, Burton asked me why I had chosen him to play Wagner. 'Ah,' I replied. 'First, you are both called Richard; second, you both have the gift of the gab, even if some of the 'stories' are somewhat exaggerated. Third, you both drink rather more than is wise. Fourth, you both clearly have a way with the ladies, far too many of them, in my view. And last, you are both touched with genius.'

'Ah,' Richard grunted.

Luckily he did not ask me about all the other 'stuff', as he put it. Wagner was a monster: a vegetarian, occasionally; a braggart; a thief; a liar; a scoundrel...and so on. Richard Burton was none of those things. Nor was he the rabid antisemite of his namesake. We cannot blame Wagner for Hitler. But when Hitler said that Wagner's opera *Parsifal* was his favourite musical work, Hitler saw very clearly that *Parsifal* was a codification of Wagner's racial theories. What Wagner did was very, very dangerous, because his work, his mind, eventually contributed to a dreadful turn of events. Hitler's racial theories owed so much to Wagner that it's often very hard to separate one from the other. Hitler, at times, adopted Wagnerian prose, so that his style and his vocabulary were Wagnerian.

Parsifal – of which I directed the Russian première at the Mariinsky Theatre in St Petersburg in 1997, conducted by Valery Gergiev (it had never been fully staged before in Russia) – is often represented as the ultimate 'Christian' opera. People often believe that they're going to an 'Easter experience', but the opera has nothing to do with Easter, and

Parsifal has nothing to do with Christianity as preached by the Roman Catholic Church or any of the major Protestant churches. Nothing at all. Wagner takes the Communion service and gives it a new context. People still believed what Wagner thought was a terrible error: that Christ was a Jew. So Parsifal's blood had to be purified. When Wagner wrote his pamphlet, *Judaism in Music*, in the 1850s, he said there was just a possibility for Jews to become human beings. But by the time he reissued his pamphlet in 1869, he said it was impossible. This what he wrote: 'The Jew is repulsive...He rules and will continue to rule as long as money remains the power. The Jew has come to dominate public taste in music. So join in this bloody battle. Redeem yourself from the curse that weighs upon you!'

Few great actors in my experience have been so unfairly represented in their public image as has Richard Burton. Drunk, a wastrel, uncontrollable, unprofessional, besotted with glamour and wealth - these are just a few of the more generous epithets dumped on him. I made a film about him soon after he died in 1984, just in time to capture on film all his surviving siblings - he was the twelfth of thirteen children - especially his eldest sister Cecilia, 'Cis', who, after the death of their mother when Richard was two, had brought him up. What I learned from them was the horror of working down the coal mines, as their father had done, and the determination of the young Welsh-speaking Richard Jenkins that this would never be his fate. Later, as his fame and wealth increased, he never forgot his extended family; indeed, at one point he had over thirty family members on his 'payroll'.

But this 'escape' from the mining community of Pontrhydyfen in South Wales came at a considerable price. His father (Walter Jenkins) effectively 'sold' him, for money, to the local schoolmaster, Philip Burton, who changed young Richard's name and attempted to adopt him. The film *Mr Burton* demeaned Philip Burton almost to a wimp who had failed to get his 'scripts' accepted by the BBC. In fact, Philip Burton became a full-time BBC Features producer, with almost 500 broadcasts to his name, and later became a distinguished lecturer in the United States about Shakespeare; one of the many inaccuracies in that feeble film.

Meanwhile, Richard Burton's prodigious talent and good looks propelled him, thanks to the intervention of Lauren Bacall and her husband Humphrey Bogart, who had seen him as Henry V in Stratford-upon-Avon (not mentioned in *Mr Burton*), into Hollywood - a world wholly alien. That he was transformed from a scruff who earned money by collecting coal lumps from the scrap heaps around his village into one of the most famous actors in the world before he was twenty-five, was nothing short of miraculous.

But, as he told me, he hated his voice, hated his face, hated everything about himself. Not disliked; *hated*. As the great American director Mike Nichols (*Who's Afraid of Virginia Woolf*) told me, 'Richard was a man cut off from his past, a man for whom "seeming" became more real than "being".'

Paradoxically, for someone who lived most of his life in the public eye, Burton was shy, deferential, courteous and absurdly generous. He certainly knew about good food and wine. During the nine months I worked with him, I had a beautiful girl friend, to whom Richard clearly took a shine. One day he asked me if I could beg a favour of her next time she came on location. Fearing the worst, I hesitated to answer.

'What?' I asked nervously.

'Next time she visits,' said Richard, 'please ask her to bring me some kippers.'

As his godson Brook Williams told me, 'If Richard passed through your life, even if you had only worked with him for a day or even half a day, he lit something in you that I don't think ever went out.' Yes, he was wild, passionate, literate, incredibly well read (he once boasted he could recite any of Shakespeare's sonnets by heart, backwards! And he could!), but he was riddled with self-doubt. So why did he agree to make my enormous film about Wagner for comparatively little money? I believe he wanted to stick two fingers up to all those who said he was a wasted actor who had sold his soul to Hollywood. He wanted to show what he was capable of, which in his view no-one could match.

A bigger challenge was securing the services of the three grand old men of British theatre, Oliver, Gielgud and Richardson. Charles Wood had written various scenes for Ludwig of Bavaria's principal ministers, Pfordten, Pfistermeister and Pfeufer, almost in the manner of farce, as these three old codgers chewed the cud over the waywardness of their 'young king'. In one particular scene, for example (a scene which had almost given Wolfgang a seizure at our 'read through' as he had laughed so much), the three ministers were sitting in a coffee shop, supposedly in Munich, Ludwig's capital city. After bemoaning the cost to the Munich exchequer of Wagner and all his works – his silk clothes, his new house, his new music school – Pfistermeister (played by Gielgud) comes to the heart of the matter. Rocking back in his chair, holding a cup of coffee delicately between his forefinger and thumb,

Gielgud looks at the other two and says, with a sigh, 'And then there is this Ring thing,' referring, of course, to Wagner's great tetralogy *The Ring of the Nibelung*. 'Ring Thing' translates into German as 'Ring Ding', so, ever thereafter, Wolfgang referred to the film (and me) as 'Ring Ding'.

But when it came to actually filming this 'Ring Ding' scene, Gielgud merely holding a cup of coffee delicately between his forefinger and thumb and speaking the line is not what happened. As the line was such an obvious scene-stealer, there was no way in which the other two - Olivier and Richardson - were going to hand the scene to Gielgud on a plate, or even a coffee cup. First, Richardson would not sit still; he insisted on bouncing out of his chair and making for a non-existent pool table moments before Gielgud delivered the line. Then Olivier succeeded in manoeuvring himself right behind Gielgud's head and making all manner of funny faces (all absolutely in character, he assured me) just before Gielgud spoke. A more shameless example of upstaging on the part of Olivier and Richardson it was hard to imagine. Was this the secret of their unique partnership, of which one had read so much?

Round one to Olivier. But Richardson had his revenge. In a later scene, the three were theoretically watching an awards ceremony that was being presided over by the king, Ludwig II. Once more they are complaining, this time about the 'young boy's inattention to his royal duties'. Richardson is explaining to the other two that the problem lies in the king's unfortunate choice of a new minister for war, Lutz. Richardson, in all the rehearsals, refused (or forgot) to get the man's name right. Thus: Litz, Letz, Latz and similar variations. At first, this merely irritated Olivier and Gielgud, who alternately corrected the apparently forgetful Richardson. Each time Richardson apologised, and promised to get it right next time. Finally, we decided to film the little scene. Fingers crossed, here we go, and Richardson says with a smile, 'The trouble is, the new war minister, Benteelheimer...'

'Oh, for God's sake,' Gielgud shouted at me, 'Can't you get rid of that man?'

A film on the scale of *Wagner* obviously involves the talents and skills of an enormous range of personnel, from scenic artists to costume designers, from hairdressers to location caterers. The difficulty, from a director's or a producer's standpoint, is that each person arrives on location or in the studio early each morning with their individual problem, which usually has nothing to do with the work in hand: a row with the wife/husband/girlfriend/lover; a nasty letter from the bank manager; a hangover; a stomach ache.

And it is the director's job, in part, to motivate this crowd of over a hundred people into a fighting unit capable of providing the right atmosphere in which the actor or actress can give their best. Because, never forget that the actor or actress, no matter how famous or experienced, is usually terrified out of their wits by having to 'perform' in front of such an audience – in fact in front of *any* audience. And never forget also that this gaggle of workers come from widely different backgrounds: some are illiterate; some are totally ignorant of anything cultural except Donald Duck and Mickey Mouse; equally, some are more knowledgeable about film and film history than you or I will ever be; some speak sixteen languages fluently, so why the hell have they finished up moving scenery? Some are pleased to be working on this particular film and some delight in telling you – frequently – that they are doing you a favour. All, however, feel that their particular job is the one on which the entire film depends. I do not scorn this attitude; without such an attitude, many of their jobs would be intolerable. But sometimes this attitude can have unfortunate consequences.

We had much difficulty, for example, in casting the role of Ludwig II, not least because the real nineteenth century Ludwig had towered over the real nineteenth century Wagner. Ekkehard Schall, Brecht's son-in-law and the great leader of the Berliner Ensemble, told me he did not need any 'assistance'. Schall, who was a very short man, played Franz Liszt, a very tall man, but his presence and his bearing on the film set were so powerful that, somehow, you convinced yourself that Schall was, in fact, much taller than he was. Burton, on the other hand, although by no means small, always insisted on wearing shoes with built-up heels to increase his height. The shoes were uncomfortable, and his stature as an actor was more than sufficient to compensate for what he thought of as lack of physical height. It was pure vanity. But it didn't help with the problem of finding a *taller* Ludwig.

I had already found a remarkable Swiss actor who *looke*d like Ludwig, could act most of his fellows off the stage, but he was *shorter* than Burton. As the commencement date for principal photography grew ever closer, I was forced to offer him the job on condition that I would go on looking for a taller alternative until the last possible moment. And, of course, at the last possible moment, I found a very tall actor who also looked like Ludwig: A Hungarian, László Gálffi. The fact that he spoke not a word of English was not the problem it might seem; you can re-voice anyone, and you often have to. No-one understood a word Marthe Keller said, for example, and in one particular scene we had to re-voice her. No-one noticed, not even Marthe.

As for Ludwig, I returned in some triumph to a production meeting to announce that at last I had found, I hoped, the perfect Ludwig. 'What?' cried the chief make-up lady. 'You can't do that.'

'What do you mean, I can't do that?' I replied, somewhat amazed.

'You just can't do that,' she replied. 'I've already ordered the teeth.'

'The teeth?' I said, even more confused.

'Yes, the teeth,' she said triumphantly. 'The previous Ludwig had bad teeth, so I took the precaution of ordering a new set of dentures, just in case.'

The poor woman obviously believed that I would endanger such a crucial piece of casting, simply because she had ordered (without anyone's knowledge) an extremely expensive set of dentures. 'It was a matter of principle,' she said.

'So it was,' I replied, and fired her.

Finally there was the question of the music, and we needed lots of it. Remembering my experience of working as a tea boy on Solti's famous 1966 recording of *Götterdämmerung,* and given that by now Solti was reckoned to be among the greatest living conductors of Wagner's music, I thought: nothing ventured, nothing gained. I had worked with Solti several times since that remarkable 1966 recording, and I think I had even introduced him to his wife, Valerie Pitts, then a BBC newsreader.

'Come to dinner,' said Sir Georg. He was a master chef, had cooked the dinner himself, and talked endlessly about everything except Wagner. When I eventually broached the subject, I began by explaining that I really couldn't afford him, but…

'We do deal,' he said, cutting me off.

'Georg,' I said, 'I suspect we will need at least a week of sessions for all the music I need, and I might have difficulty affording just *one* session.'

'We do deal,' he kept saying. Georg was, of course, an Hungarian refugee, and incredibly proud of his two very English daughters. 'We do deal,' he repeated. 'My elder daughter, Claudia, she play the young Isolde in your film (Claudia, incidentally, later became a very distinguished theatre director.) Then I do your music for one concert fee.'

Deal done.

Later, when we were filming in Triebschen, Wagner's house by the lake of Luzern, a scene which included Claudia/Isolde, Georg insisted on coming to watch. The sequence consisted of a long tracking shot around the ground floor of the house while Cosima is instructing the various musicians assembled in preparation for the first performance of the opera *Siegfried*. As the camera was moving 360 degrees, I found a corner in which Solti could sit and observe. I also explained that we were recording sound, so the ebullient Sir Georg would have to remain uncharacteristically silent. We proceeded to film, but as the camera swung round so that Cosima (Vanessa Redgrave) could scoop up the young Isolde, Solti was heard to exclaim very loudly, 'Claudia, you must smile. *SMILE*.' It took several 'takes' before Sir Georg could be persuaded to keep quiet. But record the music he did, and wonderfully so.

Such problems are, I am sure, common enough in any great enterprise. What is peculiar about making films is the annual, or bi-annual, monthly, or daily humiliation to which any independent producer or director is subjected as he or she tries, with increasing desperation, to find *MONEY*. Because, believe it or not, films cost money, and you would be surprised by the number of so-called 'producers' who come out of the woodwork offering to produce one's next film, completely oblivious of the fact that in order to do so one needs money. And, given that many technicians – not to mention many actors and actresses – work, or want to work, in films because they are greedy, the amount of money one needs has steadily increased. So, beware film producers apparently bearing gifts.

The man who found the money for *Wagner*, for example, an honourable man in his way, became involved not least because he had a wife who was an actress. He was a stockbroker called Derek Brierley, who persuaded an investment trust in the City of London to put up sufficient funds to finance the film. The difficulties began because we, the actual makers of the film, were never allowed to talk directly to the financiers. Any budget that we prepared, therefore, passed through the hands of our stockbroker producer. You can imagine our horror when we discovered that the actual amount of cash we needed had never been accurately reported to the men with the money. Thus, as our budget had increased seven-fold – if you were dumb enough to insist on having Richard Burton in the starring role, you had to expect to pay for him; equally, the advantage of having him, if only from a commercial standpoint, was obvious – we assumed that the increase had the blessing of our money men because we were never told otherwise. It is to the credit of the London Trust, however, that when the truth finally was brought home to them, they decided to proceed, even though the stockbroker friend had by this time virtually disappeared.

When the shit was starting to hit every fan in the building, however, he did telephone to inquire if he could help. His room for manoeuvre was limited, he said, but he would do what he could. Suddenly, I heard the sound of what I thought were coins being dropped in a pay phone. Another pay phone!? 'Where are you?' I asked. (This was one week before we were supposed to start filming.) 'Oh, yes,' he said, 'I've just walked over the border to the nearest pay phone in order to stay in touch.'

'Over the border?' I said.

'Oh, yes,' he said. 'My wife is dying from cancer, and she's in a hospital in Mexico where the phones don't work properly, so I've just walked over the border into the States, but I must be going now as my coins have run out, so good luck.'

Brierley was extremely helpful, however, as the filming drew towards a close seven months later. By some miracle, we had stayed more-or-less on budget and more-or-less on schedule. One day, I received a phone call from him requesting an urgent meeting on behalf of the financiers. Fearing the worst (that is, cancellation; little did I know of what was to come) I agreed, and Brierley and his cohorts flew out to our location for a round table meeting. We convened, and to my surprise he was full of encouragement, even congratulations, for the progress we had made so far. Silence. Eventually, I asked, apologetically, 'what was the problem?'

'Oh, no problem,' said Brierley. 'We just thought we could help.'

Silence.

'Help?' I said.

Silence.

'Well, you see', he said, 'my colleagues and I have been studying your schedule.' 'But we are on time,' I interrupted.

'Yes, yes,' he admitted. 'But we noticed that at the very end, you have put aside a week for filming steam trains.'

I was immediately on the defensive. 'Wagner having lived in the nineteenth century,' I began, 'it would not have been possible for him to travel on *electric* trains, because electric trains hadn't been invented, and steam trains are very hard to find. There are a few in Hungary, some in East Germany, but the best examples still working are in private hands in England, and we thought it would be most economical if we did all the train scenes in one week. In England. At the end of the schedule when very few actors are required.' Silence.

Brierley and his colleagues shifted uncomfortably in their chairs, looking at one another, clearly preparing to bring the axe sharply down on my neck for having dared to challenge their cost-cutting expedition, and, eventually, turning to Brierley for leadership.

After a long pause, he said, 'Quite.'

'If they were setting to cut out all the train scenes,' I began again...

'Oh, no, no, no.' said Brierley. 'It was just that (nervously he looked along the line of his colleagues) we have come up with a scheme that we are sure will satisfy your artistic intentions, while undoubtedly saving us money.'

Silence.

'You see,' he went on with that half smile which you know spells trouble, 'my wife's sister-in-law has a cousin who is a wonderful scenic designer.'

Silence.

'She thought, that is my wife's sister-in-law's cousin thought, that you could save an awful lot of money – *and* time – if instead of *real* trains (think of all the dirt!), we used cardboard cut-outs.'

'What an extraordinary (and wonderful) idea,' I said, 'and how silly of me not to have thought of it. Could I have a little time to think about it?' I asked.

Of course, in the event we used real trains in the Lake District in England, up and down the same piece of track, painted green on one side for French trains and brown on the other for German trains.

When Richardson died soon after the film was completed, Olivier, in his peroration at Richardson's Westminster Abbey memorial, made especial mention of their time together during the Wagner film; the climax, said Olivier, of their long careers together, yet separate. Earlier, as their part in the filming had drawn to a close, each had decided to give a dinner party for the other two, with Vittorio Storaro, the Oscar-winning cameraman, Burton and me as guests – the final dinner of which is now the basis of a fascinating play. The three dinners, in their three different hotels on succeeding nights, were touching, sad, comic, and, ultimately, disastrous. Richardson began. But, try as he might, the service at his hotel was painfully slow and all the food arrived late, and cold. But who cared, with such company? The answer was that Richardson cared, and he almost broke down in tears as one thing after another went wrong.

Gielgud's party was next. This time Burton was jumping up and down and leaving the restaurant throughout the dinner, to the growing concern of the other guests. Every time he returned to the table, he looked increasingly downcast. Finally, we learned that, with Gielgud, he had organised presents for the other guests, but, somehow, these had failed to arrive. They did, of course, eventually, but not before the calm of the evening had been disturbed by the bouncing Burton.

Olivier was determined that no such disaster should befall his evening. He reserved a special room at his hotel; he had special menu cards printed commemorating the occasion; and he had personally ordered the food. Alas, it was one of those days when, through nobody's fault, the filming overran its schedule, and some of us were a little late arriving, including Gielgud. Olivier was distraught, again close to tears. His evening had been ruined, he said, the food had been ruined, or had at least gone cold.

'Well, well,' said Gielgud. 'Never mind; I'm starving.' More moaning, but, finally, the 'gone cold' food arrived. It was, of course, Beluga caviar, which would not have 'gone cold' had we been late by another two hours.

After all this, things could only improve for the dinner Burton gave in thanks for the other three, or at least so we all thought. Burton was an alcoholic, and, like all alcoholics, his good behaviour depended on keeping the level of alcohol in his blood at a more-or-less constant level. Contrary to popular belief, Burton was not a hell-raiser, and he much preferred bangers-and-mash (or even kippers) and a glass of beer. Often, he would make sure that you, as his guest, had the very best the menu could provide, while he would toy with something simpler. Thus, for instance, he would quietly sip from a glass of water (he was right-handed) while you quaffed the most expensive wine in the house. But, bearing in mind his alcoholism, he would usually pour a glass of red wine and place it by his *left* hand. He explained to me that this helped him *not* to drink; the mere sight of this glass by his 'wrong' hand enabled him to resist the temptation more firmly.

And so it was the last night Olivier, Gielgud, Richardson and Burton dined together to say their farewells. I cannot remember an evening so full of good cheer, of good jokes, of reminiscences stretching back through half a century of British stage and film history. The trials and tribulations of the previous evenings together were well and truly forgotten, with Burton, the glass of water by his right hand, the glass of wine by his left, at his most charming and beguiling. And then, in the midst of an excruciatingly funny story about the making of the epic film *Cleopatra*, Burton's hand slipped towards the glass of wine and, without thinking, he swallowed it. Less than ten minutes later, he was transformed: Jekyll into Hyde. From being delightful, self-effacing and brilliantly entertaining, Burton became abusive, slobbering and evil. The alcohol had poisoned his brain as surely as it had long since pickled his body.

The reaction of the three knights was equally fascinating. Gielgud, Burton's first important mentor, just said, 'Oh, no,' his voice full of sadness, full of regret. Richardson said he had to talk to his motorbike and got up to leave. But Olivier, against whom most of Burton's vitriol seemed to be directed – Burton at one point called Olivier a cunt; he also told him that he, Burton, was a far better actor than Olivier would ever be – Olivier sat watching quietly, his eyes narrowing, his imagination noting Burton's behaviour, no doubt storing the information for future use in whatever monster Olivier was next called upon to play.

Burton, exhausted by his tirade, finally looked at me, tears in his eyes, and said, 'Time to go, eh?' As I took him out to his taxi, he grasped my arm and blurted out, 'I blew it, didn't I?' Somewhere in the mists of his befuddled mind he knew the disaster he had just caused. He could not focus on it, nor explain his part in it; but he knew. The three knights forgave him, of course. Like the naughty little boy he sometimes was, Richard always seemed able to conjure up forgiveness from those he had most offended.

Burton's 'bad behaviour' has always been greatly exaggerated, especially after his transition into Movie Magazine Immortality. But on the Wagner film, for instance, we worked with him, six days most weeks, for 157 days non-stop. He was meticulous, and often infuriatingly so, to get each speech word-perfect. So a huge five-minute speech would often have to be re-filmed because he had mistaken one word. And only on two of those 157 days could he be said to have been 'under the weather': once when he had a very bad cold, the other time when it had been announced in the UK newspapers that he was being divorced by his fourth wife, Suzy Hunt.

That night, he asked me if I would mind exchanging hotel rooms with him – I assumed because he wished to avoid the inevitable plague of paparazzi. 'No problem,' I said. Actually, we were staying in the same hotel, so it was just a question of informing the concierge. At around four in the morning (again) my bedside telephone rang.

'Oh Richard, darling,' said the voice I knew well. 'Richard darling, I'm so sorry...'

'Elizabeth,' I interrupted, 'I'm afraid it's Tony Palmer.'

After a moment's pause, the tone of her voice changed: 'Where is he?' she demanded.

'Honestly Elizabeth, I do not know.'

Click. End of conversation.

The following morning Richard came over and said, 'Did she call? You didn't tell her where I was, did you!?' – panic in his eyes.

'No Richard, I did not.'

'She'll call again,' he said.

And sure enough, two nights later, the phone rang again.

'Oh *Tony* darling,' she began, 'surely there must be a teeny-weeny part for me in your wonderful film? All those great actors, Olivier and the others. (I don't think she knew any other names.) Just a little part…?'

This time, I was prepared.

'Actually, there is, Elizabeth. Remember when you did *Faustus* with Richard in Oxford, you made a brief appearance as the world's most beautiful woman, Helen of Troy. No dialogue; just a dazzling apparition. Well, there is something similar in our film,' I said.

'No dialogue; I like that,' she said. 'Tell me a bit more about the characterisation.' To this day I cannot believe that I actually said this, but I did.

'There's a tiny part for an Eskimo,' I said, holding the phone away in case of an explosion from the most famous and glamorous actress on the planet.

With only a millisecond's pause she said, 'Oh, I've always wanted to play an Eskimo.'

Richard and I drank her health the following day.

Above all, Burton was an easy man to please. Witness his last marriage (he stole the best secretary I ever had, damn him). Sally, although very sophisticated in her way, was able to make him a cup of tea, make his bed, provide him with a comfortable and contented home, just as his first wife Sybil had done all those years earlier.

After the film had been completed in 1983, in time for the hundredth anniversary of Wagner's death, Richardson was by now dead and Olivier was sick. But Gielgud came to a special screening, and he was generously (and characteristically) complimentary about Burton's titanic performance. 'His greatness as an actor is plain to see and hear,' said Gielgud. But, with that droll humour for which he was notorious, Gielgud added, 'Pity you could hear him breathing.'

So why expend all this energy on such a doubtful character? When Wagner opened his new opera house in Bayreuth in August 1876, this horrid little man stood at the top of the hill, his hill, welcoming most of the crowned heads of Europe. In all of Western, and probably Eastern, cultural and social life, there is no other instance of the artist, standing centre stage, making the political rulers of the world come to him. Not Shakespeare, not Aeschylus, not Mozart or Beethoven. It was, and remains, an astonishing achievement,

One final footnote. In 1986 the Jerusalem Cinemathéque showed the entire seven- hour and forty-seven minute (often mistakenly called 'the nine hour...') *Wagner* film before a packed audience. Trouble had been anticipated, especially as Wagner's anti-Semitism was well known and the screening was planned for the Jewish Sabbath. Armed guards patrolled the cinema. But there was no trouble, merely a request for a second screening to accommodate all those who had failed to get tickets. And my guess is that there are at least five hours of music in the film, conducted by Sir Georg Solti and played by the Vienna Philharmonic. Now, I am well aware that Daniel Barenboim has campaigned tirelessly to have Wagner's music played in Israel. But I'm just a little tired of ignorant music critics (and there are many) saying that Barenboim was the first to play Wagner in Israel with an Israeli/ Palestinian orchestra, the East-West Divan.

Barenboim was not the first to have played Wagner's music in public, in Israel.

I was.

Chapter 20

And the Wagner Family

And if you thought the life of Richard Wagner the composer was somewhat bizarre, now try the lives of his family and successors. Put simply, this story is appalling, and sometimes I find it difficult to believe I lived to tell the tale. You might have thought that, having spent several years planning, filming and then editing the life of Richard Wagner, I would have had enough. But the more I learned, and the more members of his family I met, the more extraordinary and almost unbelievable their story became.

My curiosity was aroused by my meeting with Winifred, the widow of Siegfried, Wagner's only son. As I have explained before, prior to making my Richard Burton epic, in 1978 I had requested Winifred's son, Wolfgang, to arrange a meeting with her for one specific reason: she had known Cosima, Wagner's widow, and I hoped she would be able to give me some insights into her character, which in turn might help Vanessa Redgrave, who was to play Cosima in my film. There was, however, a problem. A few years earlier, Winifred had given an interview to the distinguished German director, Hans-Jürgen Syberberg, in which she had apparently praised Hitler and the Nazi regime. Wolfgang and his late brother Wieland had gone to considerable efforts since the end of the Second World War to distance themselves from the Nazi regime, despite (for example) extant photos of the brothers sitting beside, and looking adoringly at, the Führer, whom they clearly regarded almost as a 'father figure'.

Winifred, in her interview, had upended all that. She claimed that Syberberg had deceived her by saying, 'Let's get the Hitler stuff over, and the next weekend we can discuss all the really important aspects of your life and the Bayreuth Festival which you have struggled to keep afloat.' Having got what he needed about Hitler, Syberberg never returned. Instead, he issued the interview under the title *The Confessions of Winifred Wagner.*

After some persistence on my part, Wolfgang relented and told me I could have half an hour with her, but I could not take a camera nor any recording device. To be confronted by this legendary woman was daunting. Even in her eighties, she was strong, physically large, and tough. Given what she had endured after seventy years in Bayreuth this was hardly surprising. What did surprise me was her charm. She was English, of course, having been born Winifred Marjorie Williams in Hastings on the south coast of England. It was clear that she longed to speak English, and I guess that was partly why I was 'received'.

The first thing Winifred said, almost before I had got through the door, was, 'I suppose you want to know about Cosima. She was the most evil woman I ever met.' That seemed as good a start as any, and we talked over tea for rather longer than my allotted thirty minutes. Cosima had become Wagner's mistress in the 1860s and had borne him three illegitimate children: Isolde, Eva and Siegfried, while he was living in exile in the house 'Triebschen' on the lake of Luzern, although at the time she was still married to Liszt's favourite pupil, the conductor Hans von Bülow.

Eventually Winifred produced some champagne. The conversation continued, mostly about Cosima and how she had not only dominated the Festival but had also made everyone else's life a misery. 'I think we should go and have supper,' Winifred said, now clearly relishing the chance to bitch about her mother-in-law and much else besides. So off we went to her favourite tavern in the town of Bayreuth, while the stream of funny stories flowed about the trials and tribulations of trying to prevent the Festival from collapsing due to a lack of funds, or the war, or the ineptitude of her sons, to whom the management of the Festival had been entrusted after the war – or, rather, taken away from her against her wishes. I carefully avoided any mention of Hitler, but she cheerfully brought up his name. 'I called him "Wolf" and he called me "Winnie",' she said. 'We had a very close relationship, as did the children. They all called him Wolf as well.' As I called for the bill, she became very tearful. I apologised, fearing that by bringing up all kinds of memories good, bad, or indifferent, I had caused her some distress.

'Oh no,' she said. 'I was just remembering the number of times Wolf had sat where you are sitting.'

I should declare first that without the full cooperation of Wolfgang Wagner, the composer's grandson and incumbent of Bayreuth and artistic leader of the Festival, my Richard Burton film would not have been possible. He approved the script, gave permission to film in the Festspielhaus theatre built by the composer himself and opened in 1876, came to the première and approved of the finished film. But what I unearthed was a sorry tale. To start with, Winifred had been less than straightforward about Hitler. Gottfried, her grandson, told me, 'My grandmother always said very proudly, "Yes! Hitler and I were really close." So a hospital was constructed in Bayreuth, and this was called the Winifred Wagner Krankenhaus. And there was a kind of an Aryan breeding going on; that means pure Germans in the sense of the Nazi philosophy – blond heroes who should breed with blonde, typical Nordic women. A master race, and almost next door to the Festspielhaus theatre itself!'

According to Gottfried, Hitler himself claimed he knew all of Wagner's scores; he was able not only to read the scores, but even to play them. Hitler was even, in a modest way, a composer. And still parts of his Overtures exist, apparently completely in the style of Richard Wagner, in Winifred's possession. When Gottfried had challenged his mother about her relationship with Hitler (it was even rumoured that marriage had been discussed), he got a flea in his ear. 'I said, "Listen, Omi" (as she was called by the grandchildren), "this is unsupportable. You cannot blame only the close collaborators of Hitler for what happened. That's not true. Hans Frank, who was one of your closest friends – Hans Frank, the General Governor of occupied Poland and responsible for Auschwitz – he had even a love affair with the Governess of your four children. The Governess was also a militant Nazi herself, and she was responsible for the education of your children, Wieland, Friedelind, Wolfgang and Verena."' And when I questioned her about Auschwitz, she said, "This is only the invention by certain groups, especially the New York Jews." She always had this idea there was a world conspiracy coming from Wall Street and the Jews. So she had her obsessions and did not even accept that she lived in her dream world. She believed to her dying day that Hitler was the man who had found the Holy Grail, bringing light to Bayreuth and the rest of the world.'

And Winifred's husband, Siegfried, Wagner's only son, was not much better. At Christmas 1923, he wrote to Winifred, 'We will remain true to Hitler even if it should mean going to prison ourselves. The situation in Bavaria is appalling. The Jew and the Jesuit are working hand in glove to exterminate German-ness! But Satan has miscalculated. Should the German cause really fail, then I'll believe in the God of revenge and hatred.' Of course, the irony was that Winifred knew almost from the beginning of their arranged marriage that Siegfried was homosexual. She tolerated it, never complained, or even said anything. It was as if she didn't want to know. She had to care for her very sick mother-in-law, Cosima; for the house; for the servants – but with very little money. The family was almost bankrupt. They even went to the States so that Siegfried could conduct concerts of his own music. But they were almost all cancelled because no-one wanted to hear *his* music. We also know from the diaries of Josef Goebbels, "Oh, he is disgustingly decadent. He is not even a real man." Because of his homosexuality, he was blackmailed. And the Siegfriedhaus itself, an annexe to the left of the main family house, Villa Wahnfried, was built not just so that he could withdraw to compose, but also so that he could entertain his homosexual friends away from his mother, wife and children. Not surprisingly Winifred, the orphan from Hastings, was often very lonely.

'I must confess, Hitler made a very deep impression on me as a personality,' she told Syberberg. 'His eyes were especially attractive. Very blue, large and expressive. After he was incarcerated in Landsberg Prison following a failed coup in Munich in 1923, I asked what he needed. He said, 'Lots of writing paper.' So I sent a whole load of paper from our house in Bayreuth, Villa Wahnfried, and my God, now people tell me I supplied the paper for Hitler to write *Mein Kampf*. Almost as if I am responsible for *Mein Kampf* being written.'

Even after the war Winifred was completely unrepentant. 'I admit that everything that happened in the last half of the war I totally reject,' she said, 'but I will not pour out the baby with the bathwater and I insist that what I considered good and humane about Hitler remains true. And I will not be untrue to this memory. I mean, he had such a unique personality that I would not have wanted to miss that experience.'

I met Gottfried in Cerro Maggiore in Northern Italy, where he lived with his Italian wife Teresina and adopted son Eugenio in modest, somewhat reduced circumstances, having been cut off from the Wagner inheritance by his irate father Wolfgang, who considered his son's constant criticism of the family as a betrayal. He was, however, a distinguished scholar, having written learned treatises about Bertolt

Brecht and Kurt Weill, and the basement of his apartment housed a magnificent and comprehensive archive of all matters concerning the Family Wagner. Wolfgang had even refused to acknowledge Gottfried's adopted son or receive either of them in Bayreuth, which had obviously hurt Gottfried profoundly. But his observations about the family were not bitter; they were more a genuine search for the truth.

'Just take my father's autobiography,' Gottfried told me. 'There's a statement where he says, "When Wieland and I took over in 1951, we had not the slightest need to put ashes on our hair, to feel responsible, because during the war we were much too young and had no responsibility for what was happening." But they saw in the 30s and 40s so much more than the rest of the world. They knew about Auschwitz; they *knew* what was going on. As we know, Hitler talked and talked, his talks never ended, and talked about 'his vision' after the Final Victory. And he had in mind that Wolfgang should be the General Director of all the theatres in the east, and I'm not talking about Germany, but the rest of the world; and Wieland was to be the General Director of all western opera houses. So they had these kind of completely insane, lunatic ideas about what would be done after the Final Victory.

'I'm not blaming my father for that, but when he writes a biography as a man of seventy-five years, he has to put it all on the table. But he does not even mention it. By March 1945, the world was burning. Wieland was in charge of a concentration camp in Flossenberg near Bayreuth, and yet still – with Hitler's approval – he was actually planning a new Bayreuth Festival for the summer of 1945. But this was hidden. Not mentioned in my father's autobiography, and did not come out until 1987. You might have thought that he could have at least said, "Oh I'm so sorry." I mean, you know, sixty million dead people, and nothing mentioned. That's too much.

'Falsifying the truth is, unfortunately, part of the history of the Wagner family,' Gottfried concluded. 'It started with Richard Wagner himself. If you look at his first biographical sketches in his autobiography *Mein Leben,* he is just falsifying history. He himself. He started that. Then Cosima, his second wife, she was worse. Seventy letters Wagner wrote to his mistress, Mathilde von Wesendonck – letters which had an enormous importance for his opera *Tristan and Isolde* – were burnt by Cosima.'

Nor was Gottfried's scorn reserved solely for his father or his great-grandmother Cosima. Winifred, his grandmother, had been forced by the Allies to surrender her control of the Bayreuth Festival, to her intense anger. And during her de-Nazification trial, 'my grandmother was preaching aggressively, you know, "I'm innocent. I did my duty. What the hell do they want? I never did anything wrong." And people even applauded her in the hall. But the trial was faked. Winifred said, "Oh my goodness, this American officer who is a Jew, you know, silly man if he thinks that I would give him the real, real stuff." And she always gave parties every April 20th, Hitler's birthday. She sent out invitation cards with the message: "Wonderful, I'm so happy to invite you for a special remembrance of U.S.A." But that was not the United States of America, but '*Unser Seliger Adolf*' ('Our Blessed Adolf'). And then she signed each card with an '88', which is the eighth letter in the alphabet, which is H. *Heil Hitler*.'

'We saw the collapse of all our hopes when Hitler's putsch had failed in November 1923,' Winifred remembered. 'That day, November 8th, should always be remembered as a day of National Repentance. A big celebration concert planned for that night with my husband Siegfried conducting had to be cancelled, and as a result of that collapse we have had to live with all the tragic consequences that have followed.'

Both of Winifred's sons had incredibly beautiful daughters, from whom, again, the truth had been hidden. Wieland's youngest daughter was called Daphne, to whom we had given the part of Princess Metternich in my Burton epic, not least because she was the spitting image of her great-grandfather. 'The biggest shock for me,' she told me, 'was the film which Syberberg made about my grand-mother in 1975. I was in Munich and went to see it in a local cinema and I watched those five hours in shock. Total shock. Shock. Total shock. I always had these pictures in my head of Winifred, 'Omi' we called her, sitting all day long at her typewriter. And one Christmas I saw her carrying a load of presents in a washing basket. Then I said to her, "Omi, who are all these presents for?" And she said, "For those poor pigs in the east zone."'

Wolfgang's daughter, called Eva, was also very beautiful and had ambitions to assume control of the Bayreuth Festival when her father retired. It was she who had kept encouraging me to make my film during the long struggle to get it financed and on the road. No-one who met her did not fall in love with her. Eventually she was muscled out of the job at the Festival by her half-sister Katherina (Wolfgang married twice), then she had a nervous breakdown and, as far as Bayreuth was concerned, more or less disappeared.

Of Winifred's four children, only one had stayed resolutely out of sight and had never been interviewed, Verena Lafferentz, neé Wagner. I was very curious about this missing link, found her address, wrote to her, and to my astonishment received a welcoming reply inviting me to her home in Nußdorf in Überlingen, southern Germany, on Lake Constance near the Swiss border. Ironically, this was also the spot from where Richard Wagner had fled following the failed putsch in Dresden in 1849, after which he had become a 'wanted criminal' with a price of fifty thalers on his head, dead or alive. The house where Verena received me had been the family's summer cottage, and, more importantly, the bolt hole to which her brother Wieland had fled to avoid capture by the Allies after the war. The garden of the house also turned out to be where various priceless manuscripts of Wagner's operas had been buried, again to avoid seizure.

Verena was the gentlest of women, and she plied me with cakes and sweetmeats. I kept wondering why no-one had bothered to interview this ninety-year-old woman before. 'In February, 1945, when we came here to Nußdorf, our mother gave us the original manuscript scores of *Tristan* and *Parsifal*, as well as the whole of the Wagner-Liszt correspondence. Liszt was also my grandfather, as you know,' Verena told me. 'The point was that the archive should be dispersed, so that if a bomb or the enemy destroyed something in Bayreuth, other things would survive. So first we buried the scores in the garden. They were well wrapped in my children's nappies and then wrapped further in leather and sealed with wax. We buried them out there,' she pointed towards the lake, 'during a foggy night because we had lodgers and we didn't want them to notice what we were doing and report us.

'After several weeks, I suddenly panicked. Maybe the humidity would affect the parcel. So we dug up the scores, realised everything was okay, but then buried them again, now in the walls of the house, because the walls were made of two layers of wood with a gap in between. And that's where we put them next, newly wrapped of course. But this also gave me sleepless nights. I kept thinking: what if the mice attack them? Because we had lots of mice.'

But what else? Some people have asserted that Hitler would gladly have married this granddaughter of Richard Wagner, the vivacious twenty-year-old Verena who was a frequent guest at his mountain retreat at Berchtesgaden, had he not been opposed in principle to marriages between persons of such unequal ages. In his company, she had the reputation of being his most outspoken critic, telling him in unflattering language simple truths that no Cabinet member would have dared to utter.

Then there was her actual marriage. In 1943 she had married Bodo Lafferentz, a high-ranking officer (*SS-Obersturmbannführer*) assigned to the Race and Settlement Office. According to Wieland's daughter, Daphne, Lafferentz was practically the king of Bayreuth. He was its principal employer. He controlled all the money; and he had the Festival effectively under his control. And through his marriage to Verena, he, too, became part of the 'family'. After the war, Lafferentz was interned during the Allies' de-Nazification programme, but released in 1949. Of this she made no mention during our long day together. Nor that in Bayreuth, Lafferentz had founded and overseen the Institute for Physical Research, an outpost of the nearby Flossenbürg concentration camp, to develop the V-2 rocket employing slave labour, with the resulting countless deaths.

Once again, I found it difficult to reconcile the gentle old lady in whose house I was now a guest with my knowledge of what she and her family had done during the Nazi period. I tried to put this aside while quizzing her about Cosima, her grandmother. After all, there were very few remaining living witnesses of what this titan in the story of the composer Richard Wagner was like, the widow who had ruthlessly exploited his legacy even while he was still alive. Again, I was confounded. 'My grandmother thought that all young women should be kept busy,' Verena told me, 'and so she taught us to do the dusting in her big room and to clean her books nicely. My mother [Winifred], although she spoke German, and even French, you could tell from her accent then that she was English. So every day she would have German lessons from Cosima and also read to her. It was not true that the old woman was blind, as has often been said, although she definitely had bad eyesight. Nonetheless she was very sensitive to light and always lay on her couch away from the light. But we children could go to her whenever we wanted, I was about ten at the time, and we really took advantage of that, because she was incredibly humorous and played jokes with us, and we were allowed to climb all over her back. We could do her hair. We could dress her up. Anything we wanted.'

'The most evil woman I ever met,' as Winifred had told me? I began to wonder.

I needed more information, so off I set on my travels around Europe. First stop was Salzburg, in Austria, where Nike, the second daughter of Wieland, Wolfgang's elder brother, had a house. Nike was by far the most intellectual of the children. Born in 1945 in that same house where Verena now lived, she had studied musicology, literature and theatre in Berlin. She held a Ph.D. from Northwestern University in Evanston, Illinois, obtained in 1980. She had founded the Festival in Weimar, where her great-great-grandfather Liszt had lived in 1848, and had conducted the world première of Wagner's opera *Lohengrin* while the composer was on the run from the Saxon authorities for his part in the destruction of the Dresden Opera House. Again, she was charm personified, until she spoke of her grandmother Winifred. 'She was a monster,' Nike said simply. 'An iron lady. A harsh mother. A domineering character within the family. There was no human closeness, no warmth, no real understanding. And one mustn't forget that she was still relatively young when, aged only fifty, her reign over Bayreuth was, as a result of her Nazi past, taken from her and given to her sons. Her authority, her power, was taken away from her. Who could she dominate now? So her wish to dominate was now focused on her family. And so she destroyed it.'

Next stop, Vienna, and a meeting with Brigitte Hamann, Winifred's biographer. We met at a local *heuriger*, a typical Viennese tavern where new wine was tasted, and both got rather drunk. She was a very beautiful and sexy woman, and when she invited me to escort her home, I declined, to my regret, saying I needed to prepare for our interview the following day.

And what an interview that turned out to be! Perspicacious, witty, droll and devastatingly enlightening. 'The brothers, Wieland and Wolfgang, didn't have any money after the war,' she told me. 'Wolfgang had to go around with a begging bowl. That's why the brothers kept fighting, because Wolfgang said that Wieland was wasteful and couldn't manage money. He had to borrow money from his mistress, the soprano Anja Silja. She was a good singer, but she was only eighteen or twenty and earned very little, but still always had to pay for everything. And then everyone blamed her for Wieland's later marriage difficulties – "Oh, that girl-friend et cetera, et cetera." But she practically financed him. And Winifred was always sending letters everywhere, rubbishing Wieland's wife Gertrud and describing Anja as the "whore of the Kurfürstendamm".

'And anyway, Gertrud was terrible,' Brigitte added with a chuckle. 'She was incredibly stupid. She, too, had lovers. She found some worker – she even writes about it in her *Memoirs* – and had these wonderful hours with her lover in Greece! There was this young, muscular man who came through the window and… So stupid! He was heaven on earth, this worker, a builder or something.

'Then there was Wolfgang's second wife, Gudrun, the mother of Katerina,' Brigitte continued, clearly warming to her theme. 'She was terrible. Pathological. A nymphomaniac. I knew her well, but oh my God, I said, what is happening to her? Oh yes, she's drunk today. She always had a hangover. She organised the Festival really well, one must say that. But at the end, she developed a very grey skin. She was never a beauty, but still she managed to get all those men, they said. First the singers and then the chorus. But that took a little longer.'

Nike endorsed this view. 'I can well understand the anger of Wolfgang's children he had by his first wife, Ellen Drexel,' she told me. 'That their father had then married this woman, Gudrun, the most hated person in the whole artistic world, even with the politicians. Politicians are not themselves of the finest quality, but even for them Gudrun was impossible. Her style, and the way she represented the Bayreuth Festival. But, incredibly, although Gudrun was there for over thirty years, less than two years after her death she's been completely forgotten.'

Some members of the Wagner family were so outraged by what Brigitte had said to me that they collectively sued her for defamation, Inevitably, they lost. Sadly, she died only a few years later. Strange, but I miss her bubbly enthusiasm and sexy warmth to this day.

And so, on to Berlin to see Wieland's eldest daughter, Iris. Very reserved; didn't like interviews; didn't like me. But still, the subject of Bayreuth and its future was something she felt necessary to comment upon. 'The city of Bayreuth is planning to turn our home, Wahnfried, into a theme-park museum,' she told me. 'It fills me full of anger, and also great sadness. The early death of my father Wieland (in 1966, aged only forty-nine), the usurping of power by Wolfgang Wagner and later by Gudrun and even by her daughter Katherina, the present artistic director of the Festival, that was bad enough. But what the city of Bayreuth is now doing, handling the unique cultural heritage that is Wagner so carelessly, and I would even say destructively, is terrible. My family has had to endure so many bad times, that for the city of Bayreuth itself to set about destroying what should be part of world heritage, is unforgivable. But it's become like a 'swimming pool theme park'. Nothing is any longer viewed in an intelligent, even critical, way. Everything is sucked up as a 'total experience', a social event. "I am here now! I'm in Bayreuth!" The music, and what my great-grandfather intended, has gone or become meaningless.'

While in Berlin I also wanted to talk to Oliver Hilmes, whose brilliant biography of Cosima Wagner I had long admired. Surely, there must have been more to her than I had previously discovered. First, he explained her historical background: 'Cosima and her two siblings, Blandine and Daniel, the three children of Liszt, all illegitimate, had all grown up in Paris. And because the parents didn't much care about the children and showed absolutely no interest in them, the children were in effect 'given away'. First, they were dumped on Liszt's mother, Anna, but eventually given into the care of two incredibly old governesses, Madame Patersi and her sister Madame de Saint-Mars. And these two old women 'educated' the girls as if they were still living in the *Ancien Régime* – that is, completely ignorant of all the values of the post-Revolutionary France. So Cosima was a classic *'grande dame'* in the French sense – apparently friendly, but ice cold; apparently helpful, but on a whim refusing to help *anybody*. She was a very distant but 'classy' woman, one might say. This woman, who lived until 1930, came from a completely different time, and grew up in a completely different cultural climate. Even so, there were many things she did which are horrible, terrible and inhuman.'

'When her husband the composer died in February 1883,' Hilmes continued, 'she immediately elevated his death into something absurdly tragic. She lay the whole night in bed with the dead Wagner and fell asleep with the corpse. She cuddled the corpse as if practising some bizarre cult. Only after the corpse began to decompose and stink, was she eventually forced to leave the bed. So she cut her hair off and put this hair into a small velvet cushion which she then put under the head of the corpse. It was like some pseudo-oriental Dance of Death. Nonetheless, in the first months after Wagner's death, everyone thought the Festival was finished. But Cosima very cleverly and strategically organised a coup; after all, in German law, a woman could not inherit. So she just announced that she was the new Director, simply because there was no-one else. And, as it turned out, that was her enormous contribution. In effect, she saved the Bayreuth Festival.'

But for what, I wondered? According to Cosima, Wagner left behind in Bayreuth a clear political message, not only for Germany, but also for the rest of the world. So, after his death, Cosima attracted to Bayreuth all the most radical, chauvinistic, antisemitic people she could find from all over Europe. People such as Houston Stewart Chamberlain

– who was English, by the way, and a distant cousin of the later British Prime Minister, Neville Chamberlain. And by marrying one of Cosima's daughters, Eva, Houston Chamberlain became in every sense another one of the 'family'.

'Hitler was also a big fan of Chamberlain,' Oliver Hilmes told me, 'and during his visit to Bayreuth in 1923 he went to visit Chamberlain in his sickbed and knelt before him, apparently. Hitler believed in Chamberlain's theories and later even went to his funeral. But Houston Stewart Chamberlain played a disastrous role in the history of the Wagner Family. He sent his wife out to work so that he could sit at home and 'think'. He was a windbag. A poseur, a fake, who paraded himself like a peacock. If you try to read his books today, they are rubbish.'

But the fact is that Houston Chamberlain's standard work was a best seller in Germany. There were forty-three different editions. It was lauded by Kaiser William II, with the result that the Wagner family were honoured guests of the Imperial House.

Chamberlain had had the mistaken belief, as Wagner himself had done, that Christ was not a Jew. As we have seen, when Wagner wrote *Judaism in Music* in the 1850s, he said there was a possibility for Jews to become human beings. But when he reissued his pamphlet in 1869, he said that it was impossible. According to Hilmes, it was Cosima who had persuaded her husband to re-publish a revised version of *Judaism in Music*, and it was only after its second publication that anyone took any notice. The original publication had gone totally unnoticed. But with the second edition, Bang! 'After Wagner's death, she quite simply erased any leftist-revolutionary thinking of Wagner. So all that was left is Wagner the antisemite, the German chauvinist and nationalist. And this she canonised as the 'Word of the Master'. And that is her *political* legacy, made on behalf of the dead Wagner who couldn't answer back.'

'And this is what he actually wrote,' Gottfried reminded me: "The Jew is repulsive...He rules and will continue to rule as long as money remains the power. The Jew has come to dominate public taste in music. So join in this bloody battle. Redeem yourself from the curse that weighs upon you!"'

It would be a mistake to assert that the entire Wagner family were Nazis or Nazi sympathisers. The obvious exception was Friedelind, Winifred's elder daughter, who even looked like Wagner himself and had also been photographed together with Verena on the arms of the Führer. Famously, in 1939, she fled to America at the start of the war and began broadcasting anti-Hitler propaganda. One such broadcast went: 'German listeners! I did not leave Germany easily. And I only left when the murderous intentions of the German regime became clear. And even then I asked myself: what would my grandfather, Richard Wagner, have done? Would he have left? Would he have joined the Nazis? It would not be possible. Richard Wagner loved freedom and justice more than music itself. He would not have been able to breathe in Hitler's Germany.'

And so on to Liechtenstein, where lived Eva Rieger, a distinguished historian who had spent the previous decade studying Friedelind's life. Winifred was shocked by her daughter's broadcasts, of course. Eva told me that Winifred 'had received a letter from a Nazi saying, "Would you please explain why your daughter is doing this?" And she did her best by saying, "My daughter has been influenced by Jewish people." And she was eager to explain that it was not her own free will, which, of course, was nonsense. In fact, her mother gave her four options on instructions from Himmler, the chief of the SS. One was to come back to Germany at once; Friedelind said no. Another one was to remain in a neutral country and shut up. And Friedelind said, 'No, I can't do that either.' The third was to go to an enemy country, for instance England, and shut up. She said, 'No, I can't do that.' And the fourth option, (which she chose), was to go to an enemy country and *not* shut up. But Winifred was very much afraid the Gestapo would kill her daughter.'

According to Eva Rieger, what happened subsequently was worse. Friedelind stayed away from Germany and Bayreuth until 1953, when she set foot on German soil for the first time in fifteen years. She got a very mixed reception. People didn't really want to have anything to do with her, witness the fact that her autobiography was first published in the United States in 1945 (and soon became a best seller), but not released in Germany until 1987. Even Marlene Dietrich, another émigré, was not applauded in the way that she had expected. And Friedelind was also very shocked by the way in which former Nazis were back into their old jobs again. She was disgusted by the way things had developed. She was very critical of Bayreuth. She kept on stressing that she saw former Nazis in power in and around Bayreuth. 'And of course, being Friedelind,' Eva told me, 'she said these things out loud, and this made her brother furious. Wolfgang got really mad at her.'

'Bayreuth for Hitler had been just a good cover,' Friedelind said. 'He always said that the world press would see him in Bayreuth and think he was there just because he loved Wagner. But behind the scenes, in our home, many political decisions were made. The bombing of Spain;

the invasion of Poland, using my brother's geography book; the assassination of the Austrian Chancellor, Dollfuss. And all while the world was not watching.'

You can understand why Wolfgang got mad at her.

And so, finally, all roads took me back to Bayreuth and to Wolfgang, then the artistic director of the Festival and the man who had made my Richard Burton film possible. 'After the death of my father, Wieland,' Nike told me, 'his younger brother, Wolfgang, my uncle, became the boss. He had a right, therefore, to move into Wahnfried, the family house where we, my sisters and I and our brother, had been brought up and regarded as our home. But he already had his own house where he had lived for a long time. So what did he do? Wolfgang arrived to measure all the rooms where we lived to work out what we should pay in rent. How high should the rent be. He knew very well that Wieland's widow, our mother, had no money. Indeed, there were enormous debts. We had all just started our studies; there was an obvious lack of money. We just couldn't afford any rent.'

I remembered once, during the filming in Bayreuth of my Burton Wagner epic, Daphne had asked me to take her to Wahnfried, then a museum. I asked why. Surely she knew the house where she had been born and brought up? But I agreed, and as we approached the front door, Daphne gripped my arm and burst into tears. Now I understood why. Wolfgang had effectively thrown out Wieland's family from their home.

'When my father was still in his coffin,' Daphne told me, 'Wolfgang had switched the heating off in our home, so it all started becoming damp. Then mould came. We were now all somewhere else, at university, studying. But my mother was forced to move to Sylt where we had a little house, and so Wahnfried, our family home, became more and more derelict. All our things were there: our toys, the silver cutlery, the furniture, everything was still there. My mother then sold, or rather had to sell, some of it. For me, it was an unforgettable sight, this completely desolate place where I had been born, with dead birds and cobwebs everywhere. That's how this house looked. Unliveable in. Deliberately made so. Wolfgang not only evicted us, but then sacked all the people in the Festspielhaus connected to my father. He destroyed scenery designed by my father, and worse, all the little models of the stage designs he had made. He burnt the complete correspondence between my father and various artists. This time it wasn't a book-burning, but a letter-burning. Until his brother died, Wolfgang had always been in the shadow of his big brother Wieland. But as soon as Wieland died, all of Wolfgang's jealousy came out, and it became a vendetta against the whole of Wieland's family. Everything that had to do with my father was hacked to pieces. He put my family out in the street and later, when he himself took up with a younger woman, his own wife was thrown out. And his two children, Gottfried and Eva, found their nursery furniture and toys in the yard. He just said, "Either pick them up or they will be sent to the rubbish tip." He did that even to his own children.'

Ouch.

Wolfgang had his defenders. First among them was the conductor Pierre Boulez. 'During his tenure, Wolfgang has improved the working conditions immensely,' Boulez told me. 'When I first came here in 1966 to conduct my first *Parsifal*, you had the big stage of course, and one rehearsal stage, and another smaller one. That's all – three stages together. By the time Wolfgang retired, we had seven stages, six stages for rehearsal, and most of them had the same measures as the real stage. So can you imagine the improvement of the theatre's schedule. You did not have to keep changing the scenery, for instance. And I think that this part of Wolfgang is not enough recognised. Because I think if he would not have been there, and not have done the job he did to renovate the house as he did, regularly, systematically, logically, the house would be in ruins now.'

'Bayreuth and the Wagner Family are a national symbol,' Nike told me. 'All society wants to be in Bayreuth and this gives to whoever is the director, power. Or the politics of power, or the drunkenness of power. But if everyone is kneeling in front of Wolfgang's – the grandson's – words, this position of power is being abused. It's really all about who has the power and, whatever the cost, keeping it.'

'After Wagner's death, it was Cosima who saved the Festival, which otherwise might have disappeared,' Gottfried thought. 'Winifred, my grandmother, saved it from bankruptcy and much else besides. When Winifred had first been brought to Bayreuth, aged seventeen, by an old friend of Wagner's, the pianist Klindworth, and introduced to the family during one of the tea intervals, they all said, "Um, pretty girl." Siegfried, apparently, didn't notice. But all the aunts were saying, "Um, that would be great." Because they needed a young girl for the not-so-young fifty-year-old Siegfried so that she could quickly become pregnant. They desperately needed him to have a child. None of the four sisters had any children then, and nor did Siegfried, because he was homosexual. That was the problem. He absolutely had to have a child;

otherwise the dynasty would become extinct. So Winifred rescued Bayreuth in more ways than one. Then Wieland, whatever the truth about his Nazi past, rescued the Festival artistically. And my father, Wolfgang, finally put the Festival on a secure financial footing.'

'But now? With my sisters, Eva and Katherina? They say they want to open up the archives in Bayreuth. But the really important archives are not in Bayreuth, as they know. So, unfortunately, falsification continues. To forge an honest identity must entail a very critical confrontation with your heritage, a heritage left by Wagner himself and then by the Wagner family since his death in 1883, and then in the Third Reich.'

'So who are we then as Germans and Wagners after Hitler?' Gottfried asked me. 'Can you be proud to be a Wagner?'

It had been a long journey for me to arrive at this same question.

Chapter 21

Carl Orff

Among the composers who flourished during the Nazi period in Germany, the most notable was Carl Orff; which is odd, when you consider that just one work, *Carmina Burana*, of course, is among the most popular pieces of music ever written. First performed June 1937 at the Frankfurt Opera, its première coincided with *SS-Obergruppenführer* Reinhard Heydrich issuing a secret order condemning 'race violators' to 'protective custody' upon the conclusion of any normal legal process. Buchenwald concentration camp, above Weimar, opened the same month, and a systematic seizure of Jewish property began. Nonetheless, there is at least one performance of *Carmina Burana* somewhere in the world every single day of the year, and that has been so for the last ninety years. And with over 300 different recordings extant in the catalogue today, it easily outranks even Beethoven's Fifth Symphony.

So, why notable? Was Orff really a member of the Nazi party as is often assumed? No, but there is little doubt that in 1943–44 he was positioning himself to take over as Reichsminister for Music, come the Final Victory. He was a close friend of Baldur von Schirach, the Gauleiter for Vienna and previously of the Hitler Youth, later a convicted war criminal. And when every other major composer of the Third Reich – including Richard Strauss – had refused to 're-write' *A Midsummer Night's Dream* by 'that Jew' Mendelssohn, Orff had accepted.

Moreover, Orff always maintained after the war that the Nazi Party had 'hated' *Carmina Burana* (I found a piece of archive film in which he says this). That was untrue. After its première, Goebbels declared it to be the standard by which all German music should be judged, and it rapidly became the most performed piece of 'new music' in Nazi Germany.

Music critics outside Germany were huffy at the time, and they remain huffy and even puffy today. 'A rhythmic simpleton'; 'harmonically retrogressive'; 'a primitive celebration of drinking, gluttony, gambling and lust' – these are among the more generous of criticisms I have come across. The critics completely ignore the fact that the music has been used in over a thousand commercials (literally), Old Spice, Carling Black Label and Nestlé among the more famous. It has been used to introduce *The X Factor*; used in the video game *Final Fantasy VII*; and even re-arranged by Ray Manzarek, formerly of The Doors, and by Philip Glass. Curiously, his seventieth birthday celebrations in Munich in 1965 were led by Wieland Wagner, another whose association with the Nazi Party was somewhat murky. Wagner pointed out Orff's affiliations with Monteverdi – Orff can reasonably claim to have been among the first musicians in the twentieth century to have understood Monteverdi's importance; his earliest major work in the early 1920s was a reworking of *L'Orfeo* (Orpheus) – and also of Orff's debt to Stravinsky: not just Orff's emphasis on rhythm, but on his shimmering orchestration. Wagner also noted the connections with Stravinsky's *Les Noces*. And Ingmar Bergman later admitted that *Carmina Burana* had been one of the more important influences on his classic film, *The Seventh Seal*.

While making my film about Orff, *O Fortuna*, I was astonished by the range of orchestral colours that he manages to conjure up, often with tiny resources, in this sense much like Britten in his chamber operas. Because of the frequently gargantuan performances of *Carmina Burana* with choirs a zillion strong, and orchestras thumping out the simple rhythms regardless of the fact – and it *is* a fact – that actually the 'rhythms', as they are written, are very far from four-square (but hey, it's easier to play it as if they were), we assume all too easily that the music is nothing but bombast and a few catchy melodies.

Orff wrote eighteen major works for the stage, many of which employ instruments he had discovered in his travels, such as tuned wooden xylophones, marimbas, bells of all descriptions and gongs. And I have never heard the harp sound so demonic, so demented, even in Britten, one of the great composers for the harp. Nor the celesta and piccolo used to such nightmarish effect, reminiscent here of Shostakovich. I'm not surprised that Glass was drawn to Orff. Orff was the ultimate minimalist before anyone thought of inventing it.

None of this would have fired my imagination were it not for another aspect, more complex and ultimately tragic, of the man and his music. Imagine: he was struggling to survive in a regime that he thought intellectually inferior to him. Like all his fellow musicians, he was compelled to complete a curriculum vitae to prove that he was of the purest Aryan stock. This he did, but somehow, he 'forgot' to mention that his grandparents were Jewish. Thus, from the start, he was living a lie. To make a living, he devised a system of teaching music to children called *Schulwerk* (Schoolwork), and hoped that through his friend Baldur von Schirach he would be able to sell it to the Hitler Youth. Fortunately, as it turned out, the Hitler Youth didn't care for it much. And when it came to the de-Nazification process at the end of the war, that lack of interest probably saved Orff's neck.

In late March 1946, Orff was arrested and interrogated. By an extraordinary chance, he was interviewed by an American intelligence officer, Newell Jenkins, who happened to be a former music student of Orff's. As Orff was hoping to take up a position as Intendant of the Stuttgart Opera, Newell encouraged Orff specifically to provide evidence that, contrary to all that was known about his apparent 'collaboration', including receiving an annual stipend from the Nazi Party, he had been active *against* the regime. Ah, yes, said Orff, he had co-founded the White Rose Resistance Movement, which had been active in Munich in 1942–43 until its ringleaders were arrested, tortured by the Gestapo and variously hanged or publicly beheaded. Satisfied, the intelligence officer gave Orff a clean bill of health. Newell's account of Orff's involvement with the White Rose, noted by the historian Michael Kater, has since been disputed.

But if Orff's claim of involvement was to be believed, it was another lie. In fact, it was worse than a lie. The White Rose Resistance Movement had mostly comprised students at Munich University, principally the siblings Andreas and Sophie Scholl, mostly in the class of Kurt Huber, the Professor of Music and Psychology and one of Orff's closest friends. Huber was the scholar who had brought the medieval texts of *Carmina Burana* to Orff's attention and had actually worked on their translation into 'contemporary' Latin to tone down the explicit sexual references in the original. (In our film, we restored the original meanings). Following the arrest of the Scholls by the Gestapo, Huber was seized soon after. Huber's wife, knowing of Orff's strong friendship with von Schirach and other members of the Nazi hierarchy, pleaded with him to intercede. Not only did he refuse, thus condemning his best friend to certain execution; not only did he refuse to help Huber's widow, now destitute; but later he even wrote to Huber asking for forgiveness...except that Huber was by now dead.

We found Huber's widow shortly before she herself died; for her, those horrors were still fresh in the memory. I was very shaken hearing her tell of something that had happened sixty years previously as if it were yesterday. Little wonder, therefore, that all of Orff's post-war works are consumed by the feeling of guilt – in *Antigonae* and *Oedipus at Tyrannus;* in *Prometheus,* in which the protagonist protests agonisingly against his 'punishment'. Most telling of all, in *De temporum fine comoedia* (Comedy for the End of Time), in which the narrator pleads not that his sins be forgotten, but that they be forgiven.

Yet it is arguable that Orff's enduring legacy is the system, the method, he devised for teaching music to children: *Schulwerk.* I saw it at first hand in South Africa, where it was used to bind the wounds left by Apartheid; in China and Taiwan, where it is an essential educational tool in making children aware that we must care for the planet we are busy polluting; in Japan, where it is being used to preserve ancient traditions of music-making in the face of what the Japanese think of as cultural pollution, especially from the United States; and, most extraordinarily of all, at a school in Nottingham, where it is used to help children with cerebral palsy. As one of the teachers in Nottingham told me, 'Without the Orff method these children would have very little hope of becoming fully realised human beings. With Orff's help, they have just a chance.' In view of Orff's behaviour and the lies he had told throughout his life, it is hard to imagine a greater irony.

Orff's daughter, his only child, also had a terrible story to tell. 'He did not really love people,' she told me. 'If anything, he despised people, unless they could be useful to him.' This view was confirmed by at least one of his three surviving wives; a fourth wife had died by the time I made my film. His last wife described to me in detail their simple life together in the house at Diessen, in the heart of Bavaria, where she still lived in sight of the monastery at Andechs where Orff is supposedly buried. Certainly, there is a tomb there bearing his name, but of late the suspicion has arisen that it is not his ashes that are buried there, but those of Ludwig II of Bavaria. 'He died in my arms,' Liselotte says in the film, 'and I'm so grateful. I had the feeling it was the other end of the thread – giving birth to a child and watching that child slip away at the end.' We all cried when she said it, and judging from the reaction to the film received from around the world since, others cry also.

Weeping, perhaps, for a life so full of internal agony. His third wife, Luise, described to me the many nights when she had been awoken by Orff screaming and screaming. After she had calmed him down, she asked him what was it that had so disturbed him? 'I have seen the Devil,' he said. And this is from a woman who herself had faced a Nazi firing squad and lived to describe it.

But in Orff's first major work for the stage lay, perhaps, the clue to everything that followed. *Der Mond* (The Moon), tells of a group of ruffians who attempt to rule the world by stealing the moon, stealing the light, and thus plunging the world into an unutterable darkness in which they can pilfer and rape to their heart's content. The reference to the Nazis and all their barbarism is unmistakable. I believe that just as Shostakovich is the most eloquent witness we have of Stalin's nightmare, so Orff is a vital witness to Hitler's Germany and the Nazis, in that he believed that they, too, had 'stolen the light'.

And that is a million miles from what we usually think of when we hear *Carmina Burana*.

Chapter 22

Margot Fonteyn

Not long after joining the BBC and my Huw Wheldon-inspired exile in Nottingham, I was sent on a three-month secondment to the Royal Opera House in Covent Garden. Once again, I was incredibly lucky. It so happened that Kenneth MacMillan was in full rehearsal for his epic and ground-breaking production of the Prokofiev ballet, *Romeo and Juliet,* starring Margot Fonteyn and Rudolf Nureyev. MacMillan needed every help he could get, and I was deployed as his tea-boy, fetcher of messages and general dogsbody. I remember standing on the side of the stage watching his two great dancers rehearse, and what I saw was unbelievable. How could Margot Fonteyn, then forty-six years old, appear on stage to be younger than the twenty-seven-year old Nureyev? I was gripped. Who on earth was this extraordinary woman?

Little did I know the horrors I was to discover when, years later and principally in memory of that first encounter, I began to seek out the story of how the most famous dancer that England has ever produced was deceived and betrayed by those closest to her; how a little girl named Peggy Hookham, who had been brought up in Shanghai, had told her mother she would one day become the greatest dancer in the world, and how, despite being almost unable to walk, she was still performing when she was sixty-six. It proved to be a story of courage, and tenacity, and of unbelievable devotion – to her art, and to those whom she loved. Despite Nureyev paying many of her hospital bills, others, in the end, left her penniless and alone, dying of ovarian cancer while living off cornflakes, in a hut in the middle of the Panamanian jungle near El Higo with a corrugated iron roof; no telephone, no running water, cows meandering through what passed as the kitchen; even eventually being buried, at first, in a pauper's grave.

It was the stuff of fiction – except that it turned out to be true.

To understand the story of Margot Fonteyn, it is perhaps necessary to glimpse the times in which she grew up. Men wore bowler hats, which they doffed to their female companions. Young ladies expected to be 'presented' into society, dolled up in their finest as debutantes, showing that they had reached an age of maturity, completed an education, learned to curtsy, and were ready to be introduced into the world. This meant the girl was eligible to marry, and the purpose was to display her to bachelors and their families for suitability. Tea-dances were also *de rigueur,* the man taking the lead and the woman or girl being obliged to follow. Walton, for example, with his love of titled ladies, took full advantage of this charade. Margot Fonteyn was more anarchic.

During the rehearsals for *Romeo and Juliet,* although I was formally introduced to Margot by MacMillan, I was far too tongue-tied to utter more than 'Good Morning'. She, on the other hand, was effusive and welcoming. 'Do let me know if there is anything you need,' was the first thing she ever said to me.

I was hooked.

Keith Money, her long-time secretary, later gave me a clue to her irrepressible personality. 'I think that she felt trapped in the expectations of all those people around her,' he told me, 'and she was a soul who actually tried to please. She always felt inadequate. She always wanted to do better. Every hour of the day in Margot's life there were seven people wanting something of her, and they would want it *then, that* afternoon. There would be messages stacking up saying, Would you do this? Would you do that? Oh, I haven't got seats for your performance. You promised that you'd do this for my niece.'

Later, he added, 'I mean, eventually, she only had a very passing acquaintanceship with what might be termed as a 'normal life'. She'd always been treated as something odd, special, and so in many ways controlled from a very early age. She had the expectations of her mother; of Ninette de Valois, the grande dame of the Royal Ballet. She had the expectations of Frederick Ashton, her favourite choreographer. What was in it for *them*? And so, gradually, all these pressures built up from all points of the compass, and I think it actually split her personality. I don't think that she ever really got free of that crushing burden, and I don't think she knew for a minute why she carried it. She was a driven creature,' he said sadly. 'But anyone with a stroke of genius is a driven creature. These people are sacrificed; they really are sacrificial victims. They are put on the stone, and they're pulverised.'

Ouch!

So who was this extraordinary woman? 'She was an invention really,' Meredith Daneman her biographer told me. 'She was a podgy little girl, with a basin haircut. Looked a bit Chinese. She had her nose changed since she believed that there was a kind of glamour to dancers that she felt she needed. She had a very low hairline, and so when she pulled her hair back she used to pluck the hair around her forehead to take her hairline further back and give her what she hoped would be a better line. She dyed her hair, because when she began dancing there was a sort of prejudice that you absolutely had to have black hair if you were going to succeed.'

Phoebe, her sister-in-law, agreed. 'She wanted a long neck', Phoebe told me, 'and she achieved it by holding her neck and her head in a strange position.' Next was her voice. Peter Wright, another great choreographer and a close friend, told me, 'When, as a young woman, she opened her mouth, it was dreadful. A squeaky little voice. So she went and had special voice lessons.'

'She was like a blank page,' Meredith Daneman added. 'She was something that people could write on. She was like somebody coming out of a chrysalis; a haunted, beautiful, bony face, that came out of this really unpromising material. Almost as unpromising as her name, really.'

And it was here that her mother, Hilda, later known as the Black Queen, had taken a firm hand, I was told. 'Hookham isn't a good stage name,' she announced, 'so we changed it to Fontes, my maiden name as it happens.' Not quite true. Hearing of the impending change of name, a letter came from the Fontes family saying, 'On no account will we let our name be besmirched by theatrical associations.' Today, most people think that the name which became Fonteyn was 'wonderfully' chosen. In fact, a shop in the Charing Cross Road had supplied the magic name. Rebuffed by the Fontes family, Margot and her mother went to the London telephone directory and looked down the Fs and, lo and behold, there was a hairdresser in the Charing Cross Road called 'Fonteyn', and they said, *Right*, that will do.

'The first house that I can remember,' Margot told me, 'was in the London suburb of Ealing. And there we were: a happy, ordinary little family of four, with my father and mother and my brother Felix, three years older than me.' In fact, her mother, who had been an illegitimate child, had grown up without any experience of proper mothering. She was sufficiently alarmed when she had children of her own that she actually tried to abort Margot when she was pregnant by throwing herself down the steps and taking strange potions that she had read about in books. This was certainly kept a dark family secret all through Margot's life. It never appeared in the press.

Interestingly, Margot died only two years after her mother. Her mother had therefore lived more-or-less her entire adult life with her daughter. If Margot was married to anyone in the world, I realised, she was married to her mother. They were a complete double act.

'Father had been working in London,' Margot told me. 'He used to have an office overlooking St James' Park. And when I was very tiny, I used to go up to his office and look out across the park. When he had been at Manchester University, he had met my mother, who was actually half Brazilian but had never been to Brazil in her life, because she, too, was born and brought up in Manchester. I was only eight when this happy family existence came to an end, because my father accepted a position with the British American Tobacco Company to be Chief Engineer for their whole China division. And for a variety of reasons we were in fact never again to live together as a family of four. We arrived finally at Shanghai and the ship moored up in midstream of the Wangpo River, opposite the famous Shanghai waterfront, the Bund. That must have been early 1928.'

I managed to track down someone who had actually known Margot in Shanghai: Patsy, Lady Jellicoe. 'I met Margot in Shanghai when she was seven. There were beggars everywhere. And my first memory was seeing a man in a faraway field cutting his child's leg off to make him a beggar. It was terrible. Terrible. I thought Margot would die. She appeared to have no bones. Margot floated. We called her 'the little black cat'. She's always remained the little black cat to me. She used to waft movement. Very quiet. Very reserved. Only came to life when she danced.'

'When I was fourteen,' Margot told me, 'my mother brought me back to England because she thought that if I had any talent for dancing, it was time that she took me to a professional company to see if this was so. Actually, I really didn't like ballet dancing very much because it was rather stiff and rigid and, frankly, boring. And I preferred something where I was banging a tambourine and stamping about in heeled shoes. But my mother was very persistent, and eventually took me for an audition at the Sadler's Wells Theatre, which then housed the school of the Vic-Wells Ballet. A young company, which much later became Britain's Royal Ballet, and there I met its founder, Ninette de Valois, the presiding genius of British ballet whose real name I discovered was Edris Stannus from County Wicklow in Ireland.' Later, some unkind soul described de Valois as 'that Irish washer-woman'.

And so Margot began a career of unparalleled success. And calamity. First up was the musical director of the Vic-Wells Ballet, Constant Lambert, whose son Kit, incidentally, became the manager of The Who. I asked Ashton, resident choreographer of the new company, what made Lambert such a good conductor. Ashton said, 'Very good tempi, very good ear, very good sense of balance, very large cock.' Andrew Motion, a former Poet Laureate and the biographer of the whole Lambert Family, told me he could remember finding photos of Constant looking like a kind of ash heap. 'I mean really quite disgusting, actually, with food down himself. There are plenty of stories of him falling over drunk, sometimes during a performance. This colossally bloated pastiche Churchill figure, at least one cigarette in his mouth if not several, trying to put that in my mind next to the immaculate, young, fawn-like Margot Fonteyn, and really puzzling over how it had worked.'

'She did have two abortions when she was young and working with Constant Lambert,' Meredith Daneman told me, 'and one presumes they were Constant's children. That weird thing of being in a company, knowing that this person had huge power to wield, and wanting her sexually. I think she was frightened and didn't quite know what to do. Her mother was certainly thoroughly alarmed and felt that Constant put an enormous amount of pressure on her to which she eventually succumbed. But she was forever worrying and fretting about him. The thing about abortion in those days in a ballet company was, it was the worst thing you could do really was have a baby, because dancers just didn't have children. You made a decision: were you going to dance or were you going to develop your maternal side? You *had* to absolutely cast out all thought of leading a double life.'

'People were reluctant to talk about the relationship between Constant Lambert and Margot because, strictly speaking, she was under age,' Andrew Motion told me, 'and this would not have looked good had it been brought out into the light of day. Besides, of course, it was illegal. Can you imagine her shame and embarrassment, and how hurt she must have felt, having given so much, when he turned her away and went back to somebody else?' I learnt later that she'd actually been stood up at a registry office by Constant. 'They were actually supposed to meet first at a church,' Meredith Daneman told me, 'and he just didn't turn up. And when he later married someone else, this was a terrible blow to Margot. She even cut him out of her autobiography as a professional figure, let alone as a personal one.' In Ashton's words, 'She cut the *idea* of him completely out of her life and sewed herself up and became a virgin again.'

Margot's subsequent career as the prima ballerina of what became the Royal Ballet is the stuff of legend. When the Royal Opera House re-opened after the Second World War (it had been used as a dance hall during the war), 20 February 1946, it was with a fully staged performance of *The Sleeping Beauty*, in fact, the first full-length three-act ballet ever to be staged in England. Its later transfer to New York, with Margot Fonteyn appearing simultaneously on the covers of both *Time* magazine and *Newsweek*, made her a legend overnight, although not without a certain cost. Beryl Grey, Margot's fellow principal, told me they were being paid £4 a week. And even after their huge success in *The Sleeping Beauty*, together with their other principal dancer Moira Shearer, they had to demand a pay rise from the management. Eventually, David Webster, the boss, agreed to an extra £10 a week; 'But we had to fight for it'.

Beryl Grey also had a wicked story about that first night in Covent Garden. Because of the war, nobody had new clothes to appear grand. 'So they brought out all their old evening dresses and everybody did whatever they could to dress up. But I always said that it was a Gala that smelled strongly of mothballs, because no one had worn anything like that for so long.' By contrast, that first performance in Covent Garden was also attended by King George VI and Queen Elizabeth and the Princesses, together with the old Queen Mother, Queen Mary. When Queen Mary arrived, she was conducted upstairs by David Webster to the Royal anteroom. She gave one piercing look round it and said, 'What, no food?'

But what had made Margot such an astonishing dancer? Let's start with *The Sleeping Beauty*, which I did not see but have talked to many people who did.

Performed over 200 times in the first ten years alone after its première in 1890, it tells the story of Princess Aurora, whose hand is sought in marriage by numerous suitors. Four such likely gentlemen are presented, and Aurora dances what became known as the Rose

Adagio as she moves along the line, pirouetting between each one until accepting the proffered rose. When she came to the last suitor, according to all who saw it, Fonteyn, *en pointe*, waited for what seemed forever, some said for *30 seconds*, before accepting the rose, bringing gasps of astonishment from the audience. Many years later when I interviewed Clive Barnes, the renowned ballet critic of the New York Times, he burst into tears remembering this moment. 'She must have felt that the entire prestige of Great Britain was resting on her tiny shoulders. But she just waited there, didn't even bother to take his hand for balance. Just smiled at him. En pointe, on her toes… she…I can't…' He wept. In the audience, one man had got so excited he had actually fallen out of his box. Valerie Taylor, a member of the corps de ballet that night told me, 'we were all standing in the wings. We had never seen Margot or anyone else dancing like that. Never. The audience reaction was astonishing; yelling and screaming with applause. We had never heard anything like it. When Margot got into an arabesque or something similar, there was yet another huge amount of applause. Everybody was crying.'

Desmond Kelly, a fine dancer and one of Fonteyn's favourite partners, told me that dancing with her was at first a shock. 'When I was in my thirties, I thought that technique was it. This is what dancing was about. This is what we trained to do every day of our life, to make our technique as beautiful as possible. But Margot taught me that it's not that; not technique. Of course, you have to have a technique to dance. But she had the most extraordinary way of telling a story. Of making it real from the beginning to the end, so you believed absolutely everything she was doing. No arty-farty stuff; there was nothing stitched on from the outside. It actually came from inside her. She had an amazing ability to reach people, to come across the footlights and say to a person sitting in the audience that she was actually dancing for *you*.'

I'm a clod-pole when it comes to dancing, even the waltz. But there was another element when you talked to her that it was impossible to ignore. Donald MacLeary, another fine dancer and sometimes partner of Fonteyn, pointed out to me that 'She always looked immaculate. I mean, you never saw her in a pair of jeans, or sneakers or anything like that. Heels and gloves and hats and Dior suits and always perfectly groomed. Hair always terribly tidy. She was immaculate: her dark, jet-black hair, her huge almond eyes. She always wore bright red lipstick. She radiated happiness. Something hard for people to understand nowadays, but honestly, when she came on the stage the kilowatts went up. Really they did. And we all sort of, you know, thought, God, that's what being a ballerina is all about.'

And Lynn Seymour, who had much cause to be resentful of Margot – the part of Juliet in MacMillan's Prokofiev ballet had been choreographed for her, only for her to be dumped at the last moment in favour of Fonteyn; MacMillan was furious – Lynn Seymour told me that 'even in the remote corner of wilderness in Canada where I was born, Fonteyn was a household name. She was on everyone's tea biscuit tin and all that sort of thing. I mean, she really was as big a name as the Prime Minister of England, if not more. She was up there with Churchill, even in my remote little dot on the globe. She was a household word. She represented ballet. She *was* ballerina.'

She was like the Queen,' Meredith Daneman added. 'She represented England. She was it. She was the face of the Motherland. A true heroine; you identified with her. You just identified with the fact that this woman was there, sort of doing it for you, that she was dancing in your place; that if *you* could dance, that was what you would do.'

But what of the woman? It would be wrong to say she was among the loneliest women I ever met, but she came close. The partnership with Nureyev, when she was already in her forties, certainly sparked new energy, artistically and emotionally. Whether they actually had a sexual relationship, no one knows, although there were rumours a-plenty, even talk of another abortion. The importance of that relationship, however, was that it was a distraction, a relief from an otherwise catastrophic turn of events in her life: the meeting with a Panamanian gangster named Tito Arias, who became her husband.

Her own account, in her autobiography, tells the story thus: 'It was in Cambridge in 1937 that I fell suddenly and instantly in love. Our little company used to dance every year in May in the University town of Cambridge, which coincided with the undergraduate's final examinations. But in spite of that, they somehow managed to entertain us in an almost continuous floating party. One evening I returned to find that the party had settled temporarily in our room. Two dark-haired young men were dancing. They were dancing the rumba, which at that time was practically unknown in England. I was fascinated by the younger of the two men. I found out that his name was Tito.'

Her own account, as I began to realise, was complete bunkum.

First, she had had virtually no contact with Arias after that first encounter. In fact, he had spurned her. But in the late 1950s, when she had become a global star, huge bunches of roses kept appearing after every performance. From Arias, of course, although the bill was sent to Fonteyn herself, her secretary told me. 'The relationship with Tito was something that was totally manufactured in Margot's head,' Keith Money told me. 'Margot did admit to me that she'd been bullied into the whole idea of marriage. She had had so many people pointedly saying, my dear, you'll end up as middle-aged and lonely. And she would try and stem all this, as she saw it, interference in her private life by saying, "Very well, I'll get married when I'm thirty-five." And it's an incredible chance that Tito Arias suddenly appeared in her dressing room when she was something like thirty-four and three-quarters. Even so, it took her a long while to be persuaded that this was anything other than complete folly. She knew that he was a philanderer and that he was a married man with three children. Why should she get involved with all of that? But gradually it became part of the mantra, "Well, I've got to get married at thirty-five because I've said I'm going to, and therefore it might as well be this one." And then she kind of reinvented the whole romance of her meeting in Cambridge when she was eighteen, although in fact he'd stood her up in Cambridge.'

And so, at the height of her fame as a ballerina, in 1955, Margot married Roberto 'Tito' Arias, a diplomat, politician, playboy and serial plotter of revolutions whose family was the Panamanian equivalent of, say, the Trumps. His father was president twice and his uncle, Arnulfo Arias, one of the last Latin American *caudillos*, was a mildly deranged adherent of Rosicrucian spiritualism who was elected president four times and sent packing by the army three times. As one of Arnulfo's aides put it, at the time of the 1984 election that General Manuel Antonio Noriega 'stole' from him, he needed "only his ten lucid minutes a day to dominate the Panamanian people", upon whom he had an undeniably hypnotic effect. It was into this surreal world of tropical intrigue that Margot married, and she undoubtedly found it all a bit of a lark. 'It's really like Alice in Wonderland, isn't it?' she said. Until, that is, it all got a bit more serious. Margot found herself in a new role as a gunrunner for Tito's latest attempted revolution, despite in the meantime having appointed himself 'Panamanian Ambassador to the United Kingdom' – the first such Ambassador.

'The anarchic and revolutionary tendencies in Margot Fonteyn were at this point extreme to the point of lunacy,' Keith Money confirmed. 'I almost became heavily involved myself, because after a performance for which she had insisted on being paid in cash, she took me off to a meeting with a Geneva-based arms manufacturer, Doctor W, in a very strange meeting place in north London on a very, very foggy evening. The good doctor thought he was going to sell her several million U.S. dollars' worth of armaments, which she intended to drive across the Channel and take on a plane to Panama. And at some point, to my mounting horror, I realised that although her feet appeared to be still on the ground, she believed all this was absolutely real. She ended up with a suitcase full of automatic weaponry, but it probably only took her a few performances to pay for that lot. But if we'd continued with the good doctor, she'd have been dancing 'til she was a hundred and fifty.'

Nor did it end there. With her smuggled armaments, as Margot herself recalled, 'We boarded a little launch, called the *Nola*, and we went out to sea, meeting up with a shrimp boat. Some of the arms had arrived in Panama in the false bottom of a little dinghy, but this dinghy, due to the weight of the arms, sank. Her splendid captain said, 'Oh I don't mind sharks at all', and he dived in and got the thing up, and they broke open the bottom of the dinghy and they unpacked all the guns and ammunitions and things which were then stacked all around on the deck. Before long, we noticed a plane circling round above us. Well, that was the police and they had discovered us. And I said to Tito, "What will happen if you come back to Panama?" "Oh," he said, "I'll be arrested." So Tito clambered aboard the shrimp boat, and in what seemed no time at all, he was a little speck in the distance. And we, Tito said, were to go back to Panama as a decoy.'

And when she got back to Panama, she was arrested and sent to jail. The Governor, no doubt a Scarpia figure, sent her roses from his garden. But it was a terrible jail. A bit later she was put in a car, straight from jail, and deported. It was, as she told me, all a bit of a lark.

In fact, it was also the beginning of the end of her relationship with Arias, or so she thought. Finally he agreed to a divorce. The necessary papers were drawn up, and as Joan Thring, Nureyev's personal assistant, told me, 'It was terrible timing. We were all in Rome and he was supposed to turn up it was to discuss the divorce. And he didn't turn up, because he'd been shot, at a traffic junction in Panama, by one of his mistresses' husbands. So there it was, finished. And I suppose she felt she couldn't leave him in that condition.'

'It was a Mr Vallarino who shot Arias five times,' Keith Money told me. 'What expensive five bullets those were in terms of twisting Margot's life totally.'

'Fonteyn being Fonteyn,' Joan Thring went on, 'she was not going to walk away from a husband who was turned into a quadriplegic.

Plus, once he was a quadriplegic, he was in her hands. The control had shifted. There wasn't going to be a lot of hanky and panky from then on, she thought. She had him where she wanted him.'

The point is, as Georgina Parkinson, another Royal Ballet principal dancer, told me, 'Margot needed to be needed. And Tito had never needed her, until those bullets went in his body. "Of course, it's nice for me because it means he bothers with me now," Margot said.

I said, "What do you mean?"

She said, "Well, when we were married and we were living in London, and he was the Ambassador, days would pass on end when he wouldn't talk to me except to tell me who someone was, because he thought I was stupid." But paralysed though he was, he actually ran off with his 'secretary', Marlena Worthington. I said, "How *could* he have?" Margot said, "They left me a note."'

The effect on her dancing career was appalling. 'After he was shot and came out of his coma,' Joan Thring remembered, 'he couldn't speak properly. So Margot was down at Stoke Mandeville Hospital spending nights down there and getting up at God knows what hour, insisting on feeding his breakfast to him, and then catching an early train to be in ballet class in West Kensington by 9.30.'

'She even taught herself to drive at that time,' Monica Mason, director of the Royal Ballet told me in 2005, 'so that she could get herself from the hospital to the railway station and onto the train up to London. Coming into work at Barons Court, to the rehearsal studios, looking very tired. Knowing that she'd danced the night before. But she never missed a class, she was always there. One was very aware again of this fantastic focus, that however terrible she must have been feeling, she focused on what she had to do to get through class. And she never left class early.' And, as I saw myself, she would stay right to the end.

But the end was now closing in on her. I remember going to see her in Covent Garden, backstage, to ask her permission for a last interview before what was to be her last appearance at Covent Garden in October 1984 in an *acte de présence*, a short dance written for Fonteyn and Ashton himself to perform in honour of Ashton's eightieth birthday. I was shocked at how frail she was, compared with that all-smiling, giggling little girl in *Romeo and Juliet* all those years ago. She was immaculate as ever, gracious, glamorous, poised, but obviously dangerously ill. 'Sometimes, when I danced with her when she was already in her sixties,' Desmond Kelly told me afterwards, 'I felt that she really didn't want to. I remember once I said,

"Oh Margot, it's packed out there, they've *all* come to see you." She said, "Darling, they've come to see a freak." I thought that was really sad, that she thought she was a freak, and that people would come to see this old woman still being able to dance. Then we got to the curtain call, and because they were all shouting and screaming, she suddenly clutched me and said, "Desmond, I can't walk. I can't walk out there." She said, "You have to hold me, you have to hold me up." She was so thin, I felt that if I clutched her to help her onto the stage, she'd break.'

When she died in February 1991, aged only 71, I had two phone calls, which I am now so grateful I took. The first was from her sister-in-law, then living in Mallorca. What she told me was greatly disturbing. Phoebe Fonteyn told me that when Margot was in hospital, clearly dying and possibly unconscious, a posse of Panamanians had turned up in the hospital with paperwork apparently concerned with an alteration of her will. 'I was there. And they kept asking me, "What about the farm? What has she done with the farm?" And I said - well I *should* have said - you're not supposed to tell people what's in anyone's will. So I said, "I don't know what's in her will." I said, "I couldn't tell you anyway, and I don't suppose anyone will tell you 'till they read the will." And then they went back into her room and they made her sign. She was out of it then; she didn't know what she was doing. They made her sign with a thumb-print to say that the farm should go to Roberto, Tito's son by a previous marriage. But I know she didn't want it to go to Roberto, because he used to steal all the cows, and used drugs of which she disapproved. And, surprise, surprise: they emerge with a new will, signed with an inky thumb-print. Now you have to wonder whether Margot, weeks earlier, had said, "Oh gosh, I might just want to change my will at the very last minute, so maybe I should actually go and register my thumb-print."

The second call was from a journalist whom I had never previously met: Tony Burton, based in Central America. He told me that after Fonteyn had died he was curious to see where she had been buried, and what sort of memorial stone had been put in place. 'So I went to the cemetery six months or so after her death - "the Cemetery of Peace" it was called. I went to the custodian, and he looked up in his book, but he didn't seem to know anything about Arias and Fonteyn. Eventually he found her name, misspelled, and he took me over to the plot where she had been buried. It was clearly a pauper's grave, next to a hedge. And over the hedge was a garden and a house, with washing blowing in the breeze over the grave of this magnificent ballerina. It was as though she had been put there to be forgotten.'

There was worse to come. When I went myself to find the grave some years later, there was nothing to be seen, despite my having previously asked the Arias family's permission to visit. Eventually I found the same custodian who had helped Tony Burton. 'Ah yes,' he said. 'A week ago representatives of the family arrived, dug up her remains and I believe put them in the underground family mausoleum at the Iglesia Santuario Nacional del Corazon de Maria in Panama City with a simple plaque: Dame Margot Fonteyn de Arias, her name being underneath that of her husband Roberto Arias, Tito.'

'In the end', Meredith Daneman told me, 'she knew what was required of her and she did it with such grace – that word – and such beautiful dedication that it became an expression, a true expression of her as a person. I mean, you might think that the cancer came upon her because of the unacknowledged anger that she felt at all that she'd been put through.'

Chapter 23

Shostakovich

Anyone naive enough to make films about musicians, and composers in particular, will be confronted sooner or later by the long shadow of Dmitri Shostakovich. His life and his colossal achievements bestride the twentieth century like no other composer, except perhaps his compatriot Stravinsky.

And that is not an idle comparison. I met both men. To his dying day, Stravinsky had always maintained he was a 'Russian' composer. And to *his* dying day, Shostakovich had always regretted his infamous denunciation of Stravinsky in 1949 as being 'formalist' and therefore worthless. Both knew in their hearts that, as two of the greatest composers of the century, they were the two sides of the same coin. They *were* the twentieth century in all its blood-soaked barbarism.

But whereas Stravinsky had opted for a comfortable life in the West (although he himself had been every bit as much anti-Tsarist as Shostakovich), Shostakovich had chosen to stay in Russia, despite various opportunities to leave. And therein lay the paradox which my film *Testimony* sought to explore. What is the price that any and all creative artists have to pay to reach for the stars, with their visions and their magic? And if their *life* depends on finding the answer, as it did on an almost daily basis with Shostakovich, then we are dealing with a kind of courage that is way beyond most mortals. This is why we ignore Shostakovich and his works at our peril. Not just our loss, but our peril, because he is the beacon against which all creative endeavour must be measured, even if it is invariably and inevitably found wanting.

My film came about in an unpredictable way. Solomon Volkov had published his *Memoirs of Shostakovich* (*as related to and edited by Solomon*

Volkov) in 1979, also titled *Testimony*. Although I was sceptical of some of the text, and also of some of the claims that Volkov had made in the text, doubts which subsequent research found to be more than justified, it was a startling book.

It's now almost impossible to think back to the time (only fifty years ago!) when we knew so little about Shostakovich. But, for instance, in 1973, when the Russians were finally persuaded to sign the Berne Convention for the Protection of Literary and Artistic Works, thus acknowledging the international copyrights of our music and theirs, the Russian authorities were asked for a list of Shostakovich symphonies. The list duly arrived: Symphonies No.1, 2, 3, 5, 7, 10, 11, 12, and 15. No mention of *Babi Yar* (No.13); no mention of No. 9 (the manuscript of which had been notoriously torn up in front of Shostakovich as he was being denounced), and so on. But so stupid were the Russian authorities, that they had not even bothered to re-number the symphonies; they just left blanks. And when in 1986 Shostakovich's widow, Iryna, began secretly to help with the script for our film, despite two KGB guards being at the door (literally), at the end she asked, 'Tell me, Mr Palmer, is anyone playing my husband's works in the West these days?' 1986!

In fact, I had started out with the intention of making a documentary, and to this end I had been granted an audience in 1986 with Tikhon Khrennikov, the General Secretary of the Composers' Union - the very same Khrennikov who had been Stalin's General Secretary and who remained General Secretary, in name at least, to his dying day (which was under Putin!). I had met him before, when we had agreed in 1981 on a co-production about Stravinsky with USSR State TV. If I wanted to film in the Soviet Union at that time - and I did, to trace Stravinsky's Russian origins - I had no choice but to meet with him. Little did I realise that all Khrennikov had wanted, apparently, was to get his hands on the Western material about Stravinsky which had otherwise been denied him. And this he did, re-editing my three-hour film to make his own one-hour version 'Produced by T. Khrennikov', deleting anything critical of the Soviet Union. I have a copy. I know he did it.

So there I am, drinking vodka with the very same Mr Khrennikov, he being charming and sitting beneath three big portraits, as we have seen before. To the left, Prokofiev, whose life he had made a misery; to the right, Stravinsky, whose music he had effectively banned; and in the centre, Shostakovich, the torn-up manuscript of whose 9th Symphony he had literally danced upon in triumph - a scene we eventually included in our film. 'Of course,' said Khrennikov. 'You can have everything you want. We have *miles* of film of Shostakovich.' Indeed, he had. 'Shostakovich swimming, playing the piano, smiling, receiving medals…' and so on. Then he added, with more than a touch of menace, 'But, of course, you *will* tell the true story of Shostakovich, won't you, my *friend*?' I knew immediately what that meant: perpetuating the same lies and propaganda about Shostakovich being a true Communist, son of the Fatherland, et cetera. I thanked him and left, knowing that the only possibility now was a feature film. Fiction, in other words, but, I hoped, as close to the truth as I could manage. Enter Volkov and his book. Enter Mrs Shostakovich.

A small footnote here. About a month later, I was told that a producer from the BBC named Peter Manuira had had a similar meeting with Khrennikov. He had fallen for the trick and had produced a documentary in 1987 that in my view was pure Soviet propaganda, which the BBC had then shown without demur. He was subsequently Head of Classical Music for BBC TV for a time. He has never apologised. A disgrace? Ashamed of himself? No – being from the BBC, one of the more arrogant and self-justifying organisations in the world, he was not.

But writing a full-length film script, when there was so little information about Shostakovich other than Volkov's book, was obviously not going to be easy. To start with, we were now denied access to the Soviet Union, both for research and for the actual filming. There were several expatriates, such as Rostropovich, who volunteered to help – provided they could have complete editorial control and provided their part in the story was writ large. Rostropovich, for instance, told me that Shostakovich had died in his arms, which was a lie. Such self-serving nonsense I could do without.

Eventually, I asked a great and almost forgotten British playwright, David Rudkin, if he would make an attempt. He asked to meet Volkov, now living in New York, and, like me, was soon doubtful of Volkov's claim that Shostakovich had read and approved the text of his book by 'signing every page' before publication. Nonetheless, it was all we had to go on. The extraordinary script that Rudkin produced, although based on the few facts we knew, was, in reality, pure fiction. Incredibly, I have to report that as more and more has been revealed since we made the film about Shostakovich's life and circumstances, the 'fiction' which for us was often pure guess-work, has proved to be ninety-nine per cent accurate – unnervingly so.

But where on earth could I find locations that looked like Russia in the 1920s, 1930s, 1940s and 1950s? I might want you to believe that choosing Liverpool and the old cotton-mill town of Wigan nearby was divine inspiration. But, in fact, as I am lifelong supporter of Liverpool Football Club, the entire film schedule was worked around Liverpool's home matches. I exaggerate to some extent because, when, almost ten years later, I was persuaded by Valery Gergiev to show the film in St Petersburg – Shostakovich's home town – the majority of the audience, including Mrs Shostakovich, refused to believe that the whole thing had not actually been shot in the Soviet Union.

A digression. Films cost money. Not a lot in my case, but enough. I managed to get the film half-financed by Channel Four Television in England, principally through the genius of David Rose, the founder of Film Four. But with only two weeks to go until the start of the actual filming, we still did not have the remaining fifty percent. A lawyer friend (who, ironically, subsequently went bankrupt) introduced me to an Australian entrepreneur whose principal business, I was told, was financing army vehicles such as tanks. I was given thirty minutes to 'sell' a long, black and white, apparently non-commercial film about a (then) obscure Russian composer with a long name that even the Channel Four lawyers never could spell properly. To my astonishment, and eternal gratitude, at the end of my pitch he just shook my hand and said, 'It's a deal. It'll be a hell of a lot more fun than financing tanks.' He was as good as his word, and his proudest moment was eight months later when he chartered a Boeing airplane from Australia to bring all his mates to London for the film's première at the Empire Leicester Square, one of the biggest (and best) cinemas in London, during the opening of the London Film Festival. All he wanted was to shake hands with Ben Kingsley, who gave what many (including himself) consider to be one of his finest film performances to date.

Another digression. When I had first asked Kingsley if he would consider the part (he had won the Oscar for *Gandhi* two years previously), he had agreed – very rapidly I thought – despite being warned there was no money in it. Some while later I discovered that he had not worked since *Gandhi*. This was his first 'job' since then. Such is the crazy world of film-making. Even so, the amount of money I had was only enough for five weeks filming (for a two-and-a-half hour film), involving a huge orchestra and hundreds of extras who all came from the local Job Centre ('but don't tell Equity', Kingsley said).

But it's not really a digression, because I want you to understand the haphazard way in which films are made. Time and chance happens to all men, to film makers as well as to great composers. And I firmly believe that Shostakovich would never have left us such an incredible legacy had he lived, for example, in the UK and received a generous Arts Council grant and had a 'nice house' in Hampstead. He is what he is because of where he lived and what he experienced, and one myth that the film helped to dump into the dustbin of academia is that the Symphonies are the 'public', happy, Communist Shostakovich, whereas the String Quartets are the 'private', agonised Shostakovich, implacably hostile to the regime. That is bollocks. Every note *is* the man, and the man is the time in which he lived. The idea, as proclaimed but not (we now realise) *believed* by Stravinsky, that 'music can express nothing, only itself', should be treated with the contempt it deserves.

I always wondered, for instance, why the opera *Lady Macbeth of Mtsensk* was such a runaway hit in 1934, the year of its composition (it was not denounced by *Pravda* and banned until almost two years later): then eighty-three sold-out performances in Leningrad alone the following year, and reportedly over 300 throughout the Soviet Union – three times as many as for the entire works of Puccini and Verdi put together. Whatever else, the music is decidedly not Puccini. It is angular, frequently aggressive, uncomfortable, and it has no tunes! So, why such a success?

It wasn't until well into the filming that the penny finally dropped. If a poet writes 'Stalin bad man', well, he's for the chop. Easy. If a composer writes a melody through which he intends to say 'Stalin bad man', that's more difficult to prove. The composer survives. And Shostakovich did survive, despite saying – as we have now come to understand – repeatedly and consistently, 'Stalin bad man'. With poets, playwrights, and intellectuals of all kinds being taken away and shot in the middle of the night (Shostakovich's close friend, the theatre director Meyerhold, was beaten to death, while his wife had her eyes gouged out with blunt knives); even loyal foot soldiers of the regime and personal friends of Stalin being murdered in their millions – yes, millions – their bodies thrown into stone crushers and flushed down the city sewers, what hope for the ordinary folk? With incredible bravery and ingenuity, Shostakovich became the lone voice of 'us against them', a fact huge numbers of the population of the Soviet Union heard and knew. Hence the unprecedented success of *Lady Macbeth*. Stalin knew also, and the opera 'disappeared' for twenty-seven years, until Stalin was well and truly dead. Yet, somehow, Shostakovich survived.

As an illustration of the horrors Shostakovich endured, we included a scene in our film where Shostakovich is seen half-asleep by the door of his apartment, with his hand tied to a suitcase in which was the unfinished score of his Fifth Symphony. He reasoned that if he was taken away in the night by the NKVD to the Lubyanka prison, he would have sufficient time to complete the symphony before he was taken out and shot. Later, it amused Rudkin and me to read in Julian Barnes's 2016 novel *The Noise of Time* this same scene (without any acknowledgment of course), one of several which we had invented and had no basis in historical fact.

It is clear to me now that if we want to know what it was like to live under Stalin in the Soviet Union from 1924 until 1953, the year of Stalin's death, we need to listen to Shostakovich. It's all we've got. Compared with the garbage once propagated by the Russians that they inhabited a land of freedom and democracy, Shostakovich's music is truthful, painful and horrific. No wonder that today in Russia, in the glorious years of the Putin 'democratic' dictatorship, Shostakovich's music will empty the hall. It is as if no-one wants to be reminded now of those terrible years.

When I was devising the end credits of the film, I wanted to compare and contrast the achievements of Stalin and Shostakovich. Shostakovich, 147 works, et cetera. And Stalin? In 1987 I asked Robert Conquest, the great historian of that period, to estimate the number of people killed by Stalin in *peacetime*, whether murdered or deliberately starved to death. 'Easy,' he said. (Don't forget, this was estimated in 1987.) 'You can put any figure between fifteen and forty-five million,' he said, 'and no one will be able to prove you wrong.' Eventually, in the end credits, I put thirty million murdered by Stalin in peacetime. Gorbachev eventually admitted that Stalin had been 'responsible for the deaths of perhaps two to three million'. We now know that my figure was more accurate.

So, in this sense, the music of Dmitri Shostakovich is the most powerful memorial imaginable to the greatest number of innocent souls destroyed by a tyrant in all of recorded history. Hitler and the Jews? Appalling though the Holocaust was, in terms of numbers, it was just small potatoes. After all, there's always Chairman Mao - another sixty million?

And that, I believe, is ultimately the significance of Volkov's book. Regardless of whether or not he invented certain passages, regardless of whether Shostakovich did in fact see and approve the text (about which endless pages of academic arse-licking have been spewed out, mostly in American universities), when the book was first published in the West in 1979, four years after Shostakovich had died in August 1975, it was the very first time that anyone grasped that Shostakovich had been through a monstrous hell, but somehow his voice could not be silenced, albeit at an awful personal cost. No other single book about Shostakovich had, or has, made that so clear and with such shocking impact.

While filming in Wigan, Volkov and his wife came from New York to watch – and no doubt correct my errors – while we were recreating Shostakovich's funeral, at which he had actually been present. The fictional Stalin was played in the film by a powerful actor called Terence Rigby. After the filming, Kingsley and I and several of the crew gathered for supper at our hotel, with Volkov and his wife as our guests. Volkov sat on my right looking towards the door of the restaurant. Suddenly, he dropped his glass of wine and, white-faced, began to tremble violently. I was sure he was having a heart attack and I began to rush for the door in search of a doctor. Then I noticed that standing in the door was Terence Rigby the actor, still dressed in that murderous villain's costume. The irony was that Rigby was one of the gentlest of men, whose personal kindness knew no limits. But twenty years later, when Volkov and I were together at a Shostakovich festival in Rome, Volkov told me that the image of Rigby standing in that Wigan doorway still haunted him.

When the film was finished, we were asked by the Soviet Embassy in London to arrange a private screening. Along came the Soviet *chargé d'affaires* 'responsible' for culture, a Georgian film director who was 'very famous', I was told, and a bald-headed man who was not introduced to me. At the end, the Soviet diplomat shouted at me that I had defamed the Soviet Union, defamed the memory of Dmitri Shostakovich, defamed the Union of Soviet Composers (Khrennikov again) *bla bla bla*. The 'very famous' Georgian director, despite only being five feet high (I am six foot), spat at me. Later, the Soviet Embassy took out an injunction against the film being screened at the London Film Festival, appropriately through an English legal firm called 'Gasters' ('Gas' in English can mean hot air, i.e., meaningless wind).

When I had recovered from being spat at, I noticed that the bald-headed man was still seated in the cinema with his back to me. As I approached him, I could see that he had been weeping. He looked at me and said, 'I wish my father had lived to see your film. He would have been deeply moved by its courage and truthfulness.'

I asked him, who was his father?

'Sergei Prokofiev,' he said.

Chapter 24

Wardour Street

Following the apparent success of my film about Shostakovich at the London Film Festival and the never-ending worldwide screenings of the Richard Burton *Wagner* film, I began to ponder the true nature of 'being an actor'. I might want to say that most actors and actresses are vain, conceited and self-obsessed…and terrified. They puff themselves up with a complete lack of regard for everyone else in sight. They have to, otherwise they could not do what they do. So I have tried to love them all. Sometimes, this can reach bizarre proportions. Ekkehard Schall, director of the Berliner Ensemble and in my view a great actor, was short. But when he was cast as Liszt in my Wagner epic, I had a problem: Liszt was very tall. We gave Ekkehard platform shoes. He told me this was an affront to his vanity, his dignity and his skill as an actor. 'I act tall,' he told me. And, my goodness, so he did.

Others insist on bringing their personal masseuse. Kim Novak, a once and still very beautiful woman when we worked together on her last major film, brought with her a very serious German masseuse who offered her 'services' to other members of the team (including the director) although I'm disappointed to say all of us politely refused since we were not too sure how it might end. Richard Burton, who had given his last great performance as the German composer Wagner, also had a masseur, a man from Texas by the name of Joe. Although it was true that when we were filming Wagner - 157 days non-stop, an extraordinary commitment from Burton, and not a day lost because of his alcoholism - he was still recovering from a serious operation which had wasted the muscles in his back; I became convinced that one of Joe's functions was as a companion for Burton immediately after each day's filming, a trusted buddy to whom Burton could pour out his troubles. Although how much actual conversation took place, I do not know, because I soon realised that even at his perkiest, Joe was monosyllabic. Each new city we arrived in, Joe's one remark as he travelled from airport to hotel in the back of his limousine was 'Gee!' Munich, Vienna, Frankfurt, Nürnberg; it didn't make the slightest difference. All Joe would say was 'Gee!'

Then, after he had settled in the hotel and we were, perhaps, having lunch or a drink in the bar, Joe would suddenly look out of the window and say 'Yup!' Again: Munich, Frankfurt or wherever, Joe's one remark would be 'Yup!' As the filming wore on, I tried to encourage him to expand his vocabulary by asking him if he had been to Europe before?

'Yup,' he said.

'Well, Joe,' I replied, 'it's been really fascinating to observe you reacting to all the places we've visited as if this were the first time you were really seeing them.'

'Yup,' he said.

'But wait a minute, Joe,' I said, 'You've assured me that you'd been to Europe before, but you now say you're seeing all these cities for the first time.'

'Yup,' he said.

And then, with a beguiling smile, he pointed to the skies and said, 'Last time I was here, we bombed the hell out of them.'

'Of course,' I said, 'how stupid of me'.

It turned out that Texas Joe had been a bomber pilot in the war, and so every time he had arrived in a new city and driven from the airport, he had marvelled at the amount of rebuilding which had gone on since his last visit (as in '*Gee!*'). And every time he stared out of his hotel room and thought he recognised a building which he'd pulverised only a few years earlier, his obvious reaction was, 'Yup!'

'Gee, Joe,' I said, 'that must have been some war.'

To which, of course, he replied, 'Yup!'

The relative notoriety of my film about Shostakovich also brought two important (if eventually inconsequential) opportunities. In the sixties and seventies the film industry in England was centred (or believed it was) around an area in London's Soho called Wardour Street, many of whose buildings then appeared, from the outside at least, to be somewhat seedy. The day after the London première of *Testimony*, I received a telephone call from someone claiming to be a mogul of Wardour Street. 'My name is Regan B. Cupcake,' I thought the voice said. 'I'm in celluloid. I saw *Testimoneey*, and I'm telling you; you could be big. Huge. Come over and see my posters. You'll be impressed. It could be a big teaser.' As it's always good to have several balls in the air, as one lady agent repeatedly told me, I accepted.

'Be here prompt at 9.50,' the voice had said. At 10.40, having drunk my fourteenth cup of Nescafé, I asked the pneumatic secretary if there was any chance that Mr Cupcake had forgotten my appointment.

'Mr Who?' she cackled.

'Cupcake,' I replied apologetically.

'Cuttcake,' she said I meant.

I said I meant Cuttcake.

'Yes,' she said, 'I know you meant to say you meant 'Cuttcake'. No, he never forgets.'

'My name's Gus,' said a young man, forty-ish, with a flowery tie and shirt. 'I do publicity.'

'Ah,' I said knowingly.

'D'you know,' he continued, 'it was fantastic. I actually got twenty seconds of full-frontal nudity onto the Mike Parkinson chat show the other night. Good old Mike. Real mucker. It cost me a bit, of course, but you should have seen the queues outside the Cameo Poly the night after. Unbelievable. I mean, it was so unbelievable, it was fantastic. Here to see Cutter, are you?' he added as he wandered off with a leer at Miss Pneumatic.

'Cuttcake was right about the poster we put out; that much was certain,' he said. 'We dare not print the original title, so put out: *The Greatest Sexcess in town. We dare you to see it.*'

'My boys, forgive me,' said a white-haired face stuffed with a cigar as Gus and I entered his office. 'Come in, come in. Take your coat off. Have some coffee. Feel at home. Be relaxed. Don't worry. Have a drink. Have a cigar. Charlie; how are you Charlie? You're looking good. Look at you, Charlie. Let me have a good look at you. You're looking good. You're looking good, Charlie.'

'You see,' said Gus now known as Charlie, 'our problem is we don't need money. Who needs it? It's irrelevant. What we need now is class. Real class. Sex *and* class, in fact. It's a knockout; *and* it'll be huge. Vast. Massive. And we wanna do you a real favour. After *Testimonial*, we are prepared to go the distance. Give you all you need. *Anything*, if you can bring it off.'

I asked about the script, the cast, the story line, and the budget of the proposed new film? 'Taken care of,' said the white face, rolling his cigar around with a pock-marked tongue. 'We had, and I hesitate to tell you this, Tony boy – you don't mind if I call you Tony boy, do you, Tone? – we had the most sensational idea. In fact, it was *Testament* that brought it up.' Cuttcake hesitated, and then (hesitantly) laid it all out. 'Vera is a Russian au pair who comes to live in Stanley Crescent with a young aristo and his wife. Vera seduces the young aristo, who turns out to be in love with his wife's brother. But the wife has already had her brother, which the wife's husband subsequently finds out. In anguish – and this is where the class comes in – in *anguish*, the husband chains his wife to the television and forces Vera to have it off with his wife. I mean, this is huge,' added Cuttcake.

'Huge,' repeated Charlie/Gus.

'We envisage,' said Cuttcake, 'a three-week shooting schedule and a maximum budget of $200,000. We'll pay you $10,000 otherwise we'll miss the Christmas trade. You'll never look back, Tone my boy.' All I see is a moustache gone yellow; greasy, silver-white hair; the pale green shirt with a gold stud in the tie; sixty years in the business and doesn't look a day over ninety. Pouchy eyes and horn-rimmed glasses; the terrible knowledge that at that time men like him controlled much of the film business, not just in England, but worldwide. To make anything worthwhile in the cinema, one had to wade through dozens of Cupcakes (whose real name, it turned out, was Kunttner). And to make anything worthwhile in television, it often seemed one had to wade through dozens of mini-Cupcakes. One such, a Miss Street-Porter (*sic*), then in charge of Youth Programmes (*sic*) at the BBC, described one of her more inspired ideas for a new programme along the following lines: 'It's a soap, actually a classical opera in soap-sized chunks, which has a vampire seducing three virgins within twenty-four hours, so it's got a lot going for it and it's incredibly evil. We're updating it to work in central London, so instead of noblemen and peasants, it's going to be about businessmen and secretaries.'

In television, it seemed, the problem was not just with sex but with the overweening self-importance of the television executive, about which more anon.

Another Street Porter I encountered was one Augustus Montilardi, who invited me, together with Colin McInnes and Anthony Burgess – both very distinguished novelists, after all – to discuss contemporary culture on an Italian/Eurovision TV spectacular to be recorded in Rome. 'The cultural input,' I was told, 'would be provided by Herb Cohen, manager of Frank Zappa and the Mothers of Invention, and producer of my infamous film, *200 Motels*.'

For those who have never visited Rome's Leonardi da Vinci international airport, a word of warning. The baggage arrivals hall had then a unique feature, consisting of two moving ramps travelling downhill while the luggage attempted to travel uphill. The effectiveness of this scheme was not immediately apparent, but I was assured by an assistant of Montilardi that it had been designed by da Vinci himself, so I should stop worrying and enjoy myself.

The journey from the airport to the Rome Hilton was indeed very relaxed, except for one collision and the arrest of our driver. He seemed a cheery fellow, if a little determined. But then, as he told me, I was a guest of Italian television, and as Italian television was controlled by either the state or the Mafia or both, no harm could come to me.

The receptionist at the Rome Hilton was polite, but had never heard of me and there was certainly no message from Italian television telling me where to go and when. But they did have a room for sixteen million lira with, I was assured, all modern comforts. I took it, and then spent some hours trying to contact the man who had begun this whole affair with a phone call to my office in London, saying, 'Hello, my name is Montilardi. I make prize-winning films and my father is dying of cancer. He is very noble.' Montilardi had gone on to explain that RAI (Italian state television) was planning a two-hour programme called *Music Today* which would 'investigate the sociological, psychological, metaphysical, harmonical, linguistical, therapeutical and sacramental elements in pop music', and would I like to take part?

Sitting among all the possible creature comforts in the Rome Hilton some days later, I now realised it was foolish of me to have attempted to ring Italian TV on a Sunday to inquire about a 'Mr Montilardi'. 'No,' said a squeaky girl, 'Signor Montali no work here.' I rang a friend in London, who went to my house to look up Montilardi's home phone number. But I soon discovered that this particular home phone number did not exist. The police asked me if I wished to arrest him – and, no, they didn't have his number either. Nor did the fire brigade, the Ministry of the Interior, Alitalia or the State Tourist Board. The Hilton switchboard thought the best thing to do was wander around Rome until I caught a glimpse of him.

Next day, the phone rang early. 'Are you Mr Palmer?' said a voice. 'This is your neighbour next door. A guy called Montalardio keeps calling, and when I tell him I am <u>not</u> Signor Palmer, he refuses to believe me. Now I know where you are, I'll divert the call next time he rings.'

Ten minutes later, and finally I make contact. 'This is the voice of Montaldini,' says the voice. 'Do not panic. You are very welcome, all of you. A car will pick you up at 2pm. Please be prompt. My father died eventually. He was very noble.'

At a quarter past four we all arrived at the TV studio, just in time for the two o'clock camera rehearsal. 'They told me I was going to the Italian Riviera,' said Colin McInnes grumpily. Each participant was given a large ear piece that refused to stay in place, but it would, we were assured, give us an instantaneous translation of anything the Italian members of the discussion panel might say. The Anglo-Saxon community, as my colleagues were referred to, comprised three Celts, two Russian Jews, one Italian-American, one German émigré, and someone from Clacton. As far as we could see, there were no Italian members of the discussion panel.

In the rehearsal, we were each asked to say something to make sure we were working. One of the Russian Jews (to whom none of us had been introduced) began reading a prepared manifesto on behalf of all Russian Jews who wished to emigrate from the Soviet Union, whereupon the floor manager yelled 'Silenzio' and told us there would now be a 'fiesta break'. The actual recording started three hours later, and although everyone spoke in English, comprehension was reduced to a minimum because all the instantaneous translations were deafening and, what's more, they were in Italian. 'I was promised the Italian Riviera,' muttered McInnes, while Montalardio's secretary told me it had been difficult to organise a car to take me back to the airport because her father had died recently.

Two weeks later, Montilardi telephoned me in London to say he was organising an international symposium on the 'psychical manifestations of ragtime' and he was certain I would want to take part. I told him I would let him know.

Chapter 25

Rachmaninoff

It was while I was directing the Russian première of Wagner's opera *Parsifal* on the stage of the Mariinsky Theatre in St, Petersburg in 1997 – it was actually the first time it had ever been fully staged in Russia, as we have seen – that its conductor, Valery Gergiev (now discredited because of his support for that mobster Putin), asked me why I had never made a film about Rachmaninoff. 'Did I not know of his association with the Mariinsky; the first performance of the Second Symphony, conducted by the composer; the first performance of the St John Liturgy, et cetera?' I confessed I did not know, whereupon I received a thirty-minute lecture from Gergiev about my ignorance and how important Rachmaninoff was to all Russian musicians, a lecture which concluded with him saying, 'You make the film; I'll conduct the music.' Since, at that time, he was one of the most highly regarded and expensive conductors in the world, it was an offer I would have been churlish to refuse.

To digress momentarily about our production of *Parsifal,* which was so wildly successful that Gergiev kept it in the repertoire for twelve years. We had a triple cast of all Russian singers, because had one singer fallen sick, the Mariinsky could not afford just to fly in a replacement, as was common practice in Europe and elsewhere. Before we began rehearsing, I told Gergiev that I would not come unless he promised me he would attend all the rehearsals. He was renowned for conducting three different concerts in three different countries on the same day, but that would not be possible for me or his company, who were together tackling a whole new world of musical excitement.

He kept his word, incidentally, and it was a joyous collaboration, especially when we discovered a new star in one of the six Flower Maidens, Anna Netrebko. The question, as always, was how to stage the opera with its strange messages of purifying the German/Aryan blood, keeping in mind that the Great Patriotic War against Germany had cost the Soviet Union at least thirty million lives; this was a German opera, and there would probably be many veterans of that war in the audience.

I decided to stage the opera as if set in a Russian village, which awakens one morning to be told the tale of a wandering scholar who had accidentally shot a swan and…the rest you can work out, if you know the original. At the reception following the première, I was introduced to numerous ambassadors, including the British ambassador, Andrew Wood (it turns out we had been at Cambridge University at the same time), and, in particular, someone whom Gergiev had especially wanted me to meet: the deputy mayor of St Petersburg, the diminutive Vladimir Putin, who congratulated me in good English.

So, back to Rachmaninoff. Upon my return to London, I contacted Rachmaninoff's publisher, Boosey and Hawkes, whose managing director, Tony Fell, had been instrumental in smoothing my path to both Stravinsky and, later, the Polish composer Górecki, and had also been a fellow pupil of our music teacher at school, Denis Fielder. 'Very difficult,' said Tony Fell. 'Rachmaninoff's grandson, Alexandre, still lives in the house on the lake of Luzern which his grandfather had built in the 1930s and named after himself and his wife, Sergei and Natalia Rachmaninoff: 'Senar'.

'And he is very protective, I might also say possessive, of his grandfather's legacy, especially after the recent Geoffrey Rush film *Shine* about the crazed Australian pianist David Helfgott and its use of the 3rd Piano Concerto, which Alexandre hated! In addition, he never answers the phone, and you have to communicate by fax (this was before the pestilence of e-mails). But let's try. And whatever you talk about, do NOT mention *Shine*.'

A few weeks later, a fax duly arrived from Alexandre informing me that he would receive me at Senar. I replied that I would drive there when he told me it was convenient. 'No,' he replied. 'I will pick you up from Zurich Airport,' which he did. Off we went to a restaurant in the mountains, and he immediately began plying me with several bottles of Aigle wine, which happened also to be Stravinsky's favourite Swiss white wine. At first, I did not notice that he was sipping water; before long, I was not sure what I was saying, let alone agreeing to. He, of course, would have total editorial control over any film, the right of veto, and, no, he would not take part himself.

All that having been made clear, he suddenly asked me if I had seen the film *Shine*, and if so, what I thought about it.

'Umm …' and before I could reply, Alexandre said, 'It made me a lot of money,' and he laughed and toasted the film. It broke the ice, and now, no longer entirely sober, he took me to Senar, a magic location even if the house was somewhat Bauhaus austere.

Down in the basement, he said, were two cupboards which he needed to show me. One cupboard contained all of his grandfather's own home movies, and in the other was a stack of his grandfather's letters, most of them unpublished.

I realised immediately that I had stumbled upon a treasure trove. The home movies, twenty-seven minutes of them, proved to be in poor condition. Eight-millimetre film from the 1930s does not have a long shelf life. But we rescued them as best we could for my film. And the letters proved a godsend in that they gave me the clue as to how to shape my film. I would construct an imaginary letter as if written by Rachmaninoff from his self-imposed exile in America (to which he had fled after the Bolshevik Revolution – the Bolsheviks having burnt down his house) to his two daughters then living in France, explaining all that had happened to him in his life. Alexandre thought this was a stroke of genius. I would say, luck. He promised to select any letters he thought would be relevant and translate them for me. And although he complained all the time about my manoeuvrings (his word) to get what I needed for the film, we became firm friends until his death some fifteen years later.

Particularly memorable was our visit to his grandfather's old estate at Ivanovka, some 500 miles south-east of Moscow. Although the house had been destroyed in 1917, using old photographs it had recently been rebuilt almost to perfection. The rebuilding, in 1992, had been undertaken by a local authority which was, irony of ironies, communist. Alexandre was reluctant to go. First it was in the middle of nowhere, he said. Secondly, would we be safe? Ivanovka had belonged, incidentally, to Rachmaninoff's cousins, the Satins, one of whom had become his wife.

As Alexandre explained to me, 'Can you appreciate that as a young man, he was under the iron discipline of his piano teacher Nikolai Zverev at the Moscow Conservatory? For the first time, he does not have to wake up at 6 a.m. in a cold room; you have two minutes to wash your hands, and then thirty seconds to reach your piano, and then you have to play one hour exactly… For the first time, he came to live with young girls who were very happy to pamper him, to bring him a rocking chair, to bring his tea for him. It was an unbelievable discovery.

'And not only the daughters of his aunt, Varvara Arkadyevna. There were also the daughters of a neighbouring family, the Skalons: Natalya, Ludmilla and Vera, the last of whom was his first love. No wonder he wrote over eighty songs, most for them, but, sadly, not often performed these days.'

In spite of a miserable journey on an extremely ancient propeller aeroplane, together with an assortment of geese and even a sheep, we made it to Ivanovka with Alexandre now less than pleased but still stoic. After all, Ivanovka had been where his grandfather had written many of his famous works, including that second piano concerto which so exemplifies his style.

The local authorities had arranged a very grand welcome for Alexandre.

'Alexander Borisovich, we are happy to welcome you to Ivanovka,' intoned the Mayor. 'According to our ancient Russian custom, please take this bread and salt. Please break the bread, put salt on it, and welcome to Ivanovka, the land of your ancestors. We have been waiting for a long time for a direct heir of the

Rachmaninoff and Satin families to visit us. On this soil, your great-great- grandfather, your great-grandfather, and your grandmother were born. And on June 21st, 1907 your mother, Tatiana Sergeieva, was born here. We are honoured to greet you here. May I present you with the Tarabovsky Chamber Choir, named in honour of your grandfather. And this is the head of the, Region, Ljubov Samodurova. And this is the Head of the District, Evgeny Taraaovich. And Nadezhda Vassilieva, from the District Council. And Ainaiada Milusheva from the Department of Culture.'

Whereupon each official presented Alexandre with an enormous bouquet of flowers, with the result that he finished up looking like a mobile flower shop.

Later we were shown around the reconstructed house, and into what was claimed to be Rachmaninoff's bedroom. 'Rubbish,' Alexandre whispered to me. 'Look at the size of the bed. My grandfather was well over six feet tall. That bed wouldn't hold a man of even five foot.' But the house was, and is, impressive, and Alexandre, despite his bluster, was close to tears.

We returned to Moscow, taking one of those dreadful overnight trains, beloved of all Russians, in which it was necessary to share sleeping cabins. I chose to share with Alexandre. A few years later, I made a film about the great American soprano Renée Fleming, during which I visited her mother in upstate New York. Having not booked a hotel, I was invited to stay in her mother's house, 'Oh, you can sleep in Renée's bed,' she had said cheerfully. So, perhaps my only claim to fame is that I have slept in the same beds as Renée Fleming *and* Rachmaninoff's grandson.

Back in London, now with an almost-completed film and a script written by me but based on the letters Alexandre had supplied, I wondered who might record the script. Not only because I had worked with him several times, but also because I knew that his sonorous tones would give my words and the film the appropriate authority, I thought of Sir John Gielgud. For such 'little jobs' (his description) he always preferred to be telephoned directly rather than having to deal through agents. So I telephoned.

'Morning Sir John,' I said. 'How are you today?'

'Creaky,' he replied.

Gielgud came to London and recorded all my/Rachmaninoff's words with heartbreaking eloquence. At the conclusion of the recording, he suddenly said, 'I saw him perform, you know.'

I desperately tried to remember when Rachmaninoff had played in London.

'Oh, 1938?' I said.

'Don't be silly, dear boy,' Gielgud replied. '1914, when I was just ten years old.'

'What was it like?' I asked immediately.

'Very odd,' Gielgud replied. 'He came onto the stage, very tall, looking cross, ignored the audience, sat down and played. At the end of each piece, when the audience began to applaud, he waved his right hand somewhat dismissively, in effect telling the audience to shut up, and proceeded with the next piece. And so on until the end of the recital, whereupon he got up, bowed to the piano, and left the stage, once again completely ignoring the audience. But he did play well,' Gielgud added with a smile.

So here I was with a first-hand account of the composer about whom I had just made a film, given by the man who had just recorded his words.

The so-called letters, which now comprised the bulk of the text that Gielgud had just recorded, were really fiction, although stitched together from actual phrases and remarks the real Rachmaninoff had spoken or written. It was, in effect, autobiography in the first person. Here are some of the extracts:

'It is a curious story. The older we get, the more we lose that divine treasure of youth, and the fewer are those moments when we believe that what we have done is any good. Nowadays, I am rarely satisfied with myself, and almost never feel that what I do is successful. I am burdened with a harvest of sorrow.

'But there is another burden, heavier still, unknown to me in my youth. It is that I have no country. You must know that I was forced to leave my homeland, where I had struggled and suffered all the sorrows of the young, and where I really did achieve great success. Now, the whole world is open to me; success, apparently, awaits me everywhere. But one place, and one place only, remains closed to me, and that is my own country, the land where I was born.

'True, I have my music, and my memories, which I now put down for you, my dearest daughters Irina and Tatiana, and your children. [Alexandre was the only child of Tatiana.] And if it is true that a composer's music is the sum total of his experiences, then it must express his love affairs, his religion, above all the country of his birth. And I was born in Russia!

'My father had been in the army, and married a wealthy general's daughter, which perhaps accounts for my own military bearing. But... my father drank, enjoyed his women, and gambled, and soon we were forced to sell our estates and move to "temporary" accommodation in the great city of St. Petersburg.

'My studies went badly, and when my sister Sofya died of diphtheria, my mother decided this was the last straw, and blamed my father for our slum-like circumstances. Shortly after, she left him, and I never saw my father again.

'When I married your Mother, as she was my cousin, wedding in a church was forbidden by the Orthodox religion, so we had to marry in a military barracks!

'My 1st Symphony, written at Ivanovka when I was twenty-two and first performed in the Philharmonic Hall in St. Petersburg, was a disaster. My wife later thought the conductor, Glazunov, was drunk. One critic wrote: "If there were a Music Conservatory in hell, and one of its students was compelled to write a programme symphony on the seven plagues of Egypt, then Mr Rachmaninoff has done it. The inhabitants of hell must be delighted." As you know, the Symphony has never been performed again in my lifetime, or even published, and I'm pleased to report that the manuscript will never be found. In the Philharmonic Hall, I hid during the entire performance. I refused to come on stage at the end, and fled into the night. You can imagine how I felt. I sought refuge at Ivanovka, but was unable to compose again for almost three years.

'When I was still in despair about my 1st Symphony, I was taken to meet Leo Tolstoy, the author of *War and Peace*. It was thought he might help me restore a little faith in myself. He stroked my knees and said, "You must work, young man, work. Work every day, just as I do." Later I played for him. He asked me, "Tell me, does anybody really need music like that?" A doctor Dahl also examined me, although in truth I fancied his daughter, and this put me back on the weary road of composition with the completion of my ubiquitous Second Piano Concerto.

'And when I heard that the Bolsheviks had looted and burned down Ivanovka, our hearts were broken. The train carrying us away had been halted at the border, and we were forced to continue our winter journey by sledge. When we eventually arrived in Stockholm, we were frozen, homeless, and alone. But we were too tired to weep. After all, it was Christmas Eve.

'Eventually we arrived here, in America. I had been before, been successful, but had not liked it, not liked the crowds, although in 1909, I had given the world première of my 3rd Piano Concerto in New York, with a second performance conducted by Gustav Mahler no less. But now? I was forty-four years old, homeless and in debt. When the Boston Symphony again asked me – a hundred concerts in just thirty weeks – I was tempted, but refused. After all, I spoke not a word of the language. How would I manage?

'A terrible pain in my head resulted in surgery, although the news that I was in hospital was interpreted back in Russia that I had died. Thomas Edison asked me to make some recordings for his new invention, the gramophone. But I never cared for these, and always destroyed any pressings I thought less than perfect. And my concert debut was on December 5th in Providence, Rhode Island. Little did I know that I was to give over 1,000 concerts in America alone during the next twenty years. The only thing that suffered was my composition – not a single line. I just didn't feel like it.

'America! What madness! We found some consolation each summer by renting a house out at Locust Point in New Jersey, about an hour from New York City. I employed a Russian secretary, a Russian cook and, because I had failed my American driving test, a Russian chauffeur. We all spoke in Russian together, observed Russian customs, and surrounded ourselves with Russian friends, some of whom already lived here, and some of whom joined us in exile. Stanislavsky was there with people from the Arts Theatre. And Chaliapin, whom I adored. We had first met in Moscow when I was conducting at a private opera house, and Chaliapin was an up-and-coming singer. I also became quite a good horseman, until one day I fell off the horse and your mother said, 'That's it, no more.'

'But nothing could give us back what we most desired: our homeland. For the exile, whose musical roots have been annihilated, there remains no desire for self-expression. A friend wrote about his feelings of being a "nobody". Such feelings are probably unknown to me, he said. How wrong he is. I am filled to the brim with such feelings.

'Meanwhile, news from Russia became ever more distressing. Stalin and his bullies seemed determined to destroy the Russia we loved. In 1931, with Count Ilya Tolstoy and others, I wrote a letter to the *New York Times* in which I said. "At no time, and in no country, has there ever existed a government responsible for so many cruelties, wholesale murders and common-law crimes, as those perpetrated by the Bolsheviks. For thirteen years now, the communist oppressors have subjected the Russian people to indescribable torture. They are nothing but a group of professional murderers!" My music was now forbidden at the Moscow and St. Petersburg – now called Leningrad – Conservatories, where I had been a student all those years ago. I know now that, for me, Russia was forever closed. Dies Irae!

'Only art that is free, has meaning. Only creativity that is free, can be joyful. In Russia, there are no "free artists", only victims without rights. The title "free artist" is now a bitter joke.

'I bought a new boat for my house in Senar. It only cost me 1,600 francs. Plus 100 francs to the neighbour who drove me to the auction. Plus, oh dear, oh dear, 200 francs for the little dog we ran over on the way. Despite its great age – I'm talking about the motor, not me – it works magnificently. And if 1 do change it, it will only be because 1 want to go faster.

'In future, I intend to limit the number of concerts, or find some cure for old age. Old age! Perhaps it is that I'm lazy. My fingers are giving me real trouble, and the little finger on my left hand threatens to go the same way as the one on the right. Music should bring relief; it should rehabilitate the mind and soul. It cannot be just rhythm and colour. It must reveal, as simply as possible, the emotions of the heart. I have made immense efforts to understand the music of today, but I cannot. Perhaps it is that the music I care to write is not acceptable today. But time may change the technique of music; it cannot alter its fundamental mission.

'I sometimes feel all my audience wants is noise and excitement. On a recent tour of America, for instance, I played my *Corelli Variations* about fifteen times, but only one of these performances was any good. The others were...slapdash. I even – for the first time in my life – had a memory lapse and, to the audience's great consternation, tried for a long time to remember what came next. I was usually guided by the amount of coughing in the audience. Whenever the coughing increased, I would just leave out a variation. In one concert, the coughing was so violent that I only bothered to play about half the variations.

'But now the blood vessels on my finger-tips have begun to burst; bruises are forming. When that happens, I can't play for about two minutes, so I just strum some chords. But take me away from my concerts, and that will be the end of me.

'And did I tell you about my 3rd Symphony? They played it in New York, Philadelphia, Chicago and elsewhere. And they played it wonderfully. But one "critic" wrote: "Oh, Rachmaninoff. Does he *have* a third symphony in him?"

"*Cut, cut, cut,*" they said. It's like cutting out pieces of my heart. I wish to say, simply and directly, what I feel. And if that be love, or sadness, or bitterness, well, so be it. My music is perhaps a long dark coda into the night.

'In New Orleans, I definitely noticed that my cough was getting worse. Soon, I shall not be able to get up, sit or lie down. Like Chekov, I keep spitting phlegm into paper bags, phlegm covered with blood. Too many cigarettes. I am frightened, embarrassed, and guilty.

'And so, finally, as I end this long letter to you my dear Irina and Tatiana, I feel that my mournful features are clearing. I have signed myself up for a course of "healing by music". What other function can music have, but to make us whole again? As you know, the title of one of my first published songs was *The Harvest of Sorrow*. Perhaps now we can gather in the harvest, and heal our sorrow. Farewell. Farewell my hands.'

I must be careful not to make too many parallels between what Rachmaninoff wrote – even if re-written by me – and my own beliefs.

But I began to wonder if what he had said accurately reflected what I felt.

Sergei Vasilyevich Rachmaninoff died in Beverly Hills on 8 March 1943, a few days short of his seventieth birthday. He had composed four piano concertos, three operas, eighty songs and over a hundred pieces for piano, including two sonatas, numerous choral works for the church, and three symphonies: the second of which Rachmaninoff himself conducted the première, in St. Petersburg, on 26 January 1908, in the Mariinsky Theatre. After his death, since the return of a body to Europe was impossible in wartime, he was buried in a cemetery in Kensico outside New York that he and his wife had chosen, known locally and appropriately as 'Valhalla', the place of the Gods.

Alexandre urged me to visit the grave, pointing out three things. First, his grandfather had never spelt his name as 'Rachmaninov'. Secondly, although born in Paris as Alexandre Borisovich Conus (his mother Tatiana had married Boris Yulievich Conus), he had become so exasperated when replying to letters addressed to 'Mr Rachmaninoff' – to which he had replied signing himself as 'A. Conus', only to receive another letter saying, 'No, I want to hear from Mr Rachmaninoff' – that eventually he changed his name by deed poll to Rachmaninoff to save himself further trouble.

Finally, Alexandre reminded me that on his grandfather's death certificate it said simply: 'Composer'.

Chapter 26

Holst

Making a film - any film - is a journey of exploration. If you knew at the beginning what you know at the end, why would you bother to make a film? Writing it down is considerably easier - and cheaper. This is not the least reason I am spurned by those transitory creatures called 'commissioning editors': I begin with no script, no schedule and certainly no 'agenda' (their favourite word). Not much of a budget either, come to think of it.

It was forty years earlier, when filming Benjamin Britten, that the thought of making a film about Gustav Holst first lodged in my brain. I had noticed a photograph of the young Holst in Britten's music room, and had had the cheek to ask him why. 'Apart from Frank Bridge,' he told me, 'I owe him more than I can tell you.' Which was odd, because you seldom heard the name of Holst mentioned among the pantheon of great composers - and I do mean 'great' - of the twentieth century.

Imogen, Holst's feisty daughter, lived in Aldeburgh and worked as Britten's copyist and occasional editor. She was also one of the co-founders of the Aldeburgh Festival. Not surprisingly, she pressed me endlessly to make a film about her father, but somehow, everything she told me about him didn't quite add up. Was he really the shy, small, reclusive lover of English folk songs who taught at St Paul's Girls' School and just happened to have written *The Planets*? No matter that this is the most recorded piece of British music in the repertoire - recorded internationally, moreover. No matter that its famous melody from *Jupiter* is played at every Remembrance Day service, was played at Princess Diana's funeral, and was used as the anthem for the 1991 Rugby World Cup either as *I Vow To Thee My Country* or as *The World in*

Union. No matter that in every lazy piece of television journalism, *Mars* props up images of war and carnage. Holst? Did he write anything else, I asked myself?

This ignorance extends even to our music colleges. At an early meeting with the bosses of the Royal College of Music, for example (I was hoping somehow to involve them; after all, Holst had studied and taught there.), when I suggested we should consider a piece called *Beni Mora*. I was told that it was a rather dreary piece, hardly performed and not worthy of inclusion. The BBC had made two earlier films about Holst: the first from 1966 in black and white, which stated, 'Gustav Holst wrote *The Planets*, was much influenced by folk song and, with his friend Vaughan Williams, came from The Cotswolds.' Much of this material was recycled in a 100th birthday film in 1974. But that was it.

I made several attempts during the following several years to interest the remnants of the Music and Arts department in a film about Holst, only to be told repeatedly either 'We've done that', or 'Not particularly interesting' and 'Certainly not on our agenda' (*sic*). And certainly not on the agenda of the BBC Proms, who, years later, chose their 'fear-less front-line reporter' to introduce their 2024 Proms Season with a monologue from the egregious Clive Myrie about *The Planets*, which was insulting to anyone who cared about music and idiotic to everyone else. One viewer described him as looking like 'Mighty Mouse'. In his defence, he said his introduction was intended as a joke. It wasn't. But he certainly was.

To my surprise, therefore, back in early 2010 I was taken out to lunch by the then Director-General of the BBC, Mark Thompson (whom I didn't know), and offered the chance to make my film. The Music department didn't exactly block it, but they didn't exactly encourage it either. After all, they had blocked all my films for almost forty years, so why change now? The money I was eventually given was pitiful – a lower figure in number-of-pounds than I had been given by ITV and Melvyn Bragg for a film about Britten almost thirty years previously, not to mention the value of money having changed somewhat in the intervening years. But even if it meant re-mortgaging my house (it did), I felt I must now set out on this particular road of exploration.

I knew that Holst had lived in the Essex village of Thaxted – Imogen his only daughter repeated this fact like a mantra. Her father and Vaughan Williams had made many walking expeditions into the Essex countryside 'looking for folk songs, and in 1913 had come across this beautiful village and its imposing church', she told me. Her father had decided this was 'home'. What she did not tell me, were two astonishing facts which jumped out at me when I first visited Thaxted. First, I learnt that, contrary to myth, neither Vaughan Williams nor Holst much cared for these walks; Vaughan Williams because of his bulk, Holst because of his very poor health – neuritis, asthma, terrible eyesight. Sometimes he couldn't even recognise his own family more than two yards away. He had even learnt to play the trombone in an attempt to try and cure his asthma.

Secondly, when Holst went inside the enormous parish church at Thaxted, what he saw shocked him. Hanging there was a huge red flag and the flag of Sinn Féin, representing Free Ireland. The Union Jack, for him a symbol of imperialism, was nowhere to be seen. Which was odd, given that the Union Jack is everywhere to be seen at Remembrance Day services as the choir belts out the words sung to Holst's great melody from *Jupiter* in *The Planets*: 'I Vow to Thee, My Country'. Apparently, Holst had immediately sought out the vicar of Thaxted, a remarkable man named Conrad Noel, described at the time as the 'Red Priest', and knew he had found a true soul mate.

Suddenly, the fact that Holst had trained the Hammersmith *Socialist* Choir, that he had also taught at the newly formed Morley College (where he had given lessons on the bagpipes), whose entire purpose at the end of the nineteenth century was to bring education to the impoverished working classes, and had exhausted himself taking his 'Can't Sing Choir' to give concerts in the slums of the East End of London, all fell into place – 'Can't Sing' in the sense that everyone has a voice, he said, and therefore everyone can sing. And when teaching at Morley College, he used to cycle around the East End distributing copies of the *Socialist Worker*. In Thaxted, Conrad Noel, aided and abetted by Holst, set up a printing press publishing tract after tract about 'Freedom from Social Injustice', 'Freedom from Poverty', and 'Jesus the Revolutionary Leader', and when the First World War began, pinned notices on the church door saying such things as 'The Bell will toll at Noon for those Slain by Imperial Aggression.'

In this context I suddenly realised that the patriotic words of 'I Vow To Thee, My Country' were the complete opposite of everything that Holst believed. In everything but name, he was an extreme left-wing almost-communist in his beliefs. It transpired he had sold the rights to his melody for a mere £5, so he had no control over how his melody could be used. When he later discovered the words of Cecil Spring Rice being sung to his tune from *Jupiter*, there was nothing he could do

– except suffer. Unlike Elgar, who had never sold the copyright on his first *Pomp and Circumstance March* and was also bitterly opposed to his music being used to accompany *Land of Hope and Glory*, and had then done his utmost to prevent those chauvinistic words from ever being sung, Holst was powerless. I believe that in the end, it broke his spirit.

Holst was born in Cheltenham as Gustav von Holst, so that was my next port of call. The birthplace is now run as a 'Victorian Experience'. It has his piano, some portraits and a cot, the last of doubtful provenance. It's not their fault, those who run the 'museum'. They struggle to survive financially, being part-owned by the local council but receiving next to no support from it. Compared with the throbbing industry that is Britten's old house in Aldeburgh, it is pathetic. It peddles the familiar twaddle about folk songs and Gloucestershire and, ooh…err, *The Planets*. There had to be more to it than this. The 'von', I learnt, had been purchased by the family in the 1790s from Emperor Joseph II, the same who was Mozart's patron. But come the First World War, Holst had thought it advisable to drop the 'von', indicating that maybe he was German sympathiser, only to realise he could only do so if he *paid* to have it removed. Indeed, on the frontispiece of the *Seven Large Pieces for Orchestra,* the original title of *The Planets Suite,* you can see that the 'von' has been scratched out.

Reading through the local Cheltenham newspapers, another strange fact stared out at me: Cheltenham in the late nineteenth century (Holst was born in 1874) was famous for its curries! *Curries*? I quickly discovered that Cheltenham in the 1880s was full of retired civil servants and Army officers who had served in India, many of whom had brought Indian servants back to England with them. And the shock of listening to one of Holst's earliest orchestral works (rarely, if ever, performed) called *The Cotswold Symphony,* with its savagery and oriental sounds, made me realise his music owed little to English folk song. Its depiction of the English countryside was if anything more akin to Hardy: bleak, harsh, and unforgiving. And oriental? Maybe this is why Holst had taught himself Sanskrit and had written mesmeric piece after piece based on Hindu philosophy and the Satyagraha long before it had all been 'discovered' by minimalists such as Philip Glass.

But still the key to Holst's 'sound world' eluded me. I was aware that the very familiarity of *The Planets* had dulled our appreciation of the piece. In terms of its orchestration alone, it is totally revolutionary. The famous rhythm of the first movement, 'The Bringer of War'. five beats to the bar (for a *march*!?), is hammered out initially by the violinists hitting the strings with the wood of the bow as loudly as possible 'to make the sound of rats scurrying across a stone floor.'

So I went back to listen over and over again to every piece of music I could find by Holst: to the astonishingly lucid choral writing and its obsession with death, to the string music often in several keys at the same time, and, finally, to that piece the Royal College thought was 'not worthy', *Beni Mora,* and especially the third movement mysteriously titled *In the Street of the Ouled Naïls.* What did *that* mean? Dancing girls? Brothels? What on earth was he doing *there*?

Answer: he lived there. Given £50 by his friend Vaughan Williams, he had gone on holiday to Algiers, mostly for health reasons. There he *cycled* into the Sahara and who knows where else. Like T.E. Lawrence some ten years later, something had happened to Holst when dwarfed by those mountainous sand dunes. Imogen, in her biography of her father, never mentions it; even in the much more thorough biography of Holst by Michael Short, it merits only half a line. But when the full force of this incredible music hit me, I knew I had found the clue. 'Not worthy,' as the Royal College had said.

So, add this to Holst's passionately felt socialism and his profound understanding of Hinduism, and suddenly *The Planets* began to make sense: not as an astrological chart à la Mystic Meg, but as a *Pilgrim's Progress* from the ferocity of industrialised capitalism (*Mars*) towards a karma of enlightenment (*Neptune*), where beneficial effects are derived from past beneficial actions and harmful effects from past harmful actions. Holst never called the work *The Planets,* incidentally. He titled it simply *Seven Pieces for Large Orchestra;* the names of the planets themselves were added later.

Writing these enormous pieces of orchestral music, however, must have been very painful, so bad was his neuritis. He actually needed his pen to be tied to his middle finger to enable him to write at all. At St Paul's Girls School, where hetaught and was known as Gussie, he had two young ladies, Nora Day and Vally Lasker, waiting at the other end of his room. As soon as a page of the score was finished, they would quickly make a piano reduction and try bits out for him so that he could hear what he had written. Unfortunately, the subsequent colossal success of the *Seven Pieces* has blinded us to the mass of his other music, much of it forgotten, some still not published nearly a hundred years after his death. And the misuses and abuses of his famous melodies have frequently militated against our acknowledgement of his greatness as a composer.

Holst himself was convinced he was a failure. Many works were not performed professionally in his lifetime, or if so, more-or-less instantly forgotten thereafter. Even today he has to fight for recognition. I'm not comparing myself in any way whatsoever, but my film for the BBC, when finished, also had to fight for recognition. I was told that if I did not cut it to its ninety minutes' 'slot', 'it would fall out of the schedules'. Throughout, the BBC bureaucracy has *de facto* sought to inhibit the film. Reams and reams of form-filling, including such questions as: 'Will any of your crew be moving a trolley? If the answer is yes, please give qualifications for moving such a trolley.' At such moments, like Holst himself, I longed for the desert, its silence, its mystery, its awesome beauty and its majesty. Anywhere but the BBC.

Imogen Holst had told me once, in Aldeburgh many years earlier, why it was important to make a film about her father. 'I had a letter not long ago,' she told me, 'from one who'd been his pupil at the age of eight. And had never forgotten the passionate way that he had taught them to sing a very simple folk song with a question and answer. Absolutely in rhythm. And with very clear words. And that had been in her mind ever since. She's an old woman now. And there are others like her, who remember how he helped, not only just teaching them to do music; but how he helped, without ever saying anything about it, how he helped them to realise that music is a part of life that can't be done without.'

Chapter 27

Salzburg

As a result of my encounter, or perhaps that should be confrontation, with Oscar Kokoschka when I was Patrick Garland's tea boy all those years ago, I became fascinated by that jewel of a city and made it my home every summer until I was finally thrown out of University. What particularly intrigued me was how, in 1945, it had managed to stage its annual Music Festival within a few months of the end of the war, while there were apparently over 100,000 refugees in the city living among its ruins and existing on potatoes. As Friedrich Gehmacher, President of the International Mozarteum Foundation, told me, 'When I had my tenth birthday, that was in April 1945, I asked my mother: I have only one wish. I want to eat as many potatoes as I want. And my mother said, no, this is not possible. So you can imagine how the situation was, that a boy of ten years was not able to get enough potatoes for his birthday. We were so hungry that we went to an American camp and waited in front of where they had their dinner. Everybody had a little pot, and when the soldiers came out and didn't eat up their ration, they gave us the rest into our pot. So we were really beggars.'

Despite being warned against Salzburg by none other than the great mezzo-soprano Christa Ludwig ('Salzburg?' she told me. 'A nest of vipers!'), when I was approached in 2005 by the glamorous Gabi Burgstaller, then Governor of Land Salzburg, and asked to consider making the definitive history of the Salzburg Festival in time for the 150th anniversary celebrations of Mozart's birth, who could resist? Her, or even the Festival?

I then came across a four-volume memoir written in 1980 by Thomas Bernhard, a writer who had grown up near Salzburg and wrote that the city was 'totally anti-Semitic, completely bigoted, and that it despised anything that's new, that it despised the truth, that it only counts its enemies, whether it's the Viennese or the Germans or the Americans', and he couldn't wait to get out. Ironically, that was also the story of Mozart, the city's most famous son. He, too, had wanted to get out. He did get out, escaping not only the authority of the Prince Archbishop but also the authority of his father.

And then I remembered reading in Franz Schubert's diaries that in 1806 he had visited Salzburg for several days. Schubert adored Mozart's music, but he did not even know that Mozart had been born in Salzburg and that his widow still lived there. He also noted that the main square in the Old Town, the Residenzplatz, was covered in grass with cows happily grazing there.

Salzburg was an independent state. It was neither a part of Bavaria nor the Austrian Hapsburg Empire. It really was an independent ecclesiastical state run by the Prince Archbishop, and the Archbishop was very concerned that it be a Catholic city in terms of its population, in terms of its belief, and in terms of its authority. As a result, there had been no Jews in Salzburg from the middle of the seventeenth century. Salzburg had also expelled its Protestants in the middle of the eighteenth century. (The American city of Savannah in Georgia was founded largely by exiled Salzburg Protestants in the 1740s.)

Gabi Burgstaller suggested that I first talk to Helga Rabl-Stadler, who had been the President of the Salzburg Festival since 1995 and would go on to fulfil that role for almost twenty-six years. She was charm personified. 'Ah, Salzburg,' she said with a sigh, 'the heart of the heart of Europe.' I liked her.

She didn't like me. When she saw the finished film, for instance, she objected to the music with which the film begins. 'What was wrong with using some Mozart?' she asked. I pointed out that the music I had used was by the twenty-three-year-old Benjamin Britten, his *Frank Bridge Variations,* which had actually had its world première at the Salzburg Festival in 1937, thus demonstrating that Salzburg had long been the home of the best in new contemporary classical music – which its present-day image would not necessarily suggest. I also cheekily used the climax from Mendelssohn's *Hebrides Overture* to accompany footage of Hitler and the Nazis arriving in Salzburg in March 1938. (Mendelsohn was, of course, Jewish.)

Nor did she notice that I had begun my film with a plane descending through clouds to discover the magic city below, a clear reference to the beginning of Leni Riefenstahl's Nazi propaganda film *Triumph of the Will*, which had begun in exactly the same way.

Rabl-Stadler, although born an illegitimate child, had become co-owner of Salzburg's largest fashion shop, Resmanns. Her adopted father had been editor-in-chief of the national daily newspaper *Express* and, later, of the daily *Kurier*. For several periods, he had also served as general manager of the ORF, the Austrian state-owned radio and television channels.

So, if anyone knew the history of the Festival, Rabl-Stadler did. But in our conversations, she clearly wanted to avoid any talk of politics, although, as I came to realise, Politics with a capital 'P' was at the heart of the heart of the Salzburg Festival. After all, its most illustrious artistic director after the Second World War, Herbert von Karajan, had been a member of the Nazi party, as had several of its most distinguished participants, including Karl Böhm, the conductor, and Elisabeth Schwarzkopf, the soprano. And when a referendum had been called immediately after Hitler's 1938 annexation of Austria, 99.73 per cent had voted in favour, although 'political enemies' (communists, socialists and the like) and Austrian citizens of Roma or Jewish origin - roughly 360,000 people, or 8 per cent of the entire Austrian population - had not been allowed to vote in the plebiscite.

At the 2006 Festival, officially opened by the President of Austria, Dr Heinz Fischer, Fischer put it to me rather more succinctly, 'I think the First World War was a real shock for our citizens. I know very well that many people were in an excited mood when it started in 1914, but after millions had been killed, it seemed the whole world collapsed, and in particular in this part of the world. The Austrian–Hungarian monarchy collapsed; the German monarchy collapsed; and a new state and a new society and a new approach was necessary. And this revolution also took place in culture.'

That revolution in culture was something that Gabi Burgstaller had also emphasised.

Fischer went on, 'People had no work, not enough to eat, many of the children were homeless. So it was necessary to find something in which you could dream, and I think culture makes you dream somehow. After the First World War there was, in Austria, a situation where nobody believed in the future of this country. No one believed that such a tiny country could survive, economically. But there were just a few people who said, we *must* do something to put Austria and Salzburg on the map, as it were, and chief among these were the theatre director Max Reinhardt, his friend the composer Richard Strauss and his friend and librettist Hugo von Hofmannsthal.'

The problem? Reinhardt was Jewish, Hofmannsthal's grandfather was Jewish, as was his wife, and there was no way the Salzburg authorities were going to allow any Jew to put on a Festival in *their* city.

In 1911, Hofmannsthal had adapted the fifteenth-century English morality play *Everyman* as *Jedermann*, which had already been performed at Berlin's Schumann Circus, directed by the very same Max Reinhardt. The triumvirate decided that this production should inaugurate the birth of their new Festival. The city authorities categorically refused permission for the play to be staged at the local theatre, the Landestheater. Ironically, the situation was resolved by none other than the Prince Archbishop himself, who saw merit in a morality play about Man's salvation and gave permission for the play to be staged on the steps of his cathedral, his land, over which the city had no jurisdiction. And so that is where it was staged on 22 August 1920, and it has been performed there more or less annually ever since: five o'clock on a Sunday, every Sunday during the Festival, an undisputed highlight of Festival season, attracting great actors such as Maximillian Schell and Klaus Maria Brandauer. Set against the awe-inspiring edifice of the cathedral's west front, with the church organ thundering out when the figure of the Devil appears and the cathedral's deep bell tolling relentlessly, even in its modern dress manifestations it is theatre exemplified. One of the many ironies, therefore, was that, despite the rabid anti-Semitism in the City of Salzburg, two Jewish artists, Hofmannsthal and Reinhardt, put on a Protestant morality play, in effect protected by the Catholic Prince Archbishop, Ignaz Rieder. After the Wagner Festival in Bayreuth, Salzburg soon became only the second international festival devoted to the arts in over two thousand years – since the Greeks, in fact. It was a political as well as social and cultural statement of extraordinary vision.

Not that the *Jedermann* was without its critics. In Reinhardt's time, it was the anti-Semites who said, 'The Jews are exploiting the church.' The Nazis banned it, of course. And even after the war, so-called 'progressive' theologians said, 'The piece is not Christian.'

'I had to do it because I had promised my mother,' Brandauer told me with a giggle. 'In the 50s, I had been to the Festival and seen the great German actor Will Quadflieg perform it. He was actually born the week the First World War began. And I told my mother, 'One day I will do it.' I was born here in Altaussee in the Salzkammergut lake district.

And down the road, von Hofmannsthal actually wrote *Jedermann*. What does this play represent? The play forces you to think, what is a man in relation to his time, and to the actions of others? Man is such a small, small figure, so this play is a powerful political statement of freedom and redemption, clearly understood by Hofmannnstahl and Reinhardt when it was written, and to this day. So the most important thing for me was that it wasn't just an 'actor's job'. I am just a boy from a village here, but this boy can be in one hour in Salzburg to play *Jedermann*, not just for the ninety minutes of the play but as an inspiration for our time!'

So what of the Festival itself? By 1933, when Hitler came to power in Germany, the Festival was already a vehicle for a certain kind of self-importance and glamour. It had become a place where the social and cultural elite of Europe gathered in a very beautiful location in the summertime. Ironically, the most famous production of that time was Reinhardt's version of Goethe's *Faust*, performed in the original 'Festival Hall', again courtesy of the Prince Archbishop. The Archbishop had provided the stables of his own riding school, known as the *Felsenreitschule*, ('the riding school stables'), at the northern foot of the Mönchsberg mountain which towers above the city. On top of the Mönchsberg, incidentally, sits the *Festung* or castle where I had first met Oscar Kokoschka.

Faust: a rich man who sells his soul to the Devil in return for power. And, ironically again, the original music for that 1933 production was conducted by a very young Heribert Karajan, as he was then known.

Musically, the early Festivals were given glamour by Arturo Toscanini who, after 1933, refused to conduct in Germany, especially in Bayreuth, the shrine of Hitler's favourite composer Wagner. So when Toscanini decamped to Salzburg, where he then conducted every summer until 1938, this again was seen as a very significant political gesture. Besides being the world's most famous conductor, Toscanini had become a world hero culturally; thus, his arrival put Salzburg centre stage in the political battles to come.

'But Toscanini said,' Rabl-Stadler told me, "if you continue to offer me the Landestheater, this small theatre with such bad acoustics, I won't come here anymore." So he it was who forced Salzburg's government to construct a new, albeit small, "Festival Theatre", also cut into the rock of the Mönchsberg mountain.'

And then, in 1938, Hitler came. Toscanini left in disgust. Reinhardt had already fled to Hollywood, taking with him Salzburg's hitherto resident composer Erich Korngold. Strauss equivocated, something which he later said he always regretted. Furtwängler, the most renowned German conductor of his day, struggled to preserve his orchestra, the Vienna Philharmonic, especially when Goebbels said that the entire orchestra had to join up in the army. Furtwängler even ostentatiously wiped his hand after he was forced to shake hands with Goebbels at the end of a concert. But he stayed.

Others reacted with more obvious horror to the Nazi presence. Princess Wittgenstein, a descendant of Liszt's mistress, told me, 'When I asked my father, "Father, who are these men in brown shirts marching? We've never seen that before," he said, "Oh, terrible, terrible! They are called National Socialists." And when my father refused to say 'Heil Hitler' or whatever, he was promptly taken to Dachau concentration camp. The next thing we hear, they said he had died of pneumonia. He was, of course, killed there; his ashes were sent back to my mother who had a complete nervous breakdown and ended up in a lunatic asylum.'

Furtwängler's widow Elisabeth told me how, after the war, she remembered 'One day, we saw on television images of the Holocaust; my husband fell on the floor and beat it with his fist. "You know," he said to me, "there can be no more happiness in our life. Impossible, Elisabeth. We Germans did that, you know, we *Germans* did that!"'

I even managed to find the last surviving member of the von Trapp family, immortalised in *The Sound of Music*, ninety-four-year-old Maria. 'When Hitler came into Austria, he did horrible things, you know,' she explained to me. 'We had a lady who took care of us, and her sister was a little bit handicapped. So they took her to an institution where she was gassed, put into a *Gaswagen*, you know, these big vans which were filled with gas where they killed people.'

Even the Strauss Family was put under extreme pressure, as his great-granddaughter Madeleine recounted. 'My father was a half-Jew. According to the race laws, my grandmother was also Jewish, so her sons, including my father, had to leave their school and hide in our villa at Garmisch so that nobody would find them. Otherwise, they would have been caught up in 'Operation Death'. Cannon fodder for the Eastern front. Young children, aged only sixteen!'

Others were more 'accomodating'. Peggy Weber-McDowell was an Austrian-American businesswoman and prominent patron of Salzburg's cultural life. In 1960, she founded the candle-making company Emperor Art Creations in Little Rock, Arkansas. Their marketing concept included selling candles with sex and glamour. But she also retained her love for her homeland. Salzburg motifs repeatedly adorned her company's candles, thus contributing to the popularity of the city of Mozart among American audiences. 'We came right after *The Sound of Music*,' she told me confidently. 'As for the Nazi occupation,' she told me breezily, 'if you weren't in prison or being tortured or something, it was all very exciting, and I had to be part of it. I didn't like to march, but you know they had the Hitler Youth, like the cheerleaders for football games; they were called *"Glaube und Schönheit"*, 'Belief and Beauty'. And it was really fantastic, because we were disciplined, we were grilled, and it was a ballet type of physical discipline of the body, and an honour to be asked to participate. The morning after the 1938 occupation, our foreman, his name was Mathias, Mathias came home covered the blood and my father said, "What in the world has happened to you, Mathias?" Mathias said, "This was the night we were waiting for, for all these many, many years. We demolished all the Jews' shops."'

'Many of the officers, they loved classical music like we did,' Peggy went on, 'and with this Nazi discipline, you know they had a lot of discipline, they had fabulous music and fabulous conductors. I was as much at home in a concert then as I am today.'

Many of these 'fabulous' conductors, however, found it impossible to get work after the war ended in 1945, Furtwängler among them. Some, such as Clemens Krauss, who had led the Mozarteum Orchestra, were permanently discredited. For others, such as Karl Böhm, it could be argued that he had done what he needed to do for his career. Karajan had done the same, but Karajan was clearly a true believer; Karajan was a Nazi. When you said that someone was a Nazi, you could mean two things. A believer, or a Party member. It seems that Karajan was both. He was a believer and he was a Party member, twice. He was a member of the Austrian Nazi Party when the party was illegal in Austria in the 1930s; then, after the 1938 Anschluss (the annexation of Austria), he joined the main German Nazi Party. Karajan's influence on the Salzburg Festival was colossal, as we shall see, but in the short term, most concert impresarios shunned him.

Böhm's son Karlheinz told me with tears in his eyes that his father had suffered terribly after the war and could get no work at all. 'He must have known what was happening during the war, but always said, "Don't talk about it, no, no. That is politics; we are artists. Work on. That is finished, so we don't talk about it." And so that was one of the reasons that people attacked him; they said he had failed to make any protest. But what could he have done? Had he left, or gone in exile, his whole family (he had about twenty family members living in Graz in southern Austria) would have been put into a concentration camp and killed.'

So now I began to understand how Salzburg had managed to resurrect its Festival so soon after the Second World War. The Festival had remained in operation throughout the war, incidentally, until 1944, when it had been cancelled by the order of Reichsminister Goebbels in reaction to the 20 July plot against Hitler. In January 1945, the Russians had invaded Austria from the east. Almost immediately upon their arrival in Vienna, they had imported every great orchestra or soloist they could lay their hands on to demonstrate to the world that they were a cultured nation that could boast the finest of the finest among classical musicians. The American troops had come from the west, on the other hand, and had arrived in Salzburg in May 1945. Seeing what the Russians were doing in Vienna, the CIA, or the Office of Strategic Services, as it was known then, decided amidst the already threatening Cold War that the Salzburg Festival must once again be a beacon of artistic light, so they financed the Festival for 1945 and several years thereafter. Once again, as after the conclusion of the First World War, little Austria needed to wave a flag and say, 'Here we are, still thriving, with culture, at least.' A political statement.

'The Festival became part of an education programme,' Wilfried Haslauer, the deputy governor of Salzburg and Gabi Burgstaller's eventual successor, explained to me, 'We were a defeated country and in a defeated city.' The American occupying forces also observed that the churches were full of people, while the city itself was part destroyed. Forty-eight per cent of all houses were derelict; only the Festival Theatre, safely tucked under its mountain, had survived. 'There were thousands of refugees in the country; thousands of ex-soldiers now housed in camps. So what to give them?' Haslauer said. 'The hope of survival, the hope of a better future. To bring back a vision, a vision that had history, and to give this vision a reality was an essential part of a political game.'

In spite of the lack of world-class musicians, with American support the Festival soon found its feet again, although the initial programme in the summer of 1945 was a dismal potpourri of musical scraps: 'Csárdás' from *Die Fledermaus* by Johann Strauss; 'Liebe, du Himmel auf Erde' by Niccolò Paganini and Franz Lehár; and, inevitably, *An der schönen blauen Donau* waltz by Johann Strauss. Felix Prohaska, a long-forgotten Austrian conductor, led the Mozarteum Orchestra, whose concert hall had also been partly damaged as a result of American bombing. Remarkably, within a few years, the stars of yesteryear began to drift back; for example, the conductors Bruno Walter and Furtwängler, he with his Vienna Philharmonic Orchestra. Then, on 12 July 1950, a law was passed establishing a Salzburg Festival Fund sponsored by the Federal Government, the State and the City of Salzburg, and also by the Salzburg Tourism Board. The Festival was now given a permanent financial and legal basis.

Enter Karajan again. In spite of his past, he was appointed Artistic Director in 1956, and soon came to regard the Festival as his professional and personal fiefdom. Anyone who questioned Karajan's words of wisdom tended to cower behind the proverbial desk, fearing his wrath. But he forced through the construction of a new Großes Festspielhaus, also cut out from the Mönchsberg, which soon became the centre of the Festival's performances. With his private jet and fast cars, he projected an image of undiluted glamour which attracted the growing number of post-war European *nouveaux riches*.

Peter Gelb, soon to become General Manager of the Metropolitan Opera House in New York, described to me a car journey he had taken with Karajan. 'The very first time I arrived in Salzburg to meet Karajan,' Gelb told me, 'he took me for a drive at breakneck speed up into the mountains. I was quite scared and convinced that I was going to be killed on this drive. During the course of the drive, he explained to me that the sign of a good driver was how many dead bugs accumulated on the windshield at the end of the ride. But at a certain point in this hair-raising drive up the Alps behind his home, he slammed on the brakes and very proudly told me to look across the valley and pointed – out there was Berchtesgaden, Hitler's summer retreat. I think that he very much cherished his Austrian countryside roots, although at one point I think he also claimed he had been born on Mount Olympus.'

Karajan was short in stature, no more than five feet seven inches, vain, and wore shoes with built-in lifts. One had to be extremely careful when filming him to place the camera so that whoever he was accompanying looked shorter. This was particularly difficult, as I discovered, when he accompanied his favourite violinist, the exceptionally beautiful and gifted Anne-Sophie Mutter, who was almost six feet tall. And he could be very cruel in rehearsal. Dietrich Fischer-Dieskau told me, 'I've seen him make women cry. In every recording, he would torture someone. Tears would flow. Always. In a concert he often made the orchestra sit right on the edge of the stage, so the singers got very nervous because they had so little space. He could be really difficult.' But, as Anne-Sophie Mutter told me, 'It was his constant quest for perfection. Perfection which is obviously nothing to do with the polished surface, but perfection in finding the right shape of architecture of a piece, the beauty of *colour* in music, the beauty of emotion, the depth of emotion, the fire of a performance, the relentlessness of rehearsing the morning after a glorious performance, the very same piece again, from scratch.'

There was no denying Karajan's capacity for work. 'I never met anyone else in my entire life with such devotion to his work,' Gernot Friedel, a distinguished Austrian stage and television director (who had been responsible for over a hundred performances of *Jedermann*, for example), told me. 'Every day at 4 a.m. he was at work in his music room, in total concentration. It was always the culmination of that concentration when he went out on stage to conduct. Everything led to that. That's how he also lived his life; eating, drinking, free time, sailing, flying, fast cars. But he was also very scared of uncontrolled publicity. He had a big fear that, somehow, he would be put in the wrong light. Therefore, he was never really himself when anyone photographed him. He was constantly thinking, "Are they photographing me to look like a Neanderthal?"'

And there was no denying Karajan's musicanship. I once had the luck, courtesy of his favourite record producer, John Culshaw, of Benjamin Britten and BBC Music department fame, to film him with the Vienna Philharmonic rehearsing the third movement of Beethoven's 9th Symphony, a work they must have played a thousand times. He spent over an hour on a master class with the violinists on the proper use of the D string of their instruments: how the placement of your fingers on the neck, the pressure of the bow, the arc of your arm, how they all affected the tone you produced, and how vital this was in understanding Beethoven's intention. The Vienna Philharmonic, one of the greatest orchestras in the world, paid Karajan the greatest attention.

I also heard a performance he gave of Sibelius's 2nd Symphony, taking the last movement incredibly slowly so that when it wound itself up to its mighty climax at the end, one was left pinned to one's seat by an overwhelming sense of majesty. And his performances of Richard Strauss's opera *Der Rosenkavalier* with Anneliese Rothenberger, Sena Jurinac and Elisabeth Schwarzkopf were, by common consent, sublime.

Nor was there any doubt as to Karajan's private kindness and generosity. 'He was a man of enormous emotion,' Peter Alward, head of EMI Records, recounted. 'He adored his children, and was actually a very, very kind, decent human being behind the façade. But I suppose he felt that in his professional life, he had to keep it well hidden. He could come across as being very cold. He relied more and more on having people around him who he felt really cared for him, because, at heart, he was very lonely. If you had that level of fame, to whom can you turn? Very few people. It took time, but once he accepted you, he wasn't in any way the ogre that he's often been made out to be. It's not realised, for instance, how often he helped people financially in his immediate circle who had fallen on hard times, or who needed sudden medical help. He used to pay for them to be flown hither and thither. He didn't want it to be known, but that's what happened.'

His daughter Isabella confirmed this. 'He was the simplest man you can imagine,' she told me. 'It gets me crazy sometimes, but why someone always wants to make him complicated. He was not. His house was simple [I was a guest there, so I can confirm that]; the way he dressed was simple. If he invited people to supper, he only wanted two or three people around a small table [I know; I benefited from that]. He loved to laugh. He had a very big sense of humour. I remember rehearsals where we couldn't stand anymore by laughing so much at his stories, often dirty stories. He liked walking in nature, in the forest, in the mountains. He loved water, air and all those natural elements which are so strong. And he always told me it doesn't matter what you do, you have to do it with your heart and try to do the best you can.'

After Karajan died, quite suddenly, and within hours of signing a $20 million deal with Sony for his recordings, Peter Gelb, then chief executive of Sony Records, felt that he should pay Karajan's widow, Eliette, a courtesy visit at the family home in Anif, a small village outside Salzburg. They had supper close by in Anif. Afterwards, although it was by now pouring with rain, Gelb offered to walk Eliette back to her house. On the way, they passed by the tiny cemetery where Karajan is buried. She pulled away from Gelb and went and sat by the grave. Gelb was unsure whether he should go over with his umbrella, or keep a respectful distance. Eventually, the completely soaked Eliette came back to join Gelb. She said, 'I have a message from the Maestro.' Somewhat alarmed, Gelb waited to hear the message, apparently from beyond the grave. The message was: 'Sell more records!'

But as the limousines had got longer, the jewel-encrusted dresses had got flashier and the *Café mit Schlag* got ever creamier, it was inevitable that the Festival became increasingly viewed as old-fashioned, stultified, dull. But only when Karajan died did Rabl-Stadler begin to consider a new artistic director. Enter Gérard Mortier, who, with Nike Wagner, had previously attempted, unsuccessfully, to take over the Bayreuth Festival. His successful track record running the La Monnaie Opera House in Brussels and the Opéra National de Paris marked him out as an innovative and inspirational leader who might just bring a breath of fresh air to Salzburg. He brought with him some of the most original stage directors of that time: Peter Sellars, Bob Wilson, Jean-Pierre Ponnelle, Peter Stein, even Ingmar Bergman. But Salzburg did not want the change Mortier brought, and the nests of vipers were soon out in force.

'I created once a performance outside of the Festspiel houses,' Mortier explained, '*The Magic Flute*, by Mozart after all, and directed by Achim Fryer, a protégé of Bertolt Brecht. It was performed in the Messehalle, a sort of exhibition hall which is on the other side of the river, where mostly poor people live. It was an enormous success, still a little expensive, but half the price of the normal tickets in the Salzburg Festival. All the performances were sold out. The City didn't like it at all, and insisted I cancel its revival the following year. When I asked why, I was told, 'Oh, because the public who went didn't spend any money in the restaurants and hotels on the proper side of the river.' It seemed it was more important to note how many big Mercedes and Rolls-Royces were standing in front of the Festspielhaus, and how many private planes were standing on the airport of Salzburg. That was one of the great attacks I suffered: that there now were fewer private planes on the airport! Nobody cared about how we played Mozart.'

Peter Sellars felt most strongly that when, for instance, Mozart wrote *The Marriage of Figaro* or *Don Giovanni*, he considered these pieces as direct challenges to his own generation: 'They are deeply concerned with the most potent and alarming political and economic questions of his period. He did not view his operas as a historical phenomenon. And you can see from the contemporary reviews that they were treated as an affront, a challenge to established structures. Those who had guided the Salzburg Festival in recent years had held themselves to be the guardians of everything that is old and, happily, dead.'

Mortier clearly had to go, and go he did. Enter Peter Ruzicka, previously Director of the Hamburg State Opera and a distinguished composer and conductor who, in his short reign, did his best to revive any 'Jewish' music previously banned by the Nazis: works by Hindemith, Wellesz, Franz Schrecker, Schönberg, Zemlinsky and, most notable of all, Erich Korngold, who, despite being born near Salzburg, was shunned by the Festival for almost four decades. He had even been refused permission after the war to buy back his family home, which he had 'abandoned' when he had gone to Hollywood in the 1930s, and which had been used during the war as the local Gestapo headquarters.

I am aware that I have only skimmed the surface of this extraordinary international Festival, which has survived against all odds, of late thanks to the enormous generosity of the American Friends of the Festival, and of one man in particular – the philanthropist Donald Kahn. He not only paid for the refurbishment of the University's concert hall, the Aula, but he also staked a sufficient sum for the original old small 'Festival Theatre', built in the early 1930s and beloved of Hitler, to be completely rebuilt and newly christened 'The Mozart House'.

Because therein lies the dilemma of Salzburg: trading relentlessly on Mozart as a brand name but often seeming to do little to espouse what a music festival should be. Mortier said to me, 'Why does art exist? An artist is someone who wants to tell in a very sensitive way about history. Theatre should always be a kind of debate. You come there to discover something about the really existential value of the world you are living in. Today we can communicate instantly the whole time, but the loneliness of his world was never as big. I never saw so many lonely people. And the Festival should be a special place where you have time to make your spirit *free*. One of my worst experiences in Salzburg was during the Easter Festival where someone said to another, "Ah, tonight it's fine, the *Brahms Requiem*. It's only an hour twenty, so we will be very soon into Goldener Hirsch" – the glossiest restaurant in Salzburg, bang opposite the Festspielhaus. I never forgot it. That public we don't need.'

But the brand itself has also become tarnished. As Herbert Brugger, then Managing Director of Salzburg Tourism, pointed out to me, 'Salzburg is now visited by over seven million visitors every year. This invasion will only increase with more planes and more flight connections. Throughout the last years, in terms of overnights, Salzburg is now among the top ten places to visit *from China*, with direct flights several times a week from Beijing. But what was embarrassing was that when we went on a delegation to China recently to promote the Mozart Brand, our hosts asked us to sing the Salzburg National Song, and all we could muster was '*Edelweiss, edelweiss...*' which is, of course, from *The Sound of Music* and not by Mozart. Unfortunately, the brand is not 'protected', so we now have Mozart sausages and Mozart beer, while in Japan they have wine covered with the Mozart logo. And the Mozartkugeln, those little small, round sugar confections made of pistachio, marzipan and nougat covered with dark chocolate, now called the *Salzburger* Mozartkugeln, sell over 100 million per year!'

With characteristic ineptitude, a recent BBC documentary about Salzburg titled *Revolution and Romance* showed a woman - now, incidentally, Head of Arts and Classical Music - sitting at a roadside café munching on a Mozartkugel, saying, "If anything can prove the importance of Mozart, this invention from his time proves his immortality," or some such garbage. Wrong. The Mozartkugel was created by Salzburg confectioner Paul Fürst in 1890, almost one hundred years after Mozart's death.

The annual Festival begins with a celebration held in the main concert hall of the Mozarteum on Mozart's birthday, 27 January. The year I made my film, 2006, the inaugural address was given by the President of Austria, Dr Heinz Fischer. I was sitting near the back; in front of me were various bejewelled ladies in their furs. As Dr Fischer spoke, these same ladies could be heard harrumphing their disapproval of what he said, until, eventually, they got noisily to their feet and left, encouraging many others to do the same.

Dr Fischer said, 'Today we celebrate the 250th birthday of Mozart. And it is also the sixty-first anniversary of the liberation of the concentration camp, Auschwitz. And however incredible it is, and however difficult it is to understand, and I believe you cannot fully understand it, that the human being is able to write such wonderful, heavenly music, and at that very same time human beings are able to behave like those who were responsible for the murders and crimes in a concentration camp like Auschwitz. Personally I feel this because my father-in-law was in a concentration camp.'

'And so we should never forget on this day, the 27th of January, in this city, with historically its anti-Semitic reputation, that the wide, wide space between heaven and hell is made apparent. The question was, and is always: which road should we take?'

Chapter 28

Why Me? First, Account For Me

At the end of the film of Peter Schaffer's play *Equus*, Dysart (played by Richard Burton), the psychologist tasked with curing a young boy, Alan Strang, who has stabbed out the eyes of the horses in his charge, stares at the camera and says, 'My desire might be to make of this boy an ardent husband, a caring citizen, a worshipper of an abstract and unifying God.' Burton always told me he felt that he spoke about himself, as do I. 'My achievement, however, is more likely to have made a ghost. I've healed the rash on his body; I've erased the welts cut into his mind. But I doubt he will be left with much *passion*. He will, however, be completely without pain. For me, the pain never stops. Why me? Why me? First, account for me.'

And so, as this partial memoir draws to a close, perhaps a staging post in the trivial journey through one's life, I am also reminded of the time I stood at the graveside of W.B. Yeats, in a windswept churchyard of St Columba's Church at Drumcliff in County Sligo under the lowering mountain Ben Bulben. On the gravestone are carved the last lines of his epitaph poem *Under Ben Bulben*. 'Cast a cold Eye, On Life, on Death. Horseman, Pass by!' Yeats, one of the many film subjects I had proposed to the BBC, only to have it rejected.

I am also aware of the many extraordinary encounters I have omitted: with Leonard Bernstein; with André Previn and Mitsuko Uchida; with John Adams and Renée Fleming; Malcolm Arnold; with the unfairly discredited conductor Valery Gergiev; with Barenboim, Boulez and Fischer-Dieskau; with life-force actors such as Warren Mitchell, Michael Ball, Kim Novak, Michael Crawford, Trevor Howard, Simon Callow and Penelope Wilton, Virginia McKenna and Robert Stephens; with

Vangelis and Leni Reifenstahl; with the 1966 World Cup-winning football team; with the South African trio of Athol Fugard, Pieter-Dirk Uys and Nadine Gordimer; with Ginger Baker and Bill Wyman and James Baldwin; with the 92-year-old Eubie Blake, who actually played piano with Scott Joplin; with the indefatigable 80-year-old Lieutenant George Washington Lee, grandson of a slave, who described black culture as 'a civilisation within a civilisation.' And, finally and especially, David Cornwell/John le Carré, who, like all the others, became friends if only for the briefest of time...*Mea culpa.*

But if there is one film by which I wish to be remembered, it is my personal interpretation of the 3rd Symphony by Henryk Górecki, titled *The Symphony of Sorrowful Songs.* The version recorded by Dawn Upshaw and the London Sinfonietta, conducted by David Zinman, caused a sensation when it was released on Elektra Nonesuch records in 1992. The CD stayed at No.1 in the UK classical record charts for 26 weeks, and sold almost three-quarters of a million copies worldwide, unmatched before or since; this despite one critic saying the symphony had three movements: slow, slower and slowest.

The symphony actually dates from 1976, when Górecki was (as he told me in my film) a 'non-person' in the political sense; when his music was banned in his native Katowice in Poland. He told me that its inspiration had come from a book he had found about the Nazi occupation of Poland. In the footnotes, there were examples of the many messages that had been scratched on the walls of the Gestapo Prison in Zakopane. One, written by a young girl, said simply, 'Mama, don't cry.' Very simple. Nothing melodramatic or even tragic. But a heartfelt cry that scorched the soul.

At an early performance in Paris, a music critic whispered their verdict in Górecki's ear: 'Merde!' And at the first screening of my film in 1993, the then commissioning editor of music programmes on Channel Four said, 'What rubbish is this?' Now, only a few years later, no-one can remember either of their names. Melvyn Bragg showed the film on *The South Bank Show,* and even managed to persuade the hierarchy of ITV that it would be an abomination to disrupt the film with any commercial breaks for, say, Durex. The fifty-four minute film was shown uninterrupted, an implicit acceptance perhaps of the urgency of its content. It remains the longest single documentary shown without commercial breaks on commercial television in the UK.

'I wanted to express a great sorrow,' Górecki said. 'The war...the rotten times under Communism...our life today...the starving. What madness! This sorrow, it burns inside me. I cannot shake it off.' If the music of the twentieth century can be said to begin with *The Rite of Spring*, then surely this extraordinary symphony bears witness to its end: to the bloodiest century in all of recorded history, and not just at the hands of monsters such as Stalin, Mao and Hitler, but also at the door of those so-called liberal democracies that have allowed countless millions to starve to death while hurtling down the path of climate desolation. Gaza, Ukraine, Sudan, Myanmar, Iran – the list is endless.

I first met Górecki at his home in southern Poland. He was amazed at the symphony's success in recent years, although the royalties had bought him a gleaming white Mercedes which amused him greatly. The more he talked about his work, the more I realised there was something more here than mere notes on a page. He pointed to the three poems that are the climax of each of the three movements. In the first, the Virgin Mary is looking at Christ on the cross and asking: 'What have you done with my son? My son, my chosen and beloved. Share your wounds with your mother, Because, dear son, I have always carried you in my heart.' In the second, inspired, as we have seen, by a simple scratched message on the wall of the Gestapo Prison in Zakopane: 'Mama, don't cry. Most chaste Queen of Heaven, Support me always.' And in the third, a woman is searching for her son after some unnamed war which has taken him away, whether kidnapped or killed in the military we do not know. 'Ah, you bad people. In the name of God, the most Holy. Tell me, why did you kill my son?'

Górecki then asked me if I had ever been to the Nazi death camp at Auschwitz, which was only a few miles away. I told him that in fact I had been some years earlier. He was not Jewish, but he remembered being taken there as a five-year-old schoolboy soon after the camp had been liberated by the Red Army, and walking along a gravel path which he suddenly realised was not gravel at all but the remains of human bones. That image had stayed with him while composing his Symphony. When I tentatively suggested that maybe we should visit Auschwitz together for the film, he said that doing that would be important to understand his music.

The day we went it had been snowing and it was icy cold. The place was deserted. We walked slowly across the vast site, filming as we went. In the middle he stopped me, and said:

'What do you hear'?

'Nothing,' I said.

'Precisely.' He went on. 'No birds, no rats – the animal kingdom has abandoned the entire area.'

Later, we moved towards the gas chambers and the crematoria. I hung back, out of respect. He beckoned me to come inside with him, and pointing at one of the grotesque trolleys on which the dead bodies had been wheeled into the furnaces, he said, 'Now you see what I was writing about.'

Later some moronic critic said that I had forced Górecki to stand inside the crematoria to get a 'cheap shot for the film'. Well, perhaps I could have forced him to stand by the gates with the infamous 'Arbeit Macht Frei' sign (I did not), but never into the crematoria themselves. 'You see,' he said, 'my music is a witness, but also a warning.'

I realised in an instant what kind of film I needed to make. Part one should be about Auschwitz and all that that implied: a witness. The second part should offer some signs of hope, and I found numerous and wonderful religious icons in the churches and on the roadside in the area around Zakopane, many depicting the Virgin Mary, which therefore reflected the scratched message, 'Mama, don't cry'. The third part should be the warning: a warning of all that we have done and are doing in the name of humanity – mass bombings, the inadvertent and sometimes deliberate starvation of entire populations, the thugs and bullies and religious fanatics and 'deal-makers' who dominate the world we have created.

Re-recording the music was not straightforward. It seemed impossible to get the London Sinfonietta, David Zinman the conductor and Dawn Upshaw, the soprano soloist, in the same city at the same time. So I decided to record the music as a 'backing track' in London, and then take this to New York, where Dawn Upshaw would sing over this 'accompaniment'. The next problem was that Dawn explained to me she had never learned the Polish text of the songs by heart; rather, she had sight-read the words from the score. 'No problem,' I said. 'We will provide "idiot boards" with all the text spelt out phonetically.' She and I then had numerous transatlantic conversations to make the necessary arrangements for the filming, but in made-up Polish, neither of us understanding a word of what we were saying. Come the day in New York, she sang her heart out, to such an extent that after we had done one take of the last movement, the cameraman turned round to me in tears and said, 'Do we really have to do that again?'

Later, a jobsworth working for the distributor tried to prove that (a) I had never actually recorded the music, which must have come as a surprise to the seventy or so members of the Sinfonietta and that (b) Dawn had never actually sung it in New York. I had just used the existing CD recording to which they had all mimed their parts. What idiots I have had to deal with.

I returned to Katowice to show the finished film to Gorecki before anyone else. He had sat silently and, in the end, wept. Nonetheless, initially, my film was savagely attacked by critics. 'Palmer Porn', one writer labelled it, claiming I had used images of suffering and distress to illustrate some unfathomable point. After all, my 1968 film *All My Loving* was often called 'The burning monk film' because of one five-second shot of a Buddhist monk self-immolating. Even my long-time supporter Tony Fell, the managing director of Boosey and Hawkes, then Górecki's publisher, felt obliged to demand that the film was not to be further distributed, although he relented in the end. Górecki was at first puzzled by what people (including some second-rate conductors) had told him about the film's reception following its screening on ITV, then angry, then came to London for a 'peace conference' to see what could be salvaged. My only defender was my friend, the great Australian director Peter Weir, whose use of Vaughan Williams' music, for instance in his sea-faring film, *Master and Commander*, had been encouraged in part by my film about Vaughan Williams.

Eventually the tide turned, as it usually does. Barry Witherden wrote the following in the BBC Music Magazine under the headline '*When all words fail*'; 'It is a tribute to the power of the music as well as Palmer's images that this film often reduced me to tears and made me feel sick to my stomach. There are no "extras" or commentary since there is nothing to say beyond what the music, images and the interview with Górecki say.' Even Classic FM, not noted for its advocacy of high culture, wrote in its magazine that 'Palmer presents a direct, deeply felt condemnation of the eternal pattern of ethnic and sectarian conflict and mankind's murderous impulses. The familiarity of the images Palmer uses, together with the raw, folk-like simplicity of Górecki's music creates an overwhelming impact forcing the viewer to move beyond the usual objectivity of television documentary and confront the darkness of actions taken in the name of nation states and tribal advancement.'

The BBC has repeatedly refused to repeat the film which, although originally made for ITV, has been offered to them free.

For a while, it became impossible to turn on the television and see *any* programme relating to war or suffering and not hear Górecki's music, often in the work of directors who had publicly attacked me and my film for its use. If I felt justified, it was not as if this were a new experience. All my career, I've had my ideas butchered, imitated and stolen, even by distributors. I have never complained; rather, I have taken heart from the words of one of my true heroes, Joseph Conrad, also beloved by Orson Welles. It seems to me to express what all the great artists whom I have encountered want to say, including me. When I once suggested a film about this great Polish/English novelist to the commissioning editor of arts programmes at the BBC, I think she thought he was a reject from *Strictly Come Dancing*.

'My destiny?' Conrad wrote in *Heart of Darkness*. 'A droll thing life is, that mysterious arrangement of merciless logic for a futile purpose. The most you can hope from it is some knowledge of yourself that comes too late, a crop of unextinguishable regrets. I have wrestled with death. It is the most unexciting contest you can imagine. It takes place in an impalpable greyness, without clamour, without glory, without the great desire of victory, without the great fear of defeat, in a sickly atmosphere of tepid scepticism, without much belief in your own right, and still less in that of your adversary. If such is the form of ultimate wisdom, then life is a greater riddle than some of us think it to be.'

Yes, the horror. That is why I did what I did in my work...while not forgetting to wriggle my toes.

Filmography

Isadora [as Producer - Director Ken Russell] (1966)
Alice in Wonderland [as Assist. Producer - Director Jonathan Miller] (1966)
The Art of Conducting - with **Georg Solti** (1966)
Up the Theatre - with **Judi Dench** (1966)
Conceit (1967)
Benjamin Britten & his Festival (1967)
Burning Fiery Furnace (1967)
Corbusier (1967)
Twice a Fortnight - with **Terry Jones & Michael Palin** (1967)
All My Loving (1968)
Cream Farewell Concert (1968)
How It Is (1968)
The World of Peter Sellers (1969)
Rope Ladder to the Moon - **Jack Bruce** (1969)
Fairport Convention & Colosseum (1970)
Glad All Over (1970)
National Youth Theatre - **Michael Croft** (1970)
200 Motels - **Frank Zappa** (1971)
Brighton Breezy (1971) *see below under The Pursuit of Happiness* (2015)
Mahler 9 (aka *Four Ways to Say Farewell*)- with **Leonard Bernstein** (1971)
Ginger Baker in Africa (1971)
Birmingham (1971) *see below under The Pursuit of Happiness* (2015)
The Pursuit of Happiness (1972) *also see below* (2015)
Bird on a Wire - with **Leonard Cohen** (1972)
The World of Liberace (1972)
The World of Hugh Hefner (1973)
International Youth Orchestra (1973)
Rory Gallagher - Irish Tour (1974)
The World of Miss World (1974)
Harriet at the Circus / Harriet at Sea / Harriet in a Balloon /Harriet at War / Harriet at the Opera / Harriet at Butlins (1974)
Tangerine Dream - live in Coventry Cathedral (1975 & 2017)
All You Need is Love - 17 hour series on the history of American Popular Music, with **Bing Crosby, Sinatra, Rolling Stones, Dylan, Muddy Waters** etc. (1975/76)

All this & World War II (1976) ***see below 2016***
The Wigan Casino – the story of **Northern Soul** & break-dancing (1977)
Biddu (1977)
The Edinburgh Festival (1977)
The Mighty Wurlitzer (1978)
The Edinburgh Festival Revisited (1978)
The Space Movie – NASA's official 10th anniversary film, music by **Mike Oldfield** (1979)
Pride of Place [6 parts] (1979)
A Time There Was – profile of **Benjamin Britten** (1979)
First Edition (1980)
At the Haunted End of the Day – profile of **William Walton** (1980
Death in Venice – opera by **Benjamin Britten** (1981)
Once, at a Border... – profile of **Igor Stravinsky** (1982)
Wagner – by **Charles Wood**, music conducted by **Georg Solti**, photographed by **Vittorio Storaro**; with **Richard Burton, Vanessa Redgrave, Laurence Olivier, John Gielgud**, (1983)
Primal Scream – **Art Janov** (1984)
Puccini – with **Virginia McKenna & Robert Stephens** (1984)
God Rot Tunbridge Wells – by **John Osborne**, with **Trevor Howard** as Handel (1984/85)
Mozart in Japan – with **Mitsuko Uchida** (1986)
Testimony – with **Ben Kingsley as Shostakovich**(1987)
Maria Callas (1987)
In From The Cold? – portrait of **Richard Burton** (1988)
Dvořak in Love? – with **Julian Lloyd Webber** (1988)
Hindemith – a Pilgrim's Progress – with **John Gielgud** (1989)
The Children – with **Kim Novak, Ben Kingsley, Geraldine Chaplin** (1989)
Menuhin, a Family Portrait (1990)
I, Berlioz with **Corin Redgrave** (1992)
The Symphony of Sorrowful Songs – **Gòrecki** (1993)
A Short Film About Loving – with **Peter Sellars** (1994)
England, my England – Henry Purcell, by **John Osborne & Charles Wood**; with **Simon Callow & Michael Ball**; music conducted by **John Eliot Gardiner** (1995)
Brahms and The Little Singing Girls – with **Warren Mitchell** (1996)
The fantastic World of Michael Crawford (1996)
Hail Bop! – a profile of **John Adams** (1997)
Parsifal – with **Placido Domingo & Valery Gergiev** (1997)
The Harvest of Sorrow – **Rachmaninoff,** with the Mariinsky Opera (1998)
The Kindness of Strangers – **André Previn** (1998)
Valentina Igoshina plays Chopin (1999)
The Strange Case of Delfina Potocka – Chopin, with **Penelope Wilton** (1999)
Foreign Aids – **Pieter-Dirk Uys** on tour (2001)
Ladies & Gentlemen, Miss Renée Fleming (2002)
Hero – The Story of Bobby Moore – produced by David Frost (2002)

Toward the Unknown Region - Malcolm Arnold, A Story of Survival (2003)
John Osborne and The Gift of Friendship (2003)
Ivry Gitlis and The Great Tradition (2004)
The Adventures of Benjamin Schmid (2005)
***Margot* - Margot Fonteyn** (2005)
The Salzburg Festival (2006)
O Thou Transcendent - The Life of Vaughan Williams (2007)
O, Fortuna!* - Carl Orff & *Carmina Burana (2008)
Vangelis and the Journey to Ithaka (2009)
The Wagner Family (2010)
Holst - In The Bleak Midwinter (2011)
Wagner Boxset (2013) - consisting of the Burton/***Wagner*** epic, Domingo's ***Parsifal, The Wagner Family,*** and a bonus disc ***Silent Wagner,*** the original 1912/13 silent biopic.
***Falls the Shadow...* Athol Fugard** (2012)
Britten at 100 Boxset (2012)
Beware of Mr Baker (2012) - [as Executive Producer, Director Jay Bulger]
***Nocturne* - Britten** (2013)
Great English Composers boxsets (2014) Italia Prize winning films
Vol 1: Vaughan Williams & Malcolm Arnold
Vol. 2: Britten & Handel
Vol. 3: Purcell & Britten's Festival
Vol. 4: Walton & Holst
Music Under The Nazis boxset (2014) **The Wagner Family, Carl Orff & Hindemith - a Pilgrim's Progress**
Silent Wagner - with the original 1913 music by Giuseppe Becce (2015)
The Pursuit of Happiness (2015) includes **Brighton Breezy, Shirley MacLaine & Birmingham**
The Space Movie - music by **Mike Oldfield** (remastered 2015)
The Beatles and World War II (2016)
Bird On A Wire - with **Leonard Cohen**. Originally filmed in 1972; rescued & restored in 2010; now including the home movies (2016)
Rachmaninoff - his letters, his home movies and his recordings (2017)
Tangerine Dream in Coventry Cathedral (revised version) (2017)
Instruments of the Orchestra, Britten's Young Person's Guide (2017)
BRITTEN box-set (2017) ***Britten in his own Words***
Stravinsky 50th anniversary box-set (2021) ***Stravinsky in his own Words***
Leonard Cohen in Concert (2022)

Most titles available from isolde@btinternet.com